CORNELL STUDIES IN SECURITY AFFAIRS

edited by Robert J. Art *and* Robert Jervis

Conventional Deterrence, by John J. Mearsheimer

Liddell Hart and the Weight of History, by John J. Mearsheimer

Inadvertent Escalation: Conventional War and Nuclear Risks, by Barry R. Posen

The Sources of Military Doctrine: France, Britain, and Germany between the World Wars, by Barry R. Posen

Dilemmas of Appeasement: British Deterrence and Defense, 1934–1937, by Gaines Post, Jr.

Winning the Next War: Innovation and the Modern Military, by Stephen Peter Rosen

Israel and Conventional Deterrence: Border Warfare from 1953 to 1970, by Jonathan Shimshoni

Fighting to a Finish: The Politics of War Termination in the United States and Japan, 1945, by Leon V. Sigal

The Ideology of the Offensive: Military Decision Making and the Disasters of 1914, by Jack Snyder

Myths of Empire: Domestic Politics and International Ambition, by Jack Snyder

The Militarization of Space: U.S. Policy, 1945–1984, by Paul B. Stares

Making the Alliance Work: The United States and Western Europe, by Gregory F. Treverton

The Origins of Alliances, by Stephen M. Walt

The Ultimate Enemy: British Intelligence and Nazi Germany, 1933–1939, by Wesley K. Wark

The Tet Offensive: Intelligence Failure in War, by James J. Wirtz

Deterrence and Strategic Culture: Chinese-American Confrontations, by Shu Guang Zhang

Dilemmas of Appeasement

BRITISH DETERRENCE AND DEFENSE, 1934–1937

GAINES POST, JR.

Cornell University Press

ITHACA AND LONDON

First published 1993 by Cornell University Press.

International Standard Book Number 0-8014-2748-7
Library of Congress Catalog Card Number 92-27606
Printed in the United States of America
*Librarians: Library of Congress cataloging information
appears on the last page of the book.*

⊗ The paper in this book meets the minimum requirements of the American National Standard for Information Sciences—
Permanence of Paper for Printed Library Materials, ANSI Z39.48-1984.

To Jeanie

Contents

Acknowledgments

My work on this book was delayed by two administrative assignments, both of which influenced it more than I would have guessed. Directing the Rockefeller Foundation's Commission on the Humanities heightened my interest in how ideas of time affect policy. Serving as Dean of Faculty at Claremont McKenna College gave me practical insights into the politics of policymaking.

When I began this project, a colleague admonished, "But you're a Germanist!" Fortunately, no one in the field of British policy in the 1930s took such a parochial view. I owe thanks to many scholars for their help and encouragement. The following saw parts of the manuscript and offered suggestions: Raymond Callahan, Ward E. Y. Elliott, Lancelot L. Farrar, Jr., Michael Geyer, P. Edward Haley, Michael Hurst, MacGregor Knox, Steven Koblik, John F. Naylor, and Robert J. Young. I profited from discussions with Brian Bond, who welcomed me to the War Studies Department at King's College London while I was on sabbatical leave. Others who assisted me in discussions or correspondence were John Barnes, Richard Harrison, Michael Howard, Jon Jacobson, John Lippincott, W. Roger Louis, Peter Mellini, George C. Peden, Robert Rhodes James, Robert Paul Shay, Jr., Malcolm Smith, John Snortum, Karl von den Steinen, and, at the Foreign and Commonwealth Office Library, Gillian Bennett, W. N. Medlicott, and Margaret Pelly.

I received invaluable advice on the entire manuscript from Alastair Parker, Zara Steiner, and especially Robert J. O'Neill. All of them were extraordinarily patient with me and generous with their time. The same can be said of Robert Jervis and Wesley K. Wark, who helped improve the final shape of the book. At Cornell University Press, I gratefully acknowledge the assistance of Roger Haydon, Teresa

Jesionowski, and Kay Scheuer, and their freelance editor Adrienne Mayor.

For permission to cite collections of private papers, and for excellent staff assistance in using them, I am obliged to the University Library, University of Birmingham; the Syndics of Cambridge University Library; Churchill College Archives Centre, Cambridge; the Trustees of the Liddell Hart Centre for Military Archives, King's College London; the Trustees of the National Maritime Museum, London; and the Harry Ransom Humanities Research Center, University of Texas at Austin. Crown copyright material from the Public Record Office appears by permission of the Controller of H.M. Stationery Office. Families and trustees have considerately allowed me to quote from the private letters of Leopold Amery, Sir Alexander Cadogan, Winston Churchill (with permission of Curtis Brown Ltd., London), Sir Maurice Hankey (Lord Hankey), Sir Samuel Hoare (Lord Templewood), Sir Thomas Inskip (Lord Caldecote), Sir John Simon (Lord Simon), and Lord Weir. My thanks also go to the libraries of the University of London, Oxford University, Stanford University and the Hoover Institution, the University of Texas at Austin, and the Claremont Colleges.

General Sir Ronald F. Adam, Captain A. W. Clarke, RN, and Sir William Hayter kindly wrote to me with recollections, and Lady Liddell Hart graciously welcomed me to her home. A former civil servant from those years, who requested anonymity, gave me an insider's view of the machinery of defense. Anthony Goodenough and David Logan, currently members of the British Foreign Service, offered instructive tips on how a major government department does business.

For grants and leaves in support of my research, I thank the American Council of Learned Societies, the American Philosophical Society, the Inter-University Seminar on Armed Forces and Society, the University Research Institute of the University of Texas at Austin, and Claremont McKenna College. All these institutions understand how valuable time is to scholars. For permission to include portions of my articles, I am grateful to *The International History Review* (for "The Machinery of British Policy in the Ethiopian Crisis," in vol. 1, 1979); and *Armed Forces and Society* (for "Mad Dogs and Englishmen: British Rearmament, Deterrence and Appeasement, 1934–35," in vol. 14, 1988). I thank Dona Curry and Stacey Garza for their typing and computer skills along the way, Pat Padilla for producing the final manuscript with finesse, and Andrew Roth for bravely tackling the index.

I am extraordinarily fortunate to have studied at Cornell and Stanford universities, institutions with historical ties and remarkable historians, and at Oxford University, where military history remains a notable field. I am particularly indebted to Richard W. Lyman, excellent teacher, careful scholar, demanding administrator, and good friend, who helped keep me thinking about British history.

My debt to family is impossible to measure or repay. My late father, Gaines Post, Sr., a medievalist raised in West Texas, exemplified academic integrity. My mother, Katherine Rike Post, could ride as well as any cowboy and knows human nature better than most historians. My brother and boon companion, John F. Post, who is equally at home in philosophy and in the wilderness, has made me aware of—if not immune to—presuppositions. My children, Katie and Daniel, remind me not to sanctify hindsight. Jean Bowers Post, my wife, has unfailingly sustained my work, with great courage under uncommon circumstances. I happily dedicate this book to her.

G. P.

Claremont, California

Abbreviations

ATB	Advisory Committee on Trade Questions in Time of War
CAS	Chief of the Air Staff
CID	Committee of Imperial Defence
CIGS	Chief of the Imperial General Staff
CNS	Chief of Naval Staff
COS	Chiefs of Staff
DCOS	Deputy Chiefs of Staff
DP(P)	Defence Plans (Policy) Committee
DPR	Defence Policy and Requirements Committee
DPR(DR)	Defence Policy and Requirements (Defence Requirements) Committee
DRC	Defence Requirements Committee
FCI	Committee on Industrial Intelligence in Foreign Countries
FPC	Cabinet Committee on Foreign Policy
IIC	Industrial Intelligence Centre
JIC	Joint Intelligence Committee
JPC	Joint Planning Committee
PSOC	Principal Supply Officers Committee
RAF	Royal Air Force
TEEC	Treasury Emergency Expenditure Committee
TISC	Treasury Inter-Service Committee

[xiii]

Dilemmas of Appeasement

For WAR, consisteth not in battle only, or the act of fighting; but in a tract of time, wherein the will to contend by battle is sufficiently known: and therefore the notion of *time,* is to be considered in the nature of war; as it is in the nature of weather. For as the nature of foul weather, lieth not in a shower or two of rain; but in an inclination thereto of many days together: so the nature of war, consisteth not in actual fighting; but in the known disposition thereto, during all the time there is no assurance to the contrary. All other time is PEACE.

—Thomas Hobbes, *Leviathan*

We sail within a vast sphere, ever drifting in uncertainty, driven from end to end. When we think to attach ourselves to any point and to fasten to it, it wavers and leaves us; and if we follow it, it eludes our grasp, slips past us, and vanishes forever. Nothing stays for us.

—Blaise Pascal, *Pensées*

Introduction

When Anthony Eden became Foreign Secretary in December 1935 shortly after the political uproar over the Hoare-Laval peace plan, he succeeded to what he later called "a wretchedly disordered heritage."[1] Eden's popularity in Britain and Geneva, his subsequent resignation in February 1938 over Neville Chamberlain's appeasement of Mussolini, and his service in Winston Churchill's War Cabinet contributed to the thesis that "guilty men" lacking moral fiber were responsible for British appeasement. Close examination of the policy that Eden inherited and conducted, however, suggests that its disorder arose less from weak personalities than from an inchoate strategy of deterrence and an indecisive machinery of policy, both of which required an indefinite period of time to prepare for the inexorable event of war on as many as three fronts.

We have learned much about British rearmament and foreign policy since the Cabinet records for the 1930s were opened. Norman Gibbs's volume in the official United Kingdom military histories of the Second World War details the deficiency and rearmament programs of the three Services. Stephen Roskill has illuminated naval policy and Sir Maurice Hankey's far-reaching influence on defense policy. The Army has been examined by Brian Bond and Peter Dennis; the Royal Air Force by, most recently, Malcolm Smith. G. C. Peden and Robert Shay show the interrelationship of rearmament, finance, and "Treasury control." Christopher Andrew and Wesley Wark have written informative accounts of British intelligence that go beyond F. H. Hinsley's official history. Reinhard Meyers and Gustav Schmidt consider the internal political and economic pressures on defense policy. Correlli Barnett

[1] Lord Avon (Anthony Eden), *Facing the Dictators* (Boston, 1962), p. 354.

[1]

links national character and "total strategy" as causes for the decay of British power from 1918 to 1945. Maurice Cowling views foreign policy and rearmament as battlegrounds for conflict inside and between British political parties.[2]

Although this book covers some of the same ground, it is different in four major respects that enlarge the field of British policy in the 1930s and introduce an analytical framework for reexamining it. First, I concentrate on the years 1934–37, both a turning point and a point of departure for Britain, years in which British policy went through four stages of development. Hitler's seizure of power caused Britain to begin to rearm in 1934–35 (Part I). From July 1935 to May 1936, the Ethiopian and Rhineland crises (Parts II and III) jolted British assumptions about rearmament, potential enemies, conciliation, and the prevention of international conflict, and both crises occurred just after London had adjusted its defense policy and machinery to assimilate recent information. Starting in the summer of 1936, the repercussions of the Spanish Civil War foreshadowed a hostile ideological coalition of Germany, Italy, and Japan, while progress on strategic plans in London accentuated the disparity between foreign risks and domestic resources (Part IV).

Second, I examine British attitudes toward deterrence more comprehensively than do other works on the period. The British predicament was whether war in Europe, the Pacific, and the Mediterranean could be prevented by accompanying conciliation with the buildup of large forces for all three Fighting Services, with strong commitments to collective security and alliances or with a powerful air force that could bomb Germany. British policymakers refused to concede that this dilemma could not be solved. Yet they disagreed over how these policies,

[2] N. H. Gibbs, *Grand Strategy*, vol. 1: *Rearmament Policy* (London, 1976); Stephen Roskill, *Naval Policy between the Wars*, vol. 2: *The Period of Reluctant Rearmament* (London, 1976); Roskill, *Hankey: Man of Secrets*, vol. 3 (London, 1974); Brian Bond, *British Military Policy between the Two World Wars* (Oxford, 1980); Peter Dennis, *Decision by Default: Peacetime Conscription and British Defence, 1919–39* (London, 1972); Malcolm Smith, *British Air Strategy between the Wars* (Oxford, 1984); G. C. Peden, *British Rearmament and the Treasury, 1932–1939* (Edinburgh, 1979); Robert P. Shay, Jr., *British Rearmament in the Thirties: Politics and Profits* (Princeton, 1977); Christopher Andrew, *Her Majesty's Secret Service: The Making of the British Intelligence Community* (New York, 1985); Wesley K. Wark, *The Ultimate Enemy: British Intelligence and Nazi Germany, 1933–1939* (Ithaca, N. Y., 1985); F. H. Hinsley, *British Intelligence in the Second World War*, vol. 1 (London, 1979); Reinhard Meyers, *Britische Sicherheitspolitik 1934–1938: Studien zum aussen- und sicherheitspolitischen Entscheidungsprozess* (Düsseldorf, 1976); Gustav Schmidt, *England in der Krise: Grundzüge und Grundlagen der britischen Appeasement Politik, 1930–1937* (Opladen, 1981); Correlli Barnett, *The Collapse of British Power* (New York, 1972); Maurice Cowling, *The Impact of Hitler: British Politics and British Policy, 1933–1940* (Cambridge, 1975). See also Brian Bond and Williamson Murray, "The British Armed Forces, 1918–39," in Allan R. Millett and Murray, eds., *Military Effectiveness*, vol. 2 (Boston, 1988), chap. 4.

singly or together, constituted deterrence, which Service deserved priority, and which enemy could be conciliated most easily to Britain's greatest advantage.

Third, although recent scholars substantiate the premise that Britain wanted to buy time for rearmament, I probe the temporal dimensions of British policy more deeply than one will find elsewhere in the literature. As Britain rearmed, the material shortages, intelligence reports, and international dangers of the moment darkened Whitehall's vision of a future state of security, the date of whose arrival receded like the door at the end of a dream's bewildering corridor.

Finally, and most important, the machinery of policy and the process of policymaking are given more emphasis than is the case in the works just cited. Whereas other authors have concentrated on the difficulties of Britain's external environment, limited resources, and domestic politics, I advance as the central thesis that the machinery's flaws caused disorder in British policy. For comprehending dictatorships, deterrence, and timetables, the British had an exquisite system of decision-making by committee, one that conventional wisdom still holds far superior to any concurrent administration in Europe. Yet this system made no decisions with promptness, unambiguous assumptions, concordant parts, and clearly defined goals, a record that cannot be attributed entirely to external threats and internal weakness. The machinery's confusion and irresolution, more pronounced for long-term planning than for responding to international crises, muddled deterrence and lost time. The machinery's defects also helped create the illusion that Chamberlain's more decisive style of policymaking could solve Britain's worsening strategic dilemma once he became prime minister.

Historians rarely study the interrelationship of policy, emergency, and administration, perhaps because it does not fit into any one of history's subdivisions. One can observe the interaction among government departments, interdepartmental committees, foreign policy, budget, and military strategy. One can also discern synapses between these phenomena, where abstract notions of time and deterrence excited or inhibited action. Both kinds of magnification reveal the complexity of appeasement and the idiosyncrasies of the nervous system that practiced it. This kind of analysis requires a fresh look at facts that are, for the most part, well known to historians of British rearmament and foreign policy. Reexamining the evidence across and within departments (Foreign Office, Treasury, Admiralty, War Office, Air Ministry) suggests new perspectives on policy, policymaking, and personalities. In 1934–35, the British Government began to develop a grand strategy for deterring Germany and Japan, but frictions in the machinery of policy hampered coordination among disparate views of time and deterrence. Late in 1935, the ambivalent and unsuccessful application of deterrence in the Italo-Ethiopian war resulted in part from the special relationship between a largely ministerial committee suddenly put in charge of the emergency (the Defence Policy and Requirements Committee), and a committee of expert advisers who would rather have been drawing up proposals for long-term rearmament in case of war with Germany or Japan (the Defence Requirements Committee). Early in 1936, the Government adopted the Foreign Office's revised formula for appeasing and deterring Germany, only to be unnerved by Hitler's sabotage of this formula in the Rhineland crisis; they were unable to reassess British policy afterward. In the winter of 1936–37, the word "policy" acquired broader connotations as those at Whitehall faced the remarkable coincidence of diplomatic failures, war plans, borrowing for defense, and the prospect of a dynamic new administration under Chamberlain.

Limiting this analysis to the years 1934–37 may seem incomplete to those who concentrate on the even more tragic time of Chamberlain's premiership, the *Anschluss*, the 1938 Munich conference, the 1939 Nazi-Soviet Pact, and the outbreak of war. There is good reason, however, for reconsidering these years as a unique chapter in British history between the world wars. The British framed new policies of appeasement, strategies of deterrence, and timetables of rearmament. They struggled over reconciling these activities with international crises that subverted hypotheses for long-term planning. They lost faith in their ability to solve strategic problems with current practices of policymaking, and they turned to Chamberlain for deliverance. There is a dramatic unity to this period.

In the shadowy region between peace and war, there were personal crises of confidence among members of a ruling elite who expressed both the smugness of customarily wielding power and the fear of losing it through uncustomary events. For self-confidence, logical thinking, optimistic problem solving, political resoluteness, and egotism, one person stands out as extraordinary—Neville Chamberlain. Eden's ambivalence toward both Italy and Germany was greater than his own memoirs suggest, and he was neither as strong a Foreign Secretary as his admirers thought nor as weak as his belittlers alleged. Sir Thomas Inskip proved more effective than critics of his appointment expected, and more independent in his judgments of defense issues than Chamberlain bargained for. Sir Maurice Hankey's mastery of the machinery of government endowed him with both extraordinary influence over policy and proprietary opposition to structural change. Sir Robert Vansittart accurately forecast the strategic repercussions of Germany's actions and the year when these would set Europe on fire, but he alienated colleagues by appearing cocksure in his predictions and doubtful in his prescriptions for British policy. A man of many contrasts, Sir Warren Fisher shared Vansittart's apprehensions about German resurgence, Chamberlain's and Eden's impatience with Vansittart, Hankey's ideal of teamwork among civil servants, the Services' uneasiness about financial and commercial restrictions on rearmament, and the Treasury's determination to maintain control over expenditure. Admiral Sir Ernle Chatfield built up the prestige of the Chiefs of Staff as a body of military experts, but his natural bias toward the Royal Navy and imperial defense in the Far East put him at odds with the Eurocentrism of planning in the other two Services and the strategic ambitions of the young Royal Air Force.

After the end of the Great War in 1919, the British Government presumed that no major war would occur for the next ten years. This policy, which was renewed annually until 1932, seemed consistent with the fact that no power seriously threatened Britain or the empire, and with the idealistic presupposition that international disputes could be settled, peacefully and collectively, through the League of Nations or regional agreements such as the Locarno Treaty of 1925. Peace was a vital interest for the world's largest imperial power, and British appeasement in the 1920s meant the use of rational argument, moral suasion, and diplomatic pressure to achieve compromise and avoid armed conflict. These considerations animated a double policy of conciliating dissatisfied powers such as Germany and containing them before they radically upset the postwar European order, which formed a bulwark against bolshevism to the east. Military forces could be reduced in the interests of world peace and national economy. Deterrence of aggression was a matter for diplomatic negotiation, not military confrontation.[3]

In the mid-1930s, British policy was confounded by Hitler's unilateral repudiation of the Treaty of Versailles and Mussolini's invasion of Ethiopia, in addition to Japanese expansion in the Far East. Although the British usually reserved the canine metaphor "mad dog" for Mussolini, they also assumed that Germany (and Japan) might launch sudden attacks because the "wild men" in these militaristic dictatorships were irrational and unchecked by democratic institutions.

---

[3] For an overview, see Paul Kennedy, "The Tradition of Appeasement in British Foreign Policy, 1865–1939," *British Journal of International Studies* 2 (1976), reprinted in his *Strategy and Diplomacy, 1870–1945* (London, 1983). See also Martin Gilbert, *The Roots of Appeasement* (London, 1966), and Wolf D. Gruner, "The British Political, Social and Economic System and the Decision for Peace and War: Reflections on Anglo-German Relations 1800–1939," *British Journal of International Studies* 6 (1980).

Should Britain be tough as well as conciliatory toward them? Could Britain reconcile national and imperial security with its collective obligations in the League of Nations and the Treaty of Locarno? Could rearmament reduce international tension, promote a European settlement, and prevent war when disarmament had failed to do so? In view of the large discrepancy between Britain's military power and its worldwide interests, could diplomacy provide the time necessary for Britain to rearm? Could British rearmament or the threat of force deter Japan, Germany, and Italy from either upsetting the status quo or changing it more than Britain could accept?

To a greater extent than most accounts of British appeasement recognize, the Government's affirmative answers to these questions pointed toward a comprehensive strategy of deterrence.[4] Certainly, Britain's military resources in the 1930s were inadequate to defend its many interests. But this fact, which could be applied to most of the history of the British Empire, has become so deeply rooted in the historiography of the period that it is easy to underestimate Britain's attempts to increase its power and develop forms of coercive diplomacy. Appeasement and deterrence were compatible in a revised version of the dual policy of the 1920s, and both required increasing Britain's military strength. Rearming and economically stable, retaining an empire with vast resources, Britain could combine conciliation with diplomatic pressure and military power in a dynamic policy that would moderate the dictators' demands, create a new balance of power, and prevent war. During the winter of 1935–36, however, practice shook theory in two theaters, and British policymakers drew conclusions that narrowed their view of deterrence and shaped policy for the next few years. The Italo-Ethiopian war dramatically illustrated that threatening or showing force in an immediate crisis entailed more risks than advantages, especially if Britain retained collective obligations that jeopardized defense of its own interests. Using military coercion to prevent or limit conflict would delay long-term rearmament, and would probably not deter "mad dogs" before rearmament was substantially com-

[4] Barnett exaggerates the degree to which British political leaders were "inseminated" by romantic and idealistic internationalists in the interwar period; *Collapse*, pp. 237–42. Like Kennedy and Barnett, Gottfried Niedhart relates appeasement to the loss of British power; "Appeasement: Die britische Antwort auf die Krise des Weltreichs und des internationalen Systems vor dem Zweiten Weltkrieg," *Historische Zeitschrift* 126 (1978). The same theme runs through essays in Wolfgang J. Mommsen and Lothar Kettenacker, eds., *The Fascist Challenge and the Policy of Appeasement* (London, 1983); particularly R. A. C. Parker, "The Failure of Collective Security in British Appeasement" (chap. 2), and Reinhard Meyers, "British Imperial Interests and the Policy of Appeasement" (chap. 24). For a cogent statement of Britain's still dominant global power before the Second World War, see B. J. C. McKercher, "'Our Most Dangerous Enemy': Great Britain Pre-eminent in the 1930s," *International History Review* 13 (1991).

pleted. The Rhineland crisis showed that Hitler could act before Britain had rearmed sufficiently to negotiate from a confident position of strength. Thus, concessions might have to be made to Germany without much hope of anything solid in return, such as arms limitation or a new western security pact.

Ideas of deterrence and their application rested on conflicting perceptions of time. For the British, the time was out of joint in estimating the German threat, scheduling rearmament, and adapting long-term plans to immediate realities. Although the majority at Whitehall concurred that Germany's totalitarian system could thoroughly control industry, quickly mobilize society, and begin war with surprise attacks, British intelligence could only guess about German intentions, and thus differences arose over the imminence of conflict with that country. Officials in the Foreign Office argued that Hitler might begin a war in Western Europe by 1939 or earlier, before Germany was militarily prepared for a major campaign. Service advisers, on the other hand, assumed that Hitler would follow the recommendations of their German counterparts and not risk war before 1942, when Germany would presumably have rearmed sufficiently. The British Government used both dates as targets for planning rearmament. The first, 1939, confounded military calculations of deterrence with political unknowns. The second, 1942, implied that German and British military leaders agreed on the best time to fight, an odd way for Britain to seek the military advantage for deterrence or war. Neither date presupposed that, because time might be on Germany's side in the long run, Britain should risk war before German rearmament and territorial expansion gave Hitler invincible superiority.

British timetables for rearmament used other unsynchronous clocks as well. In 1932, the Admiralty had laid plans for a decade of naval expenditure, with emphasis on the Japanese threat in the Far East. In 1934, the Supply Board adopted a five-year period for purposes of planning, regardless of what country was named as a potential enemy. Early in 1936, the Cabinet approved Service programs for a period of three to five years. The Treasury proposed in February 1937 a five-year plan of expenditure on rearmament. The Service departments grounded their programs for reconditioning and expansion on three contrary views of the next war, their respective roles in it, and the time needed to prepare themselves for it. The Great War had shown the need to mobilize resources for a long conflict before risking war. Development of a peacetime "shadow armament industry" to provide reserves of supply required negotiation with firms that did not normally manufacture arms. The Treasury and Cabinet decided that this should be a gradual and limited process, which would help complete the authorized programs without upsetting normal trade. Officials in the Foreign Office and Services argued for an acceleration of the shadow scheme in order to equip regular units faster and ensure sufficient reserves for war.

Finally, the realities of the present and hypotheses about the future impinged on each other in British planning. Before the Ethiopian crisis of late 1935, it was not clear whether Germany or Japan was the major short-term threat, whether changes in the international situation would affect the strategic assumptions guiding long-term rearmament, whether the very policy of rearming or demonstrations of force would deter adversaries, and whether air parity with Germany would prevent war and save the cost of substantially expanding the Army for commit-ment to the Continent in a European war.

The Ethiopian (or Mediterranean) and Rhineland crises made it all the more necessary and difficult for the British to clarify such issues of time, and therefore these episodes are pivotal in this book. The crises; the Government's recognition in 1934 that Germany was the "ultimate enemy"; London's emphasis on air deterrence against Germany: these factors bias my analysis toward Europe, although imperial defense in Asia is not overlooked. The Mediterranean crisis exposed Britain's vul-nerability and military weakness as an imperial power, raised the ques-tion of whether coercing Italy now would make it easier or harder to deter Germany later, and disrupted the long-term trajectory of plan-ning for war with Germany or Japan. Germany's remilitarization of the Rhineland, like Hitler's other major actions up to the outbreak of war, defied Britain's efforts to regulate the timing and extent of changes in the European status quo through a combination of rearmament and diplomatic brokerage.

The collision between present and future caused far more alarm in the Foreign Office than in the Treasury. At the former, some months after Germany reoccupied the Rhineland, Vansittart and Eden warned that Germany's next move—perhaps against Czechoslovakia—might come in 1937. In December 1936, Vansittart wrote: "Time is the very material commodity which the Foreign Office is expected to provide in the same way as other departments have to provide *other* war mate-rial. . . . To the Foreign Office therefore falls the task of holding the situation at least till 1939, and . . . there is no certainty of our being able to do so." A year later, William Strang recorded his alarm that "the day of security never comes any nearer, but is successively postponed to a still more distant future." At the Treasury, however, Chamberlain maintained in June 1936 that Germany's "next forward step might not necessarily lead us into war," and, early in 1937, he wondered whether it was "really necessary to stick rigidly to a date in 1939 for completion

[8]

of our programmes." Later in the year, his former colleague at the Treasury, Edward Bridges, thought it "about time" that someone said "there is no particular magic about April 1939. Of course if we knew for certain that war was going to break out on that date we should all be arming more rapidly."[5] He did not add that by now the Treasury attached far more magic to the year 1942. The contrast between these two dispositions toward time was at the heart of disputes between the Foreign Office and Treasury over policy.

Hankey, Fisher, and their contemporaries frequently used the words "machinery" and "system" to describe extraparliamentary procedures for devising, coordinating, and executing national policy. Britain eclipsed all other nations in its intricate administration of government. The civilian and military officials who tended it were capable and conscientious, and they agreed on fundamental principles such as social class, patriotism, their right to rule, and Britain's right to empire. Then why, as Lord Hankey later asked, with "a system of planning for war that possessed so many merits," was Britain caught unprepared for war in 1939? Hankey did not blame the machinery of defense, which he more than anyone else had designed, but the parliamentary system and the policy of peace that crippled the arms industry.[6] More than Hankey knew, the answer can indeed be found partly in the machinery of policy itself, one of the "structural" influences to which German historians in particular have drawn attention,[7] and one which was less orderly and efficient than it seemed.

The National Government was dominated by the Conservatives, who enjoyed large majorities. Yet its failure to solve problems in the

---

[5] Vansittart and Chamberlain at meeting of Defence Policy and Requirements Committee, 11 June 1936, CAB 16/136; Eden at Cab 63(36), 4 November, CAB 23/86; Vansittart memorandum, 31 December 1936, *Documents on British Foreign Policy, 1919–1939*, Second Series (London, 1947–84), 17, appx. II (hereafter cited as *DBFP*); Chamberlain at Cab 5(37), 3 February 1937, CAB 23/87; Strang and Bridges in Uri Bialer, *The Shadow of the Bomber: The Fear of Air Attack and British Politics, 1932–1939* (London, 1980), pp. 44, 150. Official British documents cited here and below are housed in the Public Record Office, London.

[6] Lord Hankey, *Government Control in War* (Cambridge, 1945), pp. 59, 81–83. Hankey's former colleague Lord Chatfield faulted the machinery in which individuals were mere "cogs," and which allowed strict Treasury control over the Service departments; *It Might Happen Again*, vol. 2: *The Navy and Defence* (London, 1947), p. xi.

[7] See Gruner, "British System"; Meyers, *Britische Sicherheitspolitik*; Schmidt, *England in der Krise*; Bernd Jürgen Wendt, *Economic Appeasement: Handel und Finanz in der britischen Deutschland-Politik, 1933–1939* (Düsseldorf, 1971). All four authors reflect the influence of the German school of history that stresses the "primacy of internal politics"; Meyers, Schmidt, and Wendt have also contributed essays to Mommsen and Kettenacker, *Fascist Challenge*. Among British scholars, Paul Kennedy is one of the first to use German analyses; see *The Realities behind Diplomacy: Background Influences on British External Policy, 1865–1980* (London, 1981). Except for Meyers, these historians give more attention to social and economic issues than to the machinery itself.

economy, foreign policy, and defense caused influential people to question the efficacy and durability of British institutions and to admire some of the attributes of fascist regimes. In 1934, Leopold Amery, who had liked the taste of power as an assistant secretary in David Lloyd George's War Cabinet and now had none as a critical Conservative back-bencher, advocated the peacetime establishment of a small "Policy Cabinet." He blamed the "tyranny of the agenda" and the competition among government departments for the fact that important questions were broken up. There was "no such thing as a Cabinet policy on anything, . . . [and] the whole system tends to procrastination and drift." Cabinet weakness, he warned, might so discredit the parliamentary system that Britain would "follow in the wake of Central Europe." J. L. Garvin, editor of the *Observer*, agreed with Amery that "in this more complex age the old system derived from the eighteenth century . . . simply cannot bring sufficient driving power to the political machine." Britain needed a small inner Cabinet in peace as well as in war, one that would not bog down in administrative detail.[8] These and other apprehensions about British democracy can also be found in the documents of departments, interdepartmental committees, and the Cabinet Secretariat. Some officials attributed their fatigue and frustration to having to conduct policy in a democracy. Hankey and others regretted that it took so long to educate public opinion in the importance of rearmament. Some officials implicitly blamed democracy for a foreign policy that drifted from crisis to crisis, reacting to the moves of other states without any coherent plan of its own.

In contrast to Britain and other democracies, Garvin maintained, the dictatorships were stronger militarily, they were superior "in all kinds of organizing energy and executive ability," and they were led by "big men" with youthful and dictatorial vigor. Admiration and envy of fascism, although often no more than grudging, also colored official correspondence in Whitehall. The dictatorships seemed efficient, adept at long-term planning, ingenious at deficit spending on rearmament, quickly able to instill military virtues in the population and to pursue foreign policies of action based on design. These presumptions led Garvin to the conclusion that British democracy required "executive energy" at least equal to that of the dictatorships, for "organisms perish when they cease to adapt themselves protectively to their surroundings." Democracies are "big or little according to the men that lead them . . . [and] the leaders of the democracies (except perhaps Roosevelt) are not big men today." Chamberlain was "a limited though

---

[8] Amery to Garvin, 27 March 1934, and Garvin to Amery, 3 April; Garvin Papers (Harry Ransom Humanities Research Center, University of Texas at Austin).

cool and clearcut man," who did not have energy enough to rival Hitler and Mussolini.[9] Probably few ministers and officials subscribed to such fatalistic Darwinian reasoning, but many believed that the parliamentary system must stiffen its sinews if Britain hoped to survive in an increasingly hostile environment.

Challenged by fascism, which seems to have given the phrase "mad dog" an unusually ominous meaning in the 1930s, British attitudes were ambivalent. Hitler and Mussolini were sometimes described in clinical terms as irrational, sometimes paternalistically as unruly children or unpleasant boors who violated proper standards of international decorum and, even worse, got what they wanted. They might ignore the cautious counsel of their expert advisers and rashly use war to relieve economic instability and other domestic pressures. Yet they would presumably listen to reasoned proposals for economic stability and peace, and apparently had efficient policymaking systems able to develop long-term plans. Dictatorships could easily take military action before completing long-term rearmament programs, and democracies could not. Yet Germany might wait until well prepared, and Britain could, before full rearmament, show force in the Mediterranean to deter Mussolini and could use significant progress on rearmament as a means for bargaining with Germany.

London hesitated to make bold changes in the machinery of policy or adopt fascist (or American) fiscal methods at a time when political institutions, already strained by the economic and social pressures of the Great Depression, now undertook the additional task of rearmament. Although governments elsewhere—Germany, Italy, the Soviet Union, the United States, Japan—had begun to treat politics as a perpetual state of emergency, the British clung to the belief that crises such as war, revolution, general strike, and mass unemployment occur only intermittently. "Policy analysis" and "crisis management" do not describe what the Cabinet did or what was expected of the Civil Service. These terms, and their somber implication that government is a science of emergency, belong to the period after the Second World War. On the other hand, events forced Whitehall to admit that normalcy, to which it had ostensibly returned after the Great War, belied the actual state of affairs. It was not normal to contemplate the possibility of war on three fronts—Europe, the Far East, and the Mediterranean. The fundamental crisis in Britain's global situation forced policy and policymaking into an unstable position between peace and war, between normalcy and emergency, between day-to-day exigencies and long-term planning.

[9] Ibid., Garvin's notebook entries, May–September 1935.

This dilemma underscored the interdependence of foreign policy, armaments, supply, finance, and military strategy. To correlate these areas of policy, the British Government held meetings of the full Cabinet or a few ministers, created interdepartmental committees directly responsible to the Cabinet or to the Cabinet's standing Committee of Imperial Defence (CID), instructed the Chiefs of Staff (members of the CID) to examine contingencies, established in 1936 the office of the Minister for the Coordination of Defence, and relied on the Secretariat of the Cabinet and CID to coordinate the work of committees and departments. Nothing like the CID and its Secretariat existed in the United States. The French Conseil Supérieur de la Défense Nationale, a ministerial body, did not include the Foreign Minister and met infrequently after 1935. Smaller committees (the Haut Comité Militaire, 1932–36, and its successor, the Comité Permanent de la Défense Nationale) and their permanent secretariat made some headway in coordinating departmental preparations for defense, but the French system fell short of the British in terms of political stability, administrative experience, and mutual trust between civilian and military authorities. In Nazi Germany, the Ministerial Defense Council was established in 1933 but did not meet until 1938. The process of *Gleichschaltung* (coordination) of party and state organizations, the implementation of the *Führerprinzip* (leader principle), and the intense personal rivalries in Berlin all impaired civil-military relations.

British administration was designed to ensure the efficiency of decisionmaking, lend coherence to national policy by showing the interrelationship of diverse considerations and providing a common principle or goal on which to base the choice of priorities, and promote civil-military cooperation. In practice, however, the intention did not correspond to reality. Major decisions concerning foreign policy, rearmament, and strategy were postponed. Delays occurred in drawing up war plans and creating a shadow armament industry even after civilian and military leaders had agreed in 1934 that Germany posed the greatest threat to European peace and British security. Before 1937, the Treasury's habit of financing immediate defensive needs through annual Service Estimates impeded the Cabinet's approval of long-term plans with large financial commitments. Military advisers did not agree on a common strategy for deterrence or war, and Hankey did not want to air their quarrels. They and officials in the Foreign Office continued to quarrel over the distinction between military (or technical) and political considerations, even though the meaning of "policy" became increasingly synoptic as peacetime routines shaded into preparations for war.

The CID and a number of other committees had broad terms of

reference for the comprehensive examination of foreign policy, defense, and finance. Three committees were established at critical moments when the Cabinet agreed that foreign policy and defense plans needed reassessment, coordination, and consistency: the Defence Policy and Requirements Committee (DPR) in July 1935, when the proximity of enemy threats and the priorities for British rearmament were in doubt; the Cabinet Committee on Foreign Policy (FPC) in April 1936, in response to the Mediterranean and Rhineland crises; and the Defence Plans (Policy) Committee, or DP(P), in February 1937, following the Service staffs' completion of the first of several plans for war.

Neither the CID nor any of these additional committees lived up to their panoramic billing. Like the Cabinet itself, they worked harder on particular and immediate issues, such as international crises, than on general and long-term planning. The CID, cumbrous and meeting infrequently, made the slightest contribution, at least until late 1936. Of the smaller committees, the DPR had the most far-reaching terms of reference, but was sidetracked by the Mediterranean crisis and subsequently confined to rearmament. The FPC dealt chiefly with ad hoc assignments, not overviews. The DP(P) did better than the others at fulfilling its charter, but its coexistence with them raised doubts about jurisdictions. These and other mechanisms for coordination did not produce coherence among areas of policy, articulation between present urgencies and future objectives, or clear and timely decisions. The process of policymaking resembled a rugby scrum more than a rowing eight.

This book relies heavily on official documents, although Hankey once warned "how mischievous and embarrassing" was the use of Cabinet papers for purposes other than "to facilitate the efficient conduct of public affairs."[10] Reports of interdepartmental committees frequently hid sharp differences of opinion in an effort to foster the appearance of consensus. Policy was shaped by countless undocumented conversations on the telephone, at private clubs, on walks in St. James's Park, during public school reunions, at college gaudies in Oxford and Cambridge, on weekends in the country. Official correspondence only faintly reveals that discussions of modern weapons of war took place in anachronistic settings. The Imperial Defence College was housed in what had been a nineteenth-century dwelling. The offices of the Cabinet-CID Secretariat at Whitehall Gardens had been the private residences of Robert Peel and Benjamin Disraeli, and Hankey's office, formerly Disraeli's drawing room, still had "the gilt mirror and the rather vulgar paintings of fat-tummied cherubims and pop-eyed

---

[10] Hankey memorandum, 17 July 1936, CP 198(36), CAB 24/263.

fishes."[11] Victorian trappings; the tradition of government by Old Boys who had studied classics at Oxford and Cambridge or military history at Sandhurst; the moral sensibilities inflamed by King Edward VIII's fateful decision to marry Mrs. Simpson: all these conflict with the image of an intricate machinery of policy, monitored through carefully cross-indexed records by experts who, with positivist confidence, laid plans for long-term policy. The official records can be used to show that Hankey overestimated the effectiveness of the machinery, but they give little evidence of what its deficiencies owed to intangible social forces or the "political culture" outside it.[12] While I intend no mischief toward such forces as determinants of national policy, I treat high policy largely as a matter of high bureaucratic politics.

Without trying to prove or disprove models from the social sciences, the conceptual contours of this book owe something to them. Although not always explicitly, this work of history borrows from other disciplines and may exemplify what Gerald Holton, the physicist, calls "functional incorporation," a kind of synthesis of fields which "stems from the fact that so much of modern scholarship is problem oriented rather than discipline oriented."[13]

Social scientists can help shed light on British deterrence and policy-making in the 1930s. In search of theories for preventing or limiting war in the nuclear age, scholars have defined deterrence to mean persuading an opponent that the risks and costs of a particular course of action might exceed the benefits. Deterrence can prevent an opponent from initiating such an action, or it can compel him to stop or undo one already begun. Deterrence requires the threat of force (although not necessarily the capacity to win a war), clear signs of determination to defend one's interests, and "crisis management" involving the carrot as well as the stick. The deterring nation can threaten to punish the aggressor with retaliatory nuclear strikes against civilian targets, or it can deny the enemy territorial gains by being prepared to use largely conventional forces on the battlefield. In addition to the "primary" deterrence of attack against one's own country, there is the problem of "extended deterrence" against threats to one's allies and associates, who might question the deterring power's will to defend them if not itself attacked. Deterrence and conciliation (or "reassurance") are often

[11] Lord Ismay, *The Memoirs of Lord Ismay* (London, 1960), p. 44.
[12] Paul Kennedy warns against examining "the plumbing, not the water; the wires, and not the electrical impulses"; *Realities*, pp. 252–53.
[13] Gerald Holton, "Introduction," *Daedalus* 106, no. 4 (1977), p. ix. The essays introduced by Holton contain what he calls a "mandate for incorporation [which is] . . . primarily functional rather than structural, for it comes from the here-and-now requirements of solving a problem, rather than from an overarching and ideological commitment to reorganize the bases of all scholarship."

complementary. Their effectiveness will depend on the deterring nation's military capabilities, attitude toward the status quo, credibility in honoring international commitments, reputation for firmness in emergencies, and ability to communicate resolve; and on the adversary's calculation of the advantages of compromise, the risks of going ahead, and the possibility of retaliating against deterrent moves.[14]

The usefulness of such analyses for historians is limited. By concentrating on nuclear weapons and grand strategy, deterrence theory often excludes conventional force relationships and methods of war, just as historical studies of air deterrence in the 1930s neglect land and naval forces.[15] British policymakers in the 1930s did not draw as sharp a distinction between air power and traditional military forces as modern theorists do between nuclear (punishing and highly destructive) and conventional (denying and less destructive) forms of deterrence. Nor were they as concerned as today's statesmen that appeasing one dictator might embolden others. The literature on deterrence is amorphous, and its reliance on the assumption that opponents behave rationally has been convincingly challenged.[16] By and large, these theories do not comfortably accommodate vagaries of time and personality, and they rely on counterfactual guesswork to prove that deterrence has actually succeeded or failed. Applying largely postwar American theories, which presume immense peacetime forces and a bipolar world, to prewar British practices and a multipolar world, which grew out of peacetime disarmament, is risky and anachronistic.

Nevertheless, diplomatic and military historians can benefit from social science models, particularly studies of conventional deterrence that advocate more comprehensive theory.[17] Alexander George and

[14] André Beaufre, *Deterrence and Strategy* (New York, 1966); Bernard Brodie, *Strategy in the Missile Age* (Princeton, 1959), chap. 8; Joseph I. Coffey, *Arms Control and European Security: A Guide to East-West Negotiations* (New York, 1977); Alexander L. George et al., *The Limits of Coercive Diplomacy: Laos, Cuba, Vietnam* (Boston, 1971), chaps. 1, 5 (both by A. George); Alexander L. George and Richard Smoke, *Deterrence in American Foreign Policy: Theory and Practice* (New York, 1974); Paul K. Huth, *Extended Deterrence and the Prevention of War* (New Haven, Conn., 1988); Evan Luard, "Conciliation and Deterrence: A Comparison of Political Strategies in the Interwar and Postwar Periods," *World Politics* 19 (1966–67); Richard Ned Lebow and Janice Gross Stein, "Beyond Deterrence," *Journal of Social Issues* 43 (1987); John J. Mearsheimer, *Conventional Deterrence* (Ithaca, N. Y., 1983); Patrick M. Morgan, *Deterrence: A Conceptual Analysis*, 2d ed. (Beverly Hills, 1983); Thomas C. Schelling, *Arms and Influence* (New Haven, Conn., 1966), chaps. 1, 2; Glenn H. Snyder, *Deterrence and Defense: Toward a Theory of National Security* (Princeton, 1961); Paul C. Stern et al., eds., *Perspectives on Deterrence* (New York, 1989).

[15] See George H. Quester, *Deterrence before Hiroshima: The Airpower Background of Modern Strategy* (New York, 1966), and Smith, *British Air Strategy*.

[16] See especially Robert Jervis, Richard Ned Lebow, and Janice Gross Stein, *Psychology and Deterrence* (Baltimore, 1985).

[17] For applications of theory to historical cases from the 1930s, see Huth, *Extended Deterrence*, pp. 115–38; Barry Posen, *The Sources of Military Doctrine: France, Britain, and*

[15]

Richard Smoke have differentiated three levels of deterrence in contemporary theory: strategic war, conventional limited war, and "deterrence of threats of conflict below limited war." The second and third levels, which have received scant attention in the literature, usually involve "deterrence by denial" and the commitment of the deterring nation to defend allies or neutrals against encroachment by other states. At the third level can be found coercive or "crisis diplomacy," including the prevention of crises. Deterrence at these two lower levels is complicated by many factors, such as obligations between allies.[18] Samuel Huntington advocates the use of diplomatic and economic forms of persuasion. Failing these, or in combination with them, conventional forces can deter by increasing the adversary's "uncertainties and . . . potential costs" even if one's own forces may not be sufficient for successful defense; by raising the possibility of successful defense and thus forcing the opponent to weigh the chance of being defeated; and by threatening retaliation just as in the case of strategic (nuclear) forces.[19]

Patrick Morgan distinguishes between "immediate" and "general" deterrence. In the former case, at least one of two opposing states contemplates attacking the other or seizing territory of interest to the other, and the other state threatens to defend or retaliate. General deterrence refers not to specific confrontations but to maintaining a degree of military preparedness that will discourage adversaries from resorting to force for political ends. General deterrence usually tries to reduce the likelihood of having to use immediate deterrence, but it also runs the risk of provoking such confrontations. John Mearsheimer uses British, French, and German decisions from 1938 to 1941 to illustrate his theory of conventional deterrence, underscoring "the capability of denying an aggressor his battlefield objectives with conventional forces" (notably armies) and relating deterrence to "specific military strategies."[20]

Although Whitehall did not think of deterrence in such analytical or explicit terms, British policy in the mid-1930s shows characteristics of a

---

Germany between the World Wars (Ithaca, N. Y., 1984); and Stephen G. Walker, "Solving the Appeasement Puzzle: Contending Historical Interpretations of British Diplomacy during the 1930s," *British Journal of International Studies* 6 (1980). Michael G. Fry urges historians to look explicitly at the deterrent properties of appeasement; "Historians and Deterrence," in Stern et al., *Perspectives on Deterrence*, pp. 88–91.

[18] George and Smoke, *Deterrence in American Foreign Policy*, chap. 2.

[19] Samuel P. Huntington, "The Renewal of Strategy," in *The Strategic Imperative: New Policies for American Security*, ed. Samuel Huntington (Cambridge, Mass., 1982). See also Richard K. Betts, "Conventional Deterrence: Predictive Uncertainty and Policy Confidence," *World Politics* 37 (1984–85).

[20] Morgan, *Deterrence*, chap. 2; Mearsheimer, *Conventional Deterrence*, p. 15 and chap. 2.

comprehensive strategy of deterrence. Deterrence could simultaneously be a means of foreign policy and an end of defense policy. Certainly London emphasized air power, both offensive and defensive, to prevent a "knockout" German air attack against Great Britain. But the British also viewed military deterrence more broadly to include land and naval forces, the peacetime preparation of supplies for all three Services for what might be a war of attrition, and the possibility of combined operations in Europe or the Mediterranean. They wanted to appear firm to potential enemies and allies. Implicitly extending the idea of deterrence beyond self-defense, the Government acknowledged its commitment to uphold collective and regional security and declared the integrity of France and the Low Countries a vital British interest. Against Italy, Britain used military, economic, and diplomatic pressure, before British forces were ready for a major conflict, in what later theorists might label a strategy of conventional and extended deterrence for crisis diplomacy. Combined with conciliation, this pressure might have prevented or limited Italian aggression; it might have also, especially in Eden's opinion, forewarned other disaffected powers bent on changing the status quo. Finally, Whitehall treated deterrence as both a specific and a general proposition: the prevention or limitation of war in cases of confrontation; overall strength and preparedness to restrain dictatorships in an unstable international climate.

Many counterpressures worked against forming these views into a comprehensive interpretation of deterrence. The many options for deterrence implicit in the Defence Requirements Committee's momentous report of November 1935 derived partly from disagreements among its members. Chamberlain criticized their "aggregate" proposals while he advanced the retaliatory threat of offensive air power. The Services considered deterrent forces one and the same thing as fighting forces (with reserves) ready for war. The Treasury concluded that the country's peacetime industrial and financial resources could not sustain a system of war production, and its concern for cost-effectiveness helped persuade many Cabinet members that deterrent forces were what the Royal Air Force could display in the "shop window." Unsure of its own intentions, the British Government did not engage in what could be called a common discourse with German or Italian leaders over these fundamental terms of deterrence: the limits that Britain would place upon changes in the European or Mediterranean status quo; the costs that Britain might inflict upon Germany or Italy if Hitler or Mussolini went beyond these thresholds.

The British feared that applying too much military or economic pressure against Germany or Italy might trigger retaliation, prevent recon-

[17]

ciliation, and forfeit the period of peace necessary for rearmament. They did not agree upon the levels of military force that would make coercive diplomacy effective while Britain rearmed. British intelligence found it difficult to estimate, agree upon, or distinguish between the military strength and political intentions of potential enemies. These estimates seldom dealt with how dictators might react to British deterrent policies, leaving Whitehall all the more ambivalent about how war might arise—would it come from an escalation of armaments and tension (the widely held explanation for the outbreak of the Great War), or from deliberate aggression? Viewing international interdependence as a mixed blessing, the British Government sent out mixed signals and cultivated contrary reputations. Britain would be resolute in support of the League of Nations, the Treaty of Locarno, France, and the Low Countries against aggressors, yet also fair to all parties as an international broker. London assumed it would have allies in war, yet had strong reservations about sanctions, staff talks, or dispatching an expeditionary force to the Continent, and about French alliances with countries in Eastern Europe and any obligation that might weaken national and imperial defense. The Service departments discouraged general, immediate, and extended deterrence by emphasizing Britain's worldwide responsibilities and vulnerability, advising against alliances and staff talks, questioning the imminence of the German threat, advocating rearmament in depth for all three Services over a long period as the prerequisite for deterrence, equating the effectiveness of deterrence with sufficient forces to win a war, and depicting the worst case—war on two or more fronts—if Britain used force prematurely.

The Foreign Office was more willing than the Services to show force in the Mediterranean crisis, to honor international commitments and take consequent risks in case of threats against other countries, and to use the act of rearming as a means of impressing Hitler. Late in 1935, however, most Foreign Office officials admitted that displaying strength had not halted Italian aggression, and that Britain had not rearmed sufficiently to negotiate a settlement with Germany. The Foreign Office amended this notion of general deterrence of Germany early in 1936 amid warnings that Germany planned to remilitarize the Rhineland. Particular concessions could serve as bargaining chips for reciprocal commitments from Germany, all of which would help pacify Europe and avert potentially dangerous confrontations during what Vansittart called the "interval" of British rearmament. This plan suffered defeat in the Rhineland crisis, when Hitler chose the moment to overthrow the status quo and the Locarno Pact before he offered anything in return. Together, both crises revealed Britain's strategic lia-

[18]

bilities, damaged British moral and diplomatic suasion, and constricted British suppositions about deterrence.

In the ensuing debate over how to buy time, the weight of argument began to shift toward appeasement, with the pejorative meaning of surrender that has haunted the word since the late 1930s. During the fall and winter of 1936–37, the Foreign Office lost prestige because of its internal dissension and its failure to reduce the number of Britain's potential enemies. Against the interventionist implications of its heed for the security of France and Eastern Europe, the isolationist arguments of the Service staffs gained headway through ministerial consideration of major strategic reports. Chamberlain thought Britain must extend time, not deterrence. He and the Treasury began to formulate the doctrine that economic stability is an arm of defense with great deterrent power; rearmament and foreign policy must exist according to what Britain could afford to pay for expanding its forces until 1942 and maintaining them at those levels thereafter. Supply requirements, war plans, the debate over the Army's role in a continental war, and financial limitations all converged with foreign policy early in 1937 so as to broaden the meaning of policy, to set 1942 as the date until which time must be provided, to suggest that conciliation did not require coercion from the appeaser or firm reciprocal guarantees from the appeased, and to define deterrence largely in terms of self-defense.

Social scientists have found determinants of policy in the interests and procedures of government organizations and in the internal "bargaining" among members of the bureaucracy. Some argue that policymakers do not integrate problems, but separate them to reduce anxiety and instability in the policymaking system. Decisions are not reached "rationally" by comprehensive analysis of all possible options and their long-term consequences, but "incrementally" by taking small steps that seem practicable at the moment.[21] Some decisionmakers work less to attain a particular external goal than to preserve the internal mecha-

---

[21] Graham T. Allison, *Essence of Decision: Explaining the Cuban Missile Crisis* (Boston, 1971); David Braybrooke and Charles E. Lindblom, *A Strategy of Decision: Policy Evaluation as a Social Process* (New York, 1963); Morton H. Halperin, *Bureaucratic Politics and Foreign Policy* (Washington, D.C., 1974); Charles E. Lindblom, *The Intelligence of Democracy: Decision Making through Mutual Adjustment* (New York, 1965); Richard C. Snyder et al., *Foreign Policy Decision-Making: An Approach to the Study of International Politics* (New York, 1962); John D. Steinbruner, *The Cybernetic Theory of Decision* (Princeton, 1974); Harold L. Wilensky, *Organizational Intelligence* (New York, 1967). Amitai Etzioni proposes "mixed scanning" as a third model, "less demanding" than rationalism but "more demanding" than incrementalism: see *The Active Society: A Theory of Societal and Political Processes* (New York, 1968). Herbert Simon contends that policymakers oversimplify problems and select courses of action which they consider satisfactory without weighing all the possible alternatives: *Models of Man* (New York, 1957), chap. 14.

[19]

nism of policymaking, and they try to deal with uncertainty by avoiding it.[22] International crises cause internal administrative processes to neglect other matters and individuals to lose confidence in their ability to control the course of events. In Adam Yarmolinsky's words, political leaders can adopt the military habit "of reckoning contingencies in terms of the capabilities rather than the intentions of potential enemies . . . and emphasizing readiness for the worst contingencies that might arise."[23] As Robert Jervis notes, one of the most common misperceptions shared by policymakers is that the policy of other governments is "more centralized, planned, and coordinated" than their own.[24]

It is awkward at best to apply these largely American models to a British case occurring before the war that accelerated the growth of both bureaucracy and political science.[25] Still, these models help clarify how the machinery of policy lost time through confusion while trying to buy time through conciliation. As the word "policy" outgrew its peacetime compartments and acquired intimations of war, competition among departments increased and the outcomes of bargaining among their idiosyncratic views of time and deterrence became more consequential. Even Vansittart and Fisher, high officials who prided themselves in transcending bureaucratic interests, became more and more identified with their respective departments. The Service departments were especially interested in the problem of fighting the next war, the Foreign Office in how to prevent or postpone it, the Treasury in how much to pay for prevention while maintaining normal trade. Expert advisers had great and often decisive influence on Cabinet policy. Military experts, who usually formed a united front, gained ground on those from the Foreign Office, whose own infighting weakened their position in interdepartmental debates. Both kinds of experts lost ground to the Treasury, which, partly because of the default of other departments, became the dominant force in the bureaucratic politics of rearmament and deterrence. Major committees usually examined issues of policy separately and episodically rather than comprehensively and consequentially. Whitehall reacted to international crises as if they were untimely, temporary intrusions into both the assumptions and

[22] Steinbruner, *Cybernetic Theory of Decision*, pp. 65–66. See also Robert Jervis on "cognitive consistency" in *Perception and Misperception in International Politics* (Princeton, 1976), chap. 4.

[23] J. W. Burton, *Systems, States, Diplomacy and Rules* (Cambridge, 1968), pp. 76–77; Oran R. Young, *The Politics of Force: Bargaining during International Crises* (Princeton, 1968), pp. 311–12; Adam Yarmolinsky, *The Military Establishment* (New York, 1971), p. 110.

[24] Jervis, *Perception and Misperception*, p. 319.

[25] For example, see Meyers, *Britische Sicherheitspolitik*, in which the models and the narrative tend to be divorced. Meyers prefers Charles Lindblom's theses of "muddling through" and "disjointed incrementalism" to describe British policymaking.

the machinery of long-term planning, and the committee system produced more interdepartmental consensus for ending crises than for general plans.

Finally, the proliferation of committees and overlapping of their agendas evidenced not only coordination of work, but also confusion of purpose. The complex network of committees proved far more successful at coordinating many and often inconsistent ideas, as Hankey and Prime Minister Stanley Baldwin thought it should, than reducing and integrating them in a coherent plan, as Neville Chamberlain would have preferred. The first of these methods of policymaking caused delays, sustained conflicting views of time and strategy, and reached incremental compromises among government departments. It also preserved many potential options for deterrence, since the Government had to determine the appropriate interrelationship of military forces, foreign policy, finance, and timing with each new international crisis or stage of rearmament.

The incompatibilities among immediate dangers, foreign policy, available resources, strategies for war, and long-term rearmament became acute during the Mediterranean and Rhineland crises. They remained so in 1936–37, confirmed by the Spanish Civil War, the absence of a new western security pact or general European settlement, the preparation of war plans, and inter-Service disputes regarding operations and supply. The blame for Britain's persistent difficulties fell on the actions of Britain's foes and friends, but also increasingly on the Foreign Office, the inadequacies of the committee system, and Baldwin's lethargy in the twilight of his premiership. Chamberlain shrewdly exploited the atmosphere of uncertainty along Whitehall, where a growing number of ministers and expert advisers—including Hankey—saw in him Britain's best chance for achieving efficiency, coherence, and success in correlating foreign policy, defense, and economic stability. Chamberlain was certain that he could clearly define national policy and bring order to it. He would increase the opportunities for conciliation, reduce the international and strategic options for deterrence, use 1942 to resolve contrary notions of time, systematize British defense policy with a logical plan based on air power and finance, and prevent war.

Chamberlain disdained Baldwin's indulgent style of leadership. Intolerant of muddling through, Chamberlain planned to make action, efficiency, and decisiveness the bywords of his regime, which would be a unique British reply to vigorous dictatorships abroad. With these ambitions always in mind, he strengthened his already predominant position in the Cabinet as he prepared to succeed Baldwin. Events of 1937–39 would reveal how delusionary was the idea that a fundamental change in leadership and planning could prevent war with Germany or give Britain much prospect for winning, especially if war spread to other fronts. Yet Chamberlain's succession in May 1937 made sense for Britain at the time, for the times had done much to make the man.

A more cohesive system of policymaking, with strong leadership from Baldwin, would probably not have deterred Mussolini or Hitler in 1935–36. But it might have quickened the pace of rearmament, sustained several compatible options for deterrence, and produced a genuine reassessment of policy. It might also have given Chamberlain and the Treasury less cause to see themselves as the sole guardians of orderly government and the best judges of timing. Above all, by lessening the contrast between Baldwin and Chamberlain, such a system might have dampened the beguiling assumption that only Chamberlain's new model of administration could remedy Britain's global predicament with a unified strategy of deterrence. That presumption soon carried Chamberlain to Munich with unprecedented coherence of policy and unwarranted confidence in its success.

PART I

FROM DISARMAMENT TO
REARMAMENT, 1934–1935

[1]

First Steps toward
Rearmament

In 1934–35, the British Government seriously began plans to increase Britain's military power because of Japanese aggrandizement in the Far East and Germany's newfound assertiveness under Hitler. Two new committees formed bookends for this first stage in the evolution of British policy in the mid-1930s. In February 1934 the Defence Requirements Committee (DRC) began with recommendations to rectify, in five years, most of the major deficiencies in the authorized peacetime strengths of the three Fighting Services. Rearmed, Britain could deter Japan and Germany, the latter being the "ultimate potential enemy." In the summer of 1935, the Defence Policy and Requirements Committee (DPR) was appointed "to ensure that our defensive arrangements and our foreign policy are in line."

Between these two moments perplexing questions arose about timing and deterrence, and the DRC's five-year program began to slip. It was not clear whether the German or the Japanese threat would materialize first, exactly when the Service programs would be completed, or how the Cabinet's decision to achieve parity with Germany in air forces would affect the priorities and funding for defense in general. The uncertain timetables for reconditioning the Services arose from disjointed sources. The Foreign Office guessed that Hitler might make war by 1939, Chamberlain that Germany needed more than five years, and the Chiefs of Staff that Germany would not fight before militarily prepared in 1942. The Admiralty's goal of readiness by 1942 derived from its plans of 1932 with special regard for Japan. Supply committees used five years as a convenient period for planning irrespective of particular threats. The Treasury wanted to budget and manufacture arms at a pace that Britain could economically afford. The dates 1939 and 1942 were acquiring a magical significance from various venues.

Among these, the Foreign Office could not be sure that Hitler would risk war against military advice, the Services did not explain how 1942 could be a good year for both Britain and Germany to fight, and the Treasury would not abandon the parochial tempo of normal trade. No one postulated a year when Britain might do better to risk war over German actions than to postpone it until Germany grew even stronger.

The disparity among considerations of time frustrated attempts to develop a policy of deterrence, in which the relationship between immediate actions and long-term goals was crucial. Three different views of deterrence emerged. Preoccupied with Britain's reputation and interdependencies abroad, Sir Robert Vansittart urged a bold policy of rearming all three Services—including the creation of an expeditionary force for the Continent—to impress likely enemies and allies and to prepare for the possibility of German aggression before 1939. Suspicious of international commitments, the Chiefs of Staff and Sir Maurice Hankey recommended conciliatory diplomacy without taking risks while rearming for imperial security and for a conflict with Germany that Britain would not be strong enough to win—and thus unable to prevent—before 1942, the year when they presumed Germany would be ready for war. Neville Chamberlain advocated construction of an offensive air force powerful enough to moderate Hitler's aims, stop him from launching an air attack against the United Kingdom, and spare the cost of expanding the Army for operations on the Continent. Diplomatic reconciliation with Japan would save the expense of building a two-ocean Navy. The Cabinet's decisions incorporated parts of all three of these conceptions, without determining the extent to which British deterrence should precede the completion of the Service programs, embrace air power, rely on allies, or go beyond self-defense. Meanwhile, the beginnings of British rearmament did not in fact prevent Hitler from repudiating the Treaty of Versailles in a way that was unmannerly but not irrational.

Because of frictions inherent in the machinery of policy, coordination of dissimilar views of time and deterrence proved difficult, and a coherent policy free of major incongruities was impossible. Terms of reference and other procedural language ensured neither clear definitions nor expeditious handling of "general defensive policy." The large Committee of Imperial Defence no longer examined defense policy "as a whole." The DRC, a small official committee, did so, but the urgency, range, and cost of its conclusions were diluted by an exclusively ministerial committee dominated by Chamberlain—the Ministerial Committee on Disarmament. The DPR had a mixed membership (the Chiefs of Staff served as expert advisers) and a broad charter, but these advantages for planning "general defensive policy" over the long term began immediately to fade when the committee failed to discuss the framework for that policy. Although members of the DRC freely exceeded the particular concerns of their own departments, the departmental self-interest and interdepartmental bargaining characteristic of bureaucratic politics were much in evidence. Quarrels increased inside the Foreign Office, and among the Foreign Office, Service departments, and Treasury over assessments of danger, strategies and schedules for deterrence, and claims of departmental jurisdiction, with the Treasury enjoying the great advantage of Chamberlain's preeminence in the Cabinet. Committees valued compromise more than consistency among these various positions.

By and large, this system of "mutual adjustment" satisfied Ramsay MacDonald, Stanley Baldwin, and Hankey. It did not suit Chamberlain, who deeply resented the consequences of what he considered inefficient decisionmaking: unreconciled policies, unruly timetables, unrestricted options for deterrence, and unnecessary costs. While Britain began to rearm, tension arose between this system and Chamberlain's ideal of a rational structure that would bring order to British policy and prevent war.

"DEFENCE BY COMMITTEE"

In James Ramsay MacDonald's National Government, November 1931 to June 1935, the Cabinet collectively was responsible for decisions on major issues of defense policy, but it depended on the recommendations of ministers and officials or "expert advisers" who sat on the Committee of Imperial Defence (CID) and its many subcommittees.[1] Chaired by the prime minister, the CID comprised the Lord President of the Council (Stanley Baldwin); Chancellor of the Exchequer (Neville Chamberlain); Secretaries of State for Foreign Affairs (Sir John Simon), Dominion Affairs (J. H. Thomas), India (Sir Samuel Hoare), Colonies (Sir Philip Cunliffe-Lister), War (Lord Hailsham), and Air (Lord Londonderry); First Lord of the Admiralty (Sir Bolton Eyres-Monsell); the three Chiefs of Staff; Permanent Secretary to the Treasury (Sir Warren Fisher); and Permanent Under-Secretary for Foreign Affairs (Sir Robert Vansittart). The CID had been formally established in 1904

---

[1] For histories of the CID and its network of subcommittees, see John Ehrman, *Cabinet Government and War, 1890–1940* (Cambridge, 1958); Gibbs, *Rearmament*, chap. 20; Gibbs, *The Origins of Imperial Defence* (Oxford, 1955); Lord Hankey, *Diplomacy by Conference* (New York, 1946), chap. 4; Robin Higham, *Armed Forces in Peacetime* (Hamden, Conn., 1962), chap. 7; Major General H. L. Ismay, "The Machinery of the Committee of Imperial Defence," *Journal of the Royal United Services Institute* 84 (1939); Franklyn A. Johnson, *Defence by Committee: The British Committee of Imperial Defence, 1885–1959* (London, 1960).

to remedy what the War Office (Reconstitution) Committee, chaired by Lord Esher, viewed as a major defect: "The British Empire is pre-eminently a great Naval, Indian and Colonial Power. There are, nevertheless, no means for coordinating defence problems for dealing with them as a whole, for defining the proper functions of the various elements and for ensuring that, on the one hand, peace preparations are carried out upon a consistent plan, and, on the other hand, that, in times of emergency, a definite war policy based upon solid data can be formulated."[2]

By 1934, the CID had become unwieldy and met infrequently. It was a sort of clearing house for reports that its numerous subcommittees handed up to the Cabinet and ad hoc Cabinet committees or down to departments.[3] For strategy and operations, the most important of the CID's subcommittees was the Chiefs of Staff (COS, created in 1923): Admiral Sir A. E. M. Chatfield (chairman), First Sea Lord and Chief of Naval Staff; General Sir A. Montgomery-Massingberd, Chief of the Imperial General Staff; Air Chief Marshal Sir E. L. Ellington, Chief of the Air Staff. Each chief advised his own Service's board or council. Collectively, the COS advised the CID on "defence policy as a whole," prepared an annual review of imperial defense, and could take the initiative to bring strategic matters to the attention of the Cabinet. Under the direction of the COS, the Joint Planning Committee (JPC, established in 1927) drafted strategic plans and much of the annual defense review. Its members were the Admiralty's Director of Plans (chairman), and the Deputy Directors of Operations in the War Office and Air Ministry.

Of the CID subcommittees responsible for supply, the Principal Supply Officers Committee (PSOC) was the most significant. Established in 1924 and reconstituted in 1927, the PSOC was supposed "to coordinate the war supply arrangements of the three Defence Services, to avoid the competition and delays that occurred in 1914, and to ensure that the most advantageous use should be made of British industry in an emergency."[4] The president of the Board of Trade (Walter Runciman) chaired the PSOC, which included officials from the Board of

---

[2] Quoted in CP 88(36), 2 April 1936, CAB 24/261.

[3] Coordination with the Dominions, each of which planned its own defense policy, took place at Imperial Conferences and through informal contacts between British and Dominion officials. See Gibbs, *Rearmament*, pp. 782–89; Johnson, *Defence by Committee*, pp. 213–17.

[4] From a memorandum of December 1933, in J. Hurstfield, *The Control of Raw Materials* (London, 1953), p. 433. In addition to Hurstfield and the sources cited in note 1 above, see M. M. Postan, *British War Production*, rev. ed. (London, 1975), chaps. 1, 2; William J. Reader, *Architect of Air Power: The Life of the First Viscount Weir of Eastwood, 1877–1959* (London, 1968), pp. 191–93; J. D. Scott and R. Hughes, *The Administration of War Production* (London, 1955), chap. 4.

Trade, Home Office, and Service departments. The PSOC normally met once a year to consider reports from its subcommittees. Among these subcommittees, the Board of Trade Supply Organization dealt with raw materials; the Supply Board considered the types and quantities of material needed by the Services and the peacetime capacity and wartime mobilization of industry; and the Advisory Panel of Industrialists, appointed in 1934, sought firms outside the arms industry that might immediately shift to the manufacture of munitions in case of war. This network of interdepartmental supply committees reflected Whitehall's aversion to concentrating authority over supply in a single ministry during peacetime, and indeed its hope that nothing as centralized as the previous war's Ministry of Munitions would be necessary in the next war.

Among other subcommittees of the CID, the Oversea Defence Committee dealt with matters relating to the defense of the Dominions, colonies, and protectorates. The major responsibility of the Home Defence Committee was evident in the title of its Subcommittee on the Air Defence of Great Britain. The Advisory Committee on Trade Questions in Time of War (ATB), established in 1923, and its Subcommittee on Economic Pressure (1933) moved increasingly into the area of intelligence as they assessed the vulnerability of foreign countries to economic pressures that Britain, a member of the League of Nations, might have to exert against nations that went to war in violation of the League Covenant.[5] In 1929, the CID appointed a subcommittee on Industrial Intelligence in Foreign Countries (FCI) to coordinate this subject for the Board of Trade and Service departments. By June 1932, the FCI had added a representative from the Foreign Office, and had gained CID approval for the institution of the Industrial Intelligence Centre (IIC). Major Desmond Morton, who had been seriously wounded while commanding an artillery battery at Arras in 1917, headed the IIC, whose job was "to assist in the collation, interpretation and distribution of foreign industrial intelligence . . . ; to coordinate this intelligence as far as possible for the benefit of the Admiralty, War Office, Air Ministry, the FCI Committee, and the ATB Committee of the Committee of Imperial Defence."[6]

[5] Hinsley, *British Intelligence*, pp. 30–32.

[6] FCI note of 22 February 1934 and report of 14 May, in CID 1139B, CAB 60/14; also note of 30 January 1934 on the functions of the FCI, and Morton report of 15 May 1935 on the activities of the FCI during the past twelve months, in CAB 48/4. These documents indicate that the Services and other departments had much to learn from each other, that the FCI also needed a Treasury member because of the financial intelligence received, and that each Service department could still "interpret and apply industrial intelligence for its own purposes as far as possible" (FCI note of 22 February 1934). On the organization and purview of the FCI and IIC, see Andrew, *Secret Service*, pp. 354–55; Hinsley,

The CID's Committee on the Coordination of Departmental Action on the Outbreak of War would coordinate and allocate "the responsibility for action by Government Departments on the outbreak of war."[7] The committee was responsible for the War Book, which contained detailed instructions for the departments. Periodically updated, the War Book stipulated that, in an emergency, the Secretary to the Cabinet would help the prime minister decide which of four alternative systems of "supreme control" to adopt: (1) the peacetime system of the Cabinet advised by the CID; (2) "the Cabinet assisted by a Special Cabinet Committee"; (3) "the Cabinet assisted by a 'War Committee' with fuller executive powers" than the committee mentioned previously; (4) "a War Cabinet, which absorbs the functions of both the Cabinet and the [CID]."[8]

The mixed membership and functions of the CID and its subcommittees affirmed two principles of decisionmaking: the maintenance of political control by the Cabinet while civilian and military experts supplied the practical knowledge and were allowed (as were individual ministers) some latitude in the execution of policy through their respective departments; and the interdependence of foreign policy, defense, and finance. "Defence by committee" rested on the accumulated weight of precedent, if not an unblemished record of success (the disastrous failures of planning the Dardanelles expedition in 1915 come to mind). The system remained pliable enough for the Cabinet, committees, departments, or individuals to push in particular directions with a vigor that blurred distinctions between advice and decision, or between administration and policy. The Cabinet self-consciously preserved its authority before Parliament and public opinion. In agreeing with officials on the need for secrecy and expert advice in foreign policy and defense, however, ministers subscribed to the "Whitehall" school of constitutional thought.[9]

Collaboration between civilian and military officials on issues that were strictly neither political nor military helped break down anachronistic barriers between two types of professional. The CID and its subcommittees depended on a spirit of teamwork, which seems to

---

British Intelligence, pp. 30–31; Wark, *Ultimate Enemy*, pp. 158–62; Robert J. Young, "Spokesmen for Economic Warfare: The Industrial Intelligence Centre in the 1930s," *European Studies Review* 6 (1976).

[7] CP 88(36), 2 April 1936, CAB 24/261; also Ismay, *Memoirs*, p. 54; Johnson, *Defence by Committee*, pp. 268–71.

[8] Hankey memorandum, 24 May 1928, CAB 4/17.

[9] On the "Whitehall" view versus the "Liberal" (which emphasizes parliamentary sovereignty), see A. H. Birch, *Representative and Responsible Government* (Toronto, 1964), pp. 65–81, 165–70, 238–39; H. V. Wiseman, *Parliament and the Executive* (London, 1966), pp. 16–21.

have owed its existence partly to the fact that planning, administration, and execution were combined in the committees' membership. Ministers and officials advised on interdepartmental issues yet retained allegiance to their respective departments.[10] The maxim of defense by committee was coordination, not centralization. But would the CID system accomplish its constitutional mission of dealing with defense problems "as a whole" and making peacetime preparations according to a "consistent plan"? Doubtful signs can be found as Britain began to rearm.

DEFENSE REQUIREMENTS

British defense policy after 1919 presupposed that there would be no great war for the next ten years. In July 1928 the Cabinet made the "Ten Year Rule" self-renewing from each day forward, to the chagrin of the Chiefs of Staff and Sir Maurice Hankey, who had watched the Government let military strength sink far below authorized levels after the necessary postwar demobilization. The Far East crisis caused by Japan's invasion of Manchuria in 1931 prompted the COS to recommend cancellation of the Ten Year Rule. The CID accepted this recommendation in March 1932, and the Cabinet revoked the Ten Year Rule, though without committing itself to increases in defense expenditure, and with hopes that the General Disarmament Conference, which opened in Geneva in February 1932, might achieve results that would spare Britain the need to rearm.

Hitler's seizure of power in Germany in January 1933 gave the Chiefs of Staff still more reason to press for a strong defense policy. In their annual review of October 1933, prepared as usual with assistance from the Foreign Office, the COS warned that Germany would surely rearm to the point where, in a few years, it could start a war in Europe. Britain might then be obliged by the Treaty of Locarno (1925) to intervene on the side of France; at Locarno, Britain (and Italy) had guaranteed the Franco-German border and the demilitarization of the Rhineland. Alluding to an ancient and clear national interest, the COS stated that Britain must keep any continental power from seizing the Low Countries. Britain's defenses were inadequate for its responsibilities in Europe and the Far East, where the recent Sino-Japanese truce did not remove the potential danger to the British Empire from Japan. The

---

[10] Hankey later referred to the "humanizing process" of the CID, with particular reference to civil-military cooperation; *Government Control*, pp. 75–77. Donald Cameron Watt surveys civil-military relations between the world wars in *Too Serious a Business: European Armed Forces and the Approach to the Second World War* (London, 1975).

Services needed new instructions from the Government now that the Ten Year Rule had been discarded. On 14 October, two days after the COS completed this report, Germany withdrew from the League of Nations and the Geneva Disarmament Conference. Sobered by Hitler's unilateral blow to these collective ventures in which Britain had invested heavily, the CID and Cabinet agreed in November 1933, twenty months after abandoning the Ten Year Rule, to establish the Defence Requirements Committee (DRC) to examine the country's defenses.

The DRC was an ad hoc subcommittee of the CID, consisting of Hankey (chairman), Vansittart, Fisher, and the three Chiefs of Staff. The CID instructed the DRC to "prepare a programme for meeting our worst deficiencies," basing its recommendations for the time being on these "considerations of priority . . . : the defence of our possessions and interests in the Far East; European commitments; the defence of India." Furthermore, "no expenditure should for the present be incurred on measures of defence required to provide exclusively against attack by the United States, France or Italy."[11] These guidelines fit Britain's current situation: strategically, the most likely dangers came from Japan and Germany; economically, the Government could not afford to prepare for hypothetical threats from other powers.

The DRC report of 28 February 1934 signaled a fundamental change in British defense policy, from having ruled out war for ten years, to planning for its possibility in five. In October 1933, Hankey, Vansittart, and Fisher had jointly prepared a memorandum on the danger from Germany, and the DRC report emphasized the threat of war in Europe. Although the committee did not consider Japan an immediate danger to British imperial interests, it proposed strengthening defenses in the Far East in order to be ready for any emergency there, to regain Japan's respect and friendship (the DRC blamed the deterioration in Anglo-Japanese relations since the war largely on Britain's "subservience to the United States"), and to minimize the risk that "Japan might yield to the sudden temptation of a favourable opportunity arising from complications elsewhere." Since "elsewhere" meant Europe and the danger to Britain in Europe would "only come from Germany," the DRC concluded that Germany was "the ultimate potential enemy against whom our 'long-range' defence policy must be directed." Although not presently "a serious menace" to Britain, Germany would become one "within a few years." Referring to its instructions to disregard the contingencies of war with the United States, France, and Italy, the DRC observed that Britain's "long-range policy cannot be founded ex-

[11] In DRC report (DRC 14), 28 February 1934, CAB 4/23.

clusively on what might prove to be a temporary and shifting basis, and we cannot entirely ignore the possibility of changes in the international situation." Although such possibilities did not have to "be taken into account in immediate defensive plans and preparations, they ought not to be overlooked in providing the basic elements of our defensive system, such as programmes of construction extending over a long term."[12]

The DRC did not recommend rearmament, technically speaking, but a program to remedy the worst deficiencies that disarmament and the Ten Year Rule had caused in Service programs approved by the Government in the 1920s. Even this "minimum" program, the committee feared, would meet strong opposition from a "morally disarmed" British public. The DRC hoped most deficiencies could be met in the next five years, but noted that some would take longer. The Navy required modernization of ships, reinforcement of bases, and sufficient reserves of oil and other supplies. Otherwise, even assuming that Britain's naval construction program kept pace with Japan's in the 5:3 ratio approved at the Washington (1922) and London (1930) Naval Conferences, the fleet would "not be in a proper condition to encounter an enemy fleet after its arrival in the Pacific."

Because of the German threat to the Low Countries, which were now even more vital to British security because Germany might build air bases there, the Army's major deficiency lay in the expeditionary force. As "an essential first step," the DRC recommended the capability of mobilizing, within one month, a "Regular Expeditionary Force" of four infantry divisions, one cavalry division, two air defense brigades, and a tank brigade. Supplementing this force with contingents from the Territorial Army was "a matter which will require consideration when the urgent needs of the Regular Army have been met." The Royal Air Force should expand to the fifty-two squadrons approved in 1923. Although not within the meaning of "worst deficiencies," at least another twenty-five squadrons would be necessary for home defense and other tasks, especially if Germany should rapidly expand its air forces. The DRC estimated the cost of the whole program (apart from naval construction) at about £82 million over eight or nine years; of the £71

---

[12] These quotations and those in the following paragraphs are from ibid. For the origins and work of the DRC: Brian Bond, ed., *Chief of Staff: The Diaries of Lieutenant-General Sir Henry Pownall*, vol. 1 (London, 1972), pp. 24–30, 33–38; Bond, *Military Policy*, pp. 195–99; Dennis, *Decision by Default*, pp. 34–38; Gibbs, *Rearmament*, pp. 85–87, 93–99, 120–23; John M. Lippincott, "The Strategy of Appeasement," Ph.D. diss., Oxford University, 1976, chap. 2; Meyers, *Britische Sicherheitspolitik*, pp. 231–44; Roskill, *Hankey*, 3: 86–90, 101–5; Shay, *British Rearmament*, pp. 30–33; Smith, *British Air Strategy*, pp. 121–30.; Wark, *Ultimate Enemy*, chap. 1.

million for the first five years, £40 million would go to the Army, £21 million to the Navy, and £10 million to the Royal Air Force.

The DRC outlined military strategies in the event of conflict. The Navy would have the most important role in a war against Japan. For a war with Germany, in which the committee presumed Britain would be allied to France, the duties of the Services "would not differ very much in kind from those that they filled in the last war." The Navy would protect British coasts and maritime communications while controlling the seas. The Army would provide land defense of ports, naval bases, and British shores; antiaircraft defense; and an expeditionary force for action on the Continent. The Royal Air Force (RAF) "would be responsible for defence against air attack (including counter-attack), for various forms of cooperation with the Navy and Army as well as for the provision of the air force to accompany the expeditionary force." Although acknowledging that a European war might lead to—or coincide with—trouble in the Far East and India, the DRC did not dwell upon the contingency of a two-front war. Instead, the committee assumed that reconditioning the Navy for a war in the Far East would enable it to accomplish its mission in a European war, and that strengthening the Army and Air Force for the latter case would suffice for the defense of India (and presumably for a war in the Pacific). In any theater, the Services would require "close coordination."

The DRC report, a compromise document, echoed the unresolved debate among those who signed it. The dominant personalities were Fisher and Vansittart, but Hankey and Chatfield also put their stamp on the report. Fisher thought that regaining Japan's friendship would reduce naval expenditure and would be worth sacrificing good relations with the United States, a country for which he had utmost contempt. Opposed to such an extreme view of Anglo-American relations, Hankey and Chatfield nevertheless hoped for a rapprochement with Japan. So did Vansittart, although he doubted that a durable accommodation was possible. The Foreign Office resisted the Treasury's inclination toward Japan and argued that Britain's position in the Far East depended on friendship with China. Fisher and Vansittart, preoccupied with the threat from Germany, ensured that the report named Germany as Britain's "ultimate potential enemy." Although the DRC report did not make a clear distinction between Germany's military strength and its intentions, Vansittart had begun to view Hitler as a "mad dog," and he and Fisher feared that the Nazi leader might launch a "knockout" air attack against Britain before Germany was militarily prepared for war. Vansittart was grateful for Fisher's support for more air squadrons, but regretted that the "amiable trio" of experts (the COS) could not be moved to ask for increases beyond which they expected approval.[13] Hankey's holiday in Germany in August 1933 had left him with foreboding impressions of Nazi chauvinism,[14] but he questioned the imminence of the German danger and held to Chatfield's view that Japan was Britain's major threat.

Thus, the DRC report contained two different perspectives on grand strategy, and competition between them was embedded thereafter in the politics of defense. Fisher and Vansittart represented the European position (defense of Britain against Germany), Hankey and Chatfield the imperial imperative (defense of the empire primarily against Japan).[15] Fisher and Vansittart wanted to recommend immediate authorization for expanding the Air Force beyond fifty-two squadrons. Hankey and Chatfield wished to discard the "One-Power Standard" of the 1920s and build a "two-ocean" navy capable of defending the empire against Japan while protecting home waters against the strongest European naval power. Such a force was implicit in the Admiralty's redefinition of the One-Power Standard as they prepared for the London Naval Conference scheduled for 1935. The Army was more ambivalent about sending troops to the Continent than the DRC report indicates; the General Staff also had in mind its imperial mission to help defend naval bases and territories, including especially India's Northwest Frontier.[16] Jeopardizing any military commitment to the Continent was this news from Ellington, delivered to the DRC on the day it issued its report and contradicting his earlier statements to the committee: the Air Staff could not provide any support for the expeditionary force from the authorized fifty-two squadrons.[17]

Slow to respond to the DRC report of 28 February, the Cabinet referred it to the Ministerial Committee on Disarmament, chaired by the prime minister. Set up in 1932 to deal with the Geneva Disarmament Conference, this committee had become a catchall for foreign policy and defense. Now it had on its agenda three major problems which the Government considered parts of the general policy of pacifying Europe: arms limitation, whether by reviving the Geneva Disarmament Conference (it adjourned *sine die* in May 1934) or through other interna-

[13] Lord Vansittart, *The Mist Procession* (London, 1958), p. 443. See also Norman Rose, *Vansittart: Study of a Diplomat* (London, 1978), chap. 8. In addition to the sources in the preceding note, see Schmidt, *England in der Krise*, pp. 195–221, for a summary of the views of Hankey, Vansittart, and Chatfield; and, on Fisher, see Ennan O'Halpin, *Head of the Civil Service: A Study of Sir Warren Fisher* (London, 1989), pp. 227–31.

[14] Roskill, *Hankey*, 3: 82–85.

[15] Ann Trotter examines the relationship between British defense and diplomacy in the Far East in 1934, in *Britain and East Asia, 1933–1937* (London, 1975), chaps. 4, 6. See also William Roger Louis, *British Strategy in the Far East, 1919-1939* (Oxford, 1971), chap. 7.

[16] On the Navy's plans, see Gibbs, *Rearmament*, pp. 117–20; on the Army, Bond, *British Military Policy*, pp. 198–99.

[17] Gibbs, *Rearmament*, p. 98; Smith, *British Air Strategy*, p. 129.

tional agreements; European security (the Government parried both Hitler's proposal for nonaggression pacts and France's request for specific British guarantees in case of German aggression); and a program for increasing Britain's military strength. The simultaneous pursuit of disarmament and rearmament, both of which had vociferous public advocates and were fed by fear of bombing, soon became official policy.

The Ministerial Committee discussed the DRC report at thirteen meetings from early May to late July 1934.[18] Neville Chamberlain dominated these sessions. In opposition to the implications of the DRC report, he argued that Britain could not financially afford to prepare for a two-front war in the Far East and Europe. Britain should work toward rapprochement with Japan instead of "flirting" with the United States, and must concentrate on Europe, where Hitler was the greatest long-term menace. The best, quickest, and cheapest defense against Germany would be the deterrent power of an Air Force large enough to inspire the enemy's respect; "fear of force" would prevent war.[19] The Army, a secondary line of defense, would not have to send an expeditionary force to the Continent unless the air deterrent failed. For a European war, the Navy would not need major expenditures on deficiencies in the Far East or on the construction of capital ships.

Some of Chamberlain's colleagues—notably Baldwin, Cunliffe-Lister, Simon, and Hoare—agreed with him on the importance of an air deterrent, but the committee did not unequivocally endorse Chamberlain's plan for a defense policy oriented almost entirely toward Europe and air power. First Lord of the Admiralty Eyres-Monsell insisted that the greatest danger lay in the Far East, and he was not the only minister who wanted Britain to maintain a strong naval presence there. Others included MacDonald, Simon, Hailsham, and Baldwin, who told the committee that both Japan and Germany were mad dogs, and that "'the scope for a mad dog was wider in the Far East than it was in Europe'" for the next few years.[20] Although not members of the committee, Hankey, Vansittart, and the Chiefs of Staff advised ministers to retain both the imperial and European strategic missions contained in the DRC report.

The European contingency itself was subject to different interpretations. Although intelligence disclosed that Germany was accelerating

[18] For details, see especially Gibbs, *Rearmament*, pp. 102–27; also Keith Middlemas and John Barnes, *Baldwin: A Biography* (London, 1969), pp. 756–81.
[19] Chamberlain diary, 25 March and 6 June, NC 2/23a; Chamberlain to his sisters Ida (12 May) and Hilda (28 July), Chamberlain Papers (Birmingham University Library), NC 18/1/870, 881.
[20] Shay, *British Rearmament*, p. 41.

its rearmament and expanding its aircraft production capacity, British policymakers disagreed over the imminence of the German threat and the strategy Germany would employ in a war in Western Europe. Vansittart, Simon, and Fisher thought that the DRC report did not give the German threat sufficient urgency. Hankey claimed that Germans "'are not supermen'" and faulted the Cabinet and Foreign Office for being "'rather over-obsessed with the danger from Germany.'" Chamberlain doubted that Germany could be prepared for a war against the West within five years.[21] Baldwin admitted that no one in London really knew what Germany intended to do.[22] Chamberlain, Simon, Hoare, Cunliffe-Lister, Baldwin, Vansittart, Fisher, and Ellington thought Germany would probably begin a western war with a knock-out air attack against Britain. Hailsham, Hankey, Chatfield, and Montgomery-Massingberd considered this far less likely than a main German offensive on land, yet the General Staff remained unenthusiastic about sending an expeditionary force to the Continent, and the COS strongly opposed holding staff talks with France and Belgium to coordinate plans.

On 31 July, the Cabinet approved the DRC report as amended by the Ministerial Committee.[23] The revisions, largely the work of Chamberlain, threw the DRC's balanced program out of kilter and skewed defense policy toward the German threat and expansion of the Royal Air Force. Partly in response to mounting public pressure for air defense (Winston Churchill was especially critical of the Government in the House of Commons), the Cabinet authorized an additional number of air squadrons over the next five years, with reserves to be added from 1939 to 1942. The Air Ministry viewed such a rapid expansion to 1939 without the necessary reserves as "window dressing," an ineffectual deterrent born of "air panic." But the Cabinet's decision transformed the deficiency program into a program for rearmament, at least in terms of air forces. The Cabinet had given some teeth to Stanley Baldwin's statement of 8 March to the House of Commons, that British air strength would not be inferior to that of any country within striking distance of British shores.

The Admiralty's ambitions to build a two-ocean navy, capable of defending simultaneously against Japan and a major European naval power, suffered a major setback. The Ministerial Committee and Cabinet did not accept Chamberlain's proposal to stop building battleships, but neither did they sanction a long-term program that com-

---

[21] Bialer, *Shadow*, p. 56; Roskill, *Hankey*, 3: 119; Gibbs, *Rearmament*, p. 115.

[22] Thomas Jones, *A Diary with Letters, 1931–1950* (London, 1954), p. 129.

[23] Report on Defence Requirements by the Ministerial Committee on Disarmament, 31 July, CP 205(34), in CAB 16/110.

bined deficiency and replacement expenditure—the DRC had pointed in this direction by appending the Admiralty's plans for construction of new ships over the next five years. The Admiralty would have to use the normal procedure of negotiating its expenditures annually with the Treasury, and the Navy's deficiency program was cut from £21 million to £13 million. The Cabinet's action can be explained partly by the difficulty of estimating standards and long-term costs before the expected 1935 London Naval Conference convened. At least as weighty as this, however, was Chamberlain's case for concentrating on the German threat. What Hankey viewed as Chamberlain's "'unsound strategic doctrines about the Navy'" were only partially counterbalanced by the Ministerial Committee's affirmation of "'the paramount importance of the Navy as the shield of the whole Empire and of its vital seaborne communications.'" One of Hankey's assistant secretaries, Major Henry Pownall, described Chamberlain's strategic ideas as "strangely obtuse." The chancellor was "obstinate and strategically undereducated." Limiting Britain's liability on land was "deadly dangerous," he wrote, "how the Dominions will appreciate the withdrawal of naval cover!"[24]

The Army's deficiency program was halved. Of the £20 million authorized for five years, £12 million was designated for the expeditionary force, the rest for the ground defense of overseas ports (especially Singapore) and Great Britain. The Cabinet recognized the vital importance of defending the Low Countries with land forces, but this acceptance of a continental commitment was already weakened by reservations among the Chiefs of Staff and in the War Office and Cabinet, where Chamberlain and other ministers had begun emphasizing public distaste for such terms as "expeditionary force," which brought back unpleasant memories of the Somme.[25]

Agreeing with the Treasury that financial stability was essential for national security, and readier than the DRC to spread the deficiency program out over more than five years, the Cabinet reduced the DRC's five-year budget to £50 million. Yet even this reduced amount was not firm. Chamberlain insisted that the Treasury was bound neither to the sums nor to the five-year period mentioned in the final report. He would not borrow to pay for defense. He would not sacrifice butter for guns when the Government had pledged to reduce taxes and restore cuts made in salaries in 1931.[26]

[24] Roskill, *Hankey,* 3:119, and Roskill's *Naval Policy,* p. 171; Bond, *Chief of Staff,* pp. 42, 45–46, 50.

[25] Bond, *British Military Policy,* pp. 202–10; Dennis, *Decision by Default,* pp. 40–47; Michael Howard, *The Continental Commitment* (London, 1972), pp. 107–10.

[26] Ministerial Committee meetings, May–July, and final report, 31 July, CAB 16/110; Middlemas and Barnes, *Baldwin,* pp. 771–74.

The "air panic" that seized the Government in late 1934 and early 1935 led to a still larger air program. Two distinct waves of panic occurred. The first followed reports from French intelligence in October 1934 that Germany planned to have 1,300 first-line aircraft plus reserves by October 1936 instead of 1,000 by April 1939 (the British Air Staff's estimate of summer 1934). The second came after Hitler's claim, to Simon and Eden in late March 1935, that Germany's air force was already equal to Britain's and aimed toward parity with the French Metropolitan Air Force (which London estimated at 1,500 first-line aircraft).

British intelligence about German rearmament ranged from concrete information on industrial production to hunches regarding Hitler's intentions, leaving much room for disagreement over German strength and aims. Vansittart was the ranking Whitehall member of an alarmist camp that also included Ralph Wigram, Desmond Morton, Winston Churchill, and Lord Rothermere (owner of the popular *Daily Mail*, the first Secretary of State for Air, and unlike the others in his admiration of Hitler). Vansittart was sure that Germany would soon achieve air superiority over Britain, and he reproached the Air Ministry for underestimating Germany's actual strength and industrial capacity. Churchill, to whom Morton, his neighbor in the country, gave secret information collected by the Industrial Intelligence Centre, warned that Germany would be at least as strong as Britain in the air by the end of 1935 and twice as strong in 1937. Rothermere claimed that Germany already had 10,000 airplanes and might begin an air war before the end of 1936.[27]

By April 1935, the assessments of the rate of German expansion made by the director of Air Intelligence (Group Captain Charles Medhurst) had begun to confirm those of the Foreign Office and the IIC; and a joint Foreign Office-Air Intelligence memorandum warned that Britain lacked security during the next year " 'against some wild 'coup de main' by men whose previous acts have shown the nature of their resolution and audacity.' " The Air Ministry thought British intelligence estimates too high (including those of Air Intelligence), disputed Hitler's exaggerated claim of parity with Britain, and did not see how Germany could be ready for war before 1942. Morton and the IIC were convinced that Germany was gearing up its economy for total war. The Air Ministry agreed with the Foreign Office that, in a war, Germany would use superior air power to achieve a military decision in the

[27] Vansittart memorandum, 24 April 1935, *DBFP*, 13, no. 127; Rothermere to Garvin, 3 March, Garvin Papers. On Churchill and German rearmament in 1934–35, see Martin Gilbert, *Winston S. Churchill*, vol. 5: *The Prophet of Truth, 1922–1939* (Boston, 1977), chaps. 29, 32, 33.

shortest possible time, but resented Vansittart's pushing for a more rapid pace of rearmament than seemed necessary or wise.[28]

Like the Air Force, the other Services jealously guarded their prerogative to evaluate the military significance of intelligence received by the IIC and FCI. The Admiralty and War Office also emphasized 1942 as the earliest date for German military readiness, but rejected the thesis of an early knockout blow—Germany would employ air and army units together for a decision on land. Stressing Germany's territorial ambitions in the east and its problem of securing its eastern frontiers in an unlikely western war, Colonel B. C. T. Paget of Military Intelligence advised that in 1939 Germany would lack the necessary "war-preparedness" for a successful war against Britain, France, and Belgium. Vansittart, Paget complained inaccurately, "was concerned only with air forces." He had named dates (1936, 1937, not later than 1938) without consulting the General Staff, and without regard for the interrelationship of economic, military, and political factors inside Germany. Vansittart's doubts about the reliability of France as an ally should indeed underline the necessity of reaching "a peaceful settlement with Germany [rather than] resigning ourselves to the fatalistic policy based on inevitable war" without allies and with only an Air Force.[29]

British foreign policy was both fatalistic and conciliatory. Britain tried to reassure France by reaffirming British obligations under the Treaty of Locarno at the Stresa Conference in April 1935 after Germany had publicly announced that it had begun an air force and military conscription. In what soon became known as the Stresa Front, British, French, and Italian leaders censured Germany's unilateral action and reiterated their loyalty to the Locarno Pact. Yet the British also recognized that what Germany had already done to upset the Versailles settlement could not be reversed. Thus, Britain should play the honest

---

[28] Memorandum quoted in Bialer, *Shadow*, p. 71. For the "battle of half truths" between the Foreign Office and Air Ministry concerning the rate and quantity of German air rearmament, see Wesley K. Wark, "British Intelligence on the German Air Force and Aircraft Industry, 1933–1939," *Historical Journal* 25 (1982), as well as his *Ultimate Enemy*, chaps. 2, 3. As Wark's book clearly shows, "Germany was never seen through a single lens" (p. 34). See also Andrew, *Secret Service*, pp. 388–89; Avon, *Dictators*, pp. 204–8; Bialer, *Shadow*, pp. 54, 57–58, 70–74; Gibbs, *Rearmament*, pp. 135–40; Hinsley, *British Intelligence*, pp. 59–61; R. J. Overy, "German Air Strength 1933 to 1939: A Note," *Historical Journal* 27 (1984); Rose, *Vansittart*, pp. 135–37; Roskill, *Hankey*, 3:664–65; Donald Cameron Watt, "British Intelligence and the Coming of the Second World War in Europe," in Ernest R. May, ed., *Knowing One's Enemies: Intelligence Assessment before the Two World Wars* (Princeton, 1984), pp. 255–57.

[29] Admiralty memoranda on the purview of the FCI, 26 January and 1 February 1934, CAB 48/4; Paget (MI3) minutes, 28 February and 27 April, WO 190/303, 324. On Military Intelligence, including collaboration with the IIC and disagreements with the Foreign Office, see Wark, *Ultimate Enemy*, chap. 4.

broker to conciliate Germany, even if Germany could not be brought back into the League of Nations and the Geneva Disarmament Conference. Britain should be ready to negotiate bilateral arms control agreements with Germany (such as the Naval Agreement of June 1935), unwilling to tie itself too closely to France through military staff talks, but basing defense policy on independent considerations of national and imperial security.[30]

Fatalism and conciliation also ran through the Cabinet's directions for revising the draft White Paper on Defence published on 4 March 1935. The paper should (and did) emphasize "the importance of our defence forces from the point of view of peace, defence and *deterrent* against an outbreak of war, and . . . not make specially prominent such matters as our military obligations and commitments, as well as our deficiencies from the point of view of offensive action." With the forthcoming debate on Service Estimates in mind, the paper was designed to educate the public in the need to improve Britain's defenses. Reflecting public opinion's influence on the Cabinet, the paper emphasized air defense of Great Britain, omitted mention of an expeditionary force and the implied commitment to France and Belgium, noted the Government's continued adherence to collective security and disarmament, and stressed the compatibility between deterrence and "the establishment of peace on a permanent footing."[31]

In the House of Commons on 11 March, the Government easily defeated the Opposition's motion of disapproval after a debate in which Clement Attlee (deputy leader of the Labour party) and Sir Herbert Samuel (leader of the Liberal party) labeled the White Paper a betrayal of disarmament and peace. About a week later, the Service Estimates were voted by large majorities. The estimates totaled approximately £124 million compared with £114 in 1934. The increase included costs for the first year of the five-year deficiency program, the bulk of this for the Royal Air Force.

The decision in July 1934 to expand the Air Force was caught up in the two waves of air panic as the Cabinet took a position somewhere between the Foreign Office's alarm over the unpredictability of the German threat and the Service departments' assurance that the threat could not be close at hand. In November, the Cabinet announced that most of the new air squadrons approved in July would be ready by April 1937 instead of 1939. At the end of April 1935, the Ministerial

---

[30] See R. A. C. Parker's succinct analysis, "Economics, Rearmament and Foreign Policy: The United Kingdom before 1939—A Preliminary Study," *Journal of Contemporary History* 10 (1975).

[31] Cab 11(35), 25 February, CAB 23/81; Statement Relating to Defence, CP 38(35), 4 March, CAB 24/253, Cmd. 4827.

Committee on Defence Requirements (as the Ministerial Committee on Disarmament had been renamed) appointed a small subcommittee on air parity, chaired by Cunliffe-Lister. Within a few weeks, this subcommittee's report was approved by the Cabinet and a new program of air force expansion—Scheme C—was announced to the House of Commons on 22 May. Scheme C would, by April 1937, increase the number of first-line aircraft in Britain's Metropolitan Air Force to 1,512. The subcommittee and Cabinet thought that this expansion would achieve numerical parity with Germany, and that there would be time after 1937 to augment first-line forces with reserves.[32]

Scheme C concentrated on the German threat and the possibility of a European war, but the imperial strategy was also very much alive in the winter and spring of 1935. The Principal Supply Officers Committee did not abandon the 1928 hypothesis for a non-European war. When this committee asked the CID to furnish a standard hypothesis on which to base calculations of supply, Hankey, Chatfield, and Eyres-Monsell maintained that Britain must prepare concurrently for both the European and Far Eastern contingencies, and their argument carried the day at the CID meeting of 16 April 1935. Chamberlain questioned the two-front hypothesis and advised "prudent diplomacy" toward Japan, but the CID, while acknowledging the need for prudence, directed the PSOC to base their plans on both contingencies. The White Paper on Defence, drafted by Hankey, upheld the vital importance of the Navy and its capital ships for defense of Britain's maritime communications. In their annual review of imperial defense, the Chiefs of Staff stated that the "minimum naval strategical requirement for security" was the protection of home waters against German raids and the dispatch of the main fleet to the Far East to shield British interests.[33]

Imperial strategy also informed London's reasons for concluding the Anglo-German Naval Agreement of 18 June 1935. Since December 1934, when the Japanese announced their decision to withdraw from the Washington Treaty of 1922 (renewed at the London Naval Conference of 1930), the prospects had dimmed for a new treaty in 1935

[32] Reports of the Air Parity Subcommittee, 8 and 20 May, CP 100 and 103 (35), CAB 24/255; Cab 29(35), 21 May, CAB 23/81; Bialer, *Shadow*, pp. 68–73; Basil Collier, *The Defence of the United Kingdom* (London, 1957), pp. 31–35; J. A. Cross, *Lord Swinton* (Oxford, 1982), pp. 137–42; Gibbs, *Rearmament*, pp. 175–77; Meyers, *Britische Sicherheitspolitik*, pp. 267–71; Smith, *British Air Strategy*, pp. 152–59. On the problem of how to define parity, see Gibbs, pp. 539–53; Smith, chaps. 4–7 passim; Wark, *Ultimate Enemy*, chap. 2; Sir Charles Webster and Noble Frankland, *The Strategic Air Offensive against Germany, 1939–1945*, vol. 1 (London, 1961), pp. 65–81.

[33] PSOC annual report (PSO 454), 7 January 1935, CAB 60/14; PSOC meeting, 4 April, CAB 60/4; CID meetings, 25 February and 16 April, CAB 2/6; COS annual review (COS 372), 29 April, CAB 4/23.

limiting naval tonnage. The naval powers still hoped to schedule a general conference in London before the Washington and London treaties expired at the end of 1936. Meanwhile, concerned about Germany's naval expansion over the long term, the Admiralty welcomed an agreement in which Germany promised the size of its navy would not exceed 35 percent of Britain's, a ratio that Germany would probably not reach before 1942. If Germany held to this agreement, Britain could maintain its 5:3 Washington Treaty advantage over Japan, and, if an alliance with France could be counted upon, then the Royal Navy could carry out its European and imperial missions in a two-front war.[34]

TIME AND DETERRENCE

By June 1935, British policy combined these sets of conflicting elements: rearmament and a peaceful general settlement of grievances (including arms limitation); deterrence and conciliation; national security and collective or regional security; a special relationship with France as well as honest brokerage; protests against German breaches of the Treaty of Versailles along with readiness to negotiate bilateral pacts with Germany to replace Versailles; priority of air power expansion in response to German rearmament yet retention of imperial strategic commitments in case of Japanese aggression. The Cabinet did not view any of these dualities as necessarily self-contradictory, but they were based on matters of time that muddled notions of deterrence. Was Germany or Japan the near threat? When should the defense programs be completed? The Government's answers remained imprecise, as did its thinking about deterrence.

Adequate military strength in peacetime, the DRC had asserted, was "the best possible deterrent to the ambitions of any potential enemy"; this was the goal of the deficiency program. The committee applied this general theorem to two particular threats, Germany and Japan. An Army expeditionary force, supported from the air, "would, as a deterrent [to Germany], exercise an influence for peace out of all proportion to its size." A reconditioned fleet with well-defended bases in the Far East could safeguard British imperial interests. When the DRC advocated "showing a tooth" now in the Far East, however, the committee expanded the idea of deterrence: it was not necessary to complete the deficiency program before demonstrating a willingness to use force. In

[34] On the Naval Agreement and the British path toward it: Gibbs, *Rearmament*, pp. 155–70; Hines H. Hall, "The Foreign Policy-Making Process in Britain, 1934–1935, and the Origins of the Anglo-German Naval Agreement," *Historical Journal* 19 (1976); Roskill, *Naval Policy*, chap. 10.

both the German and Japanese cases, the aim of deterrence was diplomatic reconciliation and prevention of war. Both contingencies required strengthening all three Services for a coordinated strategy, one that modern theorists might describe as a "conventional" strategy for preventing either a major war or limited conflicts.

Having related deterrence to Britain's European position and extensive overseas interests, the DRC admitted that "practical finance [made it] impossible for a world-wide Empire like our own to be equally secure at every point against every conceivable enemy." Thus, it was necessary to base defense policy on "certain assumptions on such matters as what countries have to be considered as potential enemies, allies or neutrals, and the time limits within which the different dangers are liable to develop."[35] The DRC recommended a balanced program that did not favor one Service over the others. Yet the fate of this program—and its deterrent value—depended on confused and inconsistent views of time.

The DRC's choice of five years for meeting the worst deficiencies seems to have had two separate bases, apart from financial considerations. On the one hand, the committee estimated that Germany would need five years of rearmament before it could pose a real threat to Britain. On the other, late in 1933 the CID had approved the COS recommendation for the Principal Supply Officers Committee to use five years as the "hypothetical time limit" in which to prepare plans for industrial mobilization in case of war. This period was selected because it seemed to be a practicable guideline for regulating the supply group's work, not because a potential enemy might attack in five years. Moreover, since 1928, the strategic hypothesis governing the PSOC's work was for a conflict outside Europe.[36] The five-year premise (and thus the contents and pace of the deficiency program itself) could be questioned by those who feared that Hitler might strike sooner; by those who wanted British air expansion to keep pace with Germany's; by those who wished to begin making supplies as well as plans; by those who thought Germany would not risk war before 1942; and by those, particularly in the Admiralty, who saw Japan as the major threat and 1942 as a reasonable terminus for deficiency and construction programs, irrespective of the German question.[37]

---

[35] This and preceding quotations are from the DRC report (DRC 14), 28 February 1934, CAB 4/23.

[36] Supply Board meeting, 25 October 1933, CAB 60/31; DRC report (DRC 14), 28 February 1934, CAB 4/23; PSOC meeting, 1 November 1934, CAB 60/4; Bond, *Chief of Staff*, p. 23; Gibbs, *Rearmament*, p. 96; Hurstfield, *Control of Raw Materials*, p. 35; Peden, *British Rearmament and Treasury*, p. 109; Watt, "British Intelligence," pp. 250–51.

[37] In 1932, months before Hitler became chancellor, the Admiralty prepared plans for a decade of expenditure to right all the wrongs of the Ten Year Rule; Roskill, *Naval Policy*, p. 151.

As we have seen, the DRC cautioned that long-term defense policy should not be "founded exclusively" on a current state of international relations that might prove "temporary and shifting." "Immediate defensive plans and preparations" could, however, ignore the possibilities of change in the international situation. Having made this distinction between long-range and immediate planning, the DRC in fact mixed the two. The five-year program was designed to eliminate the worst deficiencies in the "shortest practicable period"; the program should guide defense policy "for the present," and "showing a tooth" to Japan should be "an immediate and provisional" foreign policy. But a longer period would be necessary to remedy all deficiencies (let alone to expand beyond authorized levels). Long-range defense policy should recognize that Germany was "the ultimate potential enemy," yet not exclude the possibility of other contingencies. Foreign policy should aim toward an "ultimate accommodation with Japan," which could threaten British interests over the short term and might cause mischief if Britain were engaged in a European conflict. Hankey and Chatfield viewed deterrence as an imperial strategy relying on a strong navy and requiring many years to modernize or construct ships, while Fisher and Vansittart had begun to think of deterrence chiefly as a European strategy accentuating the rapid expansion of air power to counteract the threat from Germany.

The juxtaposition of immediacy and eventuality in the DRC report would contribute to the disorder in British policy thereafter. First, the financing of preparations over the next five years would raise questions about the strategic underpinnings of long-term defense policy. Who was the main enemy and what British military arm would predominate in the event of conflict? Second, hypotheses carried forward from the present might preclude or delay adding other contingencies to long-term planning. If the United States, France, or Italy should begin to threaten British interests, how long would it take Whitehall to determine whether this was a momentary aberration or longer-term danger? Third, immediate defense measures might become too firmly tied to long-range goals and thus limit rather than increase Britain's freedom of action in crises that broke out before the completion of the deficiency program. If the Services had objectives of expansion to meet by 1939, why delay their work and deplete their existing resources before then?

Finally, no clear distinction would be drawn between the possible uses and timing of deterrence. Would deterrence be feasible only after Britain upgraded its defenses? If so, how could diplomacy alone buy time? Or would the demonstrable will to strengthen its defenses enable Britain to impress both potential enemies and allies even while the five-year program was under way? Would Britain threaten to fight if friendly countries were attacked or only to defend itself? Would deterrence prevent war, or buy more time to prepare for a major conflict that an irreconcilable enemy was bound to start? Did Britain really intend to punish an aggressor by retaliation or to deny the enemy victory by mounting an effective defense? Did the success of either punishment or denial presuppose mobilizing Britain's economic potential and empire for a long war? Should priority go to one Service because of its deterrent power in the most likely contingency?

The Cabinet's approval of the revised DRC report did not resolve such conflicting ideas about strategy, time, and deterrence. Although the Cabinet gave priority to the German threat and expanding the RAF, it also preserved the imperial strategy and the possibility of constructing a two-ocean navy. Emphasizing air power, the Cabinet hoped, would both deter Germany and boost public confidence in Britain's ability to defend against air attack. But the notion of air deterrence, let alone its eventual success, was complicated.

What signals was Britain prepared to send out to potential enemies, and how would the eye of the beholder interpret them? Would the air deterrent become effective by the very policy of air force expansion, or by at least maintaining parity with Germany, or after completing the first-line squadrons, or after supplementing these with reserves? Which air strategy was more likely to deter Hitler: the threat of a punishing retaliation by British bombers (probably without fighter escorts) against German cities and industry, or the capacity to defend Britain successfully (largely with fighters and antiaircraft weapons) against German bombing raids? Could British intelligence provide the answer along with statistics about German industrial production? How could deterrence be extended to prevent attacks against allies? In the absence of preliminary staff talks with France and Belgium, and without an expeditionary force ready for combat shortly after hostilities began, how could Britain, as Chamberlain envisaged, "deter Germany from mad dogging" by bombing the Ruhr with airplanes based in Belgium? If an expeditionary force were dispatched, how much air support should accompany it and at what cost to Britain's capacity to deter Germany with squadrons based in Britain? Did the strategy of "showing a tooth" in the Far East have a European analogy? That is, if British naval power could impress and pacify Japan, could British air power have similar effect on Germany? Could Britain's determination to rearm thwart or regulate Hitler's apparent aim of disrupting European politics—and expanding to the East—with a series of aggressive moves that fell short of war? If general deterrence through rearmament did not prevent such moves, should Britain threaten force to compel Germany to give up or limit specific gains on the Continent? If this deterrent threat then failed, would Britain go to war if not itself attacked?[38]

The Cabinet's adoption of a five-year program—to start in 1934—did not answer these questions and thus did not define how comprehensively or consistently Britain would pursue deterrence. The presumption, by Chamberlain and others, that such problems could be solved in time as circumstances unfolded, was implicit in their acceptance of the DRC's principle: "Long-range policy cannot be founded exclusively on what might prove to be a temporary and shifting basis." But the Cabinet did not—and could not—disentangle present and future.

The orientation of defense policy toward Europe in 1934 presumed a period of peace for developing plans for operations and supply. The COS had instructed the Joint Planning Committee to begin preparing war plans for the possibility of conflict with Germany in five years (late 1939), even though the "original five-year period . . . already approved for the Principal Supply Officers Committee" had been extended by the Cabinet to 1942 or later for many deficiencies, and although the Chiefs of Staff themselves thought it would take more than five years for the German danger to the West "to mature fully" into aggression. The COS had wished to give the JPC a "definite hypothesis" to guide its "long-term planning," which would be subject to revision to meet changing circumstances.[39] The PSOC had also begun to discuss the contingency of a German war. Pursuant to the DRC's request (of 1 February 1934) to examine how peacetime preparations might "speed up post-mobilization industrial output" for supplying the expeditionary force, the Supply Board concluded that it would be necessary to increase available reserves and implement the "shadow armament industry" plan.[40] The PSOC's Advisory Panel of Industrialists had recommended that the Government locate numerous firms and help them prepare to convert to the production of military stores in the

[38] Chamberlain to Hilda, 1 July 1934, Chamberlain Papers, NC 18/1/877. Barry Posen considers some of these questions in *Sources of Military Doctrine*, p. 72 and chap. 5. In places, Posen may distinguish too rigidly between punishment (offense) and denial (defense) because modern deterrence theory is his reference point. Elsewhere he is more tentative, admitting that British "grand strategy only loosely fits the deterrence mold" (pp. 231–32). See also Michael Howard's discussion of air deterrence in *Continental Commitment*, pp. 110–12: deterrence will not work if the opponent can "deter you from using it." The analysis of deterrence here and in chapter 3 first appeared in my article "Mad Dogs and Englishmen: British Rearmament, Deterrence, and Appeasement, 1934–35," *Armed Forces and Society* 14 (1988).

[39] Hodsoll (acting secretary of the COS in Hankey's absence) note, 28 September 1934, CAB 53/24; COS meeting, 9 October, CAB 53/5; COS report on defense plans (COS 351), 23 October, CAB 4/23; terms of reference to JPC (including the employment of land and air forces in the Low Countries), 2 November, CAB 53/24; JPC meeting, 12 November, CAB 55/1.

[40] Supply Board report (PSO 437), 11 July 1934, CAB 60/14.

event of war, and in May 1934 the CID had approved this recommendation in principle.[41] Because the PSOC's strategic hypothesis was for an extra-European war, however, the Supply Board had not been able to respond quickly to the DRC's European case. On 1 November, the PSOC thought it was time to adopt the European hypothesis. Turning to present reality, the PSOC found the store of arms and other supplies in a "lamentable situation" in case of emergency.[42]

Deciding just what should and could be done over the next five years would depend partly on the interpretation of the CID's distinction, late in 1934, between "paper planning" and "material preparations." In October, the Chiefs of Staff recommended that preparing plans for defense of the United Kingdom "'proceed on the basis that preparations should be completed in five years from 1934 in respect of a possible conflict with Germany.'" The CID approved, but "on the understanding that no question of finance was involved," and that the action of CID subcommittees be "limited to the drawing up of plans." This artful understanding reflected Chamberlain's and the Treasury's concern for keeping down costs and adhering to normal budgetary procedure, and their refusal to be bound by the five-year program recently approved. Fisher told the CID that "it would no doubt be possible to accelerate paper planning"; since the Cabinet had not accepted the DRC's recommendation, however, "material preparations would now be difficult to accelerate." Yet at the same time, echoing Simon and Vansittart, the CID asked the Chiefs of Staff "to bear in mind that events in Europe might bring about a conflict in less than five years, even though the military preparations of nations might not be completed within that period."[43]

Restricting CID subcommittees to paper plans would limit both the supplies available for defense against a sudden attack during the next five years, and the material reserves on hand in case of war in five years or more. Moreover, the five-year period itself had begun to slip. The CID, PSOC, and DRC had begun using this "hypothetical time limit" late in 1933, the Cabinet approved it at the end of July 1934, the Treasury refused to view it as binding, and the CID authorized its use for purposes of planning in November 1934. The terminus for the new defense program was beginning to imitate the self-renewing tendency of its predecessor and nemesis, the Ten Year Rule. This delay was

[41] Reader, *Architect,* pp. 193–94; Roskill, *Hankey,* 3: 101–2; Shay, *British Rearmament,* pp. 92–93.
[42] Supply Board meeting, 12 July 1934, CAB 60/31; PSOC meeting, 1 November 1934, CAB 60/4; PSOC annual report (PSO 454), 7 January 1935, CAB 60/14.
[43] COS report on defense plans (COS 351), 23 October, CAB 4/23; CID meeting, 22 November, CAB 2/6.

hardly consistent with Germany's dramatic military and diplomatic recovery.

Prompted by German rearmament and the Cabinet's policy of air force expansion, at the end of April 1935 the Chiefs of Staff asked whether Japan or Germany were now the near threat, and by what date the Service programs should be completed. Pointing out that the deficiency program adopted in 1934 presumed Japan to be the main short-term threat, with Germany the long-term menace, they wondered whether the Government still adhered to this policy. The COS doubted that Germany would, as Vansittart repeatedly warned, start a war before 1942, for the Germans would not be militarily ready. Officials in the Foreign Office, particularly Vansittart and Ralph Wigram (head of the central department), observed that Government policy could no longer appropriately describe the German threat and European contingency as "long-range." Perhaps the French General Staff was overanxious in putting the date as early Spring 1936; but other governments named 1937, and Vansittart "had met nobody who dared to put it later than early in 1938." To postpone the date to 1942, Vansittart wrote, was "to make a wish father to a comfortable thought." Germany's military preparedness was not the only question: "We have to remember that in the triumvirate (Hitler, Goering and Goebbels)— even if they are increasingly falling under the influence of the General Staff and the officials—we are not dealing with men who can be judged by ordinary standards." The Nazi oligarchy might be tempted "to precipitate a foreign crisis as a means of saving the regime from internal catastrophe." In the end, "it may well not be the complete technical readiness of Germany which will decide, but rather certain psychological and non-military factors."[44]

The Chiefs of Staff drew attention to the implications of accelerating both the air force expansion program and antiaircraft defenses. Even before the Government adopted Scheme C, the policy of expansion put the Air Force out of step with the deficiency programs of the other two Services. And the more demands that were placed on the War Office for air defense units, the longer it would take to equip the expeditionary force (now called the Field Force), which the War Office advised would take at least until 1944 because of current financial strictures. The advent of air power had made "the integrity of the Low Countries of greater importance than ever in our history, and the Army must be prepared, in conjunction with the French, to attempt to deny those

---

[44] Foreign Office (central department) memorandum (on COS report on German and British air strength of 29 April), 28 May, C3944/55/18, FO 371/18840; Vansittart memorandum, 24 April, *DBFP*, 13, no. 127.

countries to German invasion." The needs of the Field Force "should be provided concurrently with" those of air defense. If the Foreign Office were correct that the German menace necessitated a date of completion "much in advance of 1942" (the COS doubted this), then all defense measures must be accelerated if Britain were to be in a position to deter Germany.[45]

Implicit in the queries of the COS was this conclusion in the Foreign Office: some authorities in London tended to regard air parity more as a political necessity "than from the point of view of national defence." Vansittart had lobbied for air power expansion, but he and his colleagues in the central department wanted all three Services to be strengthened as quickly as possible. Noting that the newest air program (Scheme C) took 1937 as its date of completion, Vansittart and the central department agreed with the COS that a "Government decision" was needed as to the date for completing Britain's defensive preparations. This date should apply to "*all* our preparations . . . [and] be fixed without further delay." The Services should indeed assume "that a war with Germany would be fought in alliance with France and Belgium." The Chiefs of Staff were correct to recognize the importance of the Low Countries and to recommend accelerating the preparation of the Field Force "if any early date of preparedness is contemplated."[46]

Any Government decision on deadlines would have to weigh different years targeted in various departments and committees, with 1939 and 1942 mentioned most frequently. First, the Foreign Office now considered both Japan and Germany to be "near menaces" and warned of war with Germany before 1939 because Hitler might "go mad." Second, the Principal Supply Officers Committee now had to prepare plans for the possibility of war in Europe or the Far East in 1939. This CID hypothesis of war "in five years from 1934" was not based entirely on perceptions of Germany and Japan, but still to some degree on what seemed to be a practical schedule for the machinery of supply when no dramatic increase in expenditure on armaments was anticipated. Third, the Service departments saw 1942 as the earliest year in which Germany would have the military capability to risk war. Fourth, because of Cabinet decisions, budgetary restrictions, Britain's limited industrial capacity for war, and the Services' preference for slow expansion in order to ensure high quality, the Services themselves could not

---

[45] COS annual review (COS 372), 29 April, CAB 4/23; COS report of 29 April (see preceding note); COS report on air defense (COS 376), 14 May, in CP 144(35), CAB 24/256. In the War Office, the Field Force Committee and Army Council had begun to focus on the "Western Plan" for engaging the Field Force in a European war; documents in WO 163/40–42, and 33/1377.

[46] See note 44 above; also Creswell minute, 24 May, C4150/55/18, FO 371/18842.

be ready for war before 1942 at the earliest. The DRC had warned that not all deficiencies could be remedied by 1939. The Air Force would need reserves to replace inevitable losses in first-line aircraft in the early months of war. The Navy's plans for future construction awaited the possibility of a new London Naval Conference and would then, if approved by the Cabinet, take at least until 1942 to complete. Preparations of the Army's Field Force would probably not be completed before 1944. The PSOC's five-year hypothesis related to the preparation of plans for wartime supply; little progress had been made in establishing a peacetime "shadow" armaments industry.[47] Finally, the policy of air parity with Germany created a sense of immediacy in contrast to the more deliberate schedules for completing the deficiency programs of the Navy and Army.[48]

The Government could not choose any meaningful timetable for rearmament without at least implicitly defining deterrence and appeasement. Since 1933, the notion of deterrence had rested partly on suppositions about how Hitler would react to British defense policy. British intelligence did not devote much time to psychoanalysis, and Whitehall could not determine whether Hitler was a reasonable man, a temperamental child, a "mad dog," or a complex personality with all three traits. If he was rational, would British rearmament necessarily make him conciliatory and could appeasement satisfy his appetite? If he was mad, how could he be deterred or appeased?

Some ministers assumed that their very policy of air power expansion would check Hitler's demands, persuade him to negotiate an agreement to limit air armaments, and help reconcile Europe.[49] Yet British defense policy since July 1934 had not prevented Hitler from taking bold measures to overthrow the system of the Treaty of Versailles. Hitler's initial reply to the White Paper on Defence of 4 March 1935 was a "diplomatic cold" that forced postponement of Sir John Simon's visit to Berlin. Chamberlain viewed this as a "childish exhibition of bad manners" on Hitler's part, and referred to Joachim von Ribbentrop as a "mischievous meddler."[50] German manners deteriorated further when Hermann Goering declared (9 March) the existence of the Luftwaffe and Hitler announced (16 March) the introduction of conscription. Nevertheless, in May 1935 the Cabinet decided to move up a

[47] Major Pownall scoffed that it was all very well for the CID to tell the Supply Officers to be ready by 1939, "but nobody ever will be." Bond, *Chief of Staff,* p. 69.

[48] In the Foreign Office, Wigram saw this inconsistency and at the same time thought Scheme C would not enable Britain to keep pace with Germany; minute of 14 May, C3780/55/18, FO 371/18839.

[49] Smith, *British Air Strategy,* chaps. 4, 5.

[50] Chamberlain to Hilda, 9 March, Chamberlain Papers, NC 18/1/908.

debate in the House of Lords on foot-and-mouth disease in order to give Hitler time to make a statement on German policy before the Air Secretary delivered his own statement on British air policy. After Hitler's address, Chamberlain was relieved by what the Cabinet perceived to be Hitler's conciliatory mood. This change brought a "definite détente" during which Britain had time to build the RAF into a "truly formidable" deterrent and avoid "panicky and wasteful" proposals. The Government would have to convince both the House of Commons and Hitler that Britain had a striking force that "could hit very hard."[51]

Chamberlain's attitude begged questions asked in other quarters. Military Intelligence warned against an air arms race based on the elusive idea of parity: Vansittart wanted Britain to play a stabilizing role, yet the crux of his proposals envisaged "a policy of force, or at least the threat of it," and this would surely lead to an arms race and instability. Hitler was willing to negotiate, and Britain should not neglect the opportunities to reach a peaceful settlement.[52] Yet was not a childish or mad dictator just as likely to increase his demands, accelerate rearmament, or precipitate war as he was to agree to arms limitation or a general settlement? Officials in the Foreign Office certainly thought so, as did the French, who feared that any Anglo-German agreement must weaken Britain's commitment to deter Germany on the Continent. If Germany continued to press its claims, would air parity deter Hitler from war? The Air Staff doubted that first-line forces equal to those of Germany but lacking sufficient reserves constituted an effective deterrent. The Admiralty, the War Office, and the Chiefs of Staff argued that Britain would have a strong deterrent upon the completion of a comprehensive scheme of national defense involving all three Services. At least until then, diplomacy must avoid war.

Vansittart did not want to burden diplomacy and jeopardize Britain's reputation for such a long period of time without military power. In 1934, he had warned that Britain would be "written off—continentally" if it did not prepare an expeditionary force, and he had pressed for air force expansion beyond the fifty-two squadrons recommended by the DRC: "The execution by 1940 of a scheme approved in 1923 is no deterrent." Air policy, he wrote in April 1935, "cannot now be divorced from foreign policy. In recent years we have been heavily handicapped by our loss of material weight. This is a view which has been uncomfortably and repeatedly confirmed from foreign sources. To impose upon

---

[51] Cab 27(35), 15 May, CAB 23/81; Chamberlain letter to Hilda, 26 May, Chamberlain Papers, NC 18/1/919; meeting of Ministerial Committee on Defence Requirements, 20 May, CAB 27/508.

[52] Paget minute on Vansittart memorandum, 27 April, WO 190/324; also MI3 note, 6 April, WO 190/317.

us inferiority till 1939 will confirm it still further. Apart from the visibly growing German menace, any continued inferiority in the air will weaken our influence throughout Europe, where we are already considered to need more support than we can give, and the difficulty of conducting an independent and effective foreign policy will increase if this general estimate of us is allowed to continue."[53]

By spring 1935, Whitehall was trying to assimilate three different correlations of time, deterrence, and diplomacy. Fearing a German attack before 1939, Vansittart wanted to increase Britain's bargaining weight in negotiations that might calm Germany, limit changes in the status quo, and prevent a European war. Although he recognized Britain's military weakness, he believed that a resolute policy of rearmament—particularly but not exclusively in air forces—would improve Britain's position even before its completion, that this general and extended policy of deterrence would reassure France and other potential allies, and that it might be impossible to appease Hitler *ad infinitum*. If this last assumption proved correct, then Hitler's refusal to be appeased would help the British Government win public and international support for going to war. The Chiefs of Staff thought they had until 1942 to prepare adequate defenses to prevent a war they supposed could be avoided, although they did not make clear how British power could prevent war in the same year that German military advisers would presumably give Hitler the green light to make war. Meanwhile, the COS and Hankey expected the Foreign Office and Cabinet to ensure peace through conciliation; bellicosely rearming for general deterrence and making commitments to France could indeed precipitate a war that Britain might not win.

Chamberlain, Cunliffe-Lister, and most of the Cabinet occupied a third position. Like Vansittart, they assigned diplomatic leverage to the policy of air parity while Britain rearmed. Unlike him, they doubted that Germany would make war in the next few years, and they did not want to commit an expeditionary force to the Continent. Air rearmament combined with appeasement would deter Hitler, prevent war, and exempt Britain from even more costly and comprehensive rearmament. All three views presumed that Britain must buy time, but Vansittart differed from Chamberlain and the COS in having these interrelated convictions: time was very short; deterrence required broad and rapid rearmament; national security entailed the resolution, credibility, and strategy to defend the Low Countries and France; appeasement

---

[53] Dennis, *Decision by Default*, p. 39; Smith, *British Air Strategy*, p. 134; memorandum of 24 April 1935, *DBFP*, 13, no. 127; also Vansittart to Foreign Secretary, 30 June 1935, W5433/950/50, FO 371/19633.

[53]

might ultimately fail even if backed by military power.[54] None of the three positions explained how rearmament chiefly for a Western European war could prevent German aggrandizement in Eastern Europe, which was left unprotected by any umbrella of British deterrence under serious consideration in London.

The Foreign Office was glad the Chiefs of Staff had raised questions about potential enemies, the timetable for defense programs, the likelihood of alliances with France and Belgium, and the preparation of the Field Force for action in the Low Countries; "for on the answers to them depends our whole defence policy in relation to Germany."[55] The Foreign Office might have added that, without clear answers, the Government would be unable to find the appropriate relationship between rearmament and peace, European and imperial strategies, deterrence and reconciliation, self-defense and defense of other nations, buying and losing time.

THE PROBLEM OF COORDINATION

The momentum created by air force expansion and the queries of the COS led to a general reassessment of defense policy. On 27 May 1935, at what proved to be its final meeting, the Ministerial Committee on Defence Requirements accepted Hankey's suggestion that he, the COS, and a Treasury representative draft terms of reference for a new "enquiry to revise the existing programme of Defence Requirements in the light of recent changes in the situation, and with special reference to financial coordination."[56] A reappraisal seemed all the more timely because of changes in the Cabinet. Early in June, Baldwin succeeded the ailing MacDonald as prime minister. Sir Samuel Hoare replaced Sir John Simon at the Foreign Office, Simon taking the Home Office. Cunliffe-Lister moved to the Air Ministry, where Lord Londonderry

[54] According to Malcolm Smith, the "conflation of Treasury and Foreign Office views" resulted in a "new concept of a limited European deterrent." And Scheme C revealed air parity as "Britain's panacea" for reaching an agreement with Germany "not only to prevent war in Europe but also to undercut the threat in the Far East, and also to relieve the national economy of the burden of armaments expenditure by paving the way for arms limitation." *British Air Strategy*, pp. 138, 158. Smith's summary of the Government's problem is incisive and generally correct, but it does not clearly distinguish between the views of the Treasury and the Foreign Office. The phrases "limited deterrent" and "panacea" fit Chamberlain, not Vansittart.

[55] Memorandum (on COS report of 29 April), 28 May, C3944/55/18, FO 371/18840. On 3 June (same file), the Foreign Secretary minuted that the Foreign Office should use this memorandum "as a quarry of useful material" for the forthcoming reexamination of defense policy.

[56] CAB 27/508.

had lacked the energy and political acumen that his colleagues deemed necessary for their air policy. Lord Halifax took over the War Office from Lord Hailsham. Anthony Eden, formerly Lord Privy Seal, became Minister for League of Nations Affairs.

The decision to reexamine defense policy is evidence that those coordinating foreign policy, strategy, supply, and finance had not reached agreement on enemy threats, British timetables for rearmament, or deterrence. Coordination itself was imperfect, subject to procedural, personal, and departmental pressures. Procedural rules were implicit in terms of reference, ministerial authority and expert advice, and political and technical considerations. These rules sometimes hindered progress on defense policy. The official DRC, which had produced its 1934 report in a little more than three months, remained inactive for over a year until revived by a new ministerial committee, the DPR. In spite of wide terms of reference, the DPR did not give the DRC any initial guidance on general questions of policy. Military and civilian officials resented being excluded from ministerial discussions that depended on their expert opinion. Vansittart, Fisher, Chatfield, and Hankey regularly advised on matters beyond their fields of expertise. Distinguishing between political and technical subjects sometimes hampered Government business, even though policy could not be neatly subdivided into bureaucratic compartments. Aware of this fact, the Foreign Office, Treasury, and Services encroached on each other as each advanced its own case for deterrence and timing. The politics inside the Foreign Office were more divisive than in any of these other departments, thus weakening the Office's bargaining power. Chamberlain's determination gave "Treasury control" over finance even more political clout than usual. The Services tried to paper over basic disagreements about air power and strategy. Hankey did not want the Chiefs of Staff to expose inter-Service arguments to ministers, and he championed the existing system of defense by committee against critics who would make the three Services treat defense as one problem.

Together, these practices caused delays, inconsistencies, and confusion in planning long-term rearmament, but also allowed some elasticity for adapting deterrence to different circumstances. Chamberlain would have welcomed a coherent policy under a decisive administration willing to narrow Britain's options for deterrence.

Terms of reference were instructions given to committees in order to define the scope of their work and preserve a constitutional chain of authority from the Cabinet downward. Ideally, these instructions blended policy with administration, reserving political authority over the findings to the Cabinet and ministerial committees, while directing civil servants to advise on how to frame and execute policy. Terms of reference could either bend or bind, depending on how committee members saw their own functions. Although terms of reference in the British system do not easily fit American models of policymaking, one might view them as an example of operational "rules," which are not always explicit and can influence the content as well as the making of policy.[57]

The terms of reference given by the CID to the Defence Requirements Committee in November 1933 were drawn up by Hankey, who knew he would chair the DRC. Hankey successfully used them to extenuate Fisher's animosity toward the United States, his opposition to the construction of capital ships, and his (and Vansittart's) pressure for an increase in the authorized standard for the Air Force. Thus, the DRC report of February 1934 avoided antagonistic references to America and recommended a balanced program for the "worst deficiencies" of all three Services in the shortest practicable time. The Cabinet referred the DRC report to the Ministerial Committee on Disarmament, but the DRC was not formally dissolved and its future was in doubt.

After sixteen months of dormancy, the DRC was resuscitated, but only after a curious process of institutional transformation. This began in 1934 when the Ministerial Committee on Disarmament discussed air rearmament. In April 1935 the name of this committee changed to the more appropriate title of Ministerial Committee on Defence Requirements. Late in May, these ministers asked Hankey to chair a small committee to draft terms of reference for a reexamination of defense policy. Hankey's committee submitted its report on 1 July. By then the Cabinet had been shuffled and the Ministerial Committee on Defence Requirements had been replaced by the Ministerial Subcommittee of the CID on Defence Policy and Requirements (DPR). The DPR's members were Lord President of the Council (Ramsay MacDonald, chairman), Chancellor of the Exchequer (Chamberlain), Service ministers (Eyres-Monsell, Halifax, and Cunliffe-Lister), Foreign Secretary (Hoare), Minister for League of Nations Affairs (Eden), president of the Board of Trade (Walter Runciman), and the Chiefs of Staff as "expert advisers." Hankey served as secretary, Commander A.W. Clarke and Lieutenant Colonel Pownall as assistant secretaries.

At the DPR's first meeting, 8 July, Ramsay MacDonald christened the committee by announcing that it had been born out of the feeling "that steps should be taken for the closer co-ordination of policy and strategy." The committee's terms of reference were intentionally wide "so that it should be free to consider the problems involved in their broad-

[57] See Allison, *Essence of Decision,* pp. 78–96, 170–71; Halperin, *Bureaucratic Politics,* pp. 104–15; Snyder et al., *Foreign Policy Decision-Making,* pp. 106–9.

est aspect and on common sense and practical lines." The DPR had four tasks: "(i) To keep the defensive situation as a whole constantly under review so as to ensure that our defensive arrangements and our foreign policy are in line. (ii) To advise the Cabinet and/or the CID, in the light of the international, political and financial situation, as to any changes in policy or in the programmes of the Defence Services that the Committee may deem necessary or desirable. (iii) To examine the plans and preparations of the CID and of its Subcommittees and of Departments concerned, in order to ensure that these are effective and consistent with our general defensive policy. . . . (iv) To deal with any questions referred to it by the Prime Minister, the Cabinet or the [CID]." Later that day the DPR remitted to the DRC the new instructions drawn up by Hankey and his colleagues: namely, to reconsider defense requirements with reference to changes in the international situation and to "financial coordination," and "to make recommendations for the future."[58]

The DPR's membership and broad terms of reference would seem to have promised authoritative answers to the questions raised two months earlier by the Chiefs of Staff. It was an opportune time for a fresh look at "general defensive policy," not only for reasons given by the COS and Foreign Office, but also because storm warnings now began to appear in a third and unexpected region—the Mediterranean and Africa, where Mussolini was moving military forces for possible war against Ethiopia. The members of the DPR might have reexamined the benefits and liabilities of collective security through the League of Nations. They might have considered whether deterrence could prevent aggression—against Britain or other countries—even before the defense program had reached its goals. They might have discussed the relationship between immediate crises and long-term planning. But the DPR showed no sign of taking such initiatives. Passing the buck back to the DRC, the DPR in effect instructed the DRC to examine what four former members of the DRC had recommended they should examine.[59] It was not unusual for the Cabinet or an important committee to depend on experts for advice or for drawing up terms of reference. In the unusual circumstances of the summer of 1935, however, the ministers on the DPR should have explored these terms on their own if they wished to guide experts in correlating policy and strategy.

[58] DPR meeting, CAB 16/136; terms of reference (DPR 1), 1 July, CAB 16/138.

[59] "What a show!" Pownall recorded in his diary (27 May). The politicians "couldn't decide what to do, though pressed very hard by the COS to give decisions without which . . . the Services could not put up their Estimates—policy must be decided before details can be considered." Bond, *Chief of Staff*, p. 73.

The proliferation of a hierarchy of committees did not always bridge differences between ministers and officials or clearly distinguish between political and technical matters.[60] In April 1934, Hankey hoped the DRC could be reassembled from time to time as a kind of link between the expert advice of the departments and the policies of the Cabinet. He and his colleagues in the Secretariat soon resented the fact that the Ministerial Committee on Disarmament considered the advice of military experts as an afterthought at best.[61] In February 1935, Vansittart and Fisher blamed the Cabinet for ruining, "by habitual overcaution," the draft White Paper on Defence, which they had intended to be a dramatic warning to the British public as well as Germany.[62] Earlier in the month, Hankey bitterly protested against the Cabinet's disregard for the military experts' opinion about a possible air pact.[63] Avoiding such incidents and counterbalancing the ministers' bias toward the RAF were in Hankey's mind when he made sure that the DPR would include the Chiefs of Staff as expert advisers, and when he arranged the revival of the DRC in the summer of 1935.

The distinction between political and military or technical considerations was quite straightforward in theory. The COS and military writers often referred to policy and decisions as matters for politicians, while military staffs gave technical advice concerning operations and supply. The province of the Foreign Office was "political," and of the Treasury, "financial." The CID connected these jurisdictions and made recommendations to the Cabinet. It was the Cabinet's responsibility to set policy through its decisions, and these were to take into account the

[60] On the difficulty of distinguishing between the advisory role of experts and the policymaking role of ministers, see Max Beloff, "The Whitehall Factor: The Role of the Higher Civil Service, 1919–39," in Gillian Peele and Chris Cook, eds., *The Politics of Reappraisal, 1918–1939* (London, 1975), pp. 214, 217; John P. Mackintosh, *The British Cabinet*, 2d ed. (London, 1968), pp. 550–51. Samuel H. Beer notes that "discussions at the official level tend to reflect the probabilities of decision at the ministerial level"; *Treasury Control: The Co-ordination of Financial and Economic Policy in Great Britain,* 2d ed. (London, 1957), p. 118.

[61] COS meeting, 24 April, CAB 53/4. See also Pownall's criticism in Bond, *Chief of Staff,* pp. 42–43; and Wing Commander E. J. Hodsoll (Assistant Secretary, CID) to Air Chief Marshal Sir Robert Brooke-Popham (Air Officer Commanding, Air Defence), 29 October 1934, Brooke-Popham Papers (Liddell Hart Centre for Military Archives [LHCMA], King's College London), I/1/5. According to Hodsoll, the first Labour Government (1924) had started the practice of using Cabinet committees "deliberately to shut out expert advice as far as possible which might not be particularly welcome, or might not fit in with the policies of that Government."

[62] Vansittart minute, 26 February, W1897/950/50, FO 371/19633; O'Halpin, *Head of the Civil Service,* pp. 240–41; Roskill, *Hankey,* 3: 149.

[63] Hankey to Prime Minister, 4 February, and notes of 15 February, CAB 63/50; also Roskill, *Hankey,* 3: 155–64, and Bond, *Chief of Staff,* pp. 61–63.

recommendations of "technical men" in the Service departments and officials in the Foreign Office and Treasury.[64]

The reality was not so clear. Negotiations with the French in February 1935 concerning the proposed multilateral air pact illustrated that officials themselves could be divided by the distinction between political and technical considerations. The Foreign Office angered Hankey by going around the established "advisory machinery" for consultation with the CID, the Service departments, and the COS.[65] Once the machinery did begin to function in the manner deemed appropriate by Hankey, Admiral Chatfield told the CID that the Chiefs of Staff realized the proposed convention contained "both political and military implications . . . and that it was not for them to say which were the most important." In advising against the pact, the COS "had tried not to remark on the political considerations, but the two were so intermingled that it was difficult to keep them separate."[66]

In fact, political and technical implications often overlapped in the departments, committees, and Cabinet, in ways that reveal how anachronistic it had become to think of civil-military relations as largely the clash between "frocks" and "brasshats." Fisher, Vansittart, Hankey, and Chatfield did not view themselves as mere experts. Fisher also spoke for the others when he observed that permanent heads of departments should not be experts but the best people for the job, and that competence to advise on issues of national policy did not necessarily require "*technical* training."[67] Moreover, the meanings attached to the words "political" and "technical" could be narrow and misleading. By "political," the Service departments and Foreign Office usually meant foreign policy, an old connotation that still provided the Office with a procedural instrument for restricting the Chiefs of Staff to tech-

[64] COS meeting, 24 April 1934, CAB 53/4; Frank T. Ashton-Gwatkin, *The British Foreign Service* (Syracuse, 1950), pp. 49–50; Chatfield, *Navy and Defence*, pp. 49, 85; Walter Elliot, "Co-ordination of Imperial Defence," *Journal of the Royal United Services Institute* 75 (1930); Lord Hailsham's introduction to Hampden Gordon, *The War Office* (London, 1935), pp. v-vi.

[65] Hankey to prime minister, 4 February, and notes of 15 February, CAB 63/50. For Hankey's similar reaction to the Government's negotiations for the Geneva Protocol and Treaty of Locarno in 1924–25, see John F. Naylor, *A Man and an Institution: Sir Maurice Hankey, the Cabinet Secretariat, and the Custody of Cabinet Secrecy* (Cambridge, 1984), pp. 169–71; and Stephen Roskill, *Hankey: Man of Secrets*, vol. 2 (London, 1972), pp. 396–97.

[66] Extract from minutes of CID meeting, 25 February, CP 43(35), CAB 24/253; see also *DBFP*, 12, no. 483.

[67] Fisher to Hankey, 26 January 1934, CAB 21/434; Geoffrey K. Fry, *Statesmen in Disguise* (London, 1969), p. 57; Peden, *British Rearmament and Treasury*, p. 35; F. F. Ridley, *The Study of Government: Political Science and Public Administration* (London, 1975), pp. 9–12, 190–91 (British higher civil servants see their role as "policymaking" more than execution or management).

nical advice. The term "technical" was usually applied to the work of the Service departments, often to that of the Treasury, rarely to that of the Foreign Office. But these usages obscured a more complex truth: wherever it was discussed in the machinery of policy, an issue was political if it affected the economic, social, international, and strategic interests of the state.[68]

By this broad epistemological standard, every department gave advice that was in some sense political, no matter how much this might confuse or delay a particular question of policy. It was in the interests of each department to emphasize the importance of its own counsel, to admonish other departments to subordinate their respective concerns to defense policy as a whole, and to influence the pace of business accordingly. All of this required a balancing act between protecting departmental autonomy and promoting interdependence. The Foreign Office and Treasury performed this act energetically, the latter enjoying the advantages of financial control and Chamberlain's strong leadership.

The province of the Foreign Office was weakened by internal dissension and circumscribed by other departments. In May 1935, Baldwin lamented that "'he did not know where he was'" because the Foreign Office seemed to be pursuing pro-French and pro-German policies simultaneously.[69] Having decided to replace Simon with Hoare as Foreign Secretary, Baldwin created another potential source of conflicting advice by appointing a second minister, the Minister for League of Nations Affairs—Anthony Eden. Eden at first declined Baldwin's offer, but later accepted the position on a temporary basis, for he thought it unwise to have two ministers in the Office and to separate League of Nations affairs from foreign affairs.[70]

Both Hoare and Eden found the atmosphere in the Foreign Office tense and personal relationships divided. Vansittart awakened memories of Sir Eyre Crowe, who before the First World War had advocated a strong Anglo-French stand against German hegemony on the Continent, in sharp contrast to the Palmerstonian tradition of Britain's serving as a detached broker for European affairs. A man who never minced words, Vansittart's strident memoranda and Germanophobia reinforced the view of the central department that war with Nazi Germany was inevitable because Hitler was advancing step by step toward world domination. Most of his colleagues admired the brilliance and wit of Vansittart, an Old Etonian who had lost a brother in the Great

---

[68] See, for example, Squadron Leader J. C. Slessor, "The Co-ordination of the Fighting Services," *Journal of the Royal United Services Institute* 76 (1931).

[69] Sir Walford Selby, *Diplomatic Twilight 1930–1945* (London, 1953), p. 46.

[70] Avon, *Dictators*, pp. 241–45; Middlemas and Barnes, *Baldwin*, pp. 822–24.

War and who did not feel "at home" in the 1930s. But even his admirers thought his pertinacity antagonized enough officials and ministers to reduce his influence on the Cabinet. Ralph Wigram, another Old Etonian, led a group of "Young Turks" in the Foreign Office who looked to Vansittart for firmness against Germany. Wigram insisted that any document relating to Germany be under his control, and he provided Churchill with secret evidence of German rearmament. Wigram liked the French and loathed National Socialism, and his pessimism about negotiating with Hitler made some of his colleagues think that his conception of diplomacy virtually negated diplomacy.[71]

The memoirs of a number of British diplomats call attention to the usurpation of the authority of the Foreign Office in the interwar years, the era of the "New Diplomacy." Diplomacy was conducted not only by professional diplomats but also from other departments, by Cabinet ministers, and by private individuals or firms. Parliamentary control over foreign policy increased. Prime ministers, often relying on unofficial advisers and small circles of favorite ministers, intervened in the formulation of policy. Fisher and the Treasury asserted control over both the organization and the policies of the Foreign Office.[72] These allegations hold some truth, but they also betray a nostalgia for the preeminence the Office once enjoyed, and a myopic view of relations with the Treasury.

With perhaps unseemly imperiousness, since 1919 the Treasury had indeed claimed more and more responsibility for the "financial di-

---

[71] Avon, *Dictators*, pp. 195, 270–71; Robert Cecil, *A Divided Life: A Biography of Donald Maclean* (London, 1988), pp. 43–45; David Dilks, ed., *The Diaries of Sir Alexander Cadogan 1938–1945* (New York, 1972), p. 28; Sir David Kelly, *The Ruling Few* (London, 1952), p. 210; Valentine Lawford, *Bound for Diplomacy* (London, 1963), chap. 6; Lord Strang, *Home and Abroad* (London, 1956), p. 121; Viscount Templewood (Samuel Hoare), *Nine Troubled Years* (London, 1954), pp. 137–38; Vansittart, *Mist*, p. 453. Cecil recalls that the Foreign Office in the 1930s did not understand other ideologies or impose one of its own, and suggests that Wigram's leaking of information to Churchill may have influenced Donald Maclean to give information to the Soviet Union during the Cold War.

[72] Ashton-Gwatkin, *British Foreign Service*, and "Thoughts on the Foreign Office: 1918–1939," *Contemporary Review* 188 (1955); Selby, *Diplomatic Twilight*; Sir Victor Wellesley, *Diplomacy in Fetters* (London, 1944). See also "John Connell" (John Robertson), *The "Office"* (New York, 1958), and Gordon A. Craig, "The British Foreign Office from Grey to Austen Chamberlain," in Craig and Felix Gilbert, eds., *The Diplomats, 1919–1939* (Princeton, 1953). On the organization and constitutional position of the Foreign Office: Donald G. Bishop, *The Administration of British Foreign Relations* (Syracuse, 1961), chap. 12; David Dilks, "The British Foreign Office between the Wars," in B. J. C. McKercher and D. J. Moss, eds., *Shadow and Substance in British Foreign Policy, 1895–1939* (Edmonton, Canada, 1984); Zara Steiner and M. L. Dockrill, "The Foreign Office Reforms, 1919–21," *Historical Journal* 17 (1974); Sir John Tilley and Stephen Gaselee, *The Foreign Office* (London, 1933); Donald Cameron Watt, "Divided Control of British Foreign Policy—Danger or Necessity," *Political Quarterly* 33 (1962). Steiner and Dockrill point out that, although the Foreign Office had lost its "former monopoly over foreign affairs," the reformed Office did not represent a "sharp distinction . . . between the 'old' and 'new' diplomacy" (p. 151).

plomacy" associated with war reparations, loans, credits, trade, and the international economic collapse of the early 1930s. Yet some officials in the Foreign Office just as arrogantly assumed they could either ignore or master economic affairs, and they tried but failed to gain control over areas of policy already dominated by the Treasury and Board of Trade.[73] Rivalry between the Foreign Office and Treasury buttressed Fisher's charge in February 1935, during negotiations for an air pact, that the Office had violated established procedures for conducting business in cooperation with other departments. Fisher expected the Foreign Office to agree that "in modern times the business of diplomacy is largely connected with matters in which Departments other than the Foreign Office are really the principals."[74]

Although coordination between the Foreign Office and the Services was hindered by the lack of a department inside the Office specifically charged with defense policy, it collaborated with the Service departments through its representatives on many committees, the circulation of memoranda, the preparation of the Chiefs of Staff annual review of imperial defense, and daily contacts with officials in Whitehall.[75] The Foreign Office and Service departments agreed on certain broad principles: Britain must further the general pacification of Europe, the country needed time to strengthen its armed forces, and it should base its defense policy on military and diplomatic considerations, not public opinion. Disagreements arose, however, concerning the German threat, policy toward potential allies, and the relationship between arms and diplomacy while Britain bought time.

Collaboration between the Foreign Office and the Services on intelligence developed very slowly in the 1930s. The distinction made by civilian and military experts between political, military (or technical), and economic information discouraged the growth of interdepartmental machinery to synthesize different kinds of intelligence.[76] The For-

[73] For tension between the Foreign Office and Treasury, see Trotter, *East Asia*, pp. 6–12 and chap. 9; Dilks, *Cadogan*, pp. 10–11; O'Halpin, *Head of the Civil Service*, pp. 231–37; V. H. Rothwell, "The Mission of Sir Frederick Leith-Ross to the Far East, 1935–36," *Historical Journal* 18 (1975); Donald G. Boadle, "The Foundation of the Foreign Office Economic Relations Section, 1930–1937," *Historical Journal* 20 (1977).

[74] Hankey notes of conversation with Fisher, 16 February, CAB 63/50.

[75] In fact, the Office's relations with the Service departments in the mid-1930s were "quite uncoordinated, and went through the geographical department of the F.O. concerned with the relevant area." Sir William Hayter, letter to the author, 9 April 1974. Sir David Kelly recalls that officials in the Foreign Office sought closer relations with other departments because they did not want to accept "without question" the advice of experts in other fields; *Ruling Few*, pp. 207–8.

[76] Hinsley, *British Intelligence*, pp. 4–9, 15–19, 25–26, 74–75; Wark, *Ultimate Enemy*, pp. 20–22 and passim; Watt, "British Intelligence"; Major General Sir Kenneth Strong, *Intelligence at the Top* (New York, 1969), pp. 21–24.

eign Office showed little interest in collating political information with the military intelligence of the Service departments, yet claimed superior wisdom in analyzing military information for its political implications. The Service departments averred that their proper domain was military information, yet they based their estimate of Germany's military incapacity for war partly on industrial and political data, and they presumed a close correlation between material resources and political intentions. So while the Foreign Office and the Service departments separated political and military intelligence according to their respective provinces, they also combined the political and the military in ways that reflected their departmental biases. The result was sharply divergent estimates of the date and strategy of a German attack against the West. Vansittart worried about German intentions and considered the Foreign Office a better judge of these than were the Service departments. The Chiefs of Staff emphasized capabilities. The Foreign Office warned that Germany might begin a war before 1939 with a knockout bombing assault on Britain. The Services thought Hitler would not risk war before 1942, and the Admiralty and War Office expected Hitler to employ the German army as his central strategic force.

The Chiefs of Staff and Hankey knew that Britain must have allies in the event of war, but they were more reluctant than the Foreign Office to consider holding staff talks with the French. To Hankey and the military experts, the Treaty of Locarno already implied too great a strategic commitment to France: Britain was a guarantor of provisions that declared the Franco-German border inviolate and reaffirmed the demilitarization of the Rhineland. In February 1935 they warned that the Locarno Treaty (in this case the air pact that the French wanted attached to the treaty) logically committed Britain to military talks with Germany as well as France and might even lead to French and German talks directed against Britain.

The Foreign Office rejected this argument as specious and hoped that "a spirit of realism" and "mature consideration" would show anyone the implausibility of joining Germany against France and Belgium or fighting Germany without those countries as allies.[77] Technically speaking, the COS and Hankey had a point, and they probably welcomed the chance to conflate military and political considerations. Politically, the Foreign Office was correct, but it could not deny that regional and collective security now involved military liabilities and risks which Britain might not be strong enough to assume under a broad definition of deterrence.

---

[77] Foreign Office paper, 21 February, in CP 43(35), CAB 24/253; memorandum of 28 May, C3944/55/18, FO 371/18840.

The Foreign Office and the Services recognized with increasing anxiety the interdependence of military preparedness and foreign policy. Because of contrasting perceptions of deterrence and the German threat, however, the Foreign Office was predisposed to criticize the Services for lethargy, the Service departments to blame the Office for anti-German truculence that might invite war.[78] The Office was inclined to see political and strategic advantage in making commitments to potential allies without whom Britain could not win, the Services to stress the liability of moves they feared would only heighten tension with Germany. The Foreign Office viewed rearmament as a means of impressing Hitler. The Services dreaded that openly challenging Germany to an arms race or threatening force would increase the risk of conflict before Britain had time to make its defenses adequate for war.

Neither problems inside the Foreign Office nor interdepartmental arrangements outside marked its eclipse in the making of British policy. The Office could not ignore the views of other departments, but used the machinery of policy at official and ministerial levels to rebut military or financial advice that it feared would distort the content of policy. Although the Foreign Office had lost power since the years before the Great War, it had not abdicated to the Treasury or other departments.

"Treasury control" increased soon after the First World War when administrative reforms elevated the Treasury's Permanent Secretary to the position of Permanent Head of the Civil Service, and gave the Treasury various means for coordinating and controlling the financial business of government departments. Sir Warren Fisher, whose ideal was a unified Civil Service able to advise ministers with confidence and intelligence, safeguarded and consolidated these reforms during his long tenure as Permanent Secretary (1919–39).[79] A Wykehamist who

---

[78] Wigram minute, 16 July, C5539/55/18, FO 371/18848. Someone in the War Office told R. Barrington-Ward (deputy editor of the *Times*) that the General Staff had temporarily "'given up trying to persuade Vansittart and Wigram'" to stop brandishing Sir Eyre Crowe's famous memorandum of 1908 (on German militarism). The General Staff was grateful to the *Times* for advocating concessions to Germany. Barrington-Ward quoted Wigram, "'It's curious that the W.O. should be doing the work of the F.O., and *vice versa.*'" *The History of the Times*, vol. 4: *The 150th Anniversary and Beyond, 1912–1948* (New York, 1952), p. 893. See also Marshal of the RAF Sir Arthur Harris, *Bomber Offensive* (London, 1947), p. 14, for the "slightly bellicose" tone in the Foreign Office.

[79] On the reforms, Treasury control, and the Civil Service, see Beer, *Treasury Control*; Lord Bridges, *The Treasury* (London, 1964), pp. 112, 172–76; D. N. Chester and F. M. G. Willson, *The Organization of British Central Government, 1914–1956* (London, 1957), pp. 291–94; Emmeline W. Cohen, *The Growth of the British Civil Service, 1780–1939* (London, 1941), pp. 177–84; Fry, *Statesmen in Disguise*, pp. 52–58; Sir H. P. Hamilton, "Sir Warren Fisher and the Public Service," *Public Administration* 29 (1951); Sir Ivor Jennings, *Cabinet Government*, 2d ed. (Cambridge, 1951), chap. 7; Peden, *British Rearmament and Treasury*, chap. 2; Henry Roseveare, *The Treasury* (New York, 1969), pp. 246–55. For the similar

separated from his Roman Catholic wife in 1921, Fisher's broad conception of his own advisory responsibilities gave him extra incentive to
involve himself in questions of defense and foreign policy. He regarded
the Civil Service as one of four Services of the crown, and he scorned
those officers from the three Fighting Services whose uniforms
prompted them to exaggerate his "fallibility and their supposed infalli-
bility." He viewed himself as an experienced layman and a patriotic
Englishman, one who happily listened to records of Sir Arthur Sullivan
(he was "'in the tradition of Mozart'") and Harry Lauder, and who
could transcend departmental interests while working with interdepartmental "teams" (such as the Defence Requirements Committee)
to find "the best solution" for his country's defense against the German
menace.[80]

The Treasury's interests were pervasive and very political indeed.
Fisher considered finance, industry, and trade as the "sinews of war,"
which were a "fundamental element in policy." He rejected the assumption, which he found too widely held, "that imperial defence is a
matter solely for compromise between the opinion on international
affairs of the Foreign Office and the strategical and tactical conceptions
of the Defence Departments." It was the Treasury's responsibility to
ensure compatibility between national security and national resources.[81] Fisher's views were shared by the officials to whom he left
most of the departmental work on defense policy: Sir Richard Hopkins
(Second Secretary and Fisher's deputy for financial affairs): Sir Frederick Phillips (Under-Secretary in charge of finance); J. A. N. Barlow
(Under-Secretary for supply); and Edward Bridges (Assistant Secretary,
in charge of defense matters in the supply divisions).[82]

Neville Chamberlain relied on Fisher and other officials to help him
keep Government policy within the limits of sound financial principles. Chamberlain's guardianship of financial orthodoxy was made
easier by consensus among the Treasury, industry, the Bank of England

---

social and educational background of most members of the Administrative Class of civil
servants, see R. K. Kelsall, *Higher Civil Servants in Britain* (London, 1955), chap. 7.

[80] Fisher to Chatfield, 10 November 1933, and to Hankey, 26 January 1934, CAB 21/434;
Fraser M. Cameron, "Some Aspects of British Strategy and Diplomacy 1933–39," Ph.D.
diss., Cambridge University, 1972, p. 167; O'Halpin, *Head of the Civil Service*, pp. 7–12. For
tributes to Fisher from colleagues in defense planning, see Bond, *Chief of Staff*, pp. 24–25;
Chatfield, *Navy and Defence*, p. 79; Templewood, *Nine Troubled Years*, p. 137. Donald
Cameron Watt reassesses Fisher's influence on defense policy in *Personalities and Policies:
Studies in the Formulation of British Foreign Policy in the Twentieth Century* (Notre Dame,
Ind., 1965), chap. 5; the fullest and most recent study is O'Halpin's.

[81] Fisher amendment of draft note by Hankey for prime minister, 9 February 1934, CAB
21/384 and PREM 1/153; Fisher note, 19 April 1934, CAB 16/111.

[82] For sketches of these and other Treasury officials, see Peden, *British Rearmament and
Treasury*, pp. 20–26, 203.

and the larger financial community in London, the Conservative party, and the National Government. Orthodoxy meant a balanced budget, a favorable balance of payments, and stability in prices, wages, and the value of the pound. Following these commandments would bring economic recovery, reduce unemployment, avert socialism, and help restore international financial stability following the ruinous tenure of the Labour Government of 1929–31. The Treasury was certain that major increases in defense spending would disrupt "normal trade" and the production of consumer goods, cause inflation, conflict with expenditure on social programs, require borrowing, and raise the National Debt.[83]

Apparently, Chamberlain, Fisher, and Hopkins had begun to consider the possibility of a defense loan by April 1935, knowing that Germany was rearming on a large scale and that the Cabinet would probably agree to accelerate the expansion of the Royal Air Force. With at least a hint of awe, Treasury officials noted heterodox practices in the fascist dictatorships. Germany was funding accelerated rearmament by secretly increasing its internal debt, and Italy had shown "'that very large amounts can be raised over a period of years by Government guarantees to private undertakings without substantial damage to the Budget being for the moment openly revealed.'"[84] But the Treasury's adoption of unorthodox measures was prevented, for the time being, by the conviction that economic recovery was the prerequisite for—not the result of—increasing expenditure on defense.

Chamberlain, the strongest, most able, most persuasive in argument, and in some ways most forward-looking member of the Cabinet, took the lead in ministerial discussions of defense policy. He was not as imperialistic as his father, Joseph, who in 1904 had commanded the country to "think Imperially." He was not as popular as his half-brother, Austen, a Nobel laureate for his work on the Treaty of Locarno and, unlike Neville, a product of Oxbridge (Trinity College, Cambridge). But Neville had solid experience in business, city politics (Lord Mayor of Birmingham, 1915–16), and Parliament (a Conservative MP since 1918 and a Cabinet minister in all but Labour Governments since 1923). Blending departmental advice with ideas of his own, he believed that Britain's military security and diplomatic clout could prevent war, and that these preventive instruments depended on a strong economy, as did Britain's avoidance of either fascism or communism. He advocated rapprochement with Japan, the superior deterrent force of air

---

[83] Ibid., pp. 60–70; W. K. Hancock and M. M. Gowing, *British War Economy* (London, 1949), chap. 2; Kennedy, *Realities*, pp. 230–36; Meyers, *Britische Sicherheitspolitik*, pp. 374–87; Parker, "Economics"; Shay, *British Rearmament*, pp. 11–18.

[84] Peden, *British Rearmament and Treasury*, pp. 72–74.

power, the strategic priority and economic feasibility of expanding the RAF, and the pacification of Germany and Europe by even-handed brokerage from London.[85]

Chamberlain believed that this plan alone could work, and that none of his Cabinet colleagues was capable of devising one as rational and coherent as his. Chamberlain did not exaggerate much when privately he took almost all the credit for revising the DRC report: "I have practically taken charge now of the defence requirements of the country"; "I was the only member of the [Ministerial] Committee with any plan"; "I have really won all along the line." He saw himself as the only Cabinet minister able to restrain "all the cranks and 'experts' [who] are merrily at work doling out subsidies in every direction. As long as I am in the Treasury we shall do nothing rash but I wouldn't answer for some of my colleagues if they had my place."[86] He called days and weeks "good" when they marked the Cabinet's progress on his proposals, under his guidance. In the spring of 1935, when he had become "a sort of Acting P.M.," he regretted he lacked the actual power to say "this is what you must do." In 1934, MacDonald had braked "the machine from sheer inability to face up to any decision," and now he and Baldwin were "shilly shallying" when a change in leadership was urgently needed at the Air Ministry. Chamberlain would have been "the best person" to go to the Stresa Conference, although he did not covet the position of Foreign Secretary; he could not afford it financially, would hate making trips to Geneva, "and above all . . . should loathe and detest the social ceremonies."[87]

The historian risks oversimplifying a personality that even his colleagues found impossible to know well. Still, Chamberlain's papers reveal that he viewed government as a kind of moral gymnasium in which he measured wins and losses in highly egocentric terms.[88] A

---

[85] Chamberlain Papers, passim; Sir Keith Feiling, *The Life of Neville Chamberlain* (London, 1946), pp. 251–52, 258; Lippincott, "Strategy of Appeasement," chaps. 2, 3; Iain Macleod, *Neville Chamberlain* (London, 1961), pp. 165–66, 177–79; David J. Wrench, "The Influence of Neville Chamberlain on Foreign and Defence Policy," *Royal United Services Institute Journal for Defence Studies* 125 (1980).

[86] Diary, 3 May 1934, Chamberlain Papers, NC 2/23a; Chamberlain to Ida (12 May and 4 August) and Hilda (28 July), NC 18/1/870, 881–82.

[87] Diary, 3 December 1934, 29 April and 17 May 1935, NC 2/23a; Chamberlain to sisters, 22 June and 9 December 1934, March (four letters) and 12 May 1935, NC 18/1/876, 898, 908–11. Chamberlain's papers contain numerous criticisms of Simon and Londonderry, and he was instrumental in their being replaced by Hoare and Cunliffe-Lister in June 1935.

[88] G. C. Peden contends that, when Chamberlain in 1934 questioned the usefulness of an expeditionary force, he probably did so as "devil's advocate" rather than as someone whose opinions were "fixed." *British Rearmament and Treasury*, p. 123. Here and elsewhere in his informative study, Peden is too apologetic in tone and not critical enough of how the Treasury influenced the choice of strategic priorities. Both Chamberlain's papers

man whose conceit was as extraordinary as his ability, Chamberlain worked harder than any of his colleagues and knew more about the work of departments besides his own. He considered the machinery of policy efficient insofar as it deduced congenial conclusions from his general assumptions, produced evidence to substantiate those assumptions, eliminated inconsistencies and waste, and confirmed his own decisiveness.

The Treasury claimed responsibility for ensuring that the machinery of policy promoted both interdepartmental cooperation and financial accountability. The defense programs of 1934–35 began to test whether the Treasury could maintain or indeed increase its control over expenditure. In February 1934, Eyres-Monsell and Hailsham thwarted an apparent attempt by the Treasury to give the chancellor the authority to decide how much of the annual budget could be allocated to the Service departments. This, they argued, would mean the rationing of expenditure without prior consultation with the Service ministers and without preserving the Cabinet's power of last resort in decisions on the budget.[89] In June 1935, a more cautious Treasury memorandum observed that Treasury control "is subject to the overriding claims of Government policy, but despite that limitation there is a good deal that can be, and is, done by the Treasury to moderate the demands proposed to be made on the Exchequer." Scrutiny and control over the Civil Department Estimates was greater than over the Service Estimates. Because the Treasury could not "speak with the same authority" on the subject of defense as it could on civil questions, "technical reasons therefore combine with historical reasons . . . to make Treasury control of the Defence Departments more shadowy than the control exercised over the Civil Departments."[90] Thus, although Treasury control over defense expenditure was firmly entrenched, the Treasury

and the Government documents give the indelible picture of a man whose strategic ideas were already very fixed indeed. Harold Macmillan's characterization is apt: Chamberlain had a "clear, logical mind," and was "only too sure that he was right on every question." *Winds of Change, 1914–1939* (New York, 1966), p. 467. Larry W. Fuchser finds in Chamberlain's papers "a man cynically, even ruthlessly, striving to increase his personal dominion over British society"; *Neville Chamberlain and Appeasement: A Study in the Politics of History* (New York, 1982), p. 29. This is too extreme. Closer to the mark, although in places too generous, is David Dilks's portrayal in *Neville Chamberlain*, vol. 1: *Pioneering and Reform, 1869–1929* (Cambridge, 1984): "The dividing line between those deplorable characteristics [obstinacy and arrogance] and the tenacious self-confidence which a Minister must show in controversial subjects, if he is to hold steadily to a policy and not be reduced to impotence by criticism, is a narrow one." (p. 412). By and large, Dilks places Chamberlain on the latter side of the line.

[89] Draft note (by Hankey as amended by Fisher) to prime minister, 9 February; Eyres-Monsell to Hankey, 28 February; Hailsham to Hankey, 6 March; Hankey to prime minister, 6 March; PREM 1/153.

[90] H. Wilson Smith memorandum, 14 June, T 160/580.

could bump into the Service departments and Foreign Office in this "shadowy" constitutional area.

Indeed Treasury officials began to feel the pressure of time in a number of ways. First, although the Treasury had trimmed the deficiency program and could subject it to the normal procedure of annual estimates, the existence of a multiyear plan began to generate enough momentum in the Service departments and Cabinet to challenge Treasury control. The Chiefs of Staff and Foreign Office maintained that the programs of the Army and Navy should accelerate to keep pace with that of the Air Force. The offices and committees responsible for supply showed signs of wanting to go beyond mere planning on paper to actual provision of peacetime reserves and preparation of "shadow" factories. Second, the policy of air parity with Germany required spending according to a timetable that was volatile and strategically biased toward air power. Chamberlain and Treasury officials were proponents of this policy, but Chamberlain doubted that Germany would strike in the next few years, and he chafed as urgency drove the defense budget higher. Third, Nazi Germany was, at least for the moment, successfully using unorthodox financial methods to fund the rearmament that forced Britain to increase spending on a modest and potentially inadequate scale. It had at least occurred to the Treasury that the financial methods of mad dogs might be more efficient than those of democratic Englishmen.

In the interdepartmental bargaining that dealt with such pressures, the Treasury had a powerful spokesman in Chamberlain, constitutional authority to control spending, and much experience in using the coordinating machinery to influence decisions. Above all, the Treasury thought it had a consistent plan and that its main rivals in defense policy did not. The Foreign Office pursued policies that might not avert a two-front war in Europe and the Far East, yet Britain could not afford to rearm for this contingency. Similarly, the Service departments followed both European and imperial strategies and, in a European war, proposed a substantial commitment on land. Partly because of what the Treasury viewed as default of these other departments, the Treasury thought it should shape major decisions on defense according to a cohesive formulation of policy.

The agreement among the three Services that finance alone should not dictate the course of rearmament helped foster a spirit of collegiality in a number of venues. The Chiefs of Staff together proposed a balanced program of rearmament and a foreign policy of minimum risk. Their chairman, Admiral Chatfield, had joined the Navy in 1886 at the age of thirteen and fought at Jutland thirty years later. A forceful advocate for the Navy, he was also a formidable spokesman for all the

Services before predominantly ministerial committees. The members of the Joint Planning Committee seem to have worked harmoniously for the most part. The Services and the CID Secretariat agreed that the coordination of Service intelligence was already good, and could be improved without establishing a "centralized intelligence service."[91] The Imperial Defence College, founded in 1926–27, brought together higher staff officers from the Services and the Dominions for a common course of study, and the curricula of the three separate Staff Colleges included exercises in combined operations. Coordination was good among the finance departments of the Services.[92] Service representatives on the Supply Board discussed mutual concerns as well as the special requirements of each Service, and the increasing importance of the Supply Board was recognized in April 1935 when the CID authorized it to have a full-time chairman and a full-time secretary.[93] These institutions provided far more systematic coordination than existed in Germany, where the Wehrmachtsamt (formerly the Ministeramt in the Weimar Republic) was increasing its coordination of military and civilian affairs but no regular mechanism existed for joint strategic planning until Hitler assumed command of the armed forces early in 1938 and changed the Wehrmachtsamt into the Oberkommando der Wehrmacht; or in France, where meetings of the three chiefs of general staff took place only occasionally; or in the United States, where the Joint Board of representatives from the Army and Navy had little importance until 1940–41 (replaced by the Joint Chiefs of Staff in 1942).

Beneath the surface of concord, which the Chiefs of Staff were especially determined to maintain in their reports, the Services disagreed fundamentally over the role of air power in modern warfare.[94] As long as this discord persisted, so would related disputes. Military and Air Intelligence had contradictory visions of how Germany would employ its air forces in a western war. The value of committing an expedition-

---

91 JPC meetings in CAB 55/1; personal correspondence in AIR 2/1405; Brooke-Popham (Air Ministry) and Hodsoll (CID Secretariat) correspondence, 27 and 29 October 1934, Brooke-Popham Papers, I/1/5 (LHCMA).

92 Creedy (War Office) to Hankey, 13 March 1934, CAB 21/471.

93 PSOC meeting, 4 April, CAB 60/4; CID meeting, 16 April, CAB 2/6; Gibbs, *Rearmament*, pp. 778–79; Scott and Hughes, *Administration of War Production*, p. 56.

94 See especially Bond, *British Military Policy*, pp. 191–92., 210–13; Gibbs, *Rearmament*, pp. 774–75; Robin Higham, *The Military Intellectuals in Britain: 1918–1939* (New Brunswick, N.J., 1966); Posen, *Sources of Military Doctrine*, pp. 159–63; Smith, *British Air Strategy*, chaps. 1–3; Webster and Frankland, *Strategic Air Offensive*, pp. 62–64; Howard G. Welch, "The Origins and Development of the Chiefs of Staff Sub-committee of the Committee of Imperial Defence: 1923–1939," Ph.D. diss., London University, 1973. Strategic doctrine is one of several issues of "effectiveness" outlined by Allan R. Millett, Williamson Murray, and Kenneth H. Watman, "The Effectiveness of Military Organizations," in Millett and Murray, *Military Effectiveness*, Vol. 1, chap. 1.

ary force to the Continent would depend on whether Germany began the war with a bombing attack on Britain (the Air Force view) or a land assault against the Low Countries and France (the Army view). The Admiralty wanted complete control over the Fleet Air Arm and re-opened this divisive issue in the spring of 1935.[95] The Air Staff rejected the General Staff's proposal to draw their Staff Colleges closer together geographically and increase the amount of time spent on combined studies.[96]

Although each Service department prepared its estimates separately according to its strategic responsibilities, Chatfield believed that "the three Service Departments had no difference of opinion whatever in regard to defence requirements. They all, in fact, agreed that they wanted a good deal more than they had at present." He supposed some coordination of estimates necessary in order to reinforce this unanimity against the Treasury's power to cut each Service sepa-rately.[97] The Services showed little enthusiasm, however, for coor-dinating estimates on the basis of a common strategic doctrine for national and imperial defense. Neither the COS nor the DRC produced such a doctrine. The Services simultaneously pursued European and imperial strategies, and each Service had its own tactical point of view for a war in either theater.

As Secretary to the CID (since 1912) and Cabinet (since the Great War), Sir Maurice Hankey promoted inter-Service cooperation and saw himself as "the agent for bringing the Defence Services into political questions" that concerned the Foreign Office and other departments.[98] Educated at Rugby, Hankey had joined the Royal Marines in 1895, and had lost two brothers in action—one in South Africa in 1900, the other in France in 1916. He was widely regarded as one of the most indus-trious, efficient, and humorless officials in London, and had no peer in any other European government. A "curious creature," his private secretary later recalled,[99] he inspired the kind of respect one associates

---

[95] Eyres-Monsell to MacDonald, 20 May, PREM 1/282. For matters of control and tactics of the Fleet Air Arm: Chatfield, *Navy and Defence*, chap. 15; Roskill, *Naval Policy*, chap. 7; Geoffrey Till, *Air Power and the Royal Navy, 1914–1945* (London, 1979), chaps. 4, 6.

[96] Minutes and memoranda, October–December 1934, AIR 2/717.

[97] COS meeting, 24 April 1934, CAB 53/4.

[98] Hankey notes, 16 February 1935, CAB 63/50. According to Fisher, Hankey provided the "focus point" for the deliberations of the DRC; Fisher to Chatfield, 10 November 1933, CAB 21/434. The two men had gradually developed a good working relationship since 1922, when Hankey saved the Cabinet Secretariat from being absorbed by the Treasury; see Naylor, *Man and Institution*, pp. 99–107; Roskill, *Hankey*, 2: 309–20.

[99] Lawrence Burgis, unpublished MS (Churchill College, Cambridge). The two quar-reled in 1938, and Burgis resigned after seventeen years with Hankey. Roskill omits some of the most disparaging details from his excerpts from the Burgis MS in *Hankey*, 3:21–22. Two of Hankey's assistant secretaries give contrasting impressions. There is a bitter edge

with wizards. His three decades of experience while government business increased in volume and complexity made him the foremost expert in a profession that many bureaucrats themselves could not understand.

Hankey was especially sensitive to criticism of the machinery of defense, of which he considered himself the guardian. The establishment of the Chiefs of Staff, Joint Planning Committee, Principal Supply Officers Committee, and Imperial Defence College did not silence critics of the lack of coordination among the Services. The most vociferous of these came from a small group of Conservative peers and Members of Parliament, some of them retired servicemen. In July 1934, a few of them wrote to the prime minister that the existing machinery "has in fact been built up on an underlying principle which has ceased to be valid. This principle is that the Services are essentially separate, and in consequence the elaborate machinery for coordination has as its object the minimizing, so far as this may be done, of the differences and divergences between three different Service Departments." Technological advances had blurred "the line of demarcation between the roles of the three Services." Government policy should recognize "that defence is one single problem, . . . not three distinct ones," and thus the purpose of the coordinating machinery ought to be "to ensure that each Service was given adequate liberty and scope to develop its own methods within the ambit of one accepted defence policy."[100]

Hankey orchestrated the Government's responses to attacks against the current CID system. It was "steadily evolving on right lines and . . . any drastic change would be detrimental to efficiency." The CID machinery "worked with great smoothness," and the Chiefs of Staff pulled together in the DRC "without a discordant note."[101] The COS

---

in Pownall's early diary entries critical of Hankey for aloofness, stubbornness, and trying to manage too many issues at once; Bond, *Chief of Staff*. Hankey receives glowing praise in Lieutenant General Sir Gordon Macready, *In the Wake of the Great* (London, 1965), pp. 72–74. T. E. "Shaw" (Lawrence) told B. H. Liddell Hart that "Hankey was careful to avoid having anybody [in the Secretariat] who would replace him, and thought he could go on forever. . . ." Liddell Hart note, 22 March 1935, Liddell Hart Papers, 11/1935/65 (LHCMA). Roskill's biography and Naylor's *Man and Institution* reveal both strengths and flaws of character that are noticeably lacking in Franklyn A. Johnson's *Defence by Committee*, written after extensive interviews with Hankey.

100 Wing Commander Archibald James and others, 5 July, PREM 1/151; also, in the same file, James to Hankey, 25 June. The *Journal of the Royal United Services Institute* published articles by retired and active officers recommending more inter-Service coordination— e.g., through a "combined staff" of the brightest graduates of the Imperial Defence College; volumes for 1930, 1931, 1934.

101 Baldwin (drafted by Hankey) to James, 27 July 1934, PREM 1/151; Hankey to MacDonald, 3 August 1934, CAB 21/434. Hankey attributed good inter-Service relations "largely to the fact that so many [Imperial Defence College] men are coming up into the higher posts in the various staffs"; letter to Vice Admiral Sir Herbert Richmond (former Commandant of the College), 5 February 1934, Hankey Papers (Churchill College, Cambridge), 4/26.

prepared a report on staff training to show, as Hankey suggested, "why each Service requires its own Staff College, and how far, on matters of joint concern, the Staff Colleges adopt a common doctrine." The COS affirmed that the separate colleges and the Imperial Defence College were doing a good job, but they recommended strengthening instruction in common doctrine. For those Members of Parliament who thought more "common understanding" was necessary, the Commandant of the Imperial Defence College (Admiral Sir Lionel Preston) mockingly suggested that "a course for Members of Parliament should take place before election and a course for Cabinet Ministers."[102]

Hankey adamantly opposed the creation of a Ministry of Defence, which he thought would weaken the advice of military experts, challenge the authority of the prime minister in defense matters, and rival the Secretariat as the chief instrument of coordination. He kept on file papers he had written on the subject since 1923, when he had advised—and written the report of—the Salisbury Committee, which recommended against a central ministry and formally established the Chiefs of Staff as a subcommittee of the CID. To enable Cabinet ministers to ward off critics who suffered from what a Treasury official called an "amalgamation complex," Hankey periodically dusted off or revised these papers.[103] His modest prescription for change was to "ginger up" the existing machinery and to graft new committees onto the trunk or branches of the CID. Thus, in May 1935, as the Government prepared for parliamentary debates on defense policy, he envisaged a small and powerful committee, under the aegis of the CID, to coordinate all aspects of defense and act as an embryonic War Cabinet in peacetime.[104] Although larger than what Hankey had in mind, the DPR would soon resemble his idea.

Hankey was both administrator and adviser, and even in the former capacity he did more than record and coordinate Government business.[105] He prepared the agendas for committee and Cabinet meetings. He wrote terms of reference and minutes, sometimes drafting the latter

[102] Hankey to Baldwin, 13 July 1934, and to Service ministers, 16 July, PREM 1/151; COS meetings, 9 October, 1 and 20 November, CAB 53/5; COS report (COS 356), 8 November, and Hodsoll note, 5 December, CAB 53/24; Preston to Hodsoll, 22 October, AIR 2/717.

[103] Many documents in CAB 21/351, 384, 406, 424, 471, 472; Hankey to Baldwin, 23 August 1934, Baldwin Papers (Cambridge University Library); Johnson, *Defence by Committee*, pp. 193–98; Roskill, *Hankey*, 3:51–53, 98–99.

[104] PSOC meeting, 4 April, CAB 60/4; Hankey to MacDonald, 3 May, CAB 21/406, and to Lord Mottistone, 10 May, CAB 21/472; Roskill, *Hankey*, 3:153–54, 169–70.

[105] Johnson, *Defence by Committee*; Naylor, *Man and Institution*; Roskill, *Hankey*, vols. 2 and 3. On the Cabinet Secretariat, see also Hankey, *Diplomacy by Conference*, pp. 79–82; Jennings, *Cabinet Government*, pp. 223–31; Richard K. Mosley, *The Story of the Cabinet Office* (London, 1969); John F. Naylor, "The Establishment of the Cabinet Secretariat," *Historical Journal* 14 (1971).

in advance of the meetings themselves. He distributed reminders of what decisions had been taken and who was responsible for executing them. He reminded ministers to listen to expert advisers. These functions enabled Hankey to raise questions of policy, steer committees in particular directions, prod or brake them, and alert departments that might otherwise be bypassed or taken by surprise.

Hankey expected the Secretariat to "supply the drive [and] initiate new ideas" in addition to its secretarial duties.[106] He, the assistant secretaries, and joint secretaries frequently advised the people whom they served. They drafted committee reports—notably those portions dealing with "political appreciations" or assumptions. Hankey summed up his theory of the Secretary's advisory role in a letter to B. H. Liddell Hart: "The man in my position should not put forward his suggestions officially but should try and help everyone else. He sees most of the game and consequently can often make a useful suggestion. But if he makes a proposal, say to his committee or to the Prime Minister, which comes within the sphere of a minister or General Staff, there is liable to be trouble. It is best to make it direct to the responsible man and let him have the credit if he wants."[107]

In fact, Hankey gave advice both unofficially behind the scenes and officially through committee meetings and memoranda. He turned the attention of the Chiefs of Staff from the Far East to Europe in 1933, yet as chairman of the DRC he also helped keep imperial strategy alive thereafter when, in his opinion, the Cabinet exaggerated the German threat. In February 1935, Hankey condemned the proposed air pact by which the Foreign Office and the French hoped to augment the Treaty of Locarno. It would be folly, he argued, for Britain to undertake dangerous commitments at a time when the treaty was breaking down, especially in view of the expected public opposition to British intervention should Hitler remilitarize the Rhineland, which he threatened to do "within the next year or two."[108] Before Simon departed for the Stresa Conference in April, Hankey advised him privately not to encircle Germany but "to present the German case in the most attractive form that is possible" in the interests of attaining a European settlement.[109]

Hankey believed that the Services must present a united front if they hoped to convince Parliament and public opinion of the need to rearm. Thus, he encouraged teamwork on the COS and DRC, proposed a White Paper on Defence for early 1935 as a means of bringing the

[106] Ismay, *Memoirs*, pp. 52–53.
[107] 3 December 1935, Liddell Hart Papers, 1/352 (LHCMA).
[108] Hankey to CID, 14 February, in CP 43(35), CAB 24/253.
[109] Hankey to Simon, 3 and 6 April, FO 800/291, CAB 63/50.

missions of the three Services together in a single document, kept the lid on the controversy over control of the Fleet Air Arm,[110] and advised against major changes in the machinery of defense in part because the necessary debate would surely cause a row between the Services.

Hankey regretted that democracy hampered defense by committee—"so much time wasted in preparing arguments, while a dictatorship could get on with the job of military preparation."[111] Some of his contemporaries complained that the committee system was unwieldy and slow. "We have for years laboured under the burden of these endless committees and subcommittees which spend nothing but time," Vansittart lamented.[112] Whatever its shortcomings, the machinery had been designed in part to ease the burden on the prime minister, and Ramsay MacDonald used it gratefully, though not critically. The same can be said for Stanley Baldwin, who, as Lord President, frequently handled defense questions on behalf of MacDonald before replacing him as prime minister. Baldwin's quality of leadership is still open to debate (although his love of cricket and rowing is not), but even the most sympathetic observers emphasize his reluctance to take decisions, his delegation of authority to ministers and committees, and his dependence on the advice of experts and secretaries. Usually on questions of machinery, and often on questions of defense policy, Baldwin followed Hankey's advice very closely indeed.[113]

Defense by committee encouraged cooperation and coordination, among departments, between ministers and officials, and between political and technical considerations.[114] David Lloyd George's criticism

[110] Hankey drafted Baldwin's letter of 25 July 1935 to Eyres-Monsell, in which the new prime minister opposed reopening this question because it would undermine good inter-Service relations at a time of difficulty; PREM 1/282.

[111] Liddell Hart notes of conversation with Hankey, 25 March 1935, Liddell Hart Papers, 11/1935/67 (LHCMA).

[112] Vansittart and Sargent minutes, 17 July, *DBFP*, 13, no. 413n; Ralph Wigram referred to the "laborious" reporting of committees, 16 July 1935, C5539/55/18, FO 371/18848.

[113] For a revision of the uncomplimentary picture of laziness drawn by Baldwin's official biographer (G. M. Young), see Middlemas and Barnes, *Baldwin*, chap. 18. Now that Roskill's biography of Hankey and the documents of the CID's subcommittees are available, it would appear that Baldwin provided less personal guidance and relied more uncritically on the advice of Hankey than Middlemas and Barnes surmise. See also the portrayals in Robert Rhodes James, ed., *Memoirs of a Conservative: J. C. C. Davidson's Memoirs and Papers, 1910–1937* (London, 1969), pp. 175, 380–81; Jones, *Diary*, pp. xxiv, xxx–xxxiii; Lord Swinton (Philip Cunliffe-Lister), *Sixty Years of Power* (London, 1966), pp. 72–73, 80–81.

[114] American models of policymaking deal chiefly with bureaucratic organizations and interdepartmental bargaining, rarely with mechanisms for coordination—including terms of reference and distinctions between ministers and officials, which would appear to be more explicit in British procedures than in American. Perhaps close examination of the agendas and behavior of interdepartmental committees would help substantiate the

of the CID network in 1928 remained valid, however: it was more useful for exploration than for action.[115]

The committee system brought these competing ideas to light at official and ministerial levels: the possibility of a German attack before 1939, and the unlikelihood that Germany would make war before 1942; air rearmament for a war in Europe, and naval expansion for a conflict in the Far East; deterrence as the goal of rearmament and as a complement to the policy of appeasement while rearming; self-defense and the prevention of attacks against other countries; planning toward a five-year deadline because Germany might strike by then and because supply committees would find this a practical temporal guideline; making up deficiencies in five years because of present dangers, and envisaging expansion thereafter to meet future contingencies; producing paper plans or actual materials for war; political assumptions and technical military considerations.

Coordination did not eliminate the inconsistencies in these ideas. MacDonald and Baldwin relied on Hankey and the machinery to work out compromises among them. Hankey did this with an adroitness that his private secretary later thought might have been misplaced in the perilous climate of the 1930s.[116] Hankey did not trust Chamberlain's judgment, and he encouraged Baldwin to succeed MacDonald rather than "retire in favor of Neville Chamberlain."[117] Unlike MacDonald, Baldwin, or Hankey, Chamberlain had a coherent plan. He wanted policy clearly defined and firmly based on economic considerations. Willing to face up to hard choices, Chamberlain would remain impatient with the machinery and his colleagues so long as their compromises perpetuated inconsistency and did not closely conform to his conceptual framework for policy.

Baldwin's manner of governing suited his personality, the realities of bureaucratic politics, the historical traditions of Cabinet government, and Hankey's view of policy by committee. Both men encouraged what social scientists have described as "mutual adjustment," an essentially bureaucratic system in which policymakers continually bargain and no single person or strategy dominates. By contrast, Chamberlain more than any of his colleagues fits the characterization of the "rational actor" or "analytic planner" who tries to develop an integrated policy

---

theories of Jervis *(Perception and Misperception)* and Steinbruner *(Cybernetic Theory of Decision)*. Both authors emphasize the tendency of policymakers to treat issues separately rather than to integrate them when confronting a complex situation.

[115] Johnson, *Defence by Committee*, p. 223. See also Schmidt, *England in der Krise*, pp. 529–36.

[116] Burgis MS.

[117] Hankey diary, 24 February 1935, in Roskill, *Hankey*, 3: 162–63.

free of major incongruities.[118] The first of these two methods was the less orderly and decisive, but the more adaptable to changing circumstances and the more likely to preserve a variety of options for a policy of deterrence. The second promised order and decisiveness, but also a dogmatic world view and an insular idea of deterrence. The first method invited confusion and contradiction, whereas the second presupposed that better administration under a strong prime minister would solve Britain's problems of defense.

Tension between these two styles of policymaking had increased by the summer of 1935, when British defense policy reached its first major crossroads since the Cabinet approved the deficiency program a year earlier. The decisions of 1934 had become inadequate. New ones were needed, and they would inescapably mix concrete realities of the present with imaginary presentiments of the future. Under the impact of international crises the apposition of these realms of time would become even more disquieting, the practicality of deterrence more questionable, and the strain on the machinery greater.

---

[118] See the summary and criticism of the rational decision paradigm in Steinbruner, *Cybernetic Theory of Decision.* Chamberlain's attitude toward policymaking resembles what Charles Lindblom calls a "central system" of coordination, in which one person strives for consistency among decisions; in a system of mutual adjustment, however, policymakers are content to bargain without insisting upon consistency and coherence. *Intelligence of Democracy,* p. 105 and passim. See also the discussion of "disjointed incrementalism" in Braybrooke and Lindblom, *Strategy of Decision:* policymakers do not "reach agreement through intellectual resolution of their differences" (as Chamberlain hoped to do), but by compromising and trading favors (Baldwin's and Hankey's usual practice); pp. 137–38. Chamberlain's manner contrasts against what Paul Kennedy describes as the "political style of the British elite," which considered all points of view and often postponed difficult decisions; *Realities,* pp. 254–55.

PART II

THE MEDITERRANEAN CRISIS,
JULY–DECEMBER 1935

[2]

The Italo-Ethiopian War

The Italo-Ethiopian conflict was the first in a series of international crises that crowded the five years between the Defence Requirements Committee's (DRC) report of 1934 and the outbreak of the Second World War. The Mediterranean crisis, as Whitehall called it after August 1935, was a test case not simply for the League of Nations' provisions for collective security, but also for British policy, which neither deterred Mussolini nor reconciled inherent conflicts over long-term rearmament.[1]

The crisis came upon a Government that was engaged in a complex series of debates over how best to protect Britain's interests with rearmament and reconciliation. Long-range planning of rearmament had begun, primarily in case of war with Germany, but also for the contingency of war in the Far East against Japan. The effectiveness of British deterrence would hinge on as yet unresolved questions regarding strategy, resources, time, potential enemies, and the interaction of firmness and conciliation. Admitting the possibility of disharmony among these issues, the Government had established the Defence Pol-

---

[1] On the international context, see George W. Baer, *The Coming of the Italian-Ethiopian War* (Cambridge, Mass., 1967), and *Test Case: Italy, Ethiopia, and the League of Nations* (Stanford, Calif., 1976); Angelo Del Boca, *The Ethiopian War, 1935–1941*, trans. P. D. Cummins (Chicago, 1969); Manfred Funke, *Sanktionen und Kanonen: Hitler, Mussolini und der internationale Abessinienkonflikt, 1934–36* (Düsseldorf, 1970); Frank Hardie, *The Abyssinian Crisis* (London, 1974); Gerhard L. Weinberg, *The Foreign Policy of Hitler's Germany: Diplomatic Revolution in Europe, 1933–36* (Chicago, 1970), chap. 9. For British military measures, see especially *DBFP*, 14–15; Arthur Marder, "The Royal Navy and the Ethiopian Crisis of 1935–36," *American Historical Review* 75 (1970); Lawrence R. Pratt, *East of Malta, West of Suez: Britain's Mediterranean Crisis, 1936–1939* (London, 1975); Rosaria Quartararo, "Imperial Defence in the Mediterranean on the Eve of the Ethiopian Crisis (July–October 1935)," *Historical Journal* 20 (1977); also Bond, *Chief of Staff*, pp. 78–93; Gibbs, *Rearmament*, chap. 6; Roskill, *Hankey*, vol. 3, chap. 5; and Esmonde M. Robertson, *Mussolini as Empire-Builder: Europe and Africa, 1932–36* (New York, 1977), chaps. 13, 14.

icy and Requirements Committee (DPR) to keep them under review and seek consistency between defense and foreign policy.

The politicians and experts in London had not anticipated an eruption like the Italo-Ethiopian war, in which Italy became the wrong adversary at the wrong time in the wrong place. The crisis increased the complexity of the questions facing Britain and heightened the urgency of answering them. London's responses to this unpredicted and eccentric emergency from July to December 1935 mark the second stage in the evolution of British policy in the mid-1930s. They will be examined from four perspectives whose interrelationship has not been explored in other accounts of the crisis: foreign policy, attitudes toward rearmament and time, notions of deterrence, and peculiar adjustments in the machinery of policymaking.

Foreign policy followed parallel courses of conciliation and sanctions, but did not satisfy or deter Italy, or restore the previous assumption of a peaceful Mediterranean in the event of war with Germany or Japan. The emergency delayed Britain's rearmament and shook its strategic premises. Shortages of supply for a Mediterranean conflict emboldened the DRC's new recommendations for strengthening the Fighting Services over the next three to five years, including adoption of the "shadow" industry scheme. The DRC's mixed timetable, which now gave more emphasis to the German threat than before, reflected contradictory assessments of it. Britain should rearm all three Services as much as practicable by early 1939, beyond which Vansittart would not count on Germany to refrain from war. The Chiefs of Staff assumed that Britain would have at least two additional years (until 1941) to reach safer levels of security (industrial production required this extra time in any case), because the COS believed that German military forces would not be prepared for war until 1942 at the earliest.

The Government treated the crisis as a case for threatening force, while rebuilding Britain's armed forces, to deter an impulsive dictator far from British shores. Showing force might thwart Mussolini's aggressive designs on Ethiopia, prevent him from attacking British forces or territories in retaliation for British support of League of Nations sanctions, and impress both potential enemies and allies with British and League firmness. The failure of the first of these aims underscored the dangers of trying to achieve it, weakened the inherently dubious argument about impressing Germany, increased British misgivings about allies, and discouraged London from accepting such extended risks again.

The Mediterranean crisis tested the machinery of British policy. Whitehall responded more assiduously to this problem than it had to the long-term one of rearmament, but solving it proved no easier. The committee system coordinated steps to pressure Italy and prepare for war, but also marshaled powerful expert advice against coercion. The Cabinet, where the Government's concern for public support of collective security was highest, assigned the DPR to handle the emergency. This action dissipated the Cabinet's own collective control over policy, intensified the advice of experts on the DRC who viewed the crisis as an irritating disruption in long-term planning, and deflected the DPR's already uncertain responsibility for "general defensive policy." The DPR's special relationship to the DRC (whose members attended DPR meetings during the emergency), the DRC's preparation of a new report on rearmament in October and November, the Foreign Office's ambivalence toward coercion, the antipathy of the Treasury and Board of Trade toward sanctions, and the Services' opposition to risking war all led away from deterrence and toward the fateful Hoare-Laval peace plan of December.

When Eden replaced Hoare in December, the heritage he accepted was doubly disordered. Britain's immediate policy toward Italy and the League was in disarray. The Government had made little progress toward solving the strategic dilemma that preceded the emergency, which now increased the number of Britain's potential enemies to three. These failures resulted not simply from international politics beyond Britain's control, but also from confusion in the aims and machinery of policy as London struggled over the collision between a real crisis and conjectures about future security.

DOUBLE POLICY AND MILITARY MEASURES

In mid-June 1935, Sir Samuel Hoare, who had served in the British military mission to Italy in the last year of the war and recently been appointed Foreign Secretary, told the Cabinet of the deterioration in relations between Italy and Ethiopia. Italy was sending forces to its colonies in Eritrea and Italian Somaliland, and the French seemed more willing to side with Italy than with the League. His Majesty's Government would soon face "a most inconvenient dilemma."[2] As the European repercussions of this ostensibly colonial issue increased in significance, the British wondered how to reconcile two lines of policy: collective action against aggression; collaboration with Italy (and France) over the German question and the appeasement of Europe. Would the application of collective security against Germany in the future gain or lose credibility because of taking action now that would leave Italy hostile to both of its former partners in the Stresa Front

---

[2] Cab 33(35), 19 June, CAB 23/82.

(April 1935)? Britain needed France in case of war with Italy, but what sort of security could Britain offer France in return against Germany? Would flexing British muscles in the Mediterranean create foreign expectations and new strategic hypotheses that Britain could not possibly meet? Was it time for Britain to increase or reduce its commitments? Would Britain appear strong by risking war or weak by appeasing Mussolini? The Mediterranean crisis presented a conundrum that seemed to resist resolution by coercion, conciliation, or a combination of the two.

Membership in the League of Nations entailed an obligation, under Article 16 of the League Covenant, to participate in collective sanctions if Italy invaded Ethiopia. No such obligation had existed in the late nineteenth century when the European Great Powers scrambled for African territory and Italy's first attempt to conquer Ethiopia met humiliating defeat at Adowa in 1896. In later negotiations between Britain and Italy, such as the Treaty of London in 1915 and an exchange of diplomatic notes in 1925, Britain acknowledged Italy's interests in East Africa, which included economic influence over much of Ethiopia. Indeed, British policy toward Mussolini after his seizure of power in 1922 was often conciliatory. Sir Austen Chamberlain, Foreign Secretary from 1924 to 1929, welcomed Mussolini's commitment to regional security in Western Europe in the Treaty of Locarno (1925), and Chamberlain's willingness to make concessions to Italy in Africa paralleled Mussolini's implicit acceptance of British naval supremacy in the Mediterranean.

In the months following the clash of 5 December 1934 between Ethiopian troops and Italian-led Somali tribesmen in the Ogaden province of Ethiopia, London warned Rome that it would not support—and that British opinion would strongly oppose—an Italian invasion of Ethiopia. But Britain expressed willingness to help negotiate a compromise settlement favoring many Italian claims, chiefly because by 1935 Britain's European policy presupposed a "common front" with Italy and France as means for settling grievances peacefully. At the Stresa Conference, 11–14 April, British representatives agreed with the Italians and French to avoid the Ethiopian question during formal sessions for fear of detracting from the central issue—Germany's unilateral abrogations of the Treaty of Versailles. Sir Robert Vansittart and the British ambassador to Rome, Sir Eric Drummond, feared that Britain might drive Italy into the arms of Germany and allow Hitler to seize Austria, the independence of which had hitherto been a mutual interest of Britain, Italy, and France.[3]

---

[3] Drummond to Simon (with marginal comments by Vansittart), 1 June, and Vansittart to Hoare, 16 June, *DBFP*, 14, nos. 296 and 308; Vansittart, *Mist*, pp. 520–21.

Whereas the British Cabinet viewed the Stresa Front as consistent with its policy of reconciling Germany, the French Government defined "front" more literally in strategic terms. Added to France's mutual assistance pacts with Poland (1921), Czechoslovakia (1924), Yugoslavia (1927), and the Soviet Union (May 1935), and the Rome agreements of January 1935, the Stresa agreement would help strengthen French security by surrounding Germany. In the Rome accords, French Foreign Minister Pierre Laval gave Italy concessions in Africa in return for the renunciation of Italian rights in the French colony of Tunisia. Laval also gave Mussolini a free hand in Ethiopia, or so Il Duce thought. The Rome agreements included a pledge to consult if Germany should threaten Austrian independence, and they led to joint military accords in May and June that would enable France to concentrate its forces against Germany in a European emergency.[4] The Stresa Front was weakened from the start by different policies in London and Paris, and by the failure of one government to consult the other while reaching bilateral agreements with third parties—the Anglo-German Naval Agreement of 18 June was the most notable example. Mussolini skillfully exploited Anglo-French differences as he pursued an expansionist policy that would cripple both the Stresa Front and the League of Nations.

In June, Mussolini rejected as completely inadequate the British proposal, prescribed by Vansittart and conveyed to Rome by Anthony Eden, to compensate Ethiopia with a corridor through British Somaliland to the port of Zeila on the Gulf of Aden if Ethiopia would cede the Ogaden to Italy.[5] In July, when it appeared likely that Italy would invade Ethiopia in the autumn, the British Cabinet sought a peaceful settlement at Geneva, and began to discuss the possible repercussions of applying sanctions in the event of Italian aggression. Economic sanctions would almost certainly bring about hostilities. Britain should not apply Article 16 without French cooperation. "Playing for time" might allow Mussolini to realize the difficulties confronting him and motivate him to seek a compromise. Meanwhile, the Foreign Office and other departments should consider problems that would face Britain in case of an Italo-Ethiopian war.[6]

British experts had already examined the Ethiopian question as

---

[4] On the Rome agreements and military talks, see Avon, *Dictators*, p. 136; Baer, *Coming of Italian-Ethiopian War*, chap. 4; Robertson, *Mussolini*, pp. 114–16; Geoffrey Warner, *Pierre Laval and the Eclipse of France* (London, 1968), pp. 69–71, 94–96; Robert J. Young, *In Command of France: French Foreign Policy and Military Planning, 1933–1940* (Cambridge, Mass., 1978), pp. 89–92, and his "French Military Intelligence and the Franco-Italian Alliance, 1933–1939," *Historical Journal* 28 (1985), 157–62.

[5] *DBFP*, 14, chap. 5, especially no. 308 (Vansittart to Hoare, 16 June) and no. 325 (record of Anglo-Italian conversation, 25 June); Avon, *Dictators*, pp. 246–56.

[6] Cabs 35, 36, 39, 40, 41(35), CAB 23/82.

members of an ad hoc committee chaired by Sir John Maffey of the Colonial Office. In their report of 18 June, the Maffey committee concluded that, although an Italian conquest of Ethiopia "would not directly and immediately threaten any vital British interest, the balance of power in this area would be altered to Italy's advantage and a possible, if remote, threat to British control over the Sudan and the upper waters of the Nile must be taken into account." Still, in the committee's judgment this threat was too remote to necessitate British resistance to an Italian invasion of Ethiopia. The committee left to other advisers consideration of "the general situation in Europe . . . , the question of how far His Majesty's Government are prepared to support the League of Nations at the risk of losing Italian friendship, and the like."[7]

Experts in the Foreign Office and Service departments considered these larger questions when they began to reexamine defense policy in July. Since 1933, they had agreed that Germany and Japan posed the major threats to European peace and British interests, above all if one of these enemies were to take advantage of a conflict between Britain and the other. Britain, the Admiralty confidently presumed, would enjoy unrestricted passage through the Mediterranean to the Far East. Britain could "only fight in Europe in concert with allies," and must avoid war for the next few years.[8]

The idea of an allied effort and the avoidance of war were endangered by the Italo-Ethiopian dispute, which, as the Defence Requirements Committee noted, threatened to undermine the international front against Germany.[9] The Foreign Office emphasized that Britain must cooperate with those continental nations which were likely to be Britain's allies in case of war with Germany. Above all, Vansittart, Hoare, and Assistant Under-Secretary Orme Sargent feared that the Government's policy in the Ethiopian imbroglio was alienating both France and Italy, and reckoned that Britain should not confidently assume it would have allies in the event of war. Meanwhile, in tow of the Admiralty, the Chiefs of Staff began to formulate their case against imposing sanctions on Italy or interdicting Italian lines of supply to Ethiopia; either measure "would almost inevitably lead to war."[10]

When the Cabinet recessed at the end of July for the summer holidays, it had not reached a clear decision on policy. Should Britain, as Vansittart advocated, preserve the League Covenant, the Stresa Front,

---

[7] Report in *DBFP*, 14, appx. II. The report of 18 June was not circulated to the Cabinet until 16 August—as CP 161(35), CAB 24/256.

[8] Wigram minute and memorandum by Wigram and Creswell, 4 July, C5178/55/18, FO 371/18847; DRC Interim Report (DRC 25), 24 July, CAB 16/138.

[9] DRC Interim Report (DRC 25), 24 July, CAB 16/138.

[10] Vansittart minute, 5 July, *DBFP*, 13, no. 396; and Sargent minute, 4 July, on Wigram-Creswell memorandum cited above in note 8; COS meetings, 5 and 30 July, CAB 53/5.

and the recent Franco-Italian agreements by appeasing Italy with territorial concessions in Ethiopia? Or, as Eden advised, would not the League's future effectiveness in Europe depend on affirming its "'moral authority'" in this extra-European case?[11] Both options remained open in the Cabinet's tacit approval of conciliating Mussolini and pressuring him in cooperation with France. Hoare rightly believed that he had Cabinet support for this "double policy."[12] Like Hoare, Chamberlain viewed the two sides of this policy as compatible. If Britain and France could convince Mussolini that they would impose sanctions, and if they also assured him of their "desire to save his face and get him some compensation" from Ethiopia, then he might compromise short of war. If France did not adopt a more active policy in support of collective action, Britain should declare its policy "in a way which will not involve us in so much odium for nothing."[13]

But suppose Mussolini persistently refused to compromise and decided to save face by attacking British forces or territories? The possibility of Mussolini's starting a Mediterranean war with Britain became the central question for British foreign policy and military strategy during the period when Anglo-Italian tension was highest, from August to December 1935.

The Foreign Office expected the tripartite conference of 15–18 August to reveal whether Britain would have to take major military precautions. Before Eden and Vansittart left for this meeting with French and Italian representatives in Paris, Vansittart reiterated his concern over British military weakness and assured Chatfield that he and Eden would "do and say nothing . . . which might expose us to consequences for which we were not prepared."[14] Vansittart apparently did not inform Chatfield that the Foreign Office planned to say things to the French that might indeed lead to Italian retaliation against Britain. Hoare and Vansittart were already reminding France of the importance of Anglo-French solidarity in supporting the League, whose "unimpaired existence might well be essential for dealing with European problems surpassing even in gravity the one now being forced upon us by Italy in regard to Ethiopia."[15] If, Vansittart postulated, the French

---

[11] Vansittart to Hoare, 16 June, DBFP, 14, no. 308; Avon, Dictators, pp. 270–74; Templewood, Nine Troubled Years, pp. 152–53, 157–58.

[12] Templewood, Nine Troubled Years, pp. 160–61.

[13] Diary, 5 and 18 July, Chamberlain Papers, NC 2/23a; Chamberlain to Hilda, 14 July, NC 18/1/925; Feiling, Life of Chamberlain, p. 265.

[14] Vansittart to Chatfield, 9 August, DBFP, 14, no. 431n, in reply to Chatfield's letter of the same day (no. 431).

[15] Ibid., Hoare to Clerk, 29 July, no. 403; Vansittart note, 8 August, no. 429; record of conversation among Eden, Vansittart, Sir George Clerk (British ambassador to France), and Laval, 14 August, no. 442.

showed signs that they would take a strong line when the League Council convened in Geneva on 4 September, Britain would have to show its "full hand, in conjunction with the French and presumably with the other Members of the League" in early September, and the Services would have to be authorized to prepare for the possibility of a "mad dog coup" by Mussolini against Malta or the British Mediterranean Fleet.[16]

Vansittart doubted that an emergency situation would arise. Laval, whom Vansittart and his colleagues in the Foreign Office did not trust, would not take a firm line against Italy but, afraid of driving Mussolini toward Hitler, would try to satisfy Mussolini's demands in Ethiopia.[17] Vansittart misjudged Laval, who had become premier in June but retained the portfolio for foreign affairs. At the tripartite conference, the Frenchman's attitude was "perfectly loyal and satisfactory" from the British point of view, Eden reported. Laval and his colleagues gave sufficiently firm support to Britain and the League for Eden to advise the Cabinet to interrupt its holiday and consider appropriate precautionary measures before the League Council met in Geneva.[18]

At an emergency meeting on 22 August, the Cabinet considered recommendations made by military experts. The Service advisers, particularly the Naval Staff, warned that sanctions would lead to war. Any decision to participate in sanctions, or indeed any diplomatic action that might trigger an Italian attack, must be preceded by "sufficient warning" to the Services. The Services were unready for war and needed a minimum of two months' notice to prepare for the interruption of Italian sea communications (particularly by closing the Suez Canal) and the defense of British interests in the Mediterranean, Africa, Red Sea, and Middle East. Finally, Britain must not risk war without the "assured military support" of France.[19] On 6 August, Baldwin and Hoare had implicitly authorized the Services to take "relatively quiet steps" such as improving Malta's antiaircraft defenses.[20] Cabinet authority was needed, however, for sending the Home Fleet to the Mediterranean, mobilizing naval reserves, and moving significant Air

[16] Ibid., Vansittart to Hoare, 7 August, no. 442; Vansittart to Admiral Sir Charles Little (Deputy Chief of Naval Staff, 1932–35), 9 August, ADM 116/3038.

[17] Vansittart to Hoare and to Little (as in preceding note).

[18] Eden reports to Hoare, 15–17 August, *DBFP*, 14, nos. 452, 456, 461, the last of these circulated to the Cabinet as CP 163(35), CAB 24/256; Avon, *Dictators*, pp. 280–83.

[19] COS memorandum (COS 388), 2 August, and report (COS 392), 9 August, CAB 53/25; Chatfield to Vansittart, 8 August, *DBFP*, 14, no. 431. Admiralty appreciations formed the heart of both COS documents, the latter of which was circulated to the Cabinet on 19 August as CP 166(35), CAB 24/256.

[20] Meeting of Baldwin, Hoare, Eden, Vansittart, and Hankey, CP 159(35), CAB 24/256 (also in *DBFP*, 14, no. 426); Hankey to Dill, 6 August, WO 106/282; Hoare to Vansittart, 9 August, *DBFP*, no. 433.

Force and Army reinforcements from home to the Middle East and Malta. On 22 August the Cabinet so authorized except that it prohibited mobilization. The Cabinet also empowered the Defence Policy and Requirements Committee to "consider any matter that might arise in connection with the Italo-Abyssinian dispute," and on 23 August the DPR approved further measures of reinforcement.[21]

In a letter of 18 August asking Chamberlain to return from his holiday in Switzerland for the Cabinet meeting, Hoare foresaw "a first class crisis" in the League of Nations because of Italian intransigence. He wanted neither to provoke Mussolini nor to leave "undone anything that might make a mad dog act more dangerous." In the same spirit of anxious ambivalence, the Cabinet on 22 August approved military precautions while recognizing that war with Italy "would be a grave calamity."[22] Thus, on the eve of the League Council's reconvening in early September, British policy stood uncertainly between provoking and avoiding war. The alternatives, and the difficulty of finding solid footing between them, can be seen in London's attitudes toward the interrelated issues of collective security, economic sanctions, and imperial defense.

Collective security entailed both obligations and risks. The British public strongly supported the policy of collective economic sanctions against aggressors. Leaders of the Opposition, Conservative backbenchers such as Austen Chamberlain and Winston Churchill, and Dominion High Commissioners encouraged Hoare and Eden to declare Britain's readiness to participate in economic action, and they underlined the importance of French cooperation. On the other hand, the British public and the Dominions were less willing to support collective military measures, especially if these might lead to war. Party leaders and High Commissioners opposed unilateral economic or military action, and no one wanted war.[23] France needed Italy against

---

[21] Cab 42(35), 22 August, CAB 23/82; DPR meeting, 23 August, CAB 16/136; Marder, "Royal Navy," pp. 1329–30.

[22] Hoare to Chamberlain, Chamberlain Papers, NC 7/11/28/24 (also printed in *DBFP*, 14, appx. Ic); Temperley, *Nine Troubled Years*, p. 164; Cab 42(35), CAB 23/82. Winston Churchill asked Hoare whether adequate naval precautions were being taken, as Churchill had done in 1914 while First Lord of the Admiralty. Hoare reassured Churchill that he was aware of the risks. Correspondence of 25 and 27 August, *DBFP*, 14, appx. Ie and f, also printed in Churchill's *The Gathering Storm* (Bantam ed., New York, 1961), pp. 153–54.

[23] Meeting of ministers, 21 August, CAB 23/82; discussion between Hoare, Eden, and High Commissioners, 21 August, *DBFP*, 14, no. 482 (and statements from the Governments of Australia, New Zealand, and Canada in early September, nos. 521, 529, 530); conversations of Hoare and Eden with various politicians, 20–21 August, nos. 476, 477, 480, 481, 483, 484. On public attitudes toward collective security in the Ethiopian crisis, see Baer, *Coming of Italian-Ethiopian War*, pp. 202–8; Neville Thompson, *The Anti-*

Germany more than it wanted Britain against Italy, yet Anglo-French solidarity was essential for the League's survival. Churchill told Hoare and Eden that the collapse of the League now would divide Britain and France, and would destroy the League's effectiveness "as a deterrent to German aggression" in the future.[24] Hoare told the Dominion High Commissioners that, if Britain (and France) abandoned the League in the current crisis, the League would be virtually useless as an instrument of security against aggression in Europe. On 22 August the Cabinet agreed that mobilization would have an undesirable effect on public opinion in Britain and abroad. Britain must uphold the Covenant but "not in any quixotic spirit"; keep in step with France, avoiding "any commitment which France was not equally prepared to assume"; and not force France and other countries to advocate sanctions if they did not wish to do so.[25]

The weight of expert advice against sanctions steadily increased, exceeding ministerial qualms about the League. The Subcommittee on Economic Pressure (of the CID's Advisory Committee on Trade Questions in Time of War) drew a bleak picture of the consequent harm to British commerce, as well as the danger of declaring belligerent rights against states that refused to participate in sanctions. Sir Warren Fisher and Sargent (who represented the Foreign Office in the Subcommittee on Economic Pressure) underscored the impracticability of sanctions, the necessity of naval enforcement, and the likelihood of war with Italy so long as any non-League power—above all the United States or Germany—refused to cooperate fully with a League embargo.[26]

Chamberlain expected Germany and the United States to refrain from sanctions, and thought his Government should let the French know that it considered sanctions ineffective if this knowledge would persuade France jointly to propose a League investigation of the subject before the League actually applied Article 16.[27] But Hoare and Eden refused to predetermine the effectiveness of sanctions before the

---

Appeasers: Conservative Opposition to Appeasement in the 1930s (Oxford, 1971), chap. 4; Daniel Waley, *British Public Opinion and the Abyssinian War, 1935–6* (London, 1975).

[24] *DBFP*, 14, no. 483.

[25] Cab 42(35), 22 August, CAB 23/82.

[26] ATB(EP) 29, 18 September (circulated on 30 September as CID 1188-B), in CAB 4/23; Treasury papers and correspondence with the Foreign Office, August and early September, T 160/621 (especially Fisher to Chamberlain, 21 August), and T 172/1838 (including Fisher to Chamberlain, Hoare, and Eden, 30 August, also in *DBFP*, 14, no. 511); Sargent to Hoare, 26 August, *DBFP*, no. 496.

[27] Meeting of ministers, 21 August, CAB 23/82; Chamberlain to Hilda, 25 August, Chamberlain Papers, NC 18/1/929; Chamberlain notes on minute by F. Phillips, 26 August, T 172/1838; Sargent to Hoare, 26 August, *DBFP*, 14, no. 496.

League Council considered the question. Hoare admitted the possibility of self-contradiction in public presumptions that Britain could "stick to the Covenant and . . . keep out of war." Nevertheless, the League's machinery should be given a chance to work while the Government examined the question of sanctions. The Government "must on no account lay itself open to the charge that we have not done our utmost to make them practicable," and should not give the French reason to believe that Britain was determined either to apply or to oppose sanctions. If Britain refused either to press for sanctions or to declare they were bound to fail, Hoare reasoned, the other nations, not Britain, would be responsible should sanctions not be applied.[28]

Before 1935, Britain's strategy for imperial defense had presumed free passage for British warships through the Mediterranean to the Far East. When the Admiralty decided late in 1934 that it would send the main fleet around the Cape of Good Hope, it assumed that this change would not jeopardize British communications and interests in the Mediterranean.[29] The Mediterranean crisis upset the preconditions for this Far Eastern strategy, namely, good relations with Italy and no serious military threat in the Mediterranean, North and East Africa, and the Middle East. As Italy stepped up preparations for war against Ethiopia and rejected proposals for compromise, British policymakers reconsidered imperial defense. On the one hand, they accused Italy of throwing down the gauntlet for colonial supremacy in Africa and some contemplated picking it up. On the other, they wanted to avoid even a victorious war with Italy because of the disastrous consequences this would have for defense against future aggression by Germany or Japan.

In August 1935, ministers and officials at the Foreign Office worried about the harmful effect on British imperial interests if Italy conquered Ethiopia. Italian expansion in Africa threatened British control over Egypt and the Sudan as well as imperial communications through the Mediterranean, Suez Canal, Red Sea, and Gulf of Aden. Moreover, conflict between these two colonial powers would probably cause "an increase of nationalist feeling fanned by resentment of European imperialism."[30] Hoare considered the possibility of sending a British force to

---

[28] Oliphant to Campbell, 23 August (no. 490); Hoare to Clerk, 24 August (no. 493); Sargent to Hoare, 26 August (no. 496); *DBFP*, 14; Sargent to Fisher, 3 September, T 172/1838.

[29] Pratt, *East of Malta*, pp. 12–18, 22–24; apparently, the Navy's only plan for defense of the Suez Canal in the early 1930s assumed Japanese sabotage. On the Navy's change in strategy in late 1934, see Roskill, *Naval Policy*, pp. 186–87, 235.

[30] Campbell memorandum on the Maffey report, 9 August, *DBFP*, 14, appx. III.

Lake Tsana (inside Ethiopia) "to forestall the Italians, on the analogy of Fashoda."[31] Eden resented Italian propaganda about succeeding the effete British in Africa. Vansittart blamed Italy's defiance of Britain on the "foolish and dangerous doctrine [of] the school in Italy which believes the British Empire to be in full decrepitude and thinks that a new Roman Empire would ultimately take at least part of its place in the sun, however hot the sun." And Chatfield wondered whether now might be a good time to "'reassert our dominance over an inferior race.'"[32]

These combative overtones were much weaker than fundamental arguments against war with Italy. British defense policy since late 1933 had excluded Italy as a potential enemy chiefly because Britain could not otherwise defend a large empire with limited resources. Now the Admiralty and Chiefs of Staff warned that the cost of a Mediterranean war would be too high. Both concentrating and losing forces there would weaken air and naval defenses against German or Japanese aggression, and would disrupt the air rearmament program of attaining parity with Germany by April 1937.[33]

By the end of August, the Cabinet, Foreign Office, Treasury, and Service departments were not sure how long Britain could support the League Covenant and at the same time avoid war with Italy. Nor did they know how long the Mediterranean might remain a powder keg in Anglo-Italian relations. In this climate of uncertainty, speculation and wishful thinking flourished, and the wretched results of the Government's double policy were not easily predictable. Hoare forecast that if Italy attacked Ethiopia, either strong Anglo-French reaction would force Italy to "extricate itself" or French refusal to join Britain would eliminate the possibility of collective sanctions. Chamberlain expected that once Mussolini began his war against Ethiopia, Britain, in concert with France, would be able to persuade the League of the utter futility of sanctions because Germany and the United States would not participate. Then, he hoped, Britain could reconstruct the League "to deal

---

[31] Hoare conversation with Dominion High Commissioners, 21 August, *DBFP*, 14, no. 482; Lieutenant Colonel B. F. Webb (Assistant Secretary to the CID) memorandum, 30 August, CAB 21/573. According to Webb, the Chiefs of Staff opposed such a move as "strategically unsound" and "useless."

[32] Avon, *Dictators*, p. 288; Vansittart to Hoare, 19 August, *DBFP*, 14, appx. Id; Chatfield to Admiral Fisher, 25 August, in Marder, "Royal Navy," p. 1342. John Darwin rejects the "suspiciously whiggish view" that British leaders between the world wars saw the dissolution of the empire as inevitable and merely tried to postpone this event; "Imperialism in Decline? Tendencies in British Imperial Policy between the Wars," *Historical Journal* 23 (1980).

[33] COS report (COS 392), 9 August, in CP 166(35), CAB 24/256; Air Staff appreciations in AIR 9/68.

with European affairs" and could rearm so that British wishes could not "be flouted again as Mussolini has flouted them now."[34]

Neither Hoare's forecast nor Chamberlain's proved correct. Ministers and experts in London agreed that imposing economic sanctions could lead to war—either a "League war" or a "single-handed war" in which Britain fought alone against Italy. The British Government continued to try to support the League without provoking Mussolini or taking the lead in Geneva. The success of this policy would depend upon two speculative conditions: assurances from France and other League members that they would help Britain if Italy "went mad dog"; and the political effect of displaying force in the Mediterranean.

On 5 September, the day after the League Council convened, the DPR asserted that Britain must not adopt sanctions at Geneva unless participating nations agreed to declare war on Italy if Italy assaulted any one of them, and unless there was a "clear understanding with France" (and if possible with Yugoslavia and Greece) if Italy attacked British interests. The Chiefs of Staff noted the strategic advantage of French, Yugoslav, and Greek support. France could take responsibility for control of the western Mediterranean (except Gibraltar) and, with Yugoslavia, conduct air raids on northern Italy. Greek permission for use of "Port X" (Navarino, on the southwest coast of the Peloponnesus) would assist British control of the eastern Mediterranean. The DPR agreed with these strategic assumptions.[35] In case of either a League war or a single-handed war, the Admiralty and the COS expressed confidence that Britain could defeat Italy, whose armed forces the Chiefs of Staff disparaged, but Chatfield feared that the Navy might suffer heavy losses.[36]

In his dramatic address of 11 September before the League Assembly, which Chamberlain helped him write, Sir Samuel Hoare pledged his country's commitment to "steady and collective resistance to all acts of unprovoked aggression." Britain would be "second to none" in carrying out the obligations contained in the Covenant. Hoare hoped his "revivalist appeal" to the Assembly would give the League and his

---

[34] Hoare minute on COS report (see preceding note), 12 August, W7166/1209/98, FO 371/19686; Hoare to Chamberlain, 18 August (appx. Ic); Hoare to Clerk, 24 August (no. 493); Clerk to Hoare, 27 August (no. 498); *DBFP*, 14; Chamberlain to Hilda, 25 August, Chamberlain Papers, NC 18/1/929.

[35] DPR meetings, 5 and 11 September, CAB 16/136; COS memorandum (COS 395), 9 September, CAB 53/25.

[36] Chatfield memorandum, 3 September, CAB 16/138; Admiralty and Board of Trade memorandum, 10 September, CAB 16/138; COS meeting, 13 September, CAB 53/5, and memorandum (COS 397), 16 September, CAB 53/25. For Chatfield's fear of losses: letter to Admiral Sir Frederic Dreyer (Commander in Chief, China Station), 16 September, Chatfield Papers (National Maritime Museum, London).

Government a good chance to succeed. He and Chamberlain expected Mussolini to attack Ethiopia but, as the result of the League's pressure, to stop and negotiate after achieving what he could claim was a victory. Mussolini would have saved face, and, according to Chamberlain, the League would thus have succeeded "thanks to us." "Even Hitler may take warning . . . and be more careful about offending world opinion." If on the contrary, the League broke down "under the test," the two ministers thought it necessary to know this as soon as possible to avoid leaving Britain holding the bag.[37]

Although less enthusiastic than the League Assembly's, the reaction of the French Government to Hoare's speech was positive enough to buoy his report to the DPR on 17 September. The chances of a single-handed war with Italy had diminished, he announced, for it now appeared likely that France and other nations would take action if Italy attacked Britain or other League members. The DPR authorized the Admiralty to exchange information with the French Navy about possible joint action. After the meeting, Hoare wrote Chamberlain that events of the past week had put committee members in an optimistic mood, willing to show substantial force in the Mediterranean.[38] A week later, however, news from Geneva prompted some of Hoare's colleagues on the DPR to question French reliability and complain that Britain had been thrust "into a position of leadership" when it should "avoid the appearance of taking the lead." And while saluting Hoare for his speech to the League Assembly, the Cabinet underscored the collectiveness of sanctions and the need to keep in line with France.[39]

In fact, the Foreign Secretary's euphoria on 17 September was not based on what the DPR had called a "clear understanding with France." Numerous dispatches from Paris and Geneva to the Foreign Office conveyed the two main reasons why Laval was reluctant to commit France, as Britain wanted, before the application of Article 16 of the Covenant. First, the French needed Italian friendship in case of war with Germany. General Maurice Gamelin, Chief of the French General Staff, told the British military attaché of the "solid and definite advantages" the French Army would derive from this friendship, including the possibility of taking offensive action against Germany

---

[37] Chamberlain to Hilda, 7 September, and to wife, 15 September, Chamberlain Papers, NC 18/1/932, 1/26/512; Cab 43(35), 24 September, CAB 23/82; text of Hoare's speech in *DBFP*, 14, appx. IV; Hoare to Eden, 15 September, *DBFP*, 14, appx. Ig; Templewood, *Nine Troubled Years*, p. 166.

[38] DPR meeting, 17 September, CAB 16/136; Hoare to Chamberlain, 17 September, Templewood Papers (Cambridge University Library).

[39] DPR meeting, 23 September, CAB 16/136; Hoare to Clerk, 23 September, *DBFP*, 14, no. 629; Cab 43(35), 24 September, CAB 23/82.

should Germany try to seize Austria or Czechoslovakia.[40] On 11 September, the day when Hoare addressed the League Assembly and the DPR accepted the COS strategic assumption that France could bomb Italy in a Mediterranean war, a new round of conversations was under way in Paris between representatives of the French and Italian air staffs. Although Laval did not mention these talks, he informed Hoare and Eden that the cost of maintaining the League Covenant over Ethiopia would be too high if the result was to "denude the Brenner Pass" of Italian troops and strengthen Germany's position for aggression in Europe. Laval did not want the "Anglo-Italian crisis," as the French Government often called it, to force Italy out of the League and into the arms of Germany, yet he had learned that Mussolini was trying to obtain closer economic cooperation with Germany to guard against the possibility of League sanctions.[41]

The Foreign Office did not disregard the possibility of a rapprochement between Italy and Germany. Vansittart warned that Britain could no longer be confident that Italy would join a continental bloc against a German seizure of Austria. The German ambassador in Rome, Ulrich von Hassell, told his British counterpart how the Italians had informed Berlin that the League's movement against Italy was part of "a general offensive against fascism," which, if it succeeded now, would turn next on National Socialism. Hitler, von Hassell assured Mussolini, wanted to support Italian fascism but thought it too early for Germany to become involved in " 'a conflict between static and dynamic peoples.' "[42] Rome had already offended London with propaganda about the superiority of Italian fascism and its inevitable triumph over British democracy in Africa. Now London saw at least the phantom of an ideological conflict that would divide Europe as well.

In the second place, before promising to support Britain now, the French wanted to know "up to what point and in what conditions" Britain would execute its obligations under the League Covenant if Germany aggressively violated it in Europe, for example by attacking

---

[40] Colonel T. G. G. Heywood to the British ambassador, 5 September, C6525/55/18, FO 371/18850.

[41] Anglo-French conversations in Geneva, 11 and 13 September (nos. 553, 554, 564), and Eden report of talk with Laval, 18 September (no. 579), *DBFP*, 14. The French General Staff thought Italy could provide more immediate aid than Britain in a war against Germany; Young, "French Military Intelligence," pp. 161–62. On French policy, see also Baer, *Test Case*, pp. 52–63; Warner, *Pierre Laval*, pp. 102–8; Young, *In Command of France*, pp. 103–5.

[42] Vansittart minute, 10 September, C5685/55/18, FO 371/18849; Drummond to Hoare, 1 October, *DBFP*, 14, no. 666; Jens Petersen, *Hitler-Mussolini: Die Entstehung der Achse Berlin-Rom, 1933–1936* (Tübingen, 1973), pp. 437–54. Petersen disagrees with Funke's thesis that the German-Italian Axis was not forming late in 1935; see Funke, *Sanktionen*, pp. 41–43; 59–71, 80–81.

Austria. London replied that Anglo-French cooperation to uphold collective security now would make it a "deterrent" to Germany in the future. But the British Government would not promise unconditionally to support France if, for example, Germany attacked France after France took precautionary measures while Germany threatened to invade Austria or Czechoslovakia. Tit for tat, the French Government did not give unequivocal assurance of French military support if Italy attacked British forces before the application of Article 16. Eden described the French attitude toward the League and Europe as "clear sighted . . . [but] not long sighted." Von Hassell said the British Government's attitude toward "the obligations of the Covenant in any future disputes had been much admired in Berlin."[43]

The level of British forces in the Mediterranean theater increased considerably in September. The Navy all but mobilized. The Mediterranean Fleet moved from Malta to Alexandria, where reinforcements arrived from Britain and other naval stations. A powerful detachment of the Home Fleet reached Gibraltar on 17 September, and a naval squadron concentrated at Aden near the southern entrance to the Red Sea. Air units in the Middle East and Egypt were reinforced, as were Army garrisons in Malta and Egypt.[44]

Mussolini was not daunted by League diplomacy or by British military measures that London assured him were merely precautionary. He rejected the compromise proposals—for a transfer of territory—that the League presented on 18 September. He maintained that reinforcement of the Italian Army in Libya had been provoked by the threat of sanctions and by Britain's naval buildup in the Mediterranean. Both governments became increasingly concerned that the escalation of forces in the Mediterranean, Libya, Egypt, and the Red Sea might lead to war. Nevertheless, Eden advised against promising Italy that no military or crippling economic sanctions would be applied. Mussolini had made this promise a precondition for withdrawing reinforcements from Libya, but such a pledge would be disloyal to the League and would allow Mussolini "to carry on his Abyssinian adventure undisturbed." Eden argued that "it would be fatal in any way to reduce pressure on Signor Mussolini." The French, "powerfully impressed"

[43] Vansittart to Hoare, 10 September (no. 547); Anglo-French conversations (see note 41 above); Eden to Hoare, 24 September (no. 633); Hoare to Clerk, 24 September (no. 640); Vansittart conversation with M. Corbin (French ambassador to Great Britain), and Hoare to Corbin, 26 September (no. 650); Clerk to Hoare, 1 October (no. 665); von Hassell quoted in Drummond to Hoare, 1 October (no. 666); *DBFP*, 14.

[44] DPR meetings, 5, 11, 23 September, and 2 October, CAB 16/136; Hoare to Drummond, 19 September, *DBFP*, 14, no. 586; Hankey summary of precautionary measures, 20 September, CP 176(35), CAB 24/256; Cab 43(35), 24 September, CAB 23/82; Marder, "Royal Navy," pp. 1332–33.

by the British naval concentration in the Mediterranean, would eventually side with Britain and the League. The British Government had assured Mussolini it did not wish to humiliate or attack him, and evidence of declining confidence inside Italy meant that soon Britain need not have to fear "any mad dog act" by the dictator.[45]

On 24 September, First Lord of the Admiralty Eyres-Monsell warned the Cabinet that the Navy's situation in the Mediterranean was not as favorable "as was generally assumed." Hoare wrote Eden that feeling in the Government was "a very long way behind feeling in Geneva," and that he and Chamberlain had not been entirely successful in assuaging the Cabinet's "very deep nervousness as to our finding ourselves in an isolated position." But the outcome of Hoare's speech of 11 September had reinforced Eden's view that "effective action by the League is dependent upon a lead from us." Unmoved by Cabinet criticism he considered unconstructive, Eden continued to prescribe "no other course" for Britain than to see its policy of collective security "through to the end."[46]

On 3 October, Italy invaded Ethiopia, the Defence Requirements Committee reconvened in London to prepare a new set of proposals for rearmament, and Baldwin told his Conservative party's annual conference that the Government's policy of collective security, if backed by rearmament, offered Britain " 'greater security than can be obtained by any other policy which we have yet seen advocated.' "[47] While the DRC met (3 October–14 November), the League accused Italy of breaking the Covenant (7 October), lifted arms embargoes on Ethiopia while placing a collective one on Italy, began to impose financial and commercial sanctions on Italy, and took the first step toward adding oil to the list of commodities banned for export to Italy. In London, Baldwin's National Government fought a victorious election campaign on a platform that emphasized the compatibility of collective security and rearmament. On 14 November, the Government received nearly 54 percent of the vote, and the Conservatives remained in firm control. The problem of sanctions, the danger of a single-handed war, and the advice of the DRC drew the Government away from the public mandate for collective security and pushed it toward conciliation.

Shortly after the invasion of Ethiopia, Chamberlain hoped that Mussolini would "be frightened into negotiations," and he doubted that

---

[45] Eden to Hoare, 18, 19, 20, and 24 September, *DBFP*, 14, nos. 579, 588, 591, 633.

[46] Cab 43(35), 24 September, CAB 23/82; Eden-Hoare correspondence, 23–25 September, *DBFP*, 14, no. 619 and appx. Ih and i; Avon, *Dictators*, pp. 299, 302–3.

[47] On Baldwin's speech and the subsequent election campaign, see John Dunbabin, "British Rearmament in the 1930s: A Chronology and Review," *Historical Journal* 18 (1975), 591–95; Middlemas and Barnes, *Baldwin*, pp. 859–69.

war would break out between Britain and Italy, "for the French are determined not to fight and we are not going to act without them."[48] In fact, the prospect of a single-handed war frightened the British more than sanctions did the Italians. Echoing the opinions found in the Admiralty, Foreign Office, Board of Trade, and in the reports of inter-departmental committees directly concerned with sanctions, the Cabinet reiterated the condition that any sanctions must be collective and the apprehension that they might provoke Mussolini to make war in the Mediterranean.[49]

Sanctions did not halt Mussolini, and his warning that he would treat an oil embargo as an act of war kept the possibility of armed retaliation against Britain very much alive. Late in November, Hoare reported to the DPR that, although sanctions seemed to be slowing down the Italian campaign in Africa, Mussolini was intransigent. On 2 December, the Foreign Secretary pointed out to the Cabinet that Britain was now the only League member not to have expressed its willingness to support the oil sanction, which had been agreed to in principle in Geneva on 15 November and would be discussed by the League's Sanctions Committee on 12 December. The Cabinet approved Hoare's recommended line of policy. Britain should accept the oil sanction in principle but postpone the date of its application so long as peace talks offered reasonable prospects of a territorial settlement, and Hoare should speed up these talks when he saw Laval in Paris on his way to a brief skating holiday in Switzerland. Hoare should also ascertain whether the U.S. Government could effectively block oil exports and whether France and other Mediterranean states would offer military support if Italy attacked British forces.[50]

The French withheld promises of substantial military help to Britain in a war with Italy. At the Cabinet meeting of 16 October, Eyres-Monsell noted the discrepancy between the progress in Geneva on sanctions and the DPR's assertion early in September that adopting sanctions must be preceded by a "clear understanding" with France and other states as to the kind of support they would give Britain if

---

[48] Chamberlain to Ida, 5 October, Chamberlain Papers, NC 18/1/935.

[49] Cab 45(35), 9 October, CAB 23/82, including discussion of report of Advisory Committee on Trade Questions in Time of War, 3 October, CP 186(35), CAB 24/257; FO minutes on CP 186, 4–7 October, J6637/5499/1, FO 371/19203; report of CID's Subcommittee on Abyssinia, 8 October, CAB 16/121; also Foreign Office memorandum (prepared jointly with the Treasury and Board of Trade), 22 October, CP 203(35), CAB 24/257.

[50] DPR meeting, 26 November, CAB 16/136; Cab 50(35), 2 December, CAB 23/82. Hoare reminded the Cabinet that Iran was a major supplier of oil to Italy, and that the British Government held the largest share of interest in the Anglo-Iranian Oil Company; "a very active propaganda" in the United States and France was reproaching Britain for supporting sanctions "until the moment when our own interests were affected."

attacked. On this and other occasions, Laval was described as unreliable, intriguing behind the backs of Britain and the League in order to reach a compromise with Mussolini. The Cabinet instructed Hoare to obtain a clear answer from the French about their intentions. He should warn Laval of the likely consequences in Europe if France did not defend the sanctity of international agreements. In the Cabinet discussion, the breakdown of the Locarno Treaty was mentioned along with the argument that, if France refused to cooperate on grounds that British naval measures in the Mediterranean were provocative, then French defensive preparations might in the future be regarded as "equally provocative to a German attack."[51]

Although Laval gave a general assurance of cooperation a few days later, he remained determined to avoid war and to preserve the Franco-Italian military accords. Naval staff talks in November confirmed London's doubts that France was either willing or ready to fight Italy, although the Admiralty noticed some improvement in the French attitude. In late November and early December the DPR and Cabinet also authorized talks with French Air Force and Army staffs, so as to provide a practical test for Laval's most recent affirmation of French military support in case of war.[52]

So long as a single-handed war was possible, London would not agree to a mutual reduction of forces in the Mediterranean. In September, the British had rejected Mussolini's proposal for a military détente in return for assurances that no menacing sanctions would be taken against Italy. Once the League decided to impose sanctions, the question of a détente became more complex. Britain's prerequisites for withdrawing some ships from the Mediterranean were a firm French assurance of military support, a reduction of Italian forces in Libya, and a curtailment of Anglophobia in the Italian press. But Mussolini accused Britain of encouraging other European countries to back sanctions, and he raised his ante. As Hoare told the DPR on 26 November, Mussolini "was not interested in mere matters of detail, but wanted the whole future position in the Mediterranean to be discussed," and seemed not to wish "serious negotiations" for the moment. With the chances of détente dimmed, the DPR authorized the War Office to reinforce Egypt with mobile forces sufficient for defense against an Italian attack from

[51] Vansittart note, 5 October, *DBFP*, 15, no. 27 (see also nos. 76, 81, 87, 92, 101, 110); Cab 47(35), CAB 23/82.

[52] Hoare to Clerk, 8 November, *DBFP*, 15, no. 201; Admiralty minutes, 12 and 13 November, ADM 116/3398; Admiralty-Foreign Office correspondence, J7543/3861/1, FO 371/19199, and CAB 16/139; DPR meetings, 5 and 26 November, CAB 16/136; Cab 50(35), 2 December, CAB 23/82. On the staff talks: Gibbs, *Rearmament*, pp. 202–12; Marder, "Royal Navy," pp. 1346–49; R.A.C. Parker,"Great Britain, France and the Ethiopian Crisis 1935–36," *English Historical Review* 89 (1974), 308–10.

Libya. Hoare reasoned that this would not provoke Mussolini but deter him from "any mad act" in Libya, which would have serious political repercussions in Alexandria if successful.[53]

The question of Egyptian independence preceded, of course, the Mediterranean crisis of 1935, and awaited formal resolution in a new treaty. The crisis complicated this issue by adding the problem of external security to the already existing one of internal order. In September, the War Office described the latter as "the *real* problem" and minimized the Italian threat from Libya. Two months later, the Egyptian department in the Foreign Office cautioned that sending reinforcements for defense against an Italian attack might create difficulties at a time of internal unrest in Egypt. And Hoare reported Egyptian concern lest Britain take advantage of the crisis "to the detriment of Egyptian independence."[54] In brief, the internal stability and external defense of this part of the empire were not necessarily compatible, yet both were endangered by Italian expansionism and mad-dog propensities.

On 7 October, Hankey sent Cabinet members a chronology of progress made on defense requirements through July 1935, adding that since then the Defence Requirements Committee had been "interrupted by heavy preoccupations in connection with the Italo-Abyssinian dispute."[55] In the interval, the experts on the DRC had recommended precautionary measures in the Mediterranean but warned that imposing sanctions on Italy would heighten the risk of war, for which Britain was unprepared. The advice of these experts— Vansittart, Fisher, Hankey, Chatfield, Ellington, Montgomery-Massingberd—changed in emphasis as they met twelve times in six weeks to prepare a new set of proposals for rearmament, and as the Chiefs of Staff took up the preliminary report of the Joint Planning Committee (JPC) on strategic plans for the case of war with Germany. The consideration of long-term planning in combination with the escalation of the Mediterranean crisis caused the members of the DRC to give more weight than before to the adverse effect of the crisis on imperial defense and on the Services' programs for rearmament.

In their report of 21 November, the DRC pointed out that, unless Britain restored good relations with Italy, the danger existed of a war on three fronts, whereas by 1939 Britain could at best achieve "an adequate deterrent to Germany and Japan." Although the JPC's draft

---

[53] Cabs 47 and 48(35), 16 and 23 October, CAB 23/82; DPR meetings, 7 and 21 October, 26 November, CAB 16/136; *DBFP*, 15, nos. 81, 105, 160–61, 188–89, 222.

[54] Dill to Lieutenant General Sir George Weir (General Officer Commanding, British Troops in Egypt), 26 September, WO 106/283; R. J. Campbell (Egyptian department) minute, 24 November, J8768/3861/1, FO 371/19200; Cab 49(35), 27 November, CAB 23/82.

[55] CP 187(35), CAB 24/257.

contingency plan (dated 1 August) excluded the possibility of a German-Italian alliance, the DRC observed that "we must not underestimate the Italian capacity for mischief if we were in conflict with Germany, and Italy joined in on the German side." The DRC report underscored the view of the Chiefs of Staff and Hankey that the Services had important work to do at home on rearmament programs and could not afford to squander resources or time in the Mediterranean. In a separate report, the COS acknowledged that withdrawing forces from the Mediterranean would diminish Britain's political and military position in that region, but maintaining the present level of force there would weaken the Services, particularly the Navy, "for a major contingency once the present crisis was over."[56]

Hankey and Vansittart synthesized these points for Baldwin and Hoare in preparation for the DPR meeting of 26 November—the first such meeting since the general election. An oil embargo would bring Britain "within the danger zone of possible war with Italy." Britain was in no position to risk such a conflict because of perils in Europe and the Far East and France's unwillingness to promise adequate military support in a Mediterranean war. The DPR approved, in principle, recommendations of the COS that the Services begin gradually to reduce their strength in the Mediterranean area. Before taking any steps that might seriously weaken the forces, the Services should bear in mind the delicate situation which prompted Hoare to ask that "the less . . . done to weaken our state of readiness the better." Hankey asked for and received the DPR's permission to circulate a summary of this DPR meeting to the Cabinet for its meeting of 2 December.[57]

On that day, when the Cabinet resumed discussion of the Mediterranean crisis for the first time since 23 October, Hoare referred to the "serious gaps in our system of imperial defence" and wondered whether rearmament could not be speeded up. Service ministers Monsell and Cunliffe-Lister (now Lord Swinton) emphasized the serious

---

[56] DRC meetings, 3 October–14 November, CAB 16/112; Third Report, 21 November, in CP 26(36), CAB 24/259; JPC Provisional Report on Defensive Plans for the Event of War against Germany, 1 August, CAB 53/25, discussed by the COS on 29 October, CAB 53/5; COS meeting, 19 November, CAB 53/5, and report (COS 414), 22 November, CAB 53/26; Hankey to Vansittart, 20 and 21 November, CAB 63/50.

[57] Hankey-Vansittart-Chatfield correspondence, 19–21 November, and Hankey to prime minister, 25 November, CAB 63/50; Hankey conversation with Hoare, 25 November, in Roskill, *Hankey*, 3: 186–89; Vansittart to Hoare and Eden, 23 November, *DBFP*, 15, no. 251; Vansittart to Hoare (and other minutes), 24 November, commenting on COS report (COS 414, see preceding note), J8768/3861/1, FO 371/19200; DPR meeting, 26 November, CAB 16/136; Hankey's summary of DPR meeting, CP 220(35), CAB 24/257. Vansittart's apprehensions about reducing forces in the Mediterranean were diminished by the Admiralty's argument that the crisis slowed its rearmament program. See also Vansittart, *Mist*, pp. 522–23.

losses likely to be sustained in a war with Italy. These losses would "lower the datum point from which the expansion of our forces (as dealt with in the Report of the Defence Requirements Committee) would start." The Cabinet concurred that hostilities must be avoided.[58]

Collective security obliged Britain to join other League members in an oil sanction. The escalation of sanctions would, especially in the opinion of the DRC, lead to war and dire consequences for British defense policy. The Cabinet's pronounced tilt toward this latter reasoning by early December invigorated London's search for a peaceful compromise. Hoare's discussions with Laval on 7 and 8 December were intended to seek a settlement that would defuse the crisis, improve Anglo-French relations, and afford some chance of restoring the Stresa Front against Germany. On 2 December, the Cabinet had neither explicitly given nor denied Hoare the authority to agree to specific proposals in Paris without first consulting the Cabinet, the League, or Ethiopia. The agreement which he and Laval initialed in Paris conceded to Italy far more Ethiopian territory than envisaged in compromise plans previously considered by Britain, France, or the League.[59]

The Cabinet approved the Hoare-Laval plan on 9 December, but within ten days the parliamentary, public, and Dominion outcry against betraying the League, Ethiopia, and the Government's recent election manifesto forced Baldwin and the Cabinet to abandon Hoare along with his plan. The Cabinet's discussions during this brief period were tortuous as soul-searching commixed with the same problems the Hoare-Laval plan was meant to solve. It was pointed out that the plan rewarded the aggressor, whereas British and world opinion would accept terms that only greater pressure on Italy could achieve. An oil sanction heightened the risk of war, and apparently Eden was the only minister who considered this a lesser evil than the risk of destroying the League—and Britain's international repute—by backing away from sanctions that were likely to be effective. Most of his colleagues clung to the hope that both risks could be avoided. The Cabinet adhered to the conclusion it had reached early in the crisis. Action must be collective, French military support guaranteed and substantial. When he

[58] Cab 50(35), 2 December, CAB 23/82.

[59] Ibid. On the Hoare-Laval plan, preliminary negotiations in Paris and London, Vansittart's important part in all of this, and the plan's political repercussions, see especially *DBFP*, 15, chap. 4; Baer, *Test Case*, chaps. 5, 6; Hardie, *Abyssinian Crisis*, chap. 16; Middlemas and Barnes, *Baldwin*, chap. 31; Parker, "Ethiopian Crisis," pp. 313–24; Sir Maurice Peterson (head of the Foreign Office's newly established Abyssinian department), *Both Sides of the Curtain* (London, 1950), pp. 115–21; James C. Robertson, "The Hoare-Laval Plan," *Journal of Contemporary History* 10 (1975); Templewood, *Nine Troubled Years*, chap. 13.

returned to Geneva, Eden should ensure that the matter of an oil sanction be postponed indefinitely. Meanwhile, Eden and the Cabinet agreed, he should stress the question of whether oil sanctions would be effective as well the possible military repercussions of applying them.[60]

Nor did the military picture change significantly. Staff talks with the French Army and Air Force evidenced an "improvement in the atmosphere," according to Vansittart, but the French Army's mobilization plan would prevent it from offering much immediate assistance. And the French Air Force was too preoccupied with the German danger to move reinforcements to southeast France and Tunisia.[61] Yugoslavia, Greece, and Turkey pledged their cooperation in case of Italian aggression against Britain, but London did not know what this help "would mean in practice," Eden informed the Cabinet on 11 December, and no staff talks had been held with these countries. Also that same day, the Cabinet instructed the Admiralty to delay, "for political reasons," a redisposition of ships in the Mediterranean that the First Lord admitted might be interpreted by the public "as a weakening of the Fleet." And next day the DPR agreed to a Foreign Office request to reinforce the garrison in Egypt with an infantry brigade "from the point of view of internal security."[62]

During the furor over the Hoare-Laval plan, Chamberlain noted in his diary that the prestige of the Government and the League "has undoubtedly crumbled."[63] Britain's double policy of collective action and conciliation was in shambles. In August, London had hoped that this policy would deter and appease Mussolini, strengthen the League to check Germany in the future, and revive the Stresa Front. By December, all of these objectives were more distant, if not unreachable.

Having wanted from the start to be in a position to fault other countries if the League failed, British policymakers blamed French duplicity, Italian intransigence, and American oil for this unhappy state of affairs. Few candidly acknowledged the disarray and duplicity in their own policy. Britain had consistently pledged to uphold sanctions (including an oil embargo) if other League members did so, yet by December it was the lone member yet to declare its support for an oil sanction.

---

[60] Cabs 52–55(35), 9–17 December, CAB 23/82; Cab 56(35), 18 December, CAB 23/90B.

[61] Vansittart memorandum covering summaries of recent conversations in Paris, 11 December, CAB 63/50; copies sent to Service departments on 17 December, C9206/3861/1, FO 371/19201; Colonel Heywood report to British ambassador, 18 December, FO 371/19202.

[62] Cab 54(35), 11 December, CAB 23/82; DPR meeting, 12 December, CAB 16/136; telegrams from Yugoslavia, Greece, and Turkey, CAB 16/139 and 140.

[63] 15 December, Chamberlain Papers, NC 2/23a.

The British knew an oil sanction could damage Italy, yet they emphasized the perils of provocation in an effort to discourage others from pressing for it. On balance, like any other major power, the British were more aggressive in taking precautions and ministering collective action to aid themselves than in supporting collective security against a clear violation of the Covenant.

National, imperial, and League interests caused Britain to build up considerable military forces in the Mediterranean area. The deterrent and coercive dimensions of this substantially reinforced strategic position will be examined in the next chapter. Here it should be emphasized that the military measures adopted under the dual policy generated a momentum whose effects British policymakers could not predict with certainty. Reinforcements might be used to bargain for an Anglo-Italian détente. Or the magnitude and duration of these measures could turn the Mediterranean into a potential theater of war indefinitely, especially if British policy became captive to the strategic and racial overtones of a struggle between two imperial powers for regional supremacy.

REARMAMENT AND TIME

The Mediterranean crisis undermined the strategic hypotheses already being used before 1935 by the Defence Requirements Committee and Principal Supply Officers Committee (PSOC). The crisis also underscored Britain's material shortages and moved expert advisers to press for implementation of plans for a shadow arms industry, although they continued to dispute the proximity of the German threat. Both strategic and material considerations fostered the predisposition in Whitehall to view this emergency as a temporary aberration that interfered with long-term planning.

In July, the Defence Policy and Requirements Committee instructed the DRC to reexamine defense requirements with regard to the international situation and finance. At meetings of the DRC that month, the Chiefs of Staff and Sir Robert Vansittart renewed their disagreement over the date when Germany might start a war. The COS doubted that Germany would be materially ready for war until 1942 at the earliest; at least, Chatfield and Ellington remarked, they themselves would not risk war before then if they were commanding the German Navy and Air Force. But Vansittart and Fisher argued that Germany was rearming faster than the Chiefs of Staff thought. Vansittart warned that Britain could not depend on peace beyond January 1939 at the latest; the "technical military point of view" did not allow for the possibility that Germany might make war before being fully rearmed, especially if other states were weak. Hoare complained to the Cabinet that recently approved plans for air force expansion did not reflect the Foreign Office's view that the "critical date" might arrive "as early as 1938." Hankey recalled that the DRC's original proposals of 1934 were "based on an assumed 5-year programme, although the question of whether Germany would be ready within that period did not, at that time, enter so deeply into the question as it necessarily now did." He observed that Britain would not be completely ready for war before 1942 even with an internal defense loan. The committee accepted his suggestion that they "work to January 1939, i.e., three financial years," and they agreed to press for a loan.[64]

In their Interim Report of 24 July, the DRC mentioned the "technical military point of view" of the COS that Germany would not be ready "deliberately" to begin aggression before 1942. The DRC also referred to Vansittart's warning that Germany might make war earlier "by miscalculation or political error of judgment." The international situation was deteriorating. Japan continued to expand its armed forces, Germany was rapidly rearming with the help of huge internal loans, and relations between these two adversaries were improving while the anti-German front might be weakened by Italy's African policy. The committee recommended attaining "a reasonable state of preparedness" by January 1939, which would be impossible without loans in view of current limits on annual expenditure.

On 29 July, following the lead of the DRC, the DPR implicitly acknowledged that the subject was no longer deficiencies but rearmament. The DRC should prepare programs "on the assumption that by the end of the financial year 1938–39 each Service should have advanced its state of readiness to the widest necessary extent in relation to the military needs of national defence and within the limits of practicability." The DRC should consider what special measures would be necessary to ensure the production of materials required by 1939. In the absence of such measures, what "state of preparedness" could be reached by 1939, or how many more years would be required to attain the desired state? The DPR did not commit itself to the date (1939) or to the method for financing rearmament, and did not disallow the possibility of improving the international situation. The Cabinet's eventual decision on Service programs "would have to be taken on the widest review of the existing international, financial and political considerations."[65]

After July, the DPR set aside the question of rearmament to concen-

64 DRC meetings of July, CAB 16/112; Wigram and Vansittart minutes, 26 and 29 July, C5680/55/18, FO 371/18849; Hoare in Cab 40(35), 24 July, CAB 23/82; Pownall diary entries of July in Bond, *Chief of Staff*, pp. 75–76.
65 DRC Interim Report, 24 July, CAB 16/138; DPR meeting, CAB 16/136.

trate on the Mediterranean emergency. So did the members of the DRC until early October, by which time the international situation had worsened, chiefly because of the Italo-Ethiopian conflict. British intelligence reports included evidence of Germany's vulnerability to air attack and of expansion of the Wehrmacht at a slower pace than the French alleged. After returning from a visit to Germany in September, Director of Military Operations and Intelligence Major General John Dill reported that the German Army had "escaped the danger of political infection and is now probably the most important factor in stabilising conditions inside Germany." Nevertheless, in their Third Report, 21 November, the DRC emphasized the threat from Germany, noting that German rearmament continued "at full speed." Although intelligence provided some evidence of Germany's capacity for industrial production and offensive action, "it would be a dangerous illusion for us to infer that we have a reliable measure of what she can do; still less of what she may be able to do in the near future." One could not rule out the possibility of a sudden air attack, which might "fulfil the Teutonic conception of a short, sharp war." Germany's position had improved since July because of the dissolution of the Stresa Front and Germany's policy of "attracting into her orbit" states in Eastern Europe. The Third Reich was determined to expand to the east and southeast, and its first objectives were probably Czechoslovakia and Austria. The DRC recommended that Britain, in cooperation with France, "promote and maintain friendly relations with Germany," although the experts admitted this effort might be thwarted by Germany's "restless desire for expansion, either to the East or Southeast in Europe, or by the acquisition of colonies, or both." British concession or condonement of these German objectives would cause "widespread opposition and division of public opinion."[66]

Although the DRC did not examine in detail the possible courses of a European war, other documents reveal a number of British assumptions. In a memorandum of June, Military Intelligence advised that Britain keep clear of a "life and death struggle" with a Germany that would soon be the strongest continental power: such a conflict would ruin all participants, no matter who won. Britain should abandon the policy of upholding Austrian independence, and allow Germany to expand to the east. The one chance of defeating Germany in the east would be an alliance with Russia, but this would only increase Russia's "power for mischief as the main exploiter of the victory." German

[66] Vansittart minute on Air Staff paper on German industry, 28 July, C5607/55/18, FO 371/18849; MI3 notes on French estimates, 14 September, WO 190/350; Dill report, 27 September, CAB 16/112; DRC Third Report, in CP(36), CAB 24/259. See also reports of the Industrial Intelligence Centre and Air Ministry, 25 June and 9 September, CAB 4/23.

aggression in the east would not necessarily spread west; indeed, it might lead to a war between Germany and Russia, in which "we have little to lose, and might even gain considerably."[67]

Military experts considered the possibility that, in spite of ideological antagonism, Germany and the Soviet Union would revert to the friendly diplomatic and economic relations proclaimed in their bilateral Rapallo Treaty of 1922. If on the other hand Russia adhered to the anti-German bloc, Germany would probably ally with Japan, with potentially "disastrous consequences for Great Britain." Military Intelligence thought it very unlikely that Germany would attack France at the start of a war for eastern expansion. Germany would be able to seize Austria, crush the Czech Army, ward off any Russian intervention, and then "deliver the main attack against either Italy or France." British political support would not make the anti-German bloc "an effective alliance," and British military action would probably not turn the tide in the group's favor. The Royal Air Force would certainly strengthen allied air power against Germany, but then "we should be faced with the certainty of German attacks on London."[68]

On 29 October, the Chiefs of Staff considered the Joint Planning Committee's preliminary report on strategic plans for war with Germany in 1939. Chatfield faulted the planners for assuming that, because Germany's eastern border was secure, Germany could concentrate on moving west; on the contrary, Germany intended to expand in Czechoslovakia, Russia, and the Baltic States. Massingberd agreed that Germany looked eastward, but thought it correct for the Services to plan for "the most dangerous situation"—a German offensive to defeat France and Belgium on land. Ellington thought the report minimized the contingency of a German air offensive against Britain. Hankey observed that Germany liked to concentrate its forces and would probably strike through Belgium. Agreeing with Hankey that in any case Germany would probably not start a war in the west as early as 1939, the COS instructed the JPC to carry on with the study.[69]

These notions of the military experts included four contingencies: (1) Germany would not attack Western Europe; (2) it might do so but only

---

[67] MI3b memorandum, "Germany and British Security in the Future," 17 June, WO 190/335; also summarized in Wark, *Ultimate Enemy,* pp. 87–88. General Dill hoped Britain would not find itself on Russia's side in a war between France-Italy-Russia and Germany-Japan. Why not, he asked B. H. Liddell Hart, "let Germany expand eastwards at Russia's expense?" Liddell Hart replied that, in the long run, this would be like "feeding the tiger that might turn on you: we were the ultimate obstacle to Germany's ambition, as in the past." Note of 27 March 1935, Liddell Hart Papers, 11/1935/69 (LHCMA).

[68] Paget (MI3) to Sargent, 17 July, C5684/55/18, FO 371/18849; War Office draft "Strategical Review of Europe," 23 July, CAB 55/7; War Office (MI3?) notes, 25 July, WO 190/344.

[69] COS meeting, 29 October, CAB 53/5.

after a victorious campaign in the east; (3) Germany might invade France and Belgium before expanding to the east; and (4) the Germans would try to knock out Britain from the air at the start of a war in the west. Vansittart rejected the first of these, but seems not to have decided which of the rest was most likely to occur as Germany advanced toward continental hegemony and threatened Britain. Traces of all four possibilities—and no consensus on any one of them—can be found in the DRC Third Report, which emphasized Germany's eastern aims, yet also raised the possibility of a sudden German air attack on Britain during a period of strained diplomatic relations, "particularly if sanctions were being applied."[70]

Turning to other countries, the DRC saw the United States as "more isolationist at heart than ever before," and warned that Japan aimed "to dominate the Far East, as Germany means to dominate Europe." The Japanese threat would reach "its maximum from the point of view of both probability and extent when we are preoccupied in Europe." The DRC reiterated its strong recommendation for "an ultimate policy of accommodation and neighborliness" toward Japan, coupled with provision of adequate defenses in the Far East in case of a European war. Italy, the DRC report recalled, had been excluded from the committee's list of potential enemies. Diplomacy would have to negate the possibility of a hostile Italy on Britain's main route of imperial communications during a war in the Far East. The "cardinal principle" for national and imperial security should be "to avoid a situation in which we might be confronted simultaneously with the hostility, open or veiled, of Japan in the Far East, Germany in the West, and any Power on the line of communications between the two." The DRC was asking a great deal of British diplomacy in view of recent events and future uncertainties. The DRC thought it too early to predict what direction Italy would take after the present crisis—whether Italy would rejoin the Stresa Front or "gravitate toward Germany." Early in its report, the DRC stated that Italy "must necessarily emerge debilitated from the present crisis"; later, however, the report said that it was "premature to forecast in what kind of condition [Italy] will emerge." The DRC wanted long-range policy to ensure French military support if Britain were at war with Japan and Italy, or with Germany and Japan. Yet, as the DRC pointed out, France was not strongly backing Britain in the Mediterranean crisis, was internally divided, and could not be relied upon to help Britain unless French interests were directly and clearly threatened.

The DRC preserved the European and imperial strategies of its 1934

[70] DRC Third Report, 21 November, in CP 26(36), CAB 24/259.

report without adding the Mediterranean as a third theater. Vansittart and Fisher still emphasized the German menace and European security. The Japanese threat and imperial security, as well as improving relations with Germany, were of special concern to Chatfield and Hankey. The DRC report recommended close study of the "Mediterranean strategical problem," but concluded that Britain could not by 1939 materially provide for the case of Italian hostility. It was "neither urgently necessary nor feasible to make provision for the contingency of a permanently hostile Italy," especially if diplomacy could nullify that possibility. Thus, Britain's defense programs should continue to be based on the same hypotheses as in the DRC's report of 1934—sufficient strength to defend the United Kingdom and the empire in the event of war with Germany and Japan simultaneously, a "double emergency" that was the more likely to happen if Britain did not possess an "adequate deterrent."[71]

The DRC once again recommended a balanced program for all three Services, one that would raise "our armaments to a far more effective standard than they will attain when existing approved programmes are completed." The DRC sought to correct what the COS had pointed out the previous spring: the Government's policy of air force expansion had broken step with the mere deficiency programs of the other two Services. The DRC reiterated the Admiralty's adaptation of the One-Power Standard, which had become part of British planning for the forthcoming London Naval Conference: sufficient forces to "cover" the Japanese fleet and protect British possessions and shipping in the Far East, and also to deter or defend against the strongest European naval power. The committee then urged immediate adoption of a new standard of naval strength: forces adequate to defend British interests in the Far East and, simultaneously, "to meet the requirements of a war with Germany." Thanks to the Anglo-German Naval Agreement (the DRC report did not recall how the Admiralty had welcomed this treaty the previous June), Germany could now build up a substantial navy free of the restrictions formerly imposed by the Treaty of Versailles. The approval of what was a Two-Power Standard in all but name would enable the British Navy to begin preparing for this standard over the next three years while concentrating on total requirements for the existing authorized standard.

The DRC recommended strengthening the Army's overseas garrisons for imperial defense, and its resources for home defense against sea or air attack. The committee proposed reinforcing the Regular Field Force with three contingents (of four divisions each) from the Territorial

[71] Ibid.

Army. This would increase Britain's ability to assist "continental allies" and prevent a German occupation of the Low Countries, where Germany could build forward air bases. The DRC accepted the existing standard of air strength under Scheme C—123 home squadrons with a total of 1,512 aircraft by April 1937—as a minimum to be "kept under the closest continuous review," for it was based on the assumption of parity with Germany when there was in fact "no guarantee that she will not build up to an even higher figure of first-line strength." Going beyond Scheme C, the DRC proposed enlarging reserves of equipment and pilots by 1939, and augmenting air units overseas, the Fleet Air Arm, and the Army Cooperation Squadrons that would support the Field Force.

The DRC also raised the "standards of security" with respect to reserves of supply for all three Services, endorsing the "shadow armament industry scheme" in the strongest terms yet found in official records. When originally proposed in 1934, the shadow scheme was meant chiefly to prepare industry to convert quickly to wartime production after war began. In recommending adoption of this policy in November 1935, the DRC envisaged Government assistance—such as allocating firms and ensuring the continuity of orders—to increase the peacetime production of war materials by firms that did not usually manufacture them. This was the only way to make up large deficiencies and at the same time build up *a 'potential' for the much greater quantities required after the outbreak of war.*" Without the shadow industry, the state of preparedness of the Services would be dangerously inadequate. They would lack the "war reserves" needed to bridge the gap between the onset of war and the time at which wartime industry could meet their demands. Indeed, even with the shadow scheme, it would be "impossible to carry out the full programme of supply for the emergency of war" by March 1939.[72]

The DRC's conclusions concerning supply had been preceded by the annual report of the Supply Board, now chaired by Sir Arthur Robinson, Secretary to the Ministry of Health since 1920. The board warned of critical shortages in case of war in the Far East or war against Germany in 1939—the two hypotheses assigned to the Principal Supply Officers Committee by the CID in February 1935. Progress on deficiencies would be slow unless funding were increased. The Supply Board would have to reconsider the problem of supply after the DRC provided new guidelines.[73]

---

[72] Ibid. Details of the DRC Third Report are summarized in Gibbs, *Rearmament*, pp. 254–68, and Roskill, *Hankey*, 3: 192–95.
[73] Supply Board annual report (PSO 512), 9 October, CAB 60/15; discussed by PSOC on 24 October, CAB 60/4. Robinson, who replaced Air Marshal Sir Hugh Dowding, was at the same time vice chairman of the PSOC.

The DRC pointed out that its report was "based on a reasonable estimate," not on "every conceivable danger" such as an extremely rapid increase in German air power or Japanese naval power, nor on the possibility of "a sudden attack in time of normal diplomatic relations." Still, this estimate far exceeded the deficiency programs of 1934. The DRC named total requirements, not merely "worst deficiencies," and recommended rearmament over a period of at least five years beginning in 1936. The DRC gave "necessarily speculative" financial figures, but did not force the issue of a defense loan. Annual defense expenditure would have to increase over the 1935 estimates (£124 million) by the following amounts: £49,650,000 in 1936; £86,750,000 in 1937; £102,400,000 in 1938; £88,450,000 in 1939; £90,050,000 in 1940. For the next three years, the total increase (beyond a base of £124 million per year) would amount to about £239 million; for the entire five years, an increase of nearly £417.5 million.

Although the DPR's general instructions of July had left room for a report of this magnitude, there can be no doubt that the Mediterranean crisis encouraged the DRC to make bolder recommendations than it otherwise would have. "There's nothing like a good fright for opening the purse strings," Pownall noted in September, an expectation also voiced by the DRC when it reported two months later that the crisis had "tended to focus attention upon the degree of our weakness."[74]

In discussing supplies needed in case of war with Italy, ministers and experts broached the larger question of industrial production required for long-term rearmament. On 12 September, troubled by shortages of ammunition, the Service departments and the Treasury established the interdepartmental Treasury Emergency Expenditure Committee (TEEC), in order "to expedite the normal machinery for obtaining Treasury sanction, where required, to proposals arising out of the present Italo-Abyssinian crisis."[75] On 17 September, the DPR approved recommendations of the PSOC for increasing the supply of antiaircraft ammunition and other war stores. If cleared by the TEEC, the Service departments could reassure firms of continuity of orders by beginning to place orders over a three-year period. The Supply Board hoped that the need for machine tools could be shown in the Mediterranean emergency. If so, this important prerequisite for accelerating production over the long term could be expedited by referring it to the TEEC rather than go through the much slower channels of the PSOC and CID.[76]

---

[74] Bond, *Chief of Staff*, pp. 79–80; DRC Third Report, 21 November, in CP 26(36), CAB 24/259.

[75] TEEC meeting, 16 September, S40250/1, T 161/716; PSOC meeting, 17 September, CAB 60/4; DPR meeting, 17 September, CAB 16/136.

[76] DPR meeting, CAB 16/136; PSOC meeting, 17 September, CAB 60/4; Supply Board meeting, 9 October, CAB 60/32.

On 26 November, the DPR's discussion of the Mediterranean crisis spilled over into the question of converting from peacetime to wartime industrial production. If the latter were adopted, the Government would have to assist firms in changing to war commodities and finding additional skilled labor. Above all, it would be wise to inform the machine tool industry as soon as possible "of big orders coming to them." Even if war with Italy did not break out, the recommendations of the DRC "involved a very great increase all round in industrial production." The DPR instructed the Supply Board to investigate the question of priorities among the Services "with particular reference to the emergency at present existing."[77] Two days later, a subcommittee of the Supply Board recommended the earliest possible implementation of a shadow armament industry, including long-term contracts and continuity of orders for three to four years; the Treasury had agreed to this system for antiaircraft ammunition but not yet for other stores.[78]

Together with the DRC's Third Report, this report from the Supply Board subcommittee brought the question of production to a head by mid-December 1935. Vansittart directed Hoare's attention to the second document, asking him to bring it up at the Cabinet meeting of 2 December. There, Hoare referred both to this supply report and to the DPR's meeting of 26 November. The Mediterranean crisis revealed "serious gaps in our system of imperial defence," and he asked "whether it would not be possible to speed up the replacement of our deficiencies."[79] Hoare returned to this question on 4 December, emphasizing German expansionism, calling attention to the slow progress of Britain's defense programs, and recommending the appointment of Lord Weir—a prominent Scottish industrialist and unofficial adviser to the Government on aircraft production—to any committee that would consider the DRC's Third Report.[80]

On 6 December, the DPR authorized the Services to take steps through the TEEC to implement the shadow industry as recommended by the Supply Board subcommittee on 28 November. Five days later, informed that the DPR had found it difficult to separate supplies for the crisis "from the larger question of supplies generally," the Cabinet tried to do so. It was pointed out, probably by Chamberlain, that the Supply Board subcommittee and DPR had gone beyond the question of war with Italy. The effect of the DPR's decision "was to allow the

---

[77] DPR meeting, CAB 16/136, including evidence of Germany's willingness to sell war materials to Britain (see also MI3 note, 27 November, WO 190/373).
[78] Report of 28 November (DPR 56), in CP 237(35), CAB 24/257.
[79] Vansittart minute, 30 November, J8859/3861/1, FO 371/19200 (also in *DBFP*, 15, no. 286); Cab 50(35), 2 December, CAB 23/82.
[80] Cab 51(35), 4 December, CAB 23/82.

Government Departments concerned to create a shadow armament industry over the whole field of armament supply." The Cabinet approved the DPR's recommendations insofar as they applied to the emergency but stipulated that "a decision of such importance" as the creation of a shadow industry "should be reserved for consideration in connection with" the DRC's Third Report.[81]

In April 1935, the Chiefs of Staff had asked whether Germany or Japan was the "near menace," and when Britain should complete the defensive preparations of all three Services. As discussed in chapter 1, the Foreign Office had acknowledged that answers to these decisive questions would determine Britain's "whole defence policy in relation to Germany." The catalyst for the two queries had been German rearmament and the Government's acceleration of the expansion program for the RAF. A new catalyst of a different kind, the Mediterranean crisis confounded both issues while it magnified the contrast between present weakness and visions of future strength.

The DRC's Third Report neither eliminated past ambiguities about threats from Germany and Japan, nor decided whether Italy should now be viewed as a third potential enemy. Vansittart and Fisher considered Germany the greatest menace in both the short and long term, whereas Chatfield and Hankey remained more apprehensive about Japan. Vansittart still disagreed with the COS and Hankey—by three years or more—over the date when Germany might launch a European war, and thus over how much time Britain had to prepare its defenses. The DRC could not predict how the current crisis would affect Italy's future course in European politics. If Italy remained hostile, then the Navy's Far Eastern strategy, the Army's commitment of an expeditionary force to the Continent, and the RAF's concentration on the German threat were all at risk.

In the DRC report each Service worked by its own clock. The Navy, concerned more with Japan and the empire than with Germany and Europe, would not be able to reach the existing authorized standard for six years (1942) at the earliest, a date fixed since 1932 when the Admiralty foresaw a decade of work to repair the damage done by the Ten Year Rule. A more rapid rearmament would require "extraordinary measures" such as those adopted to expand the Royal Air Force, which the Admiralty wished to avoid for fear of prejudicing "the efficiency of the Service." In order for the Army to discharge its continental mission with a fully reinforced and equipped Field Force, and assuming the adoption of the shadow armament plan, the Army needed five years (until early 1941) "to be in sight of the complete requirements for the whole four contingents." The same period would bring within view

---

[81] DPR meeting, 6 December, CAB 16/136; Cab 54(35), 11 December, CAB 23/82.

the reequipment of the Field Artillery with new guns and adequate reserves of ammunition, and "the full suggested scale of anti-aircraft defence."

The RAF should increase its metropolitan first-line strength to 123 squadrons (1,512 aircraft) by April 1937 (the goal of Scheme C, approved in May 1935), but increases in German and French strength above 1,500 aircraft "would involve corresponding increases in our own first-line strength." Building up reserves of aircraft and pilots during the next few years would have to occur at a faster rate than was currently projected if the Air Force hoped to defend Britain, launch offensives against the enemy, support the Field Force, and strengthen the Fleet Air Arm and air units overseas. In spite of these different timetables, all three Services could increase their state of preparedness in three years (by 1939), but needed at least five years (to 1941) of heavy expenditures and a shadow armament industry to meet the standards deemed necessary for national and imperial security.[82]

Meeting these deadlines—and synchronizing them—presupposed a period of peace, yet the Mediterranean crisis, as the DRC pointed out, confirmed "the repeated warnings of the Chiefs of Staff . . . of the suddenness with which wars and crises are apt to arise," especially while Britain remained in the system of collective security.[83] This emergency exposed the large gap between paper plans and material preparations for war. The prospect of a Mediterranean war prompted the Supply Board, DRC, and DPR to recommend implementation of the shadow armament scheme for future conflict with Germany or Japan; the production of war reserves must move from plans to things. Yet the military measures in the Mediterranean dispersed—and a war there would deplete—the limited resources on which reaching long-term goals depended. In October 1934, the Chiefs of Staff had directed the Joint Planning Committee to prepare plans for the contingency of war with Germany in five years (1939). Yet the Mediterranean crisis caused the COS to postpone consideration of the JPC's preliminary report for a few months (from early August to late October). Even if this emergency did not explode in war or add Italy to the strategic hypotheses for future conflicts, prolonged tension in the Mediterranean or new international crises would continue to disrupt the Service programs, delay completion of the German war plan, and postpone starting a plan to meet the demands of a war with Japan.

In 1934, the DRC, Principal Supply Officers Committee, and JPC had used the hypothesis of five years for correcting "worst deficiencies"

---

[82] DRC Third Report, 21 November, in CP 26(36), CAB 24/259.
[83] Ibid.

and preparing plans. During the Mediterranean crisis, the DRC advised that Britain could not be fully prepared for war by 1939 even with the shadow industry scheme in effect. Perhaps without intending to imply that the questions posed by the COS in April 1935 might be unanswerable, the DRC described the future as "more than usually uncertain," and stated that neither this nor any later review of defense requirements should be treated as final. The heavy expenditure for the next few years would not suffice to meet all possible contingencies, but it would provide Britain and the empire—exposed to " 'the envy of less happier lands' "—the means to survive and continue their contributions to civilization. Rearmament was "the alternative to the epitaph 'England hath made a shameful conquest of itself.' "[84]

The DRC's stirring appeal to British patriotism looked ahead to an imagined state of strength. With varying degrees of confidence, the members of the DRC hoped that diplomacy would buy time while the Government bought arms. They disagreed over how much time Britain had (until 1939 or 1942), and how successful diplomacy could be with dictators. Britain's actual weakness would at least limit its freedom of action in international affairs, and at most proscribe taking any risks in foreign policy. If the present emergency subverted some of the assumptions guiding long-term planning, then Britain should extricate itself as quickly as possible and get on with the agenda that had preceded the Mediterranean crisis but was now all the more exigent because of it. This logic not only suffused the deliberations of the DRC, but also inhibited Whitehall's thinking about deterrence and found strong levers in the machinery of policy as the crisis complicated its work.

[84] Ibid.

[3]

Coercion Abroad and
Coordination at Home

Before the Mediterranean crisis, British policymakers had begun to formulate a comprehensive yet disjointed strategy of deterrence. The restoration of military strength, in conjunction with conciliatory diplomacy, would enable Britain to prevent German or Japanese aggression against Britain and the empire, and might also extend British deterrence to protect other countries through collective, regional, and bilateral arrangements. While rearming, Britain might show military teeth as a general deterrent to restrain potential enemies—particularly using the Navy to impress Japan, but also using expansion of the Air Force to moderate Germany's demands. The Mediterranean crisis tested both the breadth and the application of British deterrence.

The distant objective of a rearmed Britain deterring Germany and Japan did not preclude threatening force in response to immediate caprices of international politics, where Britain's reputation for firmness might be at stake. The British used deterrence against Italy, intending to uphold collective security, protect British interests in the Mediterranean, and persuade foreign governments that Britain was strong when it counted. The last of these motivations was especially important to Eden, who, unlike the DRC, saw British prowess in the Mediterranean as a warning to Hitler and thus added a new dimension to British ideas of deterrence. The scope and efficacy of deterrence, however, were reduced by uncertainties about Mussolini, collective security, and potential allies; by wondering whether showing force would encourage or alarm friendly nations; above all, by fears that risking a limited conflict with Italy in the Mediterranean now would weaken Britain's capacity to deter or defeat more likely enemies who would threaten British interests more seriously in the future. By revealing the liabilities of applying coercion in an actual emergency that need not have endangered Britain, the crisis dampened Whitehall's interest in developing a broad doctrine of deterrence for contingencies other than self-defense. The crisis confirmed the view of the Service advisers and Hankey that, while Britain rearmed, deterrence should be an end of defense policy and not a means of foreign policy.

After a slow start, Whitehall adapted its machinery to the emergency, but crisis management intertwined with long-term planning in ways that other histories of the crisis have not fully recognized. The Cabinet's control over policy diminished, and its accountability to Parliament became more vulnerable, when it allowed the DPR to function as an executive committee for war. The influence of expert advisers increased, largely because of the close connection between the DPR and the DRC, but also because of interdepartmental opposition to testing sanctions now, a concurrence that outweighed bureaucratic distinctions such as the difference between political and military points of view. Preoccupied with rearming in the face of the German and Japanese threats, the members of the DRC—Vansittart, Fisher, Hankey, and the Chiefs of Staff—viewed the crisis as a separate and transitory problem of policy, one which rudely interrupted the suppositions and procedures for long-term planning by the entire system of defense by committee.

The emergency changed the dynamics in relations between and within departments. The committee system helped to implement deterrence, yet it also built up formidable interdepartmental resistance to making it effective. The Foreign Office lost stature while the Services probably gained. The Foreign Office's early confidence of July and August 1935 declined because of internal disagreements, and it was shaken by the political reaction to the Hoare-Laval plan in December. The coercive side of the Foreign Office's dual policy, personified especially by Eden, drew united criticism from the Services. Chamberlain, who supported collective sanctions against Fisher's advice, did much more than Baldwin to hold the DPR and Cabinet together through the emergency, the general election, and the Hoare-Laval catastrophe. The Treasury improved interdepartmental coordination for materiel needed in the Mediterranean, but wondered how much the demand for rearmament, accelerated by the crisis, would reduce the Treasury's control over supply. Thus, although Fisher concurred with Vansittart about the imminence of the German threat, the Treasury would not allow the need for supplies in the emergency to precipitate establishment of a shadow armament industry before the Cabinet could discuss the DRC's new report of November. The Services skillfully coordinated precautionary measures as well as "worst case" arguments against using force, but without agreeing on whether air or sea power would prove decisive in defeating Italy, and without wanting to give ministers the excuse to choose for them. Whether for the crisis or rearmament, by presenting worst cases while hiding disagreements on strategy, the Chiefs of Staff and Hankey managed information so as to inflate the risks of deterrence and minimize its opportunities. Hankey fortified expert advice against risking war and guided the machinery back toward rearmament, but he came under increasing pressure from critics outside the Government who judged the current CID system inadequate for modern warfare.

The disorder in British policy in December resulted from its failure to prevent or halt Italian aggression, and from disruption in the machinery of policy, which both supported and subverted collective security. As an immediate emergency perturbed the long-range problem of rearmament, most ministers and officials in London concluded that the road to order required Britain to narrow the compass of deterrence, avoiding further risks and interruptions while rearming.

DETERRENCE TESTED

The British Government's attitude toward using force in the Mediterranean crisis has been obscured by oversimplified dichotomies. Indeed, the dual policy of sanctions and conciliation suggests polar opposites: between Sir Samuel Hoare's speech of 11 September before the League Assembly and his agreement of 8 December with Pierre Laval; between faith in the League as an international agency of enforcement and the emphasis on the strategic interests of Great Britain; between the new diplomacy of open covenants and the old diplomacy of secret pacts. These opposites reinforce Eden's argument that Hoare was bluffing on 11 September, and also support the thesis of many historians that Britain did not wish to pressure Mussolini by threats of force.[1] That conclusion diminishes the significance of the crisis as a case of deterrence.

From July to December 1935, the fluctuating relationship between military measures and foreign policy did not correspond neatly to pres-

---

[1] Avon, *Dictators*, p. 293; Gibbs, *Rearmament*, p. 192; Robert Rhodes James, *Anthony Eden* (London, 1986), pp. 150–51; Marder, "Royal Navy," p. 1334; Schmidt, *England in der Krise*, pp. 129–30. In a particularly contemptuous account of British policy, Correlli Barnett writes that Hoare's speech made the Cabinet "more than ever a prisoner of internationalist fantasy"; *Collapse*, p. 368. In *Test Case* (pp. 46–47), George Baer perceptively states that Britain and France viewed sanctions "within the limiting framework of the reconciliationist perspective, in which coercion was kept to a minimum and accommodation was the primary goal." But Baer places that minimum at a lower level than seems to have been the case.

suring Mussolini or conciliating him; nor was there a clear line between collective security and imperial security. Such ambiguities help substantiate theories of conventional deterrence in which many uncertainties confound the task of preventing or limiting war. Various complications burden deterrence at levels lower than "strategic war." The deterring nation's objectives are multiple and often contradictory. The opponent's will to win is unclear. The political situation is muddled, and conflicts between deterrence and other national policies are hard to resolve. Preventing conflicts beyond one's own borders raises the question of commitment to and from third parties; the credibility of extended deterrence depends on the deterring power's clear signals to friend and foe, its willingness to commit forces to the danger zone, and its leadership in establishing joint organizations to plan military responses. Policymakers cannot easily tell whether deterrence is actually working.[2] These attributes of coercive diplomacy can be found in British policy during the Mediterranean emergency, in which the United Kingdom attempted to devise what modern theorists might call a strategy of conventional and extended deterrence for crisis diplomacy or limited war.

Although assuring Mussolini they were not planning military sanctions, the British added the threat of force to a diplomatic offensive, hoping to stop the dictator without provoking him. British policy aimed to provide imperial security and support collective security at the same time. Showing force might deter Mussolini from attacking British interests, invading Ethiopia, or seizing more Ethiopian territory than was internationally acceptable; it might also caution Germany that Britain had the necessary resolve to thwart aggression in Europe. British strategy encompassed both denial and punishment: Britain prepared to defend its own interests, and envisaged retaliatory strikes against both the mainland and military forces of Italy if collective action led to war. While wielding a stick, Britain would also offer Italy a carrot in the form of concessions in Ethiopia. The conciliatory side of this dual policy rested on several calculations in London. The status quo could be revised so long as this did not harm Britain's possessions or vital strategic interests. A dictator irrational enough to act like a mad dog might also be intelligent enough to accept a compromise. A Mediterranean war now would weaken Britain's military capacity to prevent or win a European war in the future. France could not be trusted.

The major purpose of Britain's military measures was to prevent

[2] George and Smoke, *Deterrence in American Foreign Policy*, pp. 1, 48–54. See also Coffey, *Arms Control and European Security*, pp. 11–12; Mearsheimer, *Conventional Deterrence*, pp. 18–19.

Italian retaliation against British interests. Policymakers referred to re-inforcements for the Mediterranean and Egypt as a deterrent against such attacks, noting that British naval movements had helped reduce tension.[3] Imperial security had another dimensión as well. Italian ex-pansion in Africa threatened British control of the Nile headwaters, the internal stability of Egypt, and routes of communication to the Far East. Forcefully thwarting Italy's bid for hegemony in Africa and the Medi-terranean occurred to some in London, although it remained little more than implicit in the military buildup and diplomatic offensive.

Britain's policy of collective action both contemplated and employed the threat of force, a policy that assumed some compatibility between imperial and collective security. From mid-July to the tripartite talks of 15–18 August in Paris, there seemed to be a chance of preventing Mussolini from attacking Ethiopia. Chamberlain considered asking France to join Britain in a warning to Mussolini that they would meet force with force if necessary. Hoare described deterrence as "publicity and conversations with the French in order to get them to put pressure on Italy." Vansittart summarized British tactics in the event the French proved willing to stand firm: "We should make the Italians an offer with one hand, with an ill-concealed stick in the other," a position that offered "the only possibility of bringing the Italians to a peaceful ac-commodation." If the French refused to pressure Italy, Hoare con-cluded, then "coercive action drops out of the picture."[4]

The French did not refuse and Mussolini did not compromise. After the tripartite talks, London did not expect to prevent war but hoped to achieve a settlement short of a complete victory for Italy. Coercive diplomacy remained in the picture. Although the Services repeatedly warned against provoking war, their contingency planning included the possibility of conflict should the League decide to close the Suez Canal and if Italy tried to force warships through it.[5] Hoare considered economic sanctions a kind of "coercive action." On 22 August, he and Eden emphasized to the Cabinet that reinforcing the Mediterranean Fleet as soon as possible was desirable "from the point of view of foreign policy." In the first half of September, Chamberlain, Hoare,

[3] Air Staff appreciations, 12 August and 10 September, AIR 9/68; Chatfield to Fisher, 25 August, in Marder, "Royal Navy," pp. 1330–31; Hoare at DPR meeting, 26 November, CAB 16/136. Home Secretary Sir John Simon contrasted the Mediterranean case with the Far Eastern crisis of 1932, when he had been Foreign Secretary: "A demonstration by the British Fleet in the Far East in 1932 would have brought war and disaster upon our heads to a dead certainty. The movements of the British Fleet in the Mediterranean, whatever else they have done, have certainly helped to steady the situation." Simon to J. L. Garvin, 5 December, Garvin Papers.

[4] Chamberlain to Hilda, 14 July, Chamberlain Papers, NC 18/1/925; Hoare at Cab 39(35), 22 July, CAB 23/82; Vansittart to Hoare, 7 August, *DBFP*, 14, no. 427; Hoare minute, 12 August, W7166/1209/98, FO 371/19686.

[5] COS report (COS 392), 9 August, CAB 53/25.

Eden, and Vansittart agreed that combining diplomatic pressure with a show of military strength would "make things unpleasant" for Mussolini (Chamberlain) and "bring things to an issue quickly" in Geneva (Hoare). The First Lord of the Admiralty pointed out to the Cabinet on 24 September that measures taken at the Suez Canal "could not correctly be described as precautions for our own security." On the same day, Eden wired Hoare that to relax the pressure on Mussolini "could only restore his confidence and undo good work that has been done," and Pownall was pleased to see that "the megolomaniac is at last having his eyes opened"—by the British Navy—to the fact that he was treading on interests other than his own. Two months later, the First Lord reminded his Cabinet colleagues that "economic sanctions had been built up behind the strength of our Mediterranean Fleet," and Chamberlain believed that showing weakness would only "encourage Mussolini to be more intransigent."[6]

Thus, even without actual plans for military sanctions, the British Government used military power to impress Mussolini and the League of Nations by conveying determination to enforce collective action. But this form of coercive diplomacy was severely limited by British attitudes toward three interconnected questions: (1) the characteristics of a fascist dictatorship and the threat of war; (2) collective security, British power, and the German menace; and (3) the usefulness of allies. Taken together, these questions both required and inhibited a clear conception of deterrence.

Since the early 1920s, many British Conservatives, especially on the far right, had admired Mussolini for what they saw as his vigor, patriotism, sincerity, and ability to bring order to Italy when communism might otherwise have exploited the breakdown of Italian parliamentary democracy. Some viewed fascist Italy as a shield against the spread of bolshevism in Europe. Many regarded Ethiopia as a barbarous territory unfit for membership in the League and in need of Italy's civilizing hand.[7] Traces of these sentiments can be found in the documents,[8] but so can contrary attitudes, leaving composite pictures of Mussolini and

[6] Hoare conversation with A. Chamberlain, 20 August, *DBFP*, 14, no. 476; Cab 42(35), 22 August, CAB 23/82; Chamberlain to Hilda, 1 September, Chamberlain Papers, NC 18/1/930; Hoare to Eden, 15 September, *DBFP*, 14 appx. Ig; Cab 43(35), 24 September, CAB 23/82; Eden to Hoare, *DBFP*, 14, no. 633; Bond, *Chief of Staff*, pp. 81–82; Cab 50(35), 2 December, CAB 23/82; Chamberlain diary, 8 December, Chamberlain Papers, NC 2/23a.

[7] See R. J. B. Bosworth, "The British Press, the Conservatives, and Mussolini, 1920–34," *Journal of Contemporary History* 5 (1970); Thompson, *Anti-Appeasers*, pp. 67–70; Waley, *British Public Opinion*, chaps. 1, 5.

[8] For example, Phipps to Hoare, 16 December, *DBFP*, 15, no. 383. In a conversation with Phipps, Hitler criticized Britain's behavior toward Italy as "anti-fascist"; if Mussolini fell, "chaos and bolshevism would ensue in Italy and would certainly spread." Phipps replied that the British Government "felt no hostility towards fascism in other countries, and indeed, would infinitely prefer it there to chaos."

[121]

Italy that lack clarity, consistency, and consensus. Mussolini may or may not have been mad, and Italy may or may not have been solidly behind him. In May 1935, Chamberlain thought Ethiopia was Mussolini's "own adventure undertaken directly contrary to the advice of all his military and financial experts," probably in order to divert attention from financial troubles at home and possible diplomatic failure in Austria. Sir Eric Drummond reported from Rome that Il Duce seemed "like a man driven by fate," and would not be content with minor concessions.[9] In June, Eden's interviews with Mussolini revealed a "gloomy fatality" about the dictator's temper, and Mussolini insisted that Italy had "immense military, political and moral strength." When the British began taking military precautions in August, Hoare was aware of "the difficulty of applying preventive action [especially] in the case of a dictatorship that has already mobilized a million men."[10]

In September, Pownall lamented that Mussolini had his country "behind him almost to a man," whereas the French and English were "*not* wholeheartedly behind the policy of [their] leaders." Someone on the General Staff guessed that Mussolini would invade Ethiopia "and face even greater but possibly in his mind less immediate and less certain disaster" than losing face internationally and at home.[11] If Mussolini was mad, Drummond observed, he was "a very singular madman" who believed that war was "the means by which a country can be kept vigorous, young, powerful and progressive," and that Italy was the "heritor of the ancient traditions of the Roman Empire." Mussolini felt he was "acting as a predestined instrument," and Drummond's impression was "of a man who is the victim, not the master of his destiny." A Catholic who welcomed his posting to Rome in 1933, Drummond had served as the first Secretary General to the League of Nations but he now resisted using its authority to support a backward African nation against a European power. Ambassador Drummond disagreed with Eden that Mussolini was weakening or losing confidence; the fascist regime was not tottering, Mussolini still enjoyed the "blind faith" of the younger generation, and if the regime did fall in the future (because of defeat in war or "drastic and universal economic sanctions") anarchy would take its place.[12] In its report of 21 November, the Defence Requirements Committee called the Italians "complete opportunists [who] will take without scruple the course that suits them

[9] Chamberlain to Hilda, 18 May, Chamberlain Papers. NC 18/1/916; Drummond to Simon, 8 and 21 May, DBFP, 14, nos. 247, 281n.

[10] Eden to Hoare, 24 June, and Drummond to Hoare, 25 June, *DBFP*, 14, nos. 320, 325; Hoare minute, 12 August, W7166/1209/98, FO 371/19686.

[11] Bond, *Chief of Staff*, p. 80; General Staff note of 23 September, WO 106/282.

[12] Drummond to Hoare, 23 and 24 September, *DBFP*, 14, nos. 630, 638.

best at the moment." Italy would probably be weakened by a long campaign in Africa; the degree of her exhaustion would determine "the degree of rancour of an opportunist state." Drummond warned that imposing an oil sanction might lead to an "act of madness" by Mussolini against the British fleet. And in early December, Baldwin reminded his colleagues that in dealing with Mussolini they "were not dealing with a normal kind of intellect."[13]

The British tried to weave strands of psychoanalysis and political and military intelligence into estimates of the actual threat of an Italian attack. In August, Vansittart worried that Britain could not easily conceal its preparations for war, that Italy might strike before Britain was ready, and that British forces would have no warning. If attacked, British units could assume that a state of war existed and counterattack.[14] Could Britain have won? Eden appears to have been more confident than his colleagues of the outcome of a struggle between democratic Englishmen and fascist Italians. Hoare and Vansittart were sobered by the testimony of the Chiefs of Staff about Britain's military weakness, the two-month period needed to take sufficient precautionary measures, and the necessity of French military support.[15] Eden thought that such pessimism implied an unflattering comparison between British and Italian military prowess: "After all we alone have 10 battleships and battle cruisers to the Italian 2—or do we now think every Italian worth 5 Englishmen!"[16]

Was Mussolini likely to attack? London did not know. British intelligence concentrated on industrial indices and capacities of foreign countries, and tried to estimate the armed strength that potential enemies would reach by certain dates. The system of intelligence in London was not designed to predict the reaction of dictators to deterrence or the location and intensity of mad-dog attacks.[17] British deterrence was further hampered by security leaks, especially at the embassy in Rome.

[13] DRC Third Report, in CP 26(36), CAB 24/259; Drummond to Hoare, 29 November, DBFP, 15, no. 279; Cab 50(35), 2 December, CAB 23/82. Owen St. Clair O'Malley, head of the southern department in the Foreign Office, speculated that Mussolini had syphilis, which might "'produce megalomania as well as other illusions.'" Baer, Test Case, p. 83.

[14] Vansittart to Hoare, 7 August, DBFP, 14, no. 427; Vansittart minute to Hoare, 10 August, W7166/1209/98, FO 371/19686; Oliphant to Barnes (Admiralty), 27 August, DBFP, no. 501.

[15] Vansittart and Hoare minutes on COS report (COS 392; see note 5 above), 10 and 12 August, W7166/1209/98, FO 371/19686; Vansittart to Hoare, 19 August, DBFP, 14, appx. Id.

[16] Marginal comment on Vansittart minute (preceding note), 11 August. Admiral Sir William Fisher, commander in chief in the Mediterranean, thought he could block Italian communications to Ethiopia "'without active assistance of other powers'"; Marder, "Royal Navy," p. 1340, and Templewood, Nine Troubled Years, p. 191.

[17] This fact and its implications for British policy do not receive much attention in Andrew, Her Majesty's Secret Service, and Wark, Ultimate Enemy.

Mussolini himself read secret British communications, some of which indicated Britain's material shortages in the Mediterranean and its willingness to allow Italian expansion in Ethiopia.[18] Mussolini called British precautionary measures provocative, and warned that war would result from military sanctions and from economic sanctions (such as an oil embargo) which endangered the life of his nation. The Cabinet, Foreign Office, and Chiefs of Staff did not treat this warning as bluff.[19] Any temptation to do so was curbed not only by Italy's substantial concentration of forces in the Mediterranean, Libya, and the Red Sea, but also by uncertainty about what would (or would not) provoke this fascist dictator. As Chamberlain observed early in December, Britain could not "absolutely exclude the possibility [that] such a man" might be foolish enough to attack even though he had "tied a noose around his own neck" by placing most of the Italian Army on the other side of the Suez Canal "and left the end hanging out for anyone with a navy to pull."[20]

A second major obstacle to coercive diplomacy was British ambivalence toward collective security and its strategic implications. Was the League of Nations an instrument of war or not? How could economic sanctions be made effective? Was it possible to support collective security and avoid war? Was it more important to prevent Mussolini from invading Ethiopia or from attacking the British fleet? Did the greater value for British deterrence lie in applying collective security now or reserving it for future application against Germany? London's answers were equivocal. In 1940, Arnold Wolfers attributed this fact to the coexistence of "two profoundly different schools of thought" in the Government that cut across party lines. The "traditionalists" viewed the League as a conciliatory agency whose interests must either coincide with, or be secondary to the vital strategic interests of Britain and the empire. The "collectivists" thought that the League should use coer-

[18] On Italian interception of British communications in the 1930s, see David Dilks, "Flashes of Intelligence: The Foreign Office, the SIS and Security before the Second World War," in Christopher Andrew and Dilks, eds., *The Missing Dimension: Governments and Intelligence Communities in the Twentieth Century* (Urbana, Ill., 1984), pp. 106–18; Mario Toscano, *Designs in Diplomacy*, trans. and ed. George Carbone (Baltimore, 1970), pp. 412–14; MacGregor Knox, *Mussolini Unleashed, 1939–1941: Politics and Strategy in Fascist Italy's Last War* (Cambridge, 1982), pp. 6, 15; and Knox, "Fascist Italy Assesses Its Enemies," in May, *Knowing One's Enemies*, pp. 359, 369. E. M. Robertson cautions against assuming that Mussolini and his military and diplomatic advisers readily inferred from intelligence reports that Britain was merely bluffing; *Mussolini*, pp. 176–77.

[19] In November and December, leaders of the War Office thought Mussolini was bluffing; Dill to General W. H. Bartholomew (India), 28 November and 5 December, WO 106/283; Duff Cooper conversation with Liddell Hart, 14 December, Liddell Hart Papers, 11/1935/115 (LHCMA).

[20] Chamberlain to Ida, 8 December, Chamberlain Papers, NC 18/1/941. See also Baer, *Test Case*, pp. 81–83; Pratt, *East of Malta*, pp. 107–10, 117.

cion if necessary to uphold the rule of law in the community of nations.[21] But things were not so simple.

Public opinion encompassed both traditionalism and collectivism. Conservative critics of the Government emphasized traditionalist points that argued for accommodating Mussolini: Britain's military weakness, Hitler's likely exploitation of the breakdown of the Stresa Front, the importance of Italian friendship on the Mediterranean lifeline of the British Empire, the shortsightedness of discrediting the League by turning it into an instrument of war, the need to rearm, and the stupidity of risking war in the meantime by supporting sanctions against Italy. J. L. Garvin accused the Government of using "drum beating methods" with little power to back them up, and of having neglected defense so shamefully that the dictators "regard the British Empire as a stranded whale from which any bold hand may cut blubber with impunity." Churchill "dreamed of a Cromwellian Administration which would have handled the Italian Dictator in a resolute fashion," and feared that the combination of military weakness and the policy of the current Government would achieve "the lot": the crippling of the League, the humiliation of Britain, the estrangement of Italy, and the subjugation of Abyssinia.[22]

On the other hand, collectivist sentiment had found strong expression in the results of the Peace Ballot published in June. In an apparent wedding of moral principles and coercive diplomacy, 74 percent of those voting approved the use of military sanctions, through the League, against aggressors. Some Conservatives, along with Liberal and Labour leaders, wanted Britain and the League to bear down on Mussolini, and saw the Hoare-Laval plan as a disgraceful reversal of the policy on which the Government had recently won the election.[23]

[21] Arnold Wolfers, *Britain and France between Two Wars* (New York, 1940), chaps. 13, 19–21. See also the analysis of collective security (which included the idea of deterrence) in Inis L. Claude, Jr., *Power and International Relations* (New York, 1962), chaps. 4, 5.

[22] Garvin memorandum for Neville Chamberlain (not sent?), 22 August; Churchill (Paris) to Garvin, 1 September; Garvin Papers. These papers also include extracts from Garvin's editorials in the *Observer*, day-by-day notes on press reports of the crisis, and letters from Leopold Amery agreeing with Garvin that the Government's policy was a mess. See also Leopold S. Amery, *The Empire at Bay: The Leo Amery Diaries, 1929–1945*, ed. John Barnes and David Nicholson (London, 1988), p. 398. On Churchill's and Austen Chamberlain's support of both sides of the double policy and their consequent refusal to lead a back-bench revolt after the Hoare-Laval plan, see Thompson, *Anti-Appeasers*, pp. 78–82, 84–85, 89–93. In *Gathering Storm* (chap. 10), Churchill understates his ambivalence at the time and faults Baldwin and the Cabinet for lacking the will "to back words and gestures by action" (p. 164).

[23] See sources in chap. 2, note 23. On Labour's attitudes, see also John F. Naylor, *Labour's International Policy: The Labour Party in the 1930s* (Boston, 1969), chap. 4 and pp. 119–28; and for different views among pacifists, Martin Ceadel, *Pacifism in Britain 1914–1945: The Defining of a Faith* (Oxford, 1980), pp. 154–55, 180–82.

Traditionalist and collectivist attitudes alike influenced British policy, but were so combined and confused as to make artificial any separation of the Government into two distinct schools.

Part of the problem of collective security was Germany. London could not decide whether the League of Nations (possibly without Italy) or Italian solidarity with France and Britain (possibly without the League) would provide the better deterrent to German expansion.[24] The present crisis was viewed through the lenses of an imagined future contingency, a kind of vision that gave peculiar distortion to this test case for the League. Chatfield and Hankey perhaps best typified traditionalist points of view. Chatfield scarcely concealed his contempt for the League, writing that it might soon "be flouted militarily by the nation whom it was trying to coerce." Britain had alienated Italy, its longtime friend in the Mediterranean, and "this miserable business of collective security has run away with all our traditional interests and policies."[25] In November, Hankey denied that he opposed the League; but, he told Hoare, the Government's support for escalating sanctions would turn the League into "'an instrument of war instead of an instrument of peace.'"[26]

Shortly after the Hoare-Laval agreement, Eden spoke for collectivists when he reminded the Cabinet that many people expected the League to deter aggression and punish the aggressor.[27] Hoare, Chamberlain, and Vansittart occupied ground somewhere between Hankey and Eden. They agreed with Eden that Britain, France, and Italy had a common interest in preserving collective security to check Germany. But they were less committed than Eden to making the League work against Italy, and more apt to argue that the sooner Britain knew whether the League would break down under such a test, the better. Vansittart was more pessimistic than Hoare and Chamberlain about the League's future, and more interested in Italy's usefulness as a counter-

[24] British memoirs continued the debate. Eden and Lord Strang emphasized collective security: Avon, *Dictators*, pp. 273–74; Strang, *Home and Abroad*, p. 65 (the Stresa Front idea was "at best a will-o'-the-wisp"). Vansittart continued to believe that "the better deterrent was to keep Italy in line"; *Mist*, p. 545. See also Alfred Duff Cooper, *Old Men Forget* (London, 1953), pp. 190–92.

[25] Chatfield to Vansittart, 8 August, *DBFP*, 14, no. 431; to Admiral Fisher, 25 August, in Marder, "Royal Navy," p. 1342; to Admiral Dreyer, 16 September, Chatfield Papers.

[26] Hankey diary, 25 November, in Roskill, *Hankey*, 3:187–89. R. A. C. Parker blames British policy for the League's failure, in the Ethiopian crisis, to "be used in what now seems to have been its most important capacity—as a deterrent to armed aggression"; "Failure of Collective Security," in Mommsen and Kettenacker, *Fascist Challenge*, pp. 22–27. This thesis would seem to underestimate the degree of ambivalence and flux in British attitudes toward coercion in the crisis.

[27] Cab 54(35), 11 December, CAB 23/82. Corelli Barnett assails Eden for knowing nothing about "strategy or the world-balance of power, or the likely strategic consequences to England of his League idealism"; *Collapse*, p. 357.

weight to German designs on Austria. Vansittart supported the League, but because he doubted it would ever agree to confront aggression by Germany, he labored, as he later admitted, "under a dualism which might look like duplicity." On the one hand, he agreed with Hoare that Britain must show strength when the British situation seemed safer after Hoare's Assembly speech of 11 September. On the other, when Mussolini stepped up Italian military activity in the Mediterranean and North Africa and rejected the territorial compromise proposed by the League, Vansittart urged Hoare and Eden to avoid any military adventures and to consider offering Mussolini concessions exceeding those recommended by the League.[28]

The Chiefs of Staff considered collective security incompatible with imperial defense and rejected the idea that "sanctions can be enforced whenever diplomatically desirable."[29] The Service departments repeatedly advised that Britain must not risk war in the Mediterranean (and weaken its position elsewhere) by such provocative measures as were most likely to make economic sanctions effective: imposing a blockade on Italy, exercising belligerent rights, closing the Suez Canal, and taking any other steps that might be classified as military sanctions.

The Defence Requirements Committee reinforced this advice. The DRC declared that collective security was "on trial" and would have to be reconsidered unless at least partially successful in the Italo-Ethiopian crisis. In any case, Britain's educational institutions should emphasize the importance of defense "at least to the same extent as, and indeed as an integral element in, the propaganda for peace and the League of Nations that is carried on today in our schools." The Manchurian and Ethiopian crises had illustrated how suddenly Britain's commitment to collective action could arise "with very little warning" and jeopardize national and imperial defense. A militarily strong Britain would have made the League of Nations far more effective "as a deterrent to war." Indeed, military strength must be restored no matter whether Britain continued to support collective security or adopted any of three possible alternatives: regional security "on the Locarno model"; the "system of alliances and *ententes*" that existed before the Great War; or isolation. While Britain rearmed, its diplomacy must steer clear of war "in a world more dangerous than it has ever been

---

[28] Eden, Hoare, Vansittart correspondence, 23 September–1 October, *DBFP*, 14, nos. 619, 633, 662, 664; Avon, *Dictators*, pp. 292–96, 305–6; Rhodes James, *Anthony Eden*, pp. 150–54; Vansittart, *Mist*, pp. 522–23; Aaron Goldman, "Sir Robert Vansittart's Search for Italian Cooperation against Hitler, 1933–1936," *Journal of Contemporary History* 9 (1974); Rose, *Vansittart*, chap. 9. For "cross pressures" in London (i.e., consideration of the possibility of conflicts with opponents other than Italy), see Walker, "Solving the Appeasement Puzzle," pp. 230–32.

[29] COS report (COS 392), 9 August, CAB 53/25.

before." Britain could least of all afford to alienate Japan and a Mediterranean power simultaneously, or confront three enemies in three theaters, especially if it could not count on French military support.[30]

The members of the DRC were frustrated by a crisis that did not fit their earlier assumptions, preoccupied as they were with the German and Japanese threats and eager to return to the task of long-range planning. The Chiefs of Staff particularly stressed Britain's military weakness and far-flung strategic responsibilities. Rearmament against Germany and Japan would be delayed by sustaining abnormally high levels of military readiness in the Mediterranean region, where coercive diplomacy had been employed prematurely for reasons other than self-defense. Above all, the COS and Hankey regarded both general and immediate deterrence as the goal of rearmament and viewed diplomacy—without threatening force—as the way to avoid war in the meantime. In the DRC Third Report of November 1935, "showing a tooth" in the Far East or anywhere else while Britain regained its military strength was at most only an implicit option.

The DRC shared Ramsay MacDonald's opinion that Britain's diplomacy had outreached its military power even as the risk of war continued to grow.[31] If the crisis underlined this discrepancy, if deterrence required greater power and fewer commitments than Britain now had, and if attempting to deter Mussolini from weakness hindered the longer-term task of deterring Hitler from strength, then how should Britain deal with Germany? The members of the DRC disagreed over this question. Their report's reserved recommendation to appease Germany was a compromise between the views of Chatfield and Vansittart. Chatfield, who had welcomed the Anglo-German Naval Agreement of June 1935, believed that relations with Germany could be improved, that agreements with Germany could be trusted, and that war with Germany could be averted. Vansittart doubted all three of these assumptions, unless the Government was willing to affront public opinon by allowing Germany to expand to the east or regain colonies—and even then Germany would probably start expanding also to the west. The other members of the DRC—Ellington, Massingberd, Fisher, and Hankey—argued that Vansittart's fatalistic prediction of war in the next two or three years gave all the more reason to better relations with Germany.[32]

---

[30] DRC Third Report, 21 November, in CP 26(36), CAB 24/259.

[31] MacDonald to Baldwin, 28 November, Baldwin Papers.

[32] DRC meetings, 12 and 14 November, CAB 16/112; Pownall diary, 12 November, in Bond, *Chief of Staff*, p. 88; Schmidt, *England in der Krise*, pp. 217–19. See also John Dunbabin, "The British Military Establishment and the Policy of Appeasement," in Mommsen and Kettenacker, *Fascist Challenge*, chap. 12; and David Dilks, "'The Unneces-

Hoare and officials in the Foreign Office thought that greater military strength would improve Britain's position in negotiations with Germany, and, unlike the Chiefs of Staff, they did not peg the effectiveness of general deterrence to the state of preparedness envisaged in the DRC report. Sir Eric Phipps reported from Berlin that, although it was hard to say when German rearmament "will be judged to be complete," military expansion would inevitably lead to territorial expansion. Sargent admitted the possibility that Hitler might not be a "monster" for the present, "but it is more than probable that he is a Frankenstein, and has created a monster which is fast growing up." The threat of economic sanctions would not restrain German expansion. At last, Vansittart thankfully observed, Britain was strengthening its defenses. The warning was clearer than before 1914, "and we have a remedy in our hands if we are quick enough." Military strength would enable Britain to "drive a much better bargain." Britain must not bargain with Germany "until we have at least made a beginning on the requirements of the new DRC report—a beginning sufficient to show that we mean business, which many people still do not believe. And we have *done* nothing so far to prove them wrong." It was not necessary, in Vansittart's view, to wait until the DRC requirements were completed before negotiating with Germany; but "we shall lose nothing by waiting till we have made a strong and immediate beginning." Hoare conveyed the warning and reasoning of these officials to the Cabinet on 4 December. Germany might not "await the absolute completion of her preparations before demanding satisfaction on certain of her claims." Britain's "counter-armaments are . . . the essential accompaniment and, so far as possible, preliminary of" negotiating concessions to Germany. Hoare did not raise an issue that still divided Vansittart from Hankey and the Chiefs of Staff but had not been aired in their DRC report; namely, that the process of rearming could itself deter Hitler and that there was neither the material necessity nor the time to complete rearming before showing teeth in Europe.[33]

Finally, contradictory attitudes toward France and other Mediterranean powers conveyed mixed signals from London and reduced Britain's coercive leverage on Mussolini. The question facing the British, having decided that French cooperation was indispensable for collec-

---

sary War'? Military Advice and Foreign Policy in Great Britain, 1931–1939," in Adrian Preston, ed., *General Staffs and Diplomacy before the Second World War* (London, 1978), chap. 6.

[33] Phipps to Hoare, 13 November (no. 213, with minutes by Sargent and Vansittart); Vansittart to Lord Wigram (Buckingham Palace), 7 November (no. 195), and comments on Sargent/Wigram memorandum, 1 December (appx. Ic); *DBFP*, 15. Hoare note, 25 November, CP 217(35), CAB 24/257; Cab 51(35), 4 December, CAB 23/82.

tive action against Italy, was whether to press for French and League action. London itself remained unsure, unable to decide precisely what reputation it wanted to have. Reluctance to take the lead derived from a number of considerations. Britain's respectability as an international broker might suffer if firmness eclipsed fairness toward Italy. The British suspected that Pierre Laval might embarrass them diplomatically, by leaking information, and militarily, by failing to provide substantial support in the Mediterranean—all in the effort to avoid estranging Italy. Caution would also safeguard Britain against becoming isolated in Geneva. Isolation would have little public support; moreover, if isolated, Britain would be unable to blame others if the League failed to stop Mussolini, and would probably have to fight alone if he retaliated. Consequently, even after Laval had fallen in line with Britain and the League at the tripartite talks, Hoare did not want to imply "either too much or too little to the French, too much in suggesting that we are determined to apply sanctions however futile the investigation may prove them to be, too little by implying to them that we have come to the view that sanctions are impracticable."[34]

On the other hand, Britain had to take the lead if it hoped to boost London's and the League's reputation for firmness, and to ensure that France and other nations came to Britain's aid in case of war. This concern for esteem and interdependence, however, did not lead to a clear or consistent correlation of diplomacy and military measures. Just as the British wanted both to pressure and conciliate Mussolini, they wavered between wanting to impress friendly powers and not wanting to alarm them by showing military strength. On 4 August, Hoare did not wish to take any military action that might "worry the French." But two weeks later Vansittart regretted that British military weakness gave France "qualms as to which road they might have to tread—England and the League on the one side or Italy on the other."[35] British military reinforcements in late August and early September, particularly the dispatch of units of the Home Fleet to Gibraltar, added credence to the diplomatic offensive of Hoare and Eden in Geneva. On 17 September, the Defence Policy and Requirements Committee agreed with Hoare that, since the chances of Britain's having to fight Italy alone had diminished, "the more strength we show in the Mediterranean the better." At the same time, Hoare advised against discussing the contingency of war in much detail with other powers, for "the very fact of our making enquiries made nations think we are anxious." A week

---

[34] Hoare to Clerk, 24 August, *DBFP*, 14, no. 493, and comment on Sargent note, 26 August, no. 496.

[35] Hoare minute to Eden and Vansittart, W6968/1209/88, FO 371/19686; Vansittart (Paris) to Hoare, 14 August, *DBFP*, 14, appx. Id.

later, when fears of isolation had increased in London, Eden remonstrated that reducing the military concentration in the Mediterranean would undo its positive effect on France and other powers, which had "waked up to find that we are powerful and determined."[36]

In October, as the chance of a single-handed war increased, London did not reduce its strength in the Mediterranean. When Laval refused to promise full military cooperation, Hoare prescribed an approach to France no less disingenuous than Laval's policy toward Britain was held to be. Laval should be reminded that Britain had sent reinforcements to the Mediterranean for "elemental safety," and Laval could not truthfully call them provocative. Withdrawing forces in the interests of an Anglo-Italian détente was out of the question so long as the French would not "stand behind us in the event of attack," a commitment that would provide "a sufficient deterrent" to Italy. Hoare would also tell Laval that "if earlier we had felt confident of naval cooperation by France and of the availability of French ports in the event of an Italian aggression we should have sent fewer reinforcements to the Mediterranean."[37]

Hoare's argument belied the fact that his Government had since August used a show of force as a means of coercive diplomacy and imperial authority, and would continue to do so after October. Because of this, the levels of British force in the Mediterranean, Africa, and the Middle East did not rise or fall strictly according to the likelihood of a single-handed war against Italy or the degree of support expected from France and other powers. London remained torn between taking the lead and biding time, between impressing and alarming friendly powers, and between collective action to defend Britain or punish Mussolini. In December, the British wanted to withdraw forces from the Mediterranean in order to reduce the risk of war and concentrate on long-term rearmament. But they did not wish to appear weak in the Mediterranean or soft on sanctions.[38] Neither before nor during the crisis had they prepared an effective procedure for collaborating with potential allies, one which made possible joint action without formal alliance. Staff talks with France would continue into 1936, but by the end of 1935, in spite of some improvement in the atmosphere of these talks, neither Britain nor France had much faith in the political reliability or military will of the other.

[36] DPR meeting, CAB 16/136; Hoare to Chamberlain, 17 September, Templewood Papers; Eden to Hoare, 24 September, *DBFP*, 14, no. 633.

[37] Cab 47(35), 16 October, CAB 23/82.

[38] The British predicament is implicit in what Eyres-Monsell and Swinton told the Cabinet on 2 December: "If our weakness were known some of the nations supporting sanctions might show less alacrity." Cab 50(35), CAB 23/82.

In this first major test for British policy toward dictators who might act irrationally, London held doubts concerning the dividing line between security and provocation, the intentions of Italy, the threat of war, the effectiveness of collective security, the need for and reliability of allies, and the impact of war on public opinion and limited military resources. These uncertainties conflated into the most imponderable question of all: what did deterrence mean and require in this case? Lacking internal or public consensus, the Government struggled to give an answer somewhere between bluff and war, unwilling to go to the latter extreme yet willing to apply military pressure. But London's confidence in this moderate form of coercion steadily declined after mid-September as Mussolini refused to yield to collective pressure, as the threat of single-handed war remained, and as expert advisers resumed planning of rearmament for long-term contingencies in Europe and the Far East. Unwilling to abandon the stick, Britain offered conciliatory reassurances to Mussolini: military reinforcements were strictly precautionary; no military sanctions were planned; major concessions to Italy in Ethiopia were possible; a League decision on the oil sanction should wait.

After the Hoare-Laval plan backfired, some hope remained that sanctions would eventually stop Mussolini during what London presumed would be a long campaign. But on the whole, British ministers and experts had been sobered by the failure of the double policy of conciliation and sanctions to appease and check Mussolini. Never having developed a clear conception of deterrence or coercive diplomacy in this instance, the Government nonetheless began to draw some lessons from having futilely tried.

First, France was more perfidious than Albion, and hardly deserving of an unequivocal British commitment regarding Germany. Indeed, French hesitation to deter Italy in this case would diminish British willingness to deter a German threat against France in the months to come. Second, collective security was a greater strategic liability than its advocates (and even some of its detractors) had imagined, and Britain's policy of supporting it needed reassessment. Collective security had required Britain to test its military strength and ideas about deterrence against what it perceived was the wrong country at the wrong time. The general election had given the Government a mandate to support collective security and rearm; ministers and advisers now wondered whether it would be possible to discard the first half of that mandate but retain the second. Third, filling the gap between actual military strength and foreign responsibilities would require more resources and time for rearmament than had been envisioned before the summer of 1935. Meanwhile, the machinery and goals of long-term defense policy could ill afford disruption by international crises, and British options in such circumstances would therefore be constricted.

Finally, deterrence would probably not work unless Britain rearmed to levels that impressed Germany and Japan and indeed gave Britain some assurance of victory if it came to war against those powers. This lesson, more than the others, was subject to different interpretations among British policymakers. The crisis had not resolved the three correlations of time, deterrence, and diplomacy represented by Vansittart, the Chiefs of Staff and Hankey, and most of the Cabinet (see chapter 1). And Eden now presented a fourth: showing fortitude at this moment against an unexpected enemy would strengthen Britain's hand and its international credibility in the future against Germany and Japan. The DRC, DPR, and Cabinet had still not unequivocally answered the questions of the COS of April 1935. Was Germany or Japan the near menace? When should the Service programs be completed? The preeminence of the Navy in the Mediterranean crisis called into question any exclusive bias toward the deterrent power of the Royal Air Force.

Taken together, these debatable issues prevented agreement on the appropriate levels of military strength, political firmness, and commitment to friendly nations necessary for successful diplomacy in the next few years. Without such a consensus, the crisis was all the more likely to carry this warning: the capacity merely to threaten force before 1939 at the earliest would neither deter a fascist regime from territorial expansion nor buy time for Britain to rearm in depth for the more perilous contingencies that were likely to arise in the future. The Chiefs of Staff and Hankey could claim that, more than anyone else in the Government, they already knew this lesson, which they would apply to cases of immediate, general, and extended deterrence.

COORDINATION AND CONTROL

At the height of the Cabinet crisis following the Hoare-Laval plan, Lord Halifax (Lord Privy Seal since November) observed that "the whole moral position of the Government before the world" was in jeopardy.[39] Many explanations of how Britain had reached this embarrassing position concentrate on public opinion. Some former policymakers blame the British public for forcing a reluctant Government to

---

[39] Cab 56(35), 18 December, CAB 23/90B; the once top-secret minutes of this meeting to discuss Hoare's fate are summarized in Middlemas and Barnes, *Baldwin*, pp. 892–93, and Hardie, *Abyssinian Crisis*, pp. 186–90.

support sanctions without sufficient military power; in the words of one, "democracy preferred impractical idealism to practical politics."[40] The vehement public outcry, a month after the general election endorsed the Government's support of the League, has helped illustrate the premise that the National Government viewed foreign policy chiefly as a means of building or keeping a domestic consensus.[41] Without denying the importance of domestic politics, the rest of this chapter will show how the Government's disorder of December 1935 was a by-product of the machinery of policy, which the Mediterranean emergency agitated and in which the deliberations of departments and committees were shielded from parliamentary scrutiny.

In the last half of 1935, the Cabinet shared executive authority with the Defence Policy and Requirements Committee (whose existence the Government did not disclose to Parliament until March 1936), and the machinery shifted away from rearmament to concentrate on the Mediterranean crisis. After the DRC reconvened in October to prepare its new report on rearmament, the sentiment grew in London that an irrational Italian dictator was delaying rational long-term planning in a democracy. So did the tendency to view the crisis as a distinct and intrusive problem of policy that must be solved as soon as possible.

From July to December 1935, Baldwin and the Cabinet allowed committees and departments unusually wide latitude, with the result that the control of the prime minister and Cabinet over policy was sporadic and loose, while the weight of expert advice increased.[42] For the first three weeks of August, when most of the Cabinet went on holiday knowing that Mussolini would probably begin war on Ethiopia in the fall, two special meetings of a few ministers constituted the highest executive authority in London.[43] On 22 August, the full Cabinet, hastily recalled for an emergency meeting, authorized the DPR to examine any questions concerning the crisis, enlarged the committee, and put the prime minister in the chair.[44] The minutes of the DPR, along with

[40] Wellesley, Diplomacy in Fetters, pp. 77–78, 82–83. See also Peterson, Both Sides of Curtain, p. 118, and Templewood, Nine Troubled Years, p. 135.

[41] See especially Cowling, Impact of Hitler, and Schmidt, England in der Krise. Cowling (p. 97) maintains that the Hoare-Laval plan destroyed an uneasy consensus in the Conservative party. Schmidt (pp. 415–16) views the crisis as an example of British interwar governments' willingness to take risks in foreign policy if they thought this would help maintain the internal social and political order.

[42] This section draws upon Gaines Post, Jr., "The Machinery of British Policy in the Ethiopian Crisis," International History Review 1 (1979).

[43] Meetings of 6 August (Baldwin, Hoare, Eden; also Vansittart and Hankey) and 21 August (Baldwin, R. MacDonald, Simon, Chamberlain, Hoare, Eden; also two Foreign Office officials), and procedures for the recess, Cab 41(35), CAB 23/82.

[44] Cab 42(35), CAB 23/82. The new members of the DPR, in addition to Baldwin, were Malcolm MacDonald (Colonial Secretary) and Sir John Simon (Home Secretary).

other documents, show that Baldwin seldom contributed to discussions of policy, was distracted by the politics of the general election, and provided virtually no personal control over individual ministers or the DPR.[45]

During the crisis the DPR assumed emergency powers unforeseen in its terms of reference of July and at most only implicit in the Cabinet's conclusions of 22 August. The committee acquired enough power for Hankey and others to view the DPR as a kind of "War Committee."[46] From 23 August through December 1935, the DPR met thirteen times, the crisis having superseded defense requirements on its agenda. The Cabinet adjourned during most of August and September, met weekly from 24 September to 23 October, then took a long break to fight the victorious election campaign, and next discussed the Ethiopian question on 2 December. Toward the end of both of these recesses, Hankey circulated summaries of the work of the DPR to the Cabinet.[47]

Neither Hankey's briefs nor the fact that the prime minister and ten other Cabinet members now sat on the DPR prevented differences from arising between the Cabinet and the committee. The Cabinet, mindful of electoral politics, was less reluctant than the DPR to approve sanctions without first securing guarantees from France and other League members that they would declare war on Italy, should sanctions be imposed and Italy retaliate by attacking British interests. Moreover, the Cabinet authorized Hoare to begin negotiations with Italy for a military détente in the Mediterranean without waiting—as the DPR recommended—for the French to promise naval cooperation in the event that Italy attacked the British Mediterranean Fleet.[48] In these cases, the DPR placed greater emphasis on military security as a precondition for political action, advice that the committee heard directly from its own military experts.

Inescapably, especially after the DRC reconvened in October to dis-

45 For critical portrayals, see Sir Harold Nicolson, *Diaries and Letters, 1930–1939* (New York, 1966), p. 233; Swinton, *Sixty Years*, pp. 81–82; Templewood, *Nine Troubled Years*, pp. 136–37, 164, 167, 183–85; Vansittart, *Mist*, p. 541. Hoare complained to Chamberlain (vacationing in Switzerland) that Baldwin and R. MacDonald were no help; the one was indifferent, the other wanted to give in to Italy. Letter of 18 August, Chamberlain Papers, NC 7/11/28/24.

46 For the DPR's terms of reference, see chapter 1. The Committee of Imperial Defence met only once (14 October) between July and late December; its subcommittees usually reported to the DPR on the Mediterranean crisis.

47 CP 176(35), 20 September, CAB 24/256; summary of DPR meeting, 26 November, CP 220(35), CAB 24/257. Hankey sent King George V the minutes of the DPR during the crisis; correspondence in CAB 21/573. The king told Hoare to keep Britain out of war and find a compromise; Templewood, *Nine Troubled Years*, pp. 159–60.

48 DPR meetings, 5 September and 26 November, CAB 16/136; Cabs 45 (9 October), 47 (16 October), 48 (23 October), 50 (2 December), CAB 23/82; Baer, *Test Case*, pp. 85–87; Middlemas and Barnes, *Baldwin*, pp. 860–63; Parker, "Ethiopian Crisis," pp. 308–12.

cuss rearmament, the DPR began to combine the planning of supply priorities for the emergency and for rearmament. This synthesis of immediate and long-term policy problems was consonant with the DPR's sweeping terms of reference of July, and may have signaled an attempt to begin what Ramsay MacDonald found lacking—a survey of Britain's strategic position, which he thought the Cabinet was much too large to make itself. But the Cabinet took a narrower view. It confined the DPR's authority to matters directly related to the Mediterranean crisis, and established yet another committee—the DPR(DR)—to study the DRC's report of 21 November on defense requirements.[49]

It is not surprising that confusion arose over the precise functions of the DPR, for the committee had not yet examined "general defensive policy" according to its original terms of reference, and now something like a dual executive directed British policy during the Mediterranean crisis. The power of the DPR increased. The committee authorized military measures such as reinforcing the Mediterranean Fleet, and issued instructions to Hoare and Eden concerning the double policy that they pursued in Geneva and Paris. The delegation of Cabinet authority to a committee during an international crisis was grounded in past experience and in procedural documents kept on file. In one of four possible systems of "supreme control" envisioned for use in an emergency, the Cabinet would be assisted by a "War Committee" with broad executive powers (see chapter 1).

Some of the confusion over the powers of the DPR might have been avoided if the Cabinet had clearly defined them at the end of August and had met regularly during September and November. But neither the committee's function nor its decisions during the crisis can be fully understood without appreciating its close relationship with the members of the DRC: Hankey (the DPR's secretary), the Chiefs of Staff (charter members of the DPR), and Vansittart and Fisher (both of whom, beginning in September, attended most of the DPR's meetings).

Late in 1935, the DRC blamed its political superiors for having excluded from its terms of reference the contingency of war with Italy, and some ministers—notably Hoare and Eden—grumbled that the Services had done little to prepare themselves for war since August.[50] Most ministers approved the policy of collective action (so long as Britain did not take the lead), whereas the Chiefs of Staff and Hankey viewed collective security as a liability. Chatfield held "our statesmen"

[49] MacDonald to Baldwin, 28 November, Baldwin Papers. The DPR(DR) convened in January 1936, and is discussed in the next chapter.

[50] DRC Third Report, 21 November, in CP 26(36), CAB 24/259; Hankey diary, 25 November, in Roskill, *Hankey*, 3:189; Pownall diary, 4 December, in Bond, *Chief of Staff*, pp. 91–92.

responsible for alienating Italy.[51] He and others on the DRC thought the policy of sanctions was outdistancing military preparedness, and viewed coercive diplomacy in this crisis as a mistake.

Such allegations reveal discord between ministers and officials, and between political and military considerations. But by and large the mixed membership of the DRC, their common task of considering both the political and military dimensions of rearmament, and their direct influence on the DPR minimized civil-military frictions at both the official and ministerial levels. Generally, the degree of caution and the unwillingness to take military risks through a policy of coercion were greater in the DRC than in the DPR, and greater in the DPR than in the Cabinet. The DPR's decisions and recommendations usually reflected the advice of the members of the DRC. By late November, these officials wished the crisis would soon end, for it disrupted long-term planning for completely different cases of war. They wanted the DPR, other committees, and the Service staffs disencumbered of numerous studies that related specifically to the emergency. Ministers shared with officials the frustrations of having to deal with a crisis that jeopardized Anglo-Italian relations and Britain's preparations for war against Germany or Japan. Largely because of pressure from Vansittart, Fisher, and their colleagues on the DRC, the DPR and then the Cabinet gave much more attention in late November and early December than before to the harmful effects that a prolonged Mediterranean crisis would have on imperial strategy and rearmament.

In both framing and negotiating policy in the Mediterranean crisis, the Foreign Office was unquestionably the foremost department. In the spring and summer of 1935, the Cabinet had given Hoare and Eden wide discretion in conducting policy toward Italy and the League.[52] The Foreign Office worked to maintain this ascendancy during the crisis, encouraging interdepartmental consultation and acknowledging the interdependence of foreign policy and military preparedness.

Late in July, the Foreign Office proposed the establishment of an Official Subcommittee on Abyssinia, recommending that this be done without notifying the Cabinet.[53] Evidently pleased that the Cabinet

[51] Chatfield to Admiral Dreyer, 16 September, Chatfield Papers.

[52] For example, Cab 27, 28 (35), 15 and 17 May, CAB 23/81; 40, 41 (35), 24 and 31 July, CAB 23/82.

[53] Notes and correspondence in J3042/2742/1, FO 371/19191. Vansittart observed that Hoare could of course take up the matter with the prime minister, "but he is quite entitled to ask for such an interdepartmental gathering 'on his own.' It is an obviously practical measure of organisation." Hoare concurred, but Hankey, who thought that "this peace of Government machinery would be very valuable" because of the coming recess, suggested to Baldwin that he mention it to the Cabinet, which approved the new committee (chaired by a Foreign Office representative) on 24 July; Hankey to prime minister, 23 July, copy in J3127/1/1, FO 371/19119; Cab 40(35), CAB 23/82.

had recessed, Vansittart advised Hoare that the Foreign Office should keep control over policy, and he agreed with the Foreign Secretary that a Cabinet meeting was unnecessary before the tripartite talks of 15–18 August in Paris. Meanwhile, Vansittart added, the Foreign Office should keep MacDonald (acting prime minister in Baldwin's absence) apprised, but "in the form of intention rather than in a form which would be subject to any wide correction."[54] The Foreign Office dominated the informal meeting with Baldwin on 6 August—Hoare, Eden, and Vansittart, in addition to the prime minister and Hankey. Vansittart soon decided that a Cabinet meeting should be called to provide clear authority for military precautionary measures,[55] but he remained convinced that the Office should be left as much freedom as possible to determine the appropriate relationship between the two sides of the double policy.

In his memoirs, Eden recounted his differences with Hoare and Vansittart, and his dismay over conflicting instructions from London— "firm language" followed by "limiting clauses."[56] He attributed such problems in the conduct of policy to having two ministers in the Foreign Office, one of whom, Foreign Secretary Hoare, was indecisive, in poor health, and swayed by Vansittart.[57] Eden considered himself more qualified than Hoare to conduct Britain's foreign affairs. He had read oriental languages at Christ Church, Oxford, after the war and had planned to enter the foreign service. Having chosen politics instead, he served as Sir Austen Chamberlain's Parliamentary Private Secretary (1926–29), and, as a reward for loyalty to Baldwin after the Conservatives lost the general election of 1929, was appointed Parliamentary Under-Secretary at the Foreign Office when the National Government took office in 1931. As Lord Privy Seal in 1934–35, Eden had represented the Government in talks with foreign leaders in Paris, Geneva, Berlin, Rome, and Moscow. A veteran of the western front (Military Cross), he was handsome, young (thirty-eight years of age in 1935), popular with most of the British press, a rising star in the Conservative party.

Of the three major figures at the Foreign Office, Eden was the most

---

[54] Vansittart to Hoare, 2 and 3 August, FO 800/295. Vansittart thought it unwise to put ministers in ill humor by interrupting their holidays.

[55] Vansittart to Hoare, 9 August, FO 800/295; and to Admiral Little, 9 August, ADM 116/3038; Eden to Baldwin, 13 August, Baldwin Papers.

[56] Avon, *Dictators*, chaps. 12–16; also Rhodes James, *Anthony Eden*, pp. 149–56, and Rhodes James, *Davidson's Memoirs*, p. 407.

[57] Vansittart preferred working with Hoare, who was "refreshingly apt" to take the word of his subordinates "when he had taken their measure." Vansittart had "amicable but defined" differences with Eden, whom he viewed as "even more [Baldwin's] favorite than Tom Jones." Vansittart, *Mist*, p. 522.

determined for Britain to take the lead in supporting collective security, even if this meant war, and the most optimistic about Britain's military preparedness for a conflict with Italy. Vansittart was the least determined and most pessimistic. He and Ralph Wigram did not want to estrange Italy or compel France to break with Italy while Germany rearmed.[58] Hoare wavered between these two positions. He viewed Britain as the leader in Geneva, but also feared that his Government might become isolated. He would not rule out a sanction on oil, but was determined to avoid war.[59]

Yet the differences between Eden and his two colleagues, as well as the faults of "divided control" at the Foreign Office, can be exaggerated.[60] In May and June, Chamberlain praised Eden's and Hoare's plan to "let Eden do the travelling and the personal contacts for which he has a genius," even though this seemed "illogical and impracticable." Several months later, Eden told Chamberlain that he was "working admirably" with Hoare and that this had made an "incredible" difference in the Foreign Office.[61] Hoare and Vansittart wanted to exert diplomatic and military pressure on Mussolini in August and September. And Eden supported the conciliatory side of the dual policy, though he was more uneasy than Hoare and Vansittart about whether major concessions to Italy would be acceptable to Ethiopia, the League, and British opinion.

When Eden tried to take the lead in Geneva in an effort to increase pressure on Italy, the DPR and Cabinet gave him corrective reminders through Hoare.[62] Although the Cabinet and DPR braked Eden's efforts, they gave him, Hoare, and diplomatic officials the liberty to negotiate, without much correction, the line of policy that culminated in the Hoare-Laval plan which the Cabinet then approved. As public reaction mounted, Baldwin and the Cabinet pretended that they had not given Hoare such powers, but privately they realized too late that

---

[58] Lord Astor reported to J. L. Garvin that Wigram privately supported Garvin's line; letter of 11 October, Garvin Papers.

[59] In September, Hoare did not want to take the "defeatist" view of the League that he found in the Foreign Office; *Nine Troubled Years*, p. 166. Later he assured Garvin that he was doing his best to avoid war; letter of 22 October, Garvin Papers. After resigning two months later, Hoare wrote Baldwin, "I believe that I have succeeded in doing what you wanted me to do. I have kept the country out of war"; Baldwin Papers.

[60] This point is also made by David Carlton, *Anthony Eden: A Biography* (London, 1981), pp. 60–61, 67–69; Parker, "Ethiopian Crisis," pp. 318–24; and Watt, "Divided Control."

[61] Chamberlain to Hilda, 26 May, 22 June, and 1 September, Chamberlain Papers, NC 18/1/919, 923, 930. J. L. Garvin blamed the "two-headed Foreign Office" and Vansittart for gambling "that a thwarted Italy would also remain in the League." "Present policy means going to Hell for the sake of Eden," whom Mussolini regarded as "a good looking . . . shop assistant." Notes of August and September, Garvin Papers.

[62] DPR meeting, 23 September, CAB 16/136; Cab 47(35), 16 October, CAB 23/82; Hoare to Eden, 16 October, *DBFP*, 15, no. 87n.

no matter how desirable this territorial settlement might be, their instructions to Hoare had been too vague and their control over policy too loose. The appointment of Eden to replace Hoare was designed to shore up the Government's eroded standing; the damage done to the Foreign Office by the Hoare-Laval plan was harder to measure and probably also harder to repair.[63]

The numerous historical accounts of this episode have not recognized that the lapse in collective control resulted in some measure from the presence of another executive body, the DPR. The DPR had met more frequently than the Cabinet since August, providing both a more continuous source of authority and a direct link between ministers and expert advisers. Imprecisely defined, the DPR's executive power confused and weakened the principle of collective control by the Cabinet. The committee's authority added weight to the view that concessions be made to Mussolini, a policy elaborated in the Foreign Office with support from the Service departments.

Disagreement between the Foreign Office and the Services continued over a question that predated the crisis—the year when Germany might launch a European war. The DRC left unresolved the disagreement between the COS technical estimate of 1942 (or later) and the Foreign Office's political warning about 1939 (or earlier). The Foreign Office remained sensitive on this issue, in spite of concurring with military experts that Germany posed the major threat to European peace. Commenting in August on a monthly intelligence report from the War Office, in which the German Army was purported to "have great faith in Hitler's judgment," officials in the Foreign Office wished that the other department would ask them before commenting on the political situation: "It will be remembered that Lord Curzon found it necessary on a certain occasion to impress upon the [War Office] that they laboured under the delusion that the uniform but thinly disguised the statesman."[64] Concerning the Mediterranean crisis, however, the Foreign Office seldom made an issue of the fact that the COS combined

---

[63] The Cabinet's responsibility for the plan has been blurred by conflicting accounts of who authorized whom to do what. Baldwin denied that he or the Cabinet had pressed Hoare to go to Paris; Jones, *Diary*, p. 159. Chamberlain "had no idea that [Hoare] would be invited to consider detailed peace proposals," and felt Hoare and Vansittart had told two different stories about the danger of imposing an oil sanction; Chamberlain to Hilda and diary, 15 December, Chamberlain Papers, NC 18/1/942, NC 2/23a. See also Vansittart, *Mist*, pp. 538–39; Warner, *Pierre Laval*, p. 122; and the sources cited in chap. 2, note 59. Duff Cooper told Liddell Hart "it was a mistake to have two foreign ministers"; 14 December, Liddell Hart Papers, 11/1935/115 (LHCMA). But Geoffrey Dawson, editor of the *Times*, viewed "'the real culprits'" as Hoare's Cabinet colleagues, who had "'acquiesced in the slipshod manner in which the Cabinet conducts its business.'" Note of 18 December in *History of the Times*, p. 898.

[64] Creswell and Dodd minutes, 7 and 21 August, W6809/138/50, FO 371/19622.

technical military considerations and policy recommendations. When the Chiefs of Staff reported in August on the military implications of imposing sanctions, Hoare thought that they had assumed "the worst in the worst of all worlds" and had presented "typical staff" material with "plenty of hedging and no last ditches." Nevertheless, he and Vansittart concurred with the report's major conclusions. Sanctions might lead to a war for which Britain was unprepared, and military precautions must be taken in case of a sudden attack.[65] Although this agreement did not disintegrate, several issues frayed it.

First, the Foreign Office—notably Eden and Hoare—used the threat of force as an instrument of collective security, not simply imperial safety. Already opposed to collective security, the Chiefs of Staff now believed that British diplomacy was indeed outreaching military preparedness. Still willing to give the League of Nations a future, Vansittart complained of the Services' leisurely pace in increasing their readiness for war. The Mediterranean crisis had "been as plain as a pikestaff since August, and we have had a longer notice of danger than in 1914." The failure to profit from that notice, he maintained, had handicapped the Foreign Office during the crisis.[66] Second, the Foreign Office was more inclined than the Chiefs of Staff to view Italian expansion as a challenge to British imperial interests in the Mediterranean region. Hoare, Eden, and Vansittart expressed much more anxiety over the security of Egypt than did their colleagues at the War Office (where Alfred Duff Cooper replaced Lord Hailsham in November). Vansittart angrily dismissed the General Staff's implication that "any Italian menace to Egypt is a figment of the F.O. brain," and he privately told Hoare that Montgomery-Massingberd was an unsatisfactory CIGS, one who during the crisis, Vansittart later recalled, "went pheasant hunting as cheerfully as Lord George Germain in the American War of Independence."[67] Finally, the Services (especially the Navy and Air Force) were more skeptical than the Foreign Office about receiving support from France and other Mediterranean countries.

The Treasury and Board of Trade cooperated with the Foreign Office during the crisis at both official and ministerial levels. Fisher and other officials at the Treasury and Board of Trade warned that economic sanctions against Italy would injure British commerce. Moreover, sanc-

[65] Hoare minutes, 4 and 12 August, W6968/W7166/1209/98, FO 371/19686.

[66] Vansittart thought "a new broom" was needed in the field of supply. Minute of 30 November, *DBFP*, 15, no. 286.

[67] Halifax to Hoare, 27 September, and Vansittart to Hoare, 30 September, FO 800/295; Dill to Weir (Egypt), 26 September, and to Bartholomew (India), 10 October, WO 106/283; Vansittart minute, 25 September, J4889/3861/1, FO 371/19198; Vansittart to Hankey, 1 October, CAB 21/573; Vansittart, *Mist*, p. 544, describing Massingberd as "a handsome man who matched his name."

tions would be effective only if the United States participated and if League members exercised belligerent rights, but the latter would almost certainly lead to war.[68] Fisher thought "'the threat or use of force in the present emergency has nothing to commend it.'" In his opinion, the United States would "most probably veto an effective naval blockade," and war, along with "self-damaging futility," would result from undertaking partial sanctions just to "appear to be doing something."[69]

Chamberlain supported the double policy of Hoare, concurring with Treasury officials on the dangers of sanctions but deciding—contrary to Fisher's advice—that partial sanctions were better than none at all. Chamberlain expected French equivocation to give Britain an excuse for not pressing too far with sanctions and thereby weakening the League for dealing with European issues in the future. He was, according to Garvin, "determined not to let sanctions lead to war, and equally determined to use their failure as a lever for rearmament."[70] Before and after Italy invaded Ethiopia, Chamberlain favored offering territorial compensation to Mussolini. In early December he thought it would be absurd to proceed with an oil sanction so long as Hoare's forthcoming talks with Laval afforded "an opportunity of ending the war by the quickest and most satisfactory method."[71] Yet Chamberlain also agreed with—and frequently helped Hoare to articulate—the parallel policy of supporting collective action through the League. The Government, he believed, should put pressure on Mussolini in response to British opinion, in step with France, in conjunction with military precautions for a war that Britain must avoid, and in hopes that both Mussolini and the League would save face.

In late November, Chamberlain, unlike the Foreign Secretary, was willing for Britain, "in the last resort if necessary," to take the lead in making an oil sanction effective.[72] But Chamberlain and Hoare usually agreed on the main lines of policy. In September, Chamberlain recorded his satisfaction "to find one's ideas anticipated instead of always having to convince the Foreign Secretary first and then to hope that he might be able to convince others." He and Hoare "almost always seem

---

[68] Many Cabinet papers and conclusions refer to interdepartmental discussion and the Board of Trade's fear of losses to British trade. Officials from the board, Foreign Office, and Treasury often consulted informally as well as at meetings of the Economic Pressure Subcommittee and the Official Subcommittee on Abyssinia.

[69] Fisher to Chamberlain and Baldwin, 5 July, in O'Halpin, *Head of the Civil Service*, p. 255; Fisher note on Treasury paper of 26 August, T 172/1838; Fisher to Chamberlain, 21 August, T 160/621.

[70] Garvin to Mrs. Amery, 4 October 1935, and notes of 22 August (Chamberlain was "very cool and reasonable"), Garvin Papers.

[71] Diary, 8 December, Chamberlain Papers, NC 2/23a; Feiling, *Life of Chamberlain*, pp. 265, 272 (omitting the prepositional phrase about method).

[72] Diary, 29 November, Chamberlain Papers, NC 2/23a; Middlemas and Barnes, *Baldwin*, pp. 877–78.

to have the same sort of outlook on our problems so that we often arrive independently at the same solution."[73] Together, they overcame Eden's objections to postponing an oil embargo while negotiations seemed to hold promise of a territorial compromise. And they parried the more fearful counsel of Baldwin, Runciman, Eyres-Monsell, and Cunliffe-Lister (Lord Swinton from late November), all of whom considered an oil sanction much too risky.[74]

In his diary and letters, Chamberlain acknowledged Hoare's importance but also gave himself much of the credit for British policy. "So you see," he wrote to his sister late in August, "I have been very active and though my name will not appear I have as usual greatly influenced policy and, what is almost as important in these delicate situations, method also."[75] Chamberlain was very active indeed. In August, when Baldwin hoped Chamberlain "would have some idea of what to do," Chamberlain did. On 24 September, Hoare wrote to Eden that, when many Cabinet ministers had uttered forebodings about Britain's prominent position in Geneva, "Neville once again in a most masterly speech brought everyone around, some no doubt reluctantly, to our support." And in December, Chamberlain more than any other minister held the Cabinet together after the Hoare-Laval plan.[76]

Chamberlain also shaped major decisions on rearmament policy and Treasury control over expenditure. Early in August, he thought that the Government must accelerate rearmament. Germany was rapidly increasing its production of arms and might be tempted by British weakness and Mussolini's preoccupation in Africa to demand territory "in a few years time." At the same time, Labour was accusing the Government of concealing secret rearmament plans from the people. Chamberlain concluded that the Government could not deny Britain was rearming. For this reason, and because he saw rearmament as a means of relieving unemployment and deflating Labour's criticism of the Government's unemployment policy, he advised Baldwin to make rearmament a major issue in the general election.[77] In October, Cham-

---

[73] Chamberlain to Hilda, 7 and 22 September, Chamberlain Papers, NC 18/1/932, 934.

[74] Cab 50(35), 2 December, CAB 23/82; Chamberlain diary, 8 December, Chamberlain Papers, NC 2/23a. Chamberlain begged Hoare to find out exactly what policy Baldwin wanted; he asked Hoare whether "he realized that the P.M. was in his heart dead against his policy of sanctions" and that one day soon Baldwin would suddenly deduce he had always been opposed to it. "I had seen that happen before." Diary, 29 November, NC 2/23a.

[75] Chamberlain to Hilda, 25 August, Chamberlain Papers, NC 18/1/929.

[76] Ibid.; Hoare to Eden, *DBFP*, 14, appx. Ih; Cabs 53–56(35), CAB 23/82 and 23/90B.

[77] Diary, 2 August, Chamberlain Papers, NC 2/23a; excerpts in Macleod, *Chamberlain*, pp. 182–83, and Feiling, *Life of Chamberlain*, p. 266. See also Cowling, *Impact of Hitler*, pp. 91–93. A few weeks later, Garvin told Chamberlain that "the Unionist Party would not be responsible for the present humiliating and ignominious position regarding defence and that he would have to take over the party and the whole show." Note of 22 August, Garvin Papers.

berlain gave his Cabinet colleagues guidelines to observe in public speeches during the campaign: the Navy and Army had fallen behind the Air Force for financial reasons, "but now the state of the world was such that financial considerations might have to be viewed in a different light"; ministers should "avoid any suggestion of a loan."[78]

Fisher disagreed with the assumption of some of his colleagues that the Treasury could develop a long-term program of borrowing or increased taxation over the next five years. Closer to Vansittart than to Chamberlain or others in the Treasury in estimating the German menace, Fisher pointed out that it would reach its peak in the next few years. Thus, the Treasury should focus on the short term rather than too much on "years as far off as 1941–42." And he hoped that the actions of Hitler and Mussolini—"coupled now with an idea that other countries think England is afraid of the Iti's—may, pray heaven, educate [our people] to the need for our rearmament. Let your DRC continue to function and maintain a steady pressure," he encouraged Hankey.[79]

With respect to military supplies required during the crisis, the Treasury increased interdepartmental coordination by establishing, with the concurrence of the Service departments, the Treasury Emergency Expenditure Committee (TEEC). Representing the Treasury were Sir Richard Hopkins (chairman) and three other officials (including J. A. N. Barlow and Edward Bridges). Each Service department assigned two officials—a civilian and an officer—to the TEEC. An innovative adjustment in the machinery of policy, the TEEC ensured Treasury control over expenditure while expediting requests from the Services for financing emergency measures in accordance with the general guidelines of policy laid down by the DPR.[80] But neither the Treasury nor the Services could easily dissociate emergency expenses from expenditure on rearmament.[81] The Treasury's anxiety over this predicament, conveyed to the Cabinet by Chamberlain, helps explain the Cabinet's decision of 11 December to rescind the DPR's virtual authorization of the implementation of the shadow scheme for long-term

[78] Cab 45(35), 9 October, CAB 23/82. Because "the subject of Defence Policy had hitherto been dealt with by committees," Chamberlain was glad the Cabinet had this chance to discuss it. A week later, he assured members of the Federation of British Industrialists that the Government had no intention of "'nationalising or socialising industry or of imposing an organisation from without'"; Shay, *British Rearmament,* pp. 94–97.

[79] Notes by Phillips (29 November), Hopkins, and Fisher (both 2 December), T 160/688; Fisher to Hankey, 23 December, CAB 63/50.

[80] Minutes of TEEC meetings in T 161/716; Peden, *British Rearmament and Treasury,* pp. 36–37. In *British Rearmament* (pp. 99–102), Shay does not show the origins of the TEEC in the Mediterranean crisis and the impetus the crisis gave to the shadow industry scheme.

[81] PSOC meeting, 17 September, CAB 60/4; Treasury-War Office correspondence of October (especially Bridges of 22 October), T 161/712.

rearmament. Meanwhile the Cabinet ordered that "any difficulty arising in any particular case in separating supplies for the present emergency from those required generally for a major war, should be resolved by the Treasury Emergency Expenditure Committee."[82]

The TEEC neither eliminated the "shadowy" nature of Treasury control over the Service departments nor solved the problem of how to distinguish between emergency requirements and rearmament. The DPR had authorized the Service departments to determine their own needs during the emergency. This procedure, and the Treasury's usual readiness to fund these requirements through the TEEC, raised the Services' confidence in their bargaining power at a time when the combination of the emergency, the Service programs already approved, and the DRC's recommendation of rearmament beyond authorized programs all pointed toward extraordinarily high Service Estimates for 1936. In the coming year, the Treasury knew it would face a more difficult task than usual in funding and controlling the increasing expenditure on defense.

The position of the three Services in the machinery of policy during the crisis can be examined on two levels: their advice to the Foreign Office, DPR, and Cabinet; and their joint planning. The Chiefs of Staff and most other Service advisers agreed on large issues of policy and grand strategy. The Government's support of collective security conflicted with the Services' paramount task of protecting Britain's national and imperial interests. A war with Italy would alienate Britain's traditional friend in the Mediterranean. A prolonged emergency—let alone war—would tie up and weaken the fighting forces at a time when long-term planning presumed the possibility of war with Germany and Japan. Deterrence of aggression would be possible after Britain had rearmed, not beforehand. If there must be a conflict in the Mediterranean, the policy leading to it must not outpace the military and diplomatic preparations necessary for winning it. The Navy would be the principal Service in such a war, a specification that strengthened Chatfield's dominant position among the Chiefs of Staff. By and large, the Service ministers faithfully transmitted all of these conclusions to the DPR and Cabinet, where Eyres-Monsell and Cunliffe-Lister were far more forceful than Hailsham or Duff Cooper.

In their joint planning, the Services agreed to procedures for transmitting orders from London to forces in the Mediterranean, and for coordinating operations there. From the beginning of the crisis in late July and early August, the Service ministers and DPR gave the Service chiefs broad authority to plan operations. On 10 December, the Chiefs

[82] Cab 54(35), CAB 23/82.

of Staff prepared a set of general instructions that they would issue to the commanders in chief in the Mediterranean in case of hostilities. Military objectives should be selected by the local commander in chief and his respective department "at the discretion of the Chief of Staff concerned." The DPR and the prime minister approved this procedure, which was consistent with the constitutional practice of giving each Service department control over issuing orders to units in the field.[83]

But two sources of confusion remained. First, it was not clear how much discretion a Service chief had to issue orders without first obtaining the concurrence of his minister. This problem, which had many precedents in the First World War, was complicated by a second and more difficult issue that had come into focus since that war. Operations now were likely to involve all three Services, yet no constitutional procedure existed for issuing combined orders to commanders in chief in the theater of operations. At a meeting of the Chiefs of Staff on 20 December, chaired by the prime minister, Chatfield argued that the COS had the responsibility "to combine as the three official heads of their Services, and, in that capacity, they should be allowed to send combined instructions to the Commanders. In such circumstances, the Chiefs of Staff could act with the same authority as they normally had in their own Departments." Baldwin said he would consider this question, but he did not, and there the matter rested for nearly a year.[84]

In spite of this vagueness over procedure, Air Chief Marshal Sir Robert Brooke-Popham recalled that "the three Services worked very smoothly together in the Near East," partly because "the Army C-in-C. had the best cook in Cairo." The chief reasons for this harmony, Brooke-Popham went on, "were that the policy we had to implement was simple and definite; that the spheres of responsibility of the three services were clear; and that several senior officers on the different Staffs had been at the Imperial Defence College." Chatfield transmitted instructions (prepared by the JPC and COS, approved by the DPR) to the Naval commander in chief, who passed them on to the Army and Air commanders. This procedure (in which the Admiralty functioned as an operational headquarters and Chatfield as a commander in chief) was simplified by the fact that Chatfield was the senior member of the COS, and that Admiral Fisher was senior to the other two commanders in chief. Moreover, the commanders concurred that the main war object would be to cut Italy's communications to its colonies, that "Naval action would be the main factor towards the attainment" of this object,

---

[83] COS memorandum (COS 417), 10 December, CAB 53/26; DPR meeting, 12 December, CAB 16/136; COS meeting, 20 December, CAB 53/5; Monsell to Chatfield, 28 August, Chatfield Papers; Roskill, *Naval Policy*, pp. 266–67.
[84] COS meeting, CAB 53/5.

and that the primary duty of the other two Services "was to assist the Navy to carry out its offensive operations, and in particular to make the Naval base secure." Because of this agreement, and in view of Fisher's seniority and the location of his headquarters in Alexandria, the commanders felt "no need . . . for unity of command in order to enforce cooperation."[85]

Evidently, there were more conflicts and weaknesses in inter-Service relations back home than in the Mediterranean. Although accepting the primary role of the Navy for cutting Italian communications, the Service staffs did not agree on the central question—how best to defeat a maritime opponent in the new era of air power.[86] The Air Staff emphasized the vulnerability of ships and bases to Italian air attack, and questioned the effectiveness of antiaircraft fire in stopping determined raids. The Naval Staff, without admitting the vulnerability of ships, presumed that most air units should be used to defend the fleet and its bases while the Navy blocked both ends of the Mediterranean and established control over the central Mediterranean, no matter whether Malta, Alexandria, or Port X (Navarino) was the main base of operations. The Air Staff contested this presumption and maintained that an air offensive against the Italian mainland was at least as important as supporting the Navy. Before Britain could control the central Mediterranean, it must neutralize Italy's Metropolitan Air Force, whose bombers could reach Malta and Navarino. Achieving this objective as well as destroying Italian war industry would require British and French air attacks from southeastern France and Corsica against targets in northern Italy.[87]

The Air Force also found fault with the Army. Brooke-Popham reported to the Chief of the Air Staff that "the situation at Gibraltar resembles that in Whitehall; the Navy are at war, boom defence closed at night, air patrols out in the evening searching for the enemy;

[85] Brooke-Popham (Air Officer Commanding, Middle East), "Notes on the Emergency in the Near East—1935/36," 15 July 1936, AIR 9/71. Brooke-Popham contrasted the Navy's preeminence against the fact that "Air power . . . dominated the situation"— because the major Italian threat to British naval bases was from the air, the dispositions of the Navy and Army "were governed by the situation in the Air."

[86] For inter-Service differences, see Gibbs, *Rearmament*, pp. 194–95; Marder, "Royal Navy," pp. 1343–44; Pratt, *East of Malta*, pp. 120–21; Quartararo, "Imperial Defence," pp. 193–94, 214–19; Welch, "Chiefs of Staff," pp. 218–32.

[87] JPC meetings and papers, August–December, CAB 55/1 and 55/7; Chatfield memorandum, 3 September, CAB 16/138; Ellington minute, 4 September, AIR 8/188; COS meetings, 6 and 13 September, CAB 53/5; COS memorandum (COS 395), 9 September, CAB 53/25; Air Staff appreciation, 10 September, AIR 9/68; Ellington letters to Brooke-Popham, October–December, Brooke-Popham Papers, II/5, and Liddell Hart conversation with Sir Christopher Bullock (Permanent Secretary, Air Ministry), 4 October, Liddell Hart Papers, 11/1935/97 (LHCMA); Brooke-Popham "Notes" (see note 85 above).

the Army lie back and look on amusedly."[88] The Air Staff thought the Army hesitant about securing a landing area in or near Sollum in the northwest corner of Egypt, which would give British bombers the closest possible base to Libya, and would also deny the Italians an advanced base within 250 miles of Alexandria—the radius of many Italian bombers. If Britain sent air squadrons to southeastern France, Army administrative units would have to accompany them, but by December the War Office had done nothing about this contingency "as they had nothing to send."[89]

The Chiefs of Staff disguised or softened differences before reporting to the DPR. They recommended both establishing control over the central Mediterranean and attacking northern Italy by air, but they did not (like the Air Staff) advise that the latter must precede the former, and they did not explain how either of these tactics would cut Italian communications with East Africa. At the DPR meeting of 26 November, Cunliffe-Lister argued that "unless we could operate from southern France the air offensive would lie in Italy's hands."[90] But neither he nor any other minister pressed the main issue: in the event of war, what would be the primary mission of the RAF, and how would the Government determine priorities of supply as between the Air Force and Navy?

In preparing their reports, the Service staffs assumed that threatening or imposing effective sanctions on Italy would lead to war. Both before and after Italy invaded Ethiopia, the Chiefs of Staff used "worst case" estimates of the size and deployment of Italian forces—in the Mediterranean, Egypt, and Red Sea. They wanted prior assurances of support from France (and Yugoslavia, Greece, and even from non-Mediterranean states if possible), but they did not harmonize the air and naval strategies that dictated the substantial degree of the support they expected, and they did not want ministers to do so. Together, these attitudes built up formidable political and strategic preconditions for using coercive diplomacy to prevent or reverse Italian aggression against Ethiopia. The result was to help dampen the spirits of a Government that flirted with ideas of deterrence and coercion even though it too wanted to avoid war.

Inter-Service differences over the Mediterranean crisis were symptomatic of discord in long-term planning for rearmament. In a war with

[88] Brooke-Popham to Ellington, 2 October, Brooke-Popham Papers, II/6 (LHCMA). Montgomery-Massingberd recalled that "a state of almost panic prevailed in Government circles"; autobiography 159 (LHCMA).
[89] Air Staff minutes on Egypt, 23 September, and on southeastern France, 3–5 December, AIR 8/189, 190.
[90] CAB 16/136.

Germany, the General Staff continued to view the Low Countries as a vital strategic objective for both Germany and the West, to be secured early in the war with land forces supported by air squadrons. The Air Staff argued that Germany might start war with a knockout bombing attack on Britain, and that the development of long-range bombers now made the Low Countries less vital to Germany or Britain for advance bases. Formerly preoccupied with defense against air attack, the Air Staff had begun to define the RAF's primary mission as taking the offensive against Germany. Chatfield worried that basing plans on worst cases (a Germany free of eastern entanglements and able to concentrate its land and air forces in the west) might persuade the Service staffs to press continually for levels of force necessary to meet unrealistic circumstances.[91] For Chatfield and the Admiralty, war in the Far East was the worst contingency and the best reason for naval expansion. He did not mention the probability that, so long as long-term planning combined the cases assumed by each of the three Services, the Service staffs would set material and strategic prerequisites for war so high as to inhibit coercive diplomacy in international crises short of war.

Sir Maurice Hankey was probably more aware of inter-Service disagreement than anyone else in London, and certainly more determined to prevent its permeating discussions at ministerial levels. He was Secretary to the Cabinet, DPR, CID, and COS. He chaired the DRC, Deputy Chiefs of Staff (which met in October for the first time since February 1932), and Subcommittee on the Coordination of Departmental Action on the Outbreak of War. In these capacities, Hankey both coordinated and shaped policy. If Britain entered the "precautionary stage" of the War Book (in which mobilization would begin), he would advise the prime minister that the DPR "should continue to act as at present, doing duty as a War Committee."[92] Above all, Hankey amplified expert advice and emphasized how the emergency interfered with long-term planning. He did not "doubt that in the long run we could beat Italy." Agreeing with his colleagues on the DRC, however, he advised Baldwin, Hoare, and Eden that Britain could not rely upon French cooperation, and that the imposition of stiff sanctions might

---

[91] JPC Provisional Report on Defensive Plans for the Event of War against Germany, 1 August, CAB 53/35, discussed by the COS on 29 October, CAB 53/5, where someone (Hankey?) pointed out that the JPC had in fact not assumed the worst—Italy allied with Germany. See Wark's analysis of the various intelligence assumptions in the draft report, *Ultimate Enemy*, pp. 192–95. On the Air Staff's views and the shift toward a strategy of retaliation with bombers, see Bialer, *Shadow*, pp. 128–29; Quester, *Deterrence before Hiroshima*, pp. 85–92; Smith, *British Air Strategy*, pp. 86–89, 156–59.

[92] Hankey to Vansittart, 25 September, J5297/3861/1, FO 371/19199; also Hankey summary of precautionary measures, 20 September, CP 176(35), CAB 24/256.

lead to war. Britain's League policy had brought on this unnecessary confrontation. Conflict in the Mediterranean would seriously injure Britain's long-term rearmament, increase the vulnerability of Britain and the empire to German or Japanese aggression, and leave a permanently hostile Italy "athwart of our main line of communication to the Far East."[93]

The crisis took up the entire agenda at almost every meeting of the Chiefs of Staff and the Joint Planning Committee from August through December. But Hankey refused to allow the total eclipse of long-term planning, on which he wished the JPC, COS, and DPR had been able to concentrate. On 6 September, Hankey asked the COS when they would be ready for a meeting of the DRC, although he realized "how tremendously preoccupied" they were with the Mediterranean emergency.[94] As chairman of the DRC, Hankey achieved compromises between Vansittart and the COS concerning the possible date of German aggression and the likelihood of Anglo-German reconciliation. He preserved the different strategic views of the Services without insisting that they be reconciled in a common strategic doctrine. He told his colleagues that "the Mediterranean problem was a matter which would have to be dealt with separately in due course,"[95] a clear signal that he wanted the DRC to focus on Germany and Japan, with terms of reference that continued to exclude the contingency of war with Italy. He made sure that the DRC's conclusions reached the prime minister, DPR, and Cabinet by early December, and he then advised Baldwin on "the particular machinery for the consideration of the [DRC] Report."[96]

Hankey knew the crisis was not settling previous inter-Service disagreements, including the question of control over the Fleet Air Arm.[97] He was also aware that the crisis revealed weaknesses in the machinery for supply. Neither the DRC nor the Principal Supply Officers Committee recommended the establishment of a Ministry of Supply in time of peace, preferring to rely on interdepartmental committees under the aegis of the Committee of Imperial Defence. Still, there were signs of increasing uneasiness about the existing machinery. Members of the

---

[93] Hankey to Vansittart (20 and 21 November, 19 December), Baldwin (25 November), and Eden (26 December), CAB 63/50; also Hankey diary, 25 November, in Roskill, *Hankey,* 3:186–89. Hankey thought Britain was asking "rather a lot of the French," considering their hope for Italian support against Germany.

[94] Note in CAB 21/434. The JPC met seventeen times in 1935. At the first four of these meetings (January–July), they drafted plans for war with Germany. The next thirteen sessions dealt almost entirely with questions referred by the COS relating to the Mediterranean crisis.

[95] DRC meeting, 30 October, CAB 16/112.

[96] Cab 51(35), 4 December, CAB 23/82.

[97] On Hankey's unsuccessful attempt to mediate between the Admiralty and Air Ministry in the last quarter of 1935, see Roskill, *Naval Policy,* pp. 392–93; Till, *Air Power and Royal Navy,* pp. 49–50.

DRC, who hoped that the Supply Board could speed up its work on plans for the shadow industry, questioned the efficiency of relying on the PSOC to settle inter-Service differences that could not be resolved by the Supply Board. The Air Staff thought it would be impossible "in times of stress . . . to settle competing claims either interdepartmentally or in the Supply Board." And the PSOC itself drew attention to how difficult it was for the peacetime supply organization to provide executive control over production (especially of machine tools).[98]

In July, General Dill recommended to Hankey that intelligence be better coordinated. There was too much "uneconomical duplication" and delay in handling information of interest to two or more departments. Dill suggested enlarging the Committee on Industrial Intelligence in Foreign Countries (FCI) "to embrace all the subjects of intelligence on which joint plans by different Departments depend," and reorganizing the FCI according to various subcommittees (such as the IIC) dealing with specific types of intelligence. In October, the Chiefs of Staff referred this question to the Deputy Chiefs of Staff. Meanwhile, Dill received a report from Military Intelligence on German progress in coordination. All German military intelligence and counterintelligence was coordinated in the Abwehrabteilung. This department belonged to the Wehrmachtsamt, which had "gradually evolved from being primarily a secretariat and semi-civilian administrative office into the nucleus of a supreme Combined Staff." It now included a "national defence section, staffed by all three Services," which a German officer described as "the germ of a German CID Secretariat."[99]

In December, prompted by the Mediterranean crisis and the Government's proclaimed policy of rearmament, critics resumed the campaign for reform of the machinery of defense. Discussion in the *Times*—notably an editorial by B. H. Liddell Hart, military correspondent to the *Times* since the previous March, and a letter by Lord Trenchard, Chief of the Air Staff in the 1920s—called for a reorganization of the CID. A civilian Minister of Defence, aided by a combined staff, should coordinate planning in the three Service departments; the minister should serve as chairman of the CID, relieving the prime minister of daily responsibility for defense; the Secretary to the CID should not simultaneously be Secretary to the Cabinet.[100] On 13 December, in

[98] DRC meetings, 14 and 16 October, CAB 16/112; DRC Third Report, 21 November, CP 26(36), CAB 24/259; Air Staff minutes, 3–5 December, AIR 8/190; PSOC meeting, 24 October, CAB 60/4; Vansittart minute of 30 November, *DBFP*, 15, No. 286.

[99] Dill to Hankey, 22 July, in DCOS 3, CAB 54/3; MI3 appreciation for Dill, 26 August, WO 190/347.

[100] B. H. Liddell Hart, *The Memoirs of Captain Liddell Hart* (London, 1965), 1:315–17. In consultation with Liddell Hart late in November, Geoffrey Dawson (editor) and R. W. Barrington-Ward (deputy editor) "decided that *The Times* should take the initiative in pressing this urgent matter" (p. 315).

response to these and other criticisms, the COS briefly discussed and then postponed the question of whether to strengthen the Joint Planning Committee. Hankey wrote to Trenchard in an unsuccessful attempt to assure him that the current machinery did not suppress inter-Service arguments as he and other critics alleged; on the contrary, Hankey asserted, the present system fully investigated modern forms of warfare and successfully coordinated planning.[101]

Hankey's exasperation with an international crisis beyond his control probably helps account for his temperamental response to Trenchard.[102] He resented the intrusion of events upon the timetable and the machinery for rearmament. He pressed for decisions that he thought would deescalate the emergency and realign the machinery for that long-term agenda. He wanted the Chiefs of Staff to act as a collegial unit able collectively to influence policy at ministerial levels. He discouraged debate on major issues of military doctrine and encouraged the COS to put forward compromise reports that papered over unresolved differences among the Services. One result of this apparent consensus was to increase pressure on the Foreign Office and Cabinet to eschew a policy of coercive diplomacy that risked war. Yet Hankey and the Chiefs of Staff themselves took risks by failing to develop an integrated strategic plan with clear priorities among the Services. This neglect left the Services all the more vulnerable in the coming year to resolutions of problems in supply, strategy, and the machinery of coordination itself, by Chamberlain and any other ministers who preferred coherence to incongruity.

Two kinds of pressure drove the British Government's double policy into the Hoare-Laval pact of December 1935. First, the policy of rearming to meet the German and Japanese menaces rested on the principle that Britain must avoid any conflict that might drain resources, endanger the empire while Britain remained weak, deprive Britain and France of Italian assistance (or at least neutrality) in case of war with Germany, and hinder a general reconciliation of Germany and Europe. This policy equivocated about deterrence beyond self-defense, acknowledged Britain's present vulnerability, and looked toward a stronger position of military preparedness by 1939. Although London did not rule out deterrence or coercive diplomacy while rearming, its

---

[101] CAB 53/5; Hankey-Trenchard correspondence, CAB 21/424; Liddell Hart, *Memoirs*, 1:317–18; Roskill, *Hankey*, 3:180–81, 209.

[102] Hankey and Vansittart manifested what Oran Young describes as anxiety over the difficulty of predicting and planning during a crisis. Under such pressure, policymakers can become uneasy that "the situation has acquired a certain self-sustaining force or impetus of its own and that the ability of individual actors to exercise control over the course of events has therefore declined." *Politics of Force,* pp. 19–20.

concerns about enemies, allies, resources, and time limited the Government's willingness to threaten force in behalf of collective security and increased its readiness to offer concessions.

A less obvious pressure flowed from the policymaking system itself, which disabled collective security while trying unsteadily to sustain it. The Cabinet took long recesses, during which its collective control over policy lost both continuity and precision. Experts wielded telling influence. The DPR's agenda swerved abruptly from rearmament to the Mediterranean emergency and its executive authority increased, causing some confusion over the committee's functions and giving added purchase to the extremely cautious advice of the expert members of the DRC. The Foreign Office was given wide latitude to find a peaceful settlement. Civilian and military officials strengthened their collective position by agreeing among themselves on the interrelationship of political, military, and financial considerations, and by presenting a strong, and often worst case to ministers. Ministers cooperated with experts in adapting the established machinery of policy to the immediate crisis in the Mediterranean. In a manner that illustrates modern cognitive theory, ministers and experts managed the quarrel with Italy as a separate and temporary problem of policy, one that had to be solved peacefully because it upset the machinery as well as the timetable and strategic hypotheses of long-term rearmament.[103]

The Mediterranean crisis had profoundly upset long-term planning and exacerbated Britain's strategic dilemma. Collective security had failed, the Stresa Front had disintegrated, and Anglo-French relations had weakened. There was now the strong possibility of protracted Anglo-Italian enmity. Problems of supply and combined operations arose in the Mediterranean. The Third Report of the DRC recommended much higher expenditure on rearmament, including a shadow industry, than the Cabinet had expected only a few months earlier. Hitler might soon move again to overthrow the Treaties of Versailles and Locarno, undeterred by British rearmament or by Britain's show of force in the Mediterranean.

The repercussions of the present crisis on projected hypotheses called for a comprehensive reevaluation of policy. The promptness, breadth, and coherence of such a study would be influenced by several characteristics already visible in the machinery of policy. First, the like-

---

[103] Even when a high degree of interdepartmental coordination exists, policymakers can use "inconsistency-management mechanisms" to screen out variables, separate issues, and preserve stability in the machinery of policy; Steinbruner, *Cybernetic Theory of Decision*, chaps. 3, 4. "Premature cognitive closure" leads policymakers to hold on to an established view in the face of new information which upsets "image stability" and calls for a change in policy; Jervis, *Perception and Misperception*, pp. 187–91.

lihood of irresolution and delay increased because the DPR's overall responsibility for defense policy became even more uncertain. The committee's broad terms of reference, designed to achieve a comprehensive survey of policy, virtually disappeared while the DPR coordinated policy, strategy, and supply during the emergency. Second, treating the crisis as a separate question of policy inhibited analysis of the permanent effects that this present case might have on ideas of deterrence or on the accepted hypotheses of war with Germany and Japan. Third, although military advisers disagreed among themselves on strategic and material priorities, they used the machinery of coordination to present a united front to ministers—discouraging coercive diplomacy in this crisis and preferential treatment for one Service in the DRC report.

Experimenting with the coercion of Italy in 1935 had convinced these advisers and Hankey that, whether used to pacify Europe (an objective inherited from the 1920s) or to gain time to rearm (a new and recent imperative), appeasement would have to rely largely on diplomacy without showing teeth until Britain was militarily prepared for war. Meanwhile, Britain should not increase the risk of being drawn into conflict by aggravating mad dogs, especially when they were biting someone else. Although not fully embraced by the Cabinet, which continued to vacillate over Britain's international reputation and commitments, this restricted idea of deterrence was a major legacy of the Mediterranean crisis. It had gained legitimacy while the coercive side of the dual policy toward Italy had become, in the eyes of the majority in Whitehall, a symbol of the dangers of extending British deterrence and a source of the disorder about which Eden complained when he succeeded Hoare at the Foreign Office shortly before the New Year.

PART III

THE RHINELAND CRISIS, JANUARY–MAY 1936

[4]

Defense Policy and
the German Question

Erupting shortly after the Government decided to reexamine defense policy, the Mediterranean emergency had revealed weaknesses in British foreign policy and arms. As if to confirm a cycle of introspection and intrusion, the Rhineland crisis broke out in March 1936 just after the Cabinet approved proposals for rearmament and for reorganizing the machinery of defense, issues which the Mediterranean crisis had aggravated and which had displaced foreign policy on the Cabinet's agenda during January and February. The convergence of rearmament, defense coordination, strategic dispersal in the Mediterranean, and Germany's remilitarization of the Rhineland constituted the third stage in British policy since early 1934. For British ideas about deterring Germany, this was the most pivotal stage of all—until Britain guaranteed Poland early in 1939. The system of decisionmaking, internally at odds over rearming Britain and restructuring itself, was caught off-balance by Hitler's sudden action, and floundered as it began to assess the damage done to British deterrence and conciliation. For the second time in six months, an international crisis heightened disorder in British policy, confusion in its machinery, and doubts about deterrence.

Events from January to May 1936 intensified anxiety in London about time. Ministers and expert advisers used such words as "interval" and "gap" to denote a period of unknown length during which Britain must follow a policy of "cunctation" (delay) and rearmament. They recognized that the times had become extraordinary—certainly the pacific climate of the late 1920s had evaporated—and they disagreed over how best to preserve forms of normalcy while preparing for war. This basic uncertainty pervaded pressing subjects: rearmament and strategies of deterrence; reorganization of the machinery of defense; adaptation of appeasement and deterrence to Germany's timing of actions against the status quo; reexamination of foreign policy after the successes of Mussolini and Hitler; and operation of the system of decision-making.

The approval of new and larger Service programs, based on the Defence Requirements Committee's (DRC) Third Report, did not settle questions about the imminence of dangers on three fronts, the duration of rearmament, the preparation of war reserves, or the respective missions of the Royal Air Force and Army in a European war. The question of timing again brought out differences among the Foreign Office, Services, and Treasury. Intelligence reports about German rearmament gave the Foreign Office reason to fear that Germany might be militarily prepared for war before the Service staffs' estimate of 1942. The Service departments, each of which followed a peculiar schedule for rearming, wanted to have adequate "war potential" of supply. To Chamberlain, neither the Foreign Office's anxious conjecturing nor the Services' programs for expansion justified full-scale adoption of the shadow industry scheme to prepare reserves of supply for war.

Implicit in the Cabinet's halfway measures were contradictory ideas about deterrence: the DRC's versatile and incoherent plans for even-handed rearmament of all three Services; Chamberlain's narrow and cogent emphasis on offensive air power. The DRC's strategy, similar to modern theories of conventional and extended deterrence, included dispatching the Field Force to the Continent to hearten France and to deny German conquest of the Low Countries, and rapid implementation of the shadow industry plan. Chamberlain's strategy, like modern theories of nuclear deterrence in its reliance on retaliation from the air, would limit Britain's liability on the Continent, and require only partial adoption of the shadow program. The Cabinet sometimes referred to deterrence in comprehensive terms, which admitted the importance of Britain's reputation in matters of European security, but its decisions showed a preference for Chamberlain's more restrictive ideas, which suggested less concern for opinion in friendly capitals. Both of these strategies were limited in their usefulness for general deterrence while Britain rearmed, and vague about what German actions in Europe would trigger British military response.

To Hankey's dismay, Chamberlain joined the chorus of critics of the machinery of defense, doubting that it could develop a unified strategy for modern warfare. The controversy over defense organization delayed action on rearmament and led to the compromise decision to appoint a new minister without a ministry. The White Paper on Defence, published four days before German troops marched into the Rhineland on 7 March, stressed the expansion and deterrent function of the RAF, and stated confidently that the new minister would help strengthen the coordinating machinery. But Sir Thomas Inskip, appointed Minister for the Coordination of Defence a week after the Rhineland coup, soon discovered that reforming the machinery might not reconcile persistent differences over strategy and supply, both of which affected Britain's deterrent capabilities.

Just when British rearmament and suppositions about European deterrence were gathering momentum, Hitler's move into the Rhineland dashed London's hopes for actually deterring Germany through a combination of military strength and negotiation. The machinery of policy was more efficient in defusing the crisis than in foreseeing it, preventing it, or absorbing its lasting implications. With the exception of Duff Cooper at the War Office, who doubted that time was on Britain's side, ministers and officials from all the major departments agreed that this was neither the time nor the place to risk war. No such consensus simplified the bureaucratic politics of long-term planning. As a new attempt to reassess policy began late in April with the appointment of the Cabinet Committee on Foreign Policy, British foreign policy was adrift and its relationship to defense unclear. Service advisers faulted the Foreign Office for not reducing Britain's strategic liabilities. Especially to Chamberlain's regret, the committee system still lacked the necessary cohesion and decisiveness to resolve competing ideas about the interdependence of diplomacy, strategy, supply, and finance as constituents of deterrence.

REARMAMENT, TIME, AND DETERRENCE

On 4 December 1935, the Cabinet agreed that the prime minister should appoint ministers to consider the DRC's Third Report of 21 November. Two weeks later, a meeting of ministers followed Hankey's advice and referred the report to the DPR, whose membership was slightly changed for this study. In addition to the prime minister (in the chair) and other ministers, Lord Weir sat on this committee, the DPR(DR). The Chiefs of Staff, the Permanent Under-Secretary for Foreign Affairs, and the Permanent Secretary to the Treasury attended as expert advisers, except when the ministers and Lord Weir wished to meet alone. The terms of reference of the committee were to examine the DRC Third Report and make recommendations.[1] These in turn led

---

[1] Cab 51(35), 4 December, CAB 23/82; Hankey note on procedure, 16 December, CAB 21/434; meeting of ministers, 16 December, and terms of reference, 30 December, CAB 16/123. Initially, the DPR(DR) included Baldwin, Ramsay MacDonald, Chamberlain, Eden, Eyres-Monsell, Duff Cooper, Swinton, and Runciman. After the first few meetings, Simon (Home Secretary) and Lord Eustace Percy (Minister without Portfolio) joined the committee.

to Cabinet decisions for large increases in expenditure over the next five years on what could now be called a program of rearmament.

The DPR(DR) met nine times, from 13 to 31 January 1936, and submitted its report to the Cabinet on 12 February. The DRC had expressed alarm at German rearmament, the deterioration of the international situation, and the fact that collective security could involve Britain in international crises "with very little warning." The DRC called upon British diplomacy to avoid a simultaneous conflict with Germany, Japan, and Italy. Although not subscribing to every detail of the DRC's survey, the DPR(DR) agreed that Britain must become "strong and ready" no matter which of four possible policies it followed—collective security, "a more limited system of collective security on the Locarno model," alliances, or isolation. Military strength was necessary to help maintain peace (while hoping for a mutual reduction of armaments in the future), deter Germany and Japan, and defend Britain in case of war. The DPR(DR) endorsed the DRC's argument that it was not at the moment "urgently necessary nor feasible to make provision for a permanently hostile Italy," since Italian enmity might be temporary and because requirements for defense against Japan and Germany would consume all available resources for the three-year period under consideration. Even excluding Italy, however, the DRC had proposed "revised standards of security" for all three Services, and the DPR(DR) examined these critically.[2]

The DPR(DR) approved most of the DRC's recommendations that would, by 1939, bring naval strength up close to the existing approved standard: the ability to send a fleet to the Far East to defend British shipping and territory against Japanese attack, and, at the same time, "to retain in European waters a force sufficient to act as a deterrent and to prevent the strongest European naval power from obtaining control of our vital Home terminal areas while we can make the necessary redispositions." This sanctioned the modified version of the One-Power Standard that had spread from the Admiralty to the DRC and British preparations for the London Naval Conference, which opened in December 1935. But the DPR(DR) took exception to the DRC's recommendation that the Government adopt, in principle, a new (two-power) naval standard. Before taking a decision on the proposed new standard, the ministers wanted to wait "until the practical effects

---

[2] These and the following quotations are from DRC Third Report, 21 November 1935, and DPR(DR) report, 12 February 1936, CP 26(36), CAB 24/259; DPR(DR) first meeting, 13 January, CAB 16/123. On the DRC Third Report, see chapter 2. Gibbs correlates the two reports in *Rearmament*, pp. 254–68. See also Bond, *British Military Policy*, pp. 214–25; Middlemas and Barnes, *Baldwin*, pp. 900–904; Roskill, *Hankey*, 3:197–99.

[could] be more precisely estimated" after receiving the Admiralty's data and recommendations.

The DPR(DR) recommended acceptance of the DRC's proposals for improving Army garrisons at home and abroad, and air defense. And the ministers agreed with the experts that, especially in view of the strategic importance of the Low Countries (where the enemy could position air bases for bombing raids), Britain should be prepared to send a Field Force abroad to protect British interests and to honor Britain's "international obligations, particularly under the Treaty of Locarno." The War Office should concentrate on reconstituting the Regular Field Force—four infantry divisions, a mobile division, two air defence brigades, eight Army Cooperation Squadrons of the Royal Air Force, and support troops—to assist continental allies within a fortnight after the outbreak of war.

The DPR(DR) did not accept the DRC's plan, which would take more than five years, for augmenting this Field Force with twelve divisions from the Territorial Army—to be prepared for action in three contingents at intervals of four, six, and eight months after war began. For the next three years, "the prior needs of the Regular Army, not to mention those of the Navy and the Air Force, will strain to the utmost our productive capacity." The Army's program "should be accepted for a five-year period only, with a view to obtaining within that time a fully efficient Regular contingent of the Field Force, complete with personnel, material and war reserves of all kinds," the latter to include "reserves of ammunition . . . to bridge the gap from the outbreak of war until the war-expanded industry of the country can meet requirements." Meanwhile, although the War Office was authorized to work out plans for modernizing the Territorial Army, the decision whether to implement the DRC's proposals for this force (at an estimated cost of £45 million) should be postponed "for three years, or until such time as the industrial production of the country and its capacity for output brings these proposals within the range of actual possibilities—by which time other factors in the decision may have become clearer."

The DPR(DR) fueled an acceleration of planning in the Air Ministry. The ministers recommended completion of the RAF's Scheme C already authorized by the Cabinet and reiterated by the DRC—123 squadrons (1,512 first-line aircraft) for the Metropolitan Air Force by April 1937. But the DPR(DR) stressed how tentative this goal was in view of the policy of numerical parity with Germany and the "increasing evidence" that Germany would probably build at least 2,000 first-line aircraft. Moreover, the committee wanted the Air Ministry to "have latitude to vary the Royal Air Force programme so as to improve its offensive power and constitute the most effective deterrent against

German aggression," an emphasis on offensive doctrine that had not appeared in the DRC Third Report and departed from the notion of parity in numbers. This task would "involve some increase in numbers in addition to the substitution of larger and more efficient machines for those envisaged in the latter part of the present programme." Apart from reducing the number of Army Cooperation Squadrons for the Territorial Army, the DPR(DR) recommended approval of the DRC's proposals for the expansion of the RAF and the provision of war reserves—including a reserve of 200 percent for first-line aircraft by 1939.

Largely because of the needs of the RAF, the DPR(DR) sanctioned partial implementation of the shadow armament industry, recommending procedures which followed, in many respects, the advice of Lord Weir, who in 1934 had belonged to the small Advisory Panel of Industrialists that had advocated a modest version of this scheme. The ministers agreed with Weir that rearmament should not interfere with normal "production for civil and export trade," for the adverse impact on the "general prosperity of the country" would reduce its capacity to pay for defense. The problem of supply was a "dual one," as Weir had pointed out. Britain had to expand production in order to meet peacetime demand, but also "to build up a reserve of output capacity which can be brought into operation as soon as possible after the outbreak of war. Although these problems must be kept separate, the solution of the first . . . will go some ways towards the solution of the second, since the greater the peace time output the less remains to be done for war." Because imports, government factories, and private firms could not alone make up deficiencies and produce reserves for the earliest stage of war, it would be "necessary not only to create but to put into operation a part of the 'shadow industry' in peace." The committee insisted that the Treasury must maintain financial control, which was not "incompatible with rapidity."[3]

Weir thought it "wiser to develop and adapt the existing supply machinery of the Services to handle the new problems rather than to attempt to create any new Central Government Supply machine." As recommended by the DRC and Lord Weir, the DRC should be the final arbiter in case of inter-Service conflicts over priority; but the DPR(DR) urged that "every effort . . . be made to reach agreement departmentally or through the Principal Supply Officers Organisation before having resort to the [DRC]." Finally, the ministerial committee itself (as the DPR) should watch over industrial production and rearmament,

---

[3] DPR(DR) report, 12 February 1936, CP 26(36), CAB 24/259.

see that delays were overcome, and receive monthly progress reports from each Service department and from the Ministry of Labour.[4]

The DPR(DR) revised the DRC's estimates of expenditure. Compared to the 1935 original Service Estimates of £124 million, the annual budget would increase by about £50,700,000 in 1936 (including provision for special measures connected with the Mediterranean crisis); £88,800,000 in 1937; £101,500,000 in 1938; £80,500,000 in 1939; and £73,000,000 in 1940. The five-year total, £394.5 million, was about 18 percent less than that recommended by the DRC, most of the cuts to come in the financial years 1939–40. The ministerial committee's estimates were only tentative; details would "have to be worked out subsequently and agreed with the Treasury."

The committee did not conclude its report by echoing the DRC's forceful closing statement of difficulties or its Shakespearean appeal to British resolve. The DPR(DR) agreed with the DRC on the importance of inviting the cooperation of all Government departments—notably Labour and Health—to improve recruitment for the Army and to raise the standard of physical fitness. The DPR(DR) recommended that the Cabinet adopt the DRC Third Report as amended. This revised program was itself "subject to later modification, in one direction or another, in accordance with events, and changes in circumstances, which cannot for the moment be accurately foreseen, whether in Europe, the Far East, or the Mediterranean." The ministers praised the DRC as "a very strong Committee with the best technical advice available," the value of whose report would not diminish even if political and strategic considerations should change. On 25 February, the Cabinet approved "generally" the report of the DPR(DR), adding certain emphases.[5]

The Cabinet underlined the provisional nature of the recommended defense programs even more than the ministerial committee had done. These programs were liable to review and modification "in the light of changing circumstances and possibly later decisions as to the priority in which the requirements of the several Services are to be provided in view of the international situation and other factors." The Cabinet reinforced the ministerial committee's views on air power. "The developments in the range and offensive power of aircraft" constituted one of the most important "other factors" that would influence priorities. The Cabinet approved not only completion of Scheme C, but also Lord Swinton's recommendation to increase the size and range of the striking force. After replacing light with medium bombers, Britain could by

<hr>

4 Weir to DPR(DR), 27 January, CAB 16/123; DPR(DR) Report, 12 February, CP 26(36), CAB 24/259. See also Reader, *Architect*, pp. 235–37.

5 DPR(DR) report, 12 February, CP 26(36), CAB 24/259; Cab 10(36), CAB 23/83.

April 1939 have a striking force of 1,022 aircraft, among which even the smallest could reach "the whole of western Germany in their normal range." In this new Scheme F, first-line metropolitan strength would increase from 1,512 to 1,736 by April 1939, with war reserves of about 200 percent. British air rearmament, no longer "window dressing" if Scheme F were completed, now undertook a more muscular air deterrent than before, combining ideas of parity and destructive power for both diplomatic and operational uses. The Cabinet was extremely wary of any implied commitment of troops to fight on the European continent. Both the official and ministerial committees referred to the role of the Field Force largely in terms of assistance to Britain's European allies. The Cabinet, however, expunged "continental allies" and substituted the phrase "assistance required abroad."[6]

The DRC report of November 1935 did not eliminate uncertainties about time—the nearness of threats from Germany and Japan (with all but Chatfield now viewing Germany as probably the nearer), the timetables for completing Service programs, and the gap between drawing up paper plans and preparing actual materials for war. Moreover, the members of the DRC preserved both European and imperial strategies, recommended a balanced rearmament program for all three Services, and disagreed over how to deal with Germany while Britain rearmed. As a result of these multiple positions, the DRC defined deterrence very broadly—Britain must grow militarily stronger before it could hope to deter mad dogs. The revisions of the DRC report by the DPR(DR) and Cabinet indicate that some ministers—notably Chamberlain and Swinton, supported by Lord Weir—resolved to simplify the problem of defense and redefine the meaning of deterrence.

The DRC Third Report, intelligence reports on Germany, and mounting evidence that Germany planned to remilitarize the Rhineland all substantiated Vansittart's view that the threat from Germany was more proximate and serious than the danger of Japanese aggression in the Far East. The sheer quantity of intelligence had increased substantially since 1934. The Committee on Industrial Intelligence in Foreign Countries (FCI) and the Industrial Intelligence Centre (IIC) submitted reports to the Committee of Imperial Defence. The German section in the Air Staff's intelligence directorate collected data and made predictions on the size and disposition of the Luftwaffe. Vansittart augmented his own intelligence network with ominous reports from retired Group

---

[6] Cab 10(36), 25 February, CAB 23/83. The Cabinet had before it Swinton's memorandum, 10 February, CP 27(36), CAB 24/259. The Cabinet also referred to "'battleships versus bombs,'" an issue that would have to be investigated in the light of recent advances in air power. On Scheme F, see Collier, *Defence of the United Kingdom*, pp. 41–42; Gibbs, *Rearmament*, pp. 562–65; Smith, *British Air Strategy*, pp. 159–65; Webster and Frankland, *Strategic Air Offensive*, pp. 70–72.

Captain M. G. Christie, who had served as British air attaché in Berlin 1927–30 and maintained contacts with German politicians and military leaders.

Rivalry and friction among these sources was inevitable. Someone in Chancery at the British Embassy in Berlin criticized the IIC for attributing "to Germany in every respect the sort of Machiavellian superintelligence which is easier to imagine than to create." Although impressed by Foreign Office reports, Military Intelligence held that Germany would not "initiate a European war, involving operations on two fronts, until she has adequate forces to give a reasonable hope of success." In the Secret Intelligence Service (SIS or MI6), the head of European operations thought the Air Ministry and Admiralty were incompetent in the use of intelligence.[7] The General Staff argued that the Luftwaffe would support the German Army, the Air Staff that Germany would launch an air offensive, an assumption which fitted the Air Staff's own strategic thinking but ignored contrary information received by Air Intelligence. Vansittart, Ralph Wigram, and Desmond Morton, head of the IIC, periodically gave information on German air strength to Winston Churchill, who used the press, Parliament, and the CID's Subcommittee on Air Defence Research (of which he was a member) as forums for criticizing the Air Staff for minimizing the pace of German rearmament. Commenting on a "spirited" exchange between Churchill and the Air Ministry in December 1935, Edward Bridges of the Treasury thought the "honours [were] fairly evenly divided." Sir Warren Fisher disagreed and found the Air Staff "far too complaisant in their views about Germany and the air."[8] So did Vansittart, Wigram, and Morton, all of whom believed that Germany would build a Luftwaffe by 1937 larger than the force of 1,500 first-line aircraft which the British policy of parity presupposed. Indeed, Hitler had warned British diplomats that, because of the Franco-Soviet mutual assistance pact of May 1935, German air strength "must be based not on parity with France—as previously asserted—but on a calculation which would take into account Russia's air strength."[9]

As Bridges noted, estimates about Germany were "based to a very

---

[7] Chancery (Berlin) to Foreign Office, 31 December 1935, C61/4/18, FO 371/19883; War Office (MI3) note on CP 13(36) [Eden memo of 17 January], 27 January, WO 190/383. On the SIS, whose budget was increased on the recommendation of the DRC and DPR(DR), see Andrew, *Her Majesty's Secret Service*, pp. 58–59, 343–46, 377; Dilks, "Flashes of Intelligence."

[8] Gilbert, *Churchill*, pp. 685, 688–90, 701–2; Smith, *British Air Strategy*, p. 161; Vansittart, *Mist*, pp. 497–99; Bialer, *Shadow*, pp. 132–33; Bridges and Fisher minutes, 18 and 19 December, T 175/48.

[9] Vansittart memo, 3 February, CP 42(36), CAB 24/260, alluding to Phipps's report of 16 December of conversations he had recently had with Hitler, *DBFP*, 15, no. 383; Vansittart correspondence of February–July in Vansittart Papers (Churchill College, Cambridge), 3/1. See also chap. 5, note 97.

considerable extent on inference." Among the resultant flaws in British intelligence were an inflated image of German efficiency, the difficulty of assessing Germany's potential for industrial production and thus whether Germany planned limited or total war, the worst case assumption that Germany would launch a knockout air offensive against Britain at the start of a European war, and the failure to correlate Germany's economic policy, military strategy, and political objectives. With respect to British ideas of deterrence, perhaps the most serious weakness in intelligence was its lack of information about how Hitler might react to threats of force as he continued to revise the European status quo, and how much he thought Britain would concede short of war.[10]

In spite of intramural and interpretative difficulties, Whitehall was by early February 1936 closer than ever before to agreement that Germany might be ready for war sooner than expected even if industrial production—rather than Hitler's mad-dog propensity—were used as a predictive guide. In February, the Air Staff began to receive Christie's intelligence reports—very skeptically, to be sure, but with the awareness that Swinton did not want this information dismissed as unfounded.[11] Because of new evidence provided to the British military attaché by the German War Ministry, the FCI revised its previous estimate of the rate of expansion of the German Army. It was conceivable that by the summer of 1940, Germany could "have manufactured sufficient armaments to triplicate her peacetime army of thirty-six divisions" (which would be equipped by April 1937), although this was doubtful because of Germany's shortage of foreign exchange for purchasing raw materials. At the Foreign Office, Ralph Wigram was not dissuaded by the FCI's warning that "uncertainty regarding Germany's economic future makes prophecy beyond a few months ahead a hazardous undertaking." Something else caught his attention in the FCI report: whereas the FCI had assumed in June 1935 that Germany could not equip 100 divisions before 1943, this new paper suggested that, "given certain conditions, an earlier date is not impossible."[12]

If Germany could ready itself for war in the next few years, the distance would close between Vansittart's gloomy prediction that Hitler would start a war before militarily prepared (as early as 1937)

[10] Bridges minute, 18 December, T 175/48. For all but the last of these shortcomings in British intelligence, which still awaits investigation, see Hinsley, *British Intelligence*, pp. 59–61, 66–67; Wark, *Ultimate Enemy*; Watt, "British Intelligence."

[11] Wark, *Ultimate Enemy*, pp. 52–54. In early 1936, Wark maintains, the "honeymoon" in British intelligence about Germany was coming to an end; pp. 229–31.

[12] FCI memorandum on the German Army (CID 1209-B), 23 January, printed in *DBFP*, 15, no. 475; Wigram minute, 27 January, C543/4/18, FO 371/19883. On the Foreign Office and FCI, see also note 37 below.

and the Services' more optimistic view that he would not risk war until his forces were ready (no earlier than 1942). Anxiety over this possible compression of time can be seen in British arguments over supply and strategy.

Determined not to upset civil industry and export trade, Lord Weir emphasized that the deficiency program and preparations for a major war were two separate problems. This pronouncement "desperately frightened" the chairman of the Supply Board. "The plain truth," Sir Arthur Robinson wrote to Weir, "is that no really effective preparations for war have yet been made and the root reason for it is because governments have never been prepared to face the question. If anything is said which gives an opening to men to think what a lot they have done and rest on their oars, I am very nervous about the result on supply work." In fact, Robinson asserted, the deficiency program and preparations for a war had interacting needs. Thus, he hoped that Weir would be "piano . . . on the two being different problems."[13]

But Weir was *forte* and had Chamberlain's support, much as Chamberlain had admired Robinson's work at the Ministry of Health in the 1920s and now welcomed his services for rearmament. The DPR(DR) and Cabinet preserved Weir's distinction between making up peacetime deficiencies and increasing the capacity to produce supplies after the outbreak of war. The decision to implement only part of the shadow scheme did not go as far as Robinson and the DRC wished toward ensuring an adequate "war potential" through a system approaching one of war production.

Weir and Chamberlain based their view of supply largely on Britain's economic capacity, Robinson and the DRC on military requirements for defense. These premises coexisted in the recommendations of the DPR(DR) and decisions of the Cabinet. So did different timetables for the Services. The DPR(DR)'s recommendations to the Cabinet refer to the following: 1939 and 1942 as deadlines for completing different portions of the Navy's program, including the Fleet Air Arm; five years (without specifying when this period began) for reconstituting the Regular Field Force and for nearing completion of air defense measures; expansion of the RAF to April 1937 (front-line strength) and beyond (reserves and striking force) on a scale that might vary according to the Air Ministry's judgment; provision of supplies for the "3–5 years' programmes."

If each Service continued to have its own schedule for rearming, when would they together provide adequate strength to prevent Germany and Japan from causing crises, deter them in immediate confron-

---

[13] Robinson to Weir, 22 January, Weir Papers (Churchill College, Cambridge), 18/4.

tations, or win a war? Were those three different dates, or must they coincide? These questions were enmeshed in an increasingly acrimonious debate over strategy, in which diverse opinions pointed in different directions.

In broad terms, members of the DRC and Cabinet agreed that rearmament had both specific and general purposes combining military and political uses. Britain could prevent war with—or defend itself and the empire against—Germany and Japan. Greater military power would improve Britain's capacity to meet its international obligations and appease Europe, through mutual concessions with Germany that would change the status quo without causing war. Stanley Baldwin told his colleagues at the first meeting of the DPR(DR) that collective security had come to mean that every nation had to be stronger "and more ready for war than actually in fact they are today." Strengthening Britain militarily, Anthony Eden argued at the same meeting, would help "get Germany into the system of collective security."[14] In the Cabinet, Eden drew two conclusions from reports received from Phipps in Berlin: Britain must "hasten and complete" its rearmament; while rearming, the Government should "consider whether it is still possible to come to some *modus vivendi* with Germany," not an easy objective considering "the present temper of the German Government and people."[15] Hankey advised Baldwin that the real issue before the DPR(DR) was whether authoritarian systems (Germany and Japan) or democratic systems (Britain and France) would prevail, the former armed to the teeth. With "will and leadership," Britain could rearm and "prevent a war." Otherwise, "we shall perish."[16]

The prevention of war rested on conflicting military strategies: Weir, Chamberlain, and the Air Ministry against Hankey, the DRC and the War Office. Lord Weir had accepted the Government's invitation to join the ministerial committee "on the understanding that he was in all respects a full member" of it, free to offer his advice on every part of the DRC report.[17] The former Secretary of State for Air (1918) and current adviser to Lord Swinton lived in Glasgow, but had rooms in the Adelphi Hotel near Charing Cross for his frequent stays in London, and in these he often drafted his own memoranda. Weir criticized the DRC for not giving sufficient attention to the offensive use of air power. A "striking" force would deter Germany from launching a bombing attack which would paralyze Britain's "nerve centers" and

[14] DPR(DR) meeting, 13 January, CAB 16/123.

[15] Cab 3(36), 29 January, CAB 23/83.

[16] Hankey to Baldwin, 15 January, CAB 21/422.

[17] Runciman to Baldwin, 20 December 1935, CAB 21/422. More correspondence on Weir's appointment can be found in Weir Papers, 17/7.

might "wreck the Empire." He doubted that the Army's strength should be increased beyond modernization and reserves, since Britain's major contribution to its allies would be the Navy and an offensive Air Force. Weir was enthralled by air power, certain that the DRC's program could not be fulfilled in five years without upsetting peacetime industry, and opposed to such a disruption through the kinds of warlike and centralized measures taken by dictatorships. The Army's preparations should provide the strongest possible Regular Field Force within five years, and the question of later contingents (Territorial Army) should be postponed.[18]

Chamberlain subscribed to the strategic and financial implications of Weir's advice. Indeed, the chancellor took credit for Weir's appointment to the DPR(DR), and for asking Weir to write a paper substituting a "fighting Air Force" for an expeditionary force, a view that Chamberlain had held for a long time.[19] In the air deterrent and in the doctrine of "limited liability" in a war with Germany, Chamberlain thought he could reconcile strategy with financial resources and industrial capacity.[20] Chamberlain elaborated in a memorandum for the Cabinet. In a new European war, Germany would be able to occupy the Low Countries with "lightning speed" and establish air bases there before Britain could land an expeditionary force. Britain should therefore "construct the most terrifying deterrent we can think of," an Air Force that had been converted "from a defensive organ into a weapon of aggression with unprecedented powers of destruction."[21]

Chamberlain did not want to be charged with "advocating the *cheapest* way of defence instead of the best." He believed that, if Britain could keep out of war for a few years, "we shall have an air force of such striking power that no one will care to run risks with it." If the next war came, it would not be like the last one, so Britain should concentrate its resources on the Air Force and Navy rather than on "building up great armies."[22] The Mediterranean crisis and Japan's persistent belligerence—Japan insisted on naval equality with Britain and withdrew from the London Naval Conference in mid-January—had dampened Chamberlain's optimistic assumption of two years ear-

---

[18] Weir memorandum, 9 January; DPR meetings, 13 and 16 January; CAB 16/123. On Weir's strategic ideas, see Reader, *Architect*, pp. 205–7, 226–35.

[19] Chamberlain diary, 16 December and 19 January, Chamberlain Papers, NC 2/23a.

[20] DPR(DR) meeting, 14 January, CAB16/123; Bond, *British Military Policy*, pp. 221–25; Dennis, *Decision by Default*, pp. 60–63; Shay, *British Rearmament*, pp. 78–81.

[21] Chamberlain memorandum, "Defence Coordination," 11 February, CP 38(36), CAB 24/260.

[22] Chamberlain diary, 19 January, and Chamberlain to Hilda, 9 February, Chamberlain Papers, NC 2/23a, 18/1/949.

lier that Britain could conciliate Japan, avoid war in the Far East, and curtail naval rearmament.

Changes in personnel and doctrine in the Air Ministry made Chamberlain all the more confident about air power expansion. Swinton advocated the strategy of air offensive. Educated at Winchester and University College, Oxford, and a war veteran (Military Cross), Swinton was canny, capable, and knew industry well. Like Chamberlain, he thought Britain could build a powerful air force in a consumer economy that preserved capitalism and sought full employment. He and Group Captain Arthur Harris—recently appointed Deputy Director of Plans and later head of Bomber Command (1942–45)—extolled the deterrent power of a strong force of bombers which, backed by reserves and capable of offensive strikes against Germany, would make it unnecessary to send the Army to the Continent.[23]

Hankey and the War Office fought back. Hankey, who had originally wanted Weir on the DPR(DR), now spoke against him, declaring that the Army and Navy had fallen behind the Air Force in rearming, and that the DRC had agreed on a balanced plan for all three Services in order to provide an effective deterrent. For political and military reasons, the Field Force must be reinforced by the Territorial Army and ready to help prevent German seizure of the Low Countries. Pownall agreed with Hankey: limited liability was a "dangerous heresy"; if war came again, "our effort *must* be the maximum, by land, sea and air."[24] Montgomery-Massingberd, recently promoted to field marshal, contended that air power provided no proven substitute for land forces. German occupation of the Low Countries would make the effect of the air deterrent even more dubious than it already was because of London's vulnerability to air attack. Britain must be prepared to support France and drive back a German invasion of the Low Countries "at the earliest possible moment."[25] Uneasy about not having a broad base of counsel in the War Office, where some officers opposed a continental commitment, Duff Cooper sought the advice of B. H. Liddell Hart, whose position at the *Times* gave him access to policymakers as well as unofficial defense experts. In Liddell Hart's opinion, a small mechanized Field Force would be superior to a large number of infantry

[23] For the strategic views of Swinton and Harris: Swinton memorandum, 10 February, CP 27(36), CAB 24/259; Cross, *Swinton*, pp. 157–59; Smith, *British Air Strategy*, pp. 87–89, 160.

[24] DPR(DR) meeting, 14 January, CAB 16/123; Hankey to Baldwin, 15 January, CAB 21/422; Roskill, *Hankey*, 3:197; Bond, *British Military Policy*, p. 224; Bond, *Chief of Staff*, pp. 97–99.

[25] Massingberd notes: on Weir's memo of 9 January (see note 18 above), circulated to DPR(DR) on 15 January, CAB 16/123; and on Chamberlain's memo of 11 February (see note 21 above), CAB 21/424.

divisions if troops must be sent to the Continent. Better yet, air power should be used on the Continent at the start of a war, with the Army held in strategic reserve for imperial defense in the Near and Far East.[26] Unconvinced, Duff Cooper supported the DRC's recommendations. He wanted the Cabinet to decide now on the policy of reinforcing the Regular Field Force with Territorials, even if expenditure on these reserves were postponed for three years.[27]

Unwilling to choose between alternative strategies, the Government preserved the continental contingency without providing the necessary funds for the Army to execute it in strength. Baldwin and other ministers (notably Eden, who had fought in France and lost one brother there and another at Jutland) feared that public opinion "would rise up in anger at the idea of the Territorials being sent to 'another Passchendaele.'"[28] This political consideration helped persuade the DPR(DR) and Cabinet to find a middle ground between the DRC's report and the views of Chamberlain, who regarded Duff Cooper's effectiveness in the Cabinet to be limited by his penchant for shooting and champagne.[29]

In this compromise, the DPR(DR) and Cabinet implicitly endorsed contradictory strategies of deterrence, moving closer than before to Chamberlain's ideas. Already visible in 1934, the difference between these strategies crystallized in the winter months of 1935–36. For shorthand convenience, the two can be named after the DRC and Chamberlain, respectively. Neither was carefully defined as a theory for general and immediate deterrence, with an orderly sequence of propositions, evidence, and course of action. Still, at the risk of historical reductionism, one can see form in each.

The DRC strategy was the more comprehensive, versatile, and incoherent of the two. It involved thorough rearmament, the merging of

[26] Liddell Hart conversations with Duff Cooper, 14 December 1935 and 18 January 1936, and Liddell Hart to Cooper, 22 January, Liddell Hart Papers, 11/1935/115 and 1936/28, and 1/247 (LHCMA); Liddell Hart, *Memoirs*, 1:293–301. According to Liddell Hart, the Ethiopian crisis reinforced the argument for limiting the Army's role to imperial defense. See also Dennis, *Decision by Default*, pp. 54–55. For a debatable reevaluation of Liddell Hart's strategic ideas in the 1930s and his influence on policy, see John Mearsheimer, *Liddell Hart and the Weight of History* (Ithaca, N. Y., 1988), chaps. 5, 6.

[27] DPR(DR) meetings, 14 and 16 January, CAB 16/123.

[28] Bond, *Chief of Staff*, Pownall diary entry of 27 January (quoting Eden on Passchendaele), p. 99.

[29] DPR(DR) meetings, 16 and 27 January, CAB 16/123; DPR(DR) Report, 12 February, CP 26(36), CAB 24/259; Cab 10(36), 25 February, CAB 23/83; Chamberlain diary, 19 January and 10 February, Chamberlain Papers, NC 2/23a. The American Embassy reported to Washington that the "lack of precision" in British policy (rearming yet reluctant to take risks) could be traced to Whitehall's divisions over rearmament; Richard A. Harrison, "Testing the Water: A Secret Probe towards Anglo-American Military Co-operation in 1936," *International History Review* 7 (1985), 218–19.

supply for peacetime deficiencies and wartime reserves, and the commitment of air, land, and naval forces to the defense of Western Europe and the empire. Deterrence on this scale was very expensive, and it might not be palatable to the British public. Although the DRC opposed the extended show of force in the Mediterranean, it used the emergency to illustrate the importance of strengthening all three Services for contingencies that might arise without much warning, and for the possibility that the Government would employ force to prevent crises, limit conflict, and defend British interests.

Because of its advocacy of broad rearmament for many deterrent contingencies, according to the strategic plans of each Service, the DRC strategy resembles modern theories of conventional and extended deterrence. In these, the deterring nation's commitment derives credibility from its placing substantial conventional forces on or near allied territory. The "local" military capability to deny conquest of this territory may prove a more persuasive deterrent than the threat of "strategic" retaliation, which might indeed not follow an aggression against allies alone.[30]

The flexibility of the DRC strategy, however, rested in part on differences among members of the committee. Vansittart believed that rearming in breadth and adopting an emergency state of industrial production would increase Britain's diplomatic leverage on Hitler during the next few years, that a continental commitment of land forces was politically necessary (Fisher concurred), and that Britain's credibility was bound up with foreign policies not easily abandoned or immunized against the appearance of encircling Germany. Hankey and the Chiefs of Staff took a dim view of threatening force to protect other countries before the Services thought themselves ready for conflict, and would rather reduce Britain's liabilities than base its credibility on military weakness. Although Hankey and Massingberd supported a continental commitment, they and their military colleagues were much less willing than Vansittart to extend British deterrence by reassuring France or considering the security of Eastern Europe a British interest. Ellington neither rejected outright nor strongly endorsed the Army's role on the Continent. Chatfield still thought Japan more dangerous than Germany, and imperial defense more pressing than the security of Western Europe.

[30] George and Smoke, *Deterrence in American Foreign Policy*, pp. 41–42; Huntington, "Renewal of Strategy," pp. 21–23; Huth, *Extended Deterrence*, chap. 3; Mearsheimer, *Conventional Deterrence*, pp. 28–30; Robert Jervis, *The Meaning of the Nuclear Revolution: Statecraft and the Prospect of Armageddon* (Ithaca, N. Y., 1989), p. 141; Jack S. Levy, "Quantitative Studies of Deterrence Success and Failure," in Stern et al., *Perspectives on Deterrence*, pp. 107–17.

The future of the DRC strategy was as uncertain as the date when Britain might have adequate military strength to deter dictatorships—in negotiations or in dangerous political collisions, with or without allies. Vansittart would have named an earlier date than Hankey or the COS—partly because of his estimate of the German threat, partly because he thought general deterrence could precede completion of the requisite forces for preventing or winning a war in a specific crisis, and partly out of concern for Britain's political reputation abroad. But would not his own frightening appraisal of the rate of German rearmament suggest that Britain might be unable in the next few years to reach the position of strength necessary for such deterrence? If Britain's rearming did not check German rearmament or prevent explosive crises, would not the failure of general deterrence discourage potential allies, encourage enemies, and lose time for Britain? Hankey and the COS—and the Air Staff—would have given a later date. They equated both general and immediate deterrence with military preparedness for war, they perceived deterrence largely in terms of self-defense, and they thought the German threat would peak when Hitler's military advisers told him they were ready. In the meantime, however, what would prevent Germany from taking a series of steps whose cumulative effect so changed the status quo that war broke out before Britain was prepared to win it? If Hitler did wait as long as his military experts advised, why should Britain's experts adopt the same date as the best time to fight? Could the country produce the supplies and pay the costs necessary for meeting either Vansittart's or the COS timetable for deterrence?

Chamberlain criticized the DRC Third Report as "an aggregate of three Service plans," and proposed a coherent alternative.[31] He and Weir would simplify deterrence by tying it to air power and underscoring the security of the United Kingdom. By adopting this intrinsically narrow strategy, the Government could preserve normal industrial production, reduce its liability to send forces to the Continent, cut the costs and limit the period of rearmament, and win public support. Expanding the RAF was the quickest way to prepare a deterrent against Germany and would make it easier for the Government to estimate the date of readiness—an offensive force with reserves by 1939. British diplomacy would be strengthened by the palpable construction of this force, but should not take risks until it was ready. While the DRC's map for deterring Germany encompassed Western Europe, Chamberlain's was shrinking to the prevention of war against Britain, with commensurately less regard for potential allies. Like modern theories of nuclear deterrence, his European strategy gave little

[31] Chamberlain memo on defense coordination, 11 February, CP 38(36), CAB 24/260.

consideration to the use of force in limited contingencies or to "conventional" methods of war, and weakened any notion of extended deterrence insofar as allies would doubt British retaliatory intentions if Germany did not attack Britain itself.

If Hitler remained unimpressed by British air rearmament, what would prevent Germany from upsetting the status quo either before or after Britain had completed its striking force? If war broke out, would the deterrent force designed to prevent it discourage Germany from striking first or retaliating in kind after British bombing raids? If Hitler used air forces to support his armies, would the RAF support the Field Force and Britain's allies? Would this cooperation be sufficient to defend or liberate the Low Countries and France? With regard to diplomacy, operations, and supply, what differences were there between deterrence for a short war and for a long war of attrition? That Chamberlain did not dwell upon these questions may be one measure of his confidence that Hitler was not as mad as Vansittart believed and that British air power could prevent war in Western Europe.

Both strategies could be adapted to the general deterrence of Germany in European politics while Britain rearmed. Yet both also limited the capacity for general deterrence: the DRC's strategy, as visualized by Hankey and the COS, gave the Government no brief to threaten force short of completing rearmament across all three Services; Chamberlain's more logical plan reduced the suppleness of deterrence, both geographically and militarily. Both strategies envisaged the threat of British action if Germany went too far, but they left open the designation of what postwar theorists call the "trip wire" for retaliation: certainly an attack against Britain; probably unprovoked aggression against Belgium and France; probably not a war in Eastern Europe. Neither strategy could show that Hitler understood its terms—where Britain would draw the line and what costs Hitler would have to pay if he crossed it.[32]

Neither the DRC nor Chamberlain drew an explicit relationship between air defense and deterrence. Wing Commander E. J. Hodsoll, on the staff of the recently established Air Raid Precautions Department in the Home Office, assumed that Britain would come under "heavy and continuous air attack over some period." He had begun "to feel that until we have survived this attempt to disrupt our morale and disorganize our life and industry, it will be very difficult—it may even be

---

[32] For deterrence in cases of limited war or crisis prevention, a major problem is how to influence the opponent's calculation of costs and risks "rather that simply threatening overwhelming military costs"; George and Smoke, *Deterrence in American Foreign Policy*, pp. 51–52. Neither the DRC nor Chamberlain had given much thought to this problem, let alone solved it.

temporarily impossible—to initiate or maintain a land campaign on the Continent."[33] The implications of this apprehension supported neither dispatching the Field Force nor concentrating on bombers, but they corroborated the opinion of those less audible members of the Air Staff who would concentrate resources on the development of fighters for defense.

The DRC and Chamberlain strategies, the discord between them, and the questions they begged, rested partly on methods and supplies for waging war. Whether methods were integrated and supplies adequate underlay the controversy over defense coordination, in which critics blamed the existing machinery for incoherence and indecision.

REORGANIZATION AND THE WHITE PAPER ON DEFENCE

On 8 January 1936, in response to mounting pressure outside the Government for a reorganization of the machinery of defense, Hankey sent his views to the Chiefs of Staff and Sir Warren Fisher.[34] Over the next month, discussion centered on Hankey's memorandum and on the preparation of a paper by the COS. To Hankey's consternation, opinion inside the Government divided more sharply than he had expected. Supporting Hankey were Fisher, Massingberd, and Chatfield. Ellington disagreed with these former colleagues on the DRC, and soon the Air Staff wanted the question reviewed at the ministerial level, where Hankey did not like to reveal inter-Service differences, and where a number of Cabinet members proved more sympathetic to reform than Hankey had assumed. The controversy snarled Cabinet and parliamentary action on defense requirements, subsided with the appointment of a Minister for the Coordination of Defence, but never completely vanished because of nagging questions about the coordination of strategy and acceleration of supply.

Hankey rejected the critics' proposals for a civilian Minister of Defence who would chair the CID and COS. This would involve "dual control, not only between the Prime Minister and the Minister of Defence but between the Minister of Defence and the . . . Service Ministers." Experience during the Great War and in the period 1922–25 (when the prime minister had not chaired the CID or COS) had shown the weaknesses of systems of dual control. The present system worked

---

[33] Hodsoll to Hankey, 22 February, CAB 21/424.

[34] Hankey memorandum, 8 January, AIR 8/207. For other accounts of the reorganization controversy, see Johnson, *Defence by Committee*, pp. 234–36; Meyers, *Britische Sicherheitspolitik*, pp. 215–29; Middlemas and Barnes, *Baldwin*, pp. 908–12; Naylor, *Man and Institution*, pp. 242–44; Roskill, *Hankey*, 3:202–13.

smoothly during the Italo-Ethiopian crisis, when "questions have been handled expeditiously, and if there have been any slight differences of opinion they have been settled promptly without recourse to ministers." The machinery was also adequate for the rearmament programs already under way, although Hankey admitted that the organization for supply needed much improvement, blaming its inadequacies on the now defunct "Ten Year Rule" and on "the consequent lack of funds." Proposals were already under consideration to strengthen the Joint Planning Committee, the coordination of intelligence, and the Secretariat. Far from "throwing the Air Forces and mechanization generally into the background," the present system was a "progressive" one. Thanks to this machinery, to the Imperial Defence College, and above all to the spirit of teamwork, "a common doctrine [was] growing up in the three Services whose mutual requirements and interdependence [were] now generally realised."[35]

Fisher upheld Hankey in a mordant letter to Baldwin, dismissing the critics as impractical "crusaders," who neither knew nor discussed the operation of "the whole machine of government," of which defense by committee formed a part. The proposed Minister of Defence, without a department below him, would "have no executive authority"; he would damage the constitutional link between ministers and experts by supervising too closely the work of civil servants, and by himself advising his Cabinet colleagues "in lieu of their professional advisers." True, Fisher argued, the organization of industry for war must be improved, and he recommended that Lord Weir be assigned the task of coordinating and accelerating plans for supply, but this would be a far cry from a minister who presided over virtually the entire machinery of defense.[36]

The Chiefs of Staff approved the recommendations of the Deputy Chiefs of Staff that an inter-Service intelligence committee be established.[37] Chatfield favored strengthening the JPC and the machinery

---

[35] Hankey memorandum, "Defence Coordination," 7 February, CP 30(36), CAB 24/259. (This is a slightly revised version of the document cited in the preceding note.) In fact, the difference between the Admiralty and Air Ministry over the use of air forces in a war with Italy was more than slight. Pownall alluded to this debate, which had not been "presented to ministers as a conflict of opinion"; minute of 17 February, CAB 21/424.

[36] Fisher to Baldwin, 13 January, PREM 1/196; copies sent to Hankey, Chamberlain, and the Chiefs of Staff, CAB 21/424.

[37] COS meeting, 13 January, CAB 53/5; DCOS report, 1 January, CAB 4/24, and meetings of 29 October and 29 November, CAB 54/1; report by ad hoc subcommittee of DCOS, 17 December, CAB 54/3. Chaired by Hankey, the Deputy Chiefs of Staff included Vice Admiral W. M. James (Deputy Chief of Naval Staff), Major General J. G. Dill (Director of Military Operations and Intelligence), and Air Vice Marshal C. L. Courtney (Deputy Chief of the Air Staff). The DCOS also recommended (and the COS agreed) that the scope of the CID's subcommittee on Industrial Intelligence in Foreign Countries (FCI)

for supply, but not by appointing a "super staff" and a Minister of Defence. Massingberd concurred. But Ellington wanted to go further than the others. He recommended appointing a minister responsible for "industrial preparations," and held that, although assistants appointed to the JPC should of course keep in touch with their respective departments, they should be freed from all departmental duties except for the preparation of joint plans.[38]

Ellington heeded the advice of experts in the Air Ministry, where the reform movement had its strongest departmental footing. The Air Staff considered the present supply system inadequate for settling competing inter-Service claims in the event of war.[39] The Joint Planning Committee should be assisted by a permanent junior staff that could devote most of its time to planning ahead; the JPC would then be "less continually surprised by emergency situations for which no preparations have been made."[40] An official in the Air Ministry disputed the claims of both Fisher and Hankey. The critics did not charge that the machinery worked badly in the Mediterranean crisis, but that it was "defective for framing long-range policy." Controversy between a minister for defense coordination and the Service ministers "must be accepted as inevitable, and the argument for its acceptance is that the public interest would be better served by bringing legitimate differences of opinion on defence policy into an arena where they can be more freely discussed."[41]

Air Vice Marshal C. L. Courtney, Deputy Chief of Air Staff and Director of Operations and Intelligence, criticized the draft report prepared by the Secretariat following the Chiefs of Staff meeting of 13 January.[42] The report painted a "misleading picture" of the COS. It also gave the impression that the DRC Third Report presented a coordinated scheme of the roles of the three Services, whereas the DRC treated the Services separately with no general discussion of defense "as a coordinated whole" except for questions of supply and industrial mobilization. Ellington followed Courtney's line. He praised Hankey's skill in coordinating the work of the Services, but added that the sys-

---

should be expanded to include "Air Targets Intelligence." The CID approved both recommendations on 30 January. The Foreign Office representative on the FCI, F. T. A. Ashton-Gwatkin, thought this committee and the affiliated Industrial Intelligence Centre were likely to expand, "especially under a new Minister of Defence, into a general clearing house of intelligence, in which the Foreign Office would be considerably interested." Minute of 17 February, W 1382/80/50, FO 371/20453.

[38] COS meeting, 13 January, CAB 53/5.
[39] Air Staff minutes, 3–5 December 1935, AIR 8/190.
[40] Air Staff minute, 8 January, AIR 8/207.
[41] Ibid., minutes by C. C. Evans, 18 January.
[42] Ibid., COS draft report, 20 January, and Courtney minute, 21 January.

tem should not depend on the chance of personality, and that the Chiefs of Staff should have a civilian chairman. Hankey replied that this would be a disaster. Unable to persuade the other Services that the COS should be chaired permanently by a civilian who would coordinate defense planning, the Air Staff decided to rev up this question to ministers. Meanwhile, Ellington agreed to sign a compromise COS document.[43]

In its report on coordination, dated 10 February, the COS judged the present machinery adequate for both this emergency and rearmament, and advised against the appointment of a Minister of Defence and an independent joint staff under his authority. They recommended strengthening the Joint Planning Committee by the addition of a full-time secretary and three assistant members, who "must not be entirely cut off from departmental work in . . . their respective Ministries." Finally, the COS stated that the Principal Supply Officers Committee was more qualified than themselves to advise on whether to appoint a Minister of Supply.[44]

Hankey apparently assumed that the tempest of coordination could be kept in a teapot by a united Cabinet. Hankey avowed that it was "for the Government alone to decide on the machinery by which they transact business. No one else really knows anything about it."[45] He miscalculated. The reform movement gained momentum at the ministerial level, where the DRC report had recently been found wanting in offensive air doctrine. Swinton and Chamberlain identified structural flaws in the defense machinery, which the Cabinet should examine even if this delayed its consideration of the DPR(DR) report on rearmament. Indeed, they reckoned that reorganization would help them enforce their views on air power at the center of rearmament policy.

On 10 February, Swinton informed the Cabinet of his disagreement with Hankey. Swinton called for the appointment of a Minister without Portfolio who would act as deputy chairman of the CID and chairman of the COS, and who would supervise the organization of supply. Even under Hankey, the system might not be working perfectly. The Chiefs of Staff sometimes compromised "to avoid difficulties rather than to face them," at a time when "new issues must cut across traditional policy and traditional prejudices." The ministerial chairman would neither dictate policy nor "usurp the functions of the Prime Minister," but he would ensure that policies and differences of opinion were dis-

[43] Ibid., Ellington to Hankey, Chatfield, and Montgomery-Massingberd, 23 January; COS meeting, 24 January, CAB 53/5. "The silly chap" surprised the other Service chiefs and Hankey, Pownall wrote in his diary; Bond, *Chief of Staff*, p. 98.
[44] COS report, "Coordination of Defence," 10 February, CP 36(36), CAB 24/260.
[45] Hankey to Coxwell (Admiralty), 7 February, CAB 21/424.

[178]

cussed fully and frankly. Finally, the chairman should be assisted by a full-time combined staff, not parallel to but "working to" the Chiefs of Staff.[46]

Next day Chamberlain proposed an inquiry into defense coordination, but his paper revealed anxieties and contained allegations that took Hankey by surprise. The chancellor praised Hankey's "unequalled authority and experience," and he blamed financial restrictions for thwarting the Services' earnest efforts to adapt "to the new methods of warfare." But Chamberlain noted that "in planning for a given series of operations there is a choice of the relative importance of the part to be played by two or all of the Services." He doubted that, in the present system, "a completely objective view [could] be taken by the men who are themselves the heads of Services, each with specific and sometimes even diverging responsibilities." He reproved the DRC for not giving sufficient attention to modern air power, and for submitting a report that appeared to be the sum of three plans, "rather than a joint plan conceived *ab initio* in the light of recent developments. No alternative was put before us, and there was no source from which such an alternative could be requested."[47]

Hankey was shaken by Chamberlain's memorandum, and also by the Commons Debate of 14 February. In the debate, Clement Attlee called for "a unity of defence doctrine, not three separate doctrines." Leopold Amery agreed. Austen Chamberlain declared that war was now "an affair of nations," and defense encompassed strategy, economic resources, civil activities, and labor. Appointing a full-time minister to coordinate these activities would help assure the country "that everything is being done to prevent a continuance or recurrence of such events as those [miscalculating German air strength and negotiating the Hoare-Laval pact] for which the Prime Minister has twice stood at the Table of this House within the last two years, to ask the pardon of the House."[48]

Now Hankey was sure that "some concession" would have to be made. He therefore proposed to Baldwin a compromise plan, one that would not "upset the psychology of the whole machine" and force him to resign the following year.[49] The prime minister would remain chair-

[46] Swinton memorandum, "Coordination of Defence," 7 February, CAB 21/424.

[47] Chamberlain memorandum, "Defence Coordination," 11 February, CP 38(36), CAB 24/260. In this paper, he did not propose any specific reforms, for they "would at once have been damned by the Chiefs of Staff"; Chamberlain to Ida, 16 February, Chamberlain Papers, NC 18/1/949.

[48] 308 *HC Debates*, 14 February, *Parliamentary Debates*, Commons, Fifth Series, cols. 1295–1378; Amery, *Empire at Bay*, p. 408.

[49] Hankey to Baldwin, 14 February, PREM 1/196; copy and letter to Fisher in CAB 21/424.

man of the CID, but a deputy chairman would preside over meetings of that committee and the DPR in the prime minister's absence. The deputy would also chair the Chiefs of Staff whenever he thought it desirable or when the chiefs requested it, but he would normally leave questions of strategic planning to the chiefs "to discuss alone," and the COS must retain "the right of initiative." The deputy would replace the president of the Board of Trade as chairman of the PSOC.

Baldwin had hoped that the Cabinet would be able to discuss the report of the DPR(DR) at a special meeting on Monday, 17 February. At this Cabinet, however, he declared that consideration of the question of organization, in which "Parliament was now taking a lively interest," should precede discussion of defense requirements.[50] Baldwin, Lord Eustace Percy, and some other members of the Cabinet were especially impressed by the "large measure of assent" that had greeted Austen Chamberlain's criticism of the Chiefs of Staff in the Commons Debate of 14 February. Having been recently preoccupied with the illness, death (20 January), and funeral of King George V, the prime minister admitted to the Cabinet that he had not been able to deal effectively with the enormous increase in defense activities. The Government could satisfy the House of Commons by appointing a minister, and should also "reply to the many unfair things that had been said about the present organisation." The general mood at this Cabinet meeting was disposed to reform, partly in response to parliamentary pressure, partly from an awareness—heightened by Swinton and Chamberlain—that defense coordination actually needed improvement.

The Cabinet Committee on Coordination of Defence, which met on 18 and 19 February, acknowledged both the merits of the existing system and the need to improve coordination because of the increasing importance of defense policy. On the nineteenth, the committee discussed a draft prepared by Baldwin, Chamberlain, Simon, and Hankey. The draft proposals resembled Hankey's compromise plan, but were amended, on Hankey's advice, to prevent the new joint planners from becoming independent of the Service staffs and presenting different advice to the Chiefs of Staff.[51]

Before the Cabinet considered the revised draft on coordination, Baldwin had begun the search for someone to fill the post that the Government was about to create. Baldwin's interest in appointing Chamberlain indicates that he wanted the new position to be an im-

---

[50] Cab 7(36), 7 February, CAB 23/83.
[51] Meetings of 18 and 19 February, CAB 27/600. Members of the committee: Baldwin, Ramsay MacDonald, Chamberlain, Hailsham (Lord Chancellor), Simon, Eden, the three Service ministers, William Ormsby-Gore, Ernest Brown, and Percy.

portant one. Chamberlain declined and recommended Hoare, arguing that "the Cabinet was not strong enough in debating power to be able to afford the luxury of Sam as critic," and that the new post would require "a great deal of initiative."[52] Duff Cooper doubted that the duties of the new minister would lighten the prime minister's burden or increase coordination and efficiency.[53] Hankey concurred. He was "far from satisfied," but hoped that "British common sense will prevail and that we shall shake down to a system as promising as the starting point of these changes."[54]

On 24 February, the Cabinet approved with minor changes the recommendations of the Committee on Coordination. A deputy chairman of the CID would be appointed, without altering the constitutional duties of the Chiefs of Staff.[55] The reforms were less than many critics desired, more than Hankey would have preferred in his compromise plan. The deputy chairman would have the following duties:

(i) The general day-to-day supervision and control on the Prime Minister's behalf of the whole organisation and activity of the Committee of Imperial Defence; the co-ordination of executive action and of monthly progress reports to the Cabinet or any Committee appointed by them on the execution of the reconditioning programmes; discernment of any points which either have not been taken up or are being pursued too slowly and (in consultation with the Prime Minister or other Ministers or Committees as required) of appropriate measures for their rectification;

(ii) In the Prime Minister's absence taking the chair at the Committee of Imperial Defence and the Defence Policy and Requirements Committee;

(iii) Personal consultation with the Chiefs of Staff together, including the right to convene under his Chairmanship the Chiefs of Staff whenever he or they think desirable;

(iv) The Chairmanship of the Principal Supply Officers Committee, which will include the Chief Industrial Adviser to His Majesty's Government or his deputy, the Permanent Secretary to the Board of Trade and the Permanent Secretary to the Ministry of Labour;

(v) Making recommendations as to any improvements that he thinks necessary in the organisation of the Committee of Imperial Defence.

[52] Chamberlain diary, 11, 16, 21 February, Chamberlain Papers, NC 2/23a; Feiling, *Life of Chamberlain*, pp. 277–78; Macleod, *Chamberlain*, p. 192. After breakfasting with Baldwin on 20 February, Tom Jones concluded that Hoare was now Baldwin's choice, which would disappoint "those who desired Winston" and please "those who dreaded Eustace Percy." Jones, *Diary*, p. 175.

[53] Duff Cooper to Hankey, 21 February, CAB 21/424.

[54] Hankey to Duff Cooper, ibid. Pownall thought "the right man" could have "plenty of scope . . . though Hank would never admit it"; Bond, *Chief of Staff*, p. 103.

[55] Cab 9(36), CAB 23/82.

The Chiefs of Staff would preserve "unimpaired the right to submit confidential reports of their collective military view to the Chairman or Deputy Chairman of the [CID]." The deputy chairman would not "normally" attend the meetings of the COS, but would "supplement the present activities and initiative of the [COS] by guidance and initiative of his own," ensuring that the COS fully and frankly considered "every aspect" and differences of opinion as well. The three additional officers of the JPC, to be graduates of the Imperial Defence College, would remain in close touch with their departments in the preparation of joint plans for the Chiefs of Staff. A deputy secretary would be appointed to the CID, as well as an extra officer who would serve as full-time secretary to the new planning staff of the JPC. Finally, the Government would prepare to announce these steps in the approaching parliamentary debates "and to rebut the mis-statements and injustices regarding the existing organisation and its achievements."[56]

Having agreed upon these modest reforms in defense coordination, the Cabinet turned to defense requirements and the forthcoming White Paper on Defence. The Cabinet's approval of the DPR(DR) report may be said to mark the formal beginning of British rearmament, yet in the White Paper the Cabinet did not wish to give the full extent of its decisions. The paper should not mention the possibility of adopting a new naval standard, or the exact number of capital ships and aircraft carriers provisionally approved for construction beyond 1936, or the increase in funds for the Secret Intelligence Service. Any reference made to Lord Weir should be very discreet. And, Chamberlain advised, the White Paper should "avoid figures which could be added up to a larger amount than public opinion was anticipating."[57]

Progress on the White Paper had been delayed by the discussion of defense coordination and, consequently, by the postponement of the Cabinet's consideration of defense requirements. By 25 February, Hankey was sure that the White Paper would include something on coordination, although he was still unable to tell the prime minister exactly what lines the entire paper would take.[58] Parliament forced the Government's hand. Lord Halifax was unable to persuade Lord Salisbury to postpone from 27 February his motion for a debate on coordination, and the Cabinet agreed that it would be damaging to try once again to "stonewall" in Parliament. Not wanting to offend the House of Commons, which expected to be the first to hear the announcement of

---

[56] Cab 9(36), 24 February, CAB 23/83; CP 51(36) Revise, 24 February, CAB 24/260, formally approved by the Cabinet on 26 February, Cab 11(36), CAB 23/83.
[57] Cab 10(36), 25 February, CAB 23/83.
[58] Hankey to Wilson, 25 February, PREM 1/196.

important decisions, Baldwin informed the House that the Government had decided to appoint a deputy chairman for defense matters, add three officers to the Joint Planning Committee, and augment the Secretariat.[59] In the House of Lords, Swinton spoke to Salisbury's motion, but he implicitly attributed more power to the deputy chairman than the Cabinet as a whole had intended.[60]

Because of parliamentary pressure and the possibility of slips like Swinton's, the Cabinet needed to declare its policy clearly and soon. The Cabinet discussed the draft White Paper at two special meetings on Monday, 2 March. Chamberlain advised against giving precise figures of expense to the House of Commons because of the uncertainty of the future and because the original Service Estimates of 1936 already exceeded those of 1935 without including expenditure on the measures recommended by the ministerial committee on defense requirements, costs that would necessitate supplementary estimates.[61] (The original estimates for 1936, published later in the week, provided for expenditures of £158 million—34 million more than the original estimates for the previous year.) The Cabinet approved this and other amendments to the draft. The revised White Paper, published on 3 March, outlined the DPR(DR)'s recommendations as filtered by the Cabinet's conclusions of 25 February.[62] Britain must recondition and modernize defense forces so that it could discharge its worldwide responsibilities—including collective security and international understanding—at a time when Germany and other nations were rearming. Expanding the RAF (to a first-line strength of approximately 1,750 aircraft excluding the Fleet Air Arm, which was still under the RAF's control) and increasing its "striking power" was "the most urgent and important of our defence requirements," and the RAF's primary function was "to provide an effective deterrent" against any attack on Britain or its overseas interests. Imperial defense and the protection of commerce were the Navy's chief responsibility. The Army should be prepared to send a force overseas "wherever it may be wanted"; the country's limited industrial capacity would not permit reequipping the Territorial Army

[59] Cab 9(36), 24 February, CAB 23/83; 309 *HC Debates*, 27 February, cols. 653–57. In his statement to the House of Commons, Baldwin alluded—the first such public reference—to the DPR, which would "keep the defensive situation as a whole constantly under review."

[60] 99 *HL Debates*, 27 February, *Parliamentary Debates*, Lords, Fifth Series, cols. 807–59. Chatfield was irritated by Swinton's departure from the "very clear and satisfactory" wording used by Baldwin in the House of Commons, that the new minister "would not *normally*" attend meetings of the COS; Chatfield to Hankey, 28 February, CAB 21/424.

[61] Cabs 12 and 13(36), CAB 23/83.

[62] The following quotations are from the revised White Paper, Statement Relating to Defence, CP 62(36), 3 March, CAB 24/260; Cmd. 5107.

while attending to the needs of the Regular Army. Because the international situation was "constantly changing," the Government might have to modify defense measures from time to time. No date was given for completing the new program.

The White Paper also mentioned the official and ministerial committees on defense requirements (but did not name the former), and summarized the reorganization of the machinery of defense approved by the Cabinet on 24 February. The purposes of this reorganization were to strengthen the "apparatus for consideration of Defence problems as a whole" and to increase industrial capacity and manpower. The latter increase would require the cooperation of industry and trade unions, guarding against "extravagant profits," and peacetime preparations— notably creating "a reserve source of supply"—for converting to war production in an emergency.

Germany's remilitarization of the Rhineland on Saturday, 7 March, heightened the atmosphere of urgency in the Commons Debate and influenced Baldwin's choice of a deputy for defense. In the House, the White Paper passed easily on 10 March, surviving attacks from leaders of the Labour and Liberal parties, Winston Churchill, and David Lloyd George. Clement Attlee challenged the Government's basing defense policy on national rather than collective security, and he found the proposals for coordination "incoherent." The new minister would apparently "be like a little terrier running round barking to encourage everyone to get on with the work." Sir Archibald Sinclair, Liberal leader since Sir Herbert Samuel's defeat in the general election of November 1935, found no evidence that defense was being considered "by fresh minds, unshackled by the respective traditions of the three Services." Churchill charged that Britain was not keeping pace with Germany, and that the Government had not taken the necessary peacetime steps to ensure the immediate conversion of industry to wartime manufacture. "Will there be time," he asked, "to put our defences in order?" Lloyd George also regarded the White Paper as inadequate with respect to the organization of industry, and warned that the new minister must be an exceptional man who was not confined to advice from the Services.[63]

The Rhineland crisis convinced Baldwin and Chamberlain to find a "safe" man who would not—like Hoare or Churchill—cause misunderstandings on the Continent.[64] On 13 March, Baldwin announced that

[63] 309 *HC Debates*, 10 March, cols. 1827–1934, 1973–2090; C. R. Attlee, *As It Happened* (London, 1954), pp. 99–100. See also Hugh Dalton, *The Fateful Years: Memoirs, 1931–1945* (London, 1957), pp. 77–78.

[64] Chamberlain diary, 8 and 11 March, Chamberlain Papers, NC 2/23a; Feiling, *Life of Chamberlain*, p. 278; Macleod, *Chamberlain*, p. 193. Eden told Baldwin that Hoare's ap-

Sir Thomas Inskip would occupy the new position of Minister for the Coordination of Defence. An editorial in the *Times* called attention to the former attorney general's combination of legal training and administrative and parliamentary experience, qualities that would help him lead the Committee of Imperial Defence through its "next main stage of evolution."[65]

Recent changes in the machinery promised to improve the consideration of defense policy "as a whole" and to increase the efficiency and capacity for supply—the two objectives named in the White Paper. In his first few months in office, Inskip may have wondered whether the first of these objectives could be achieved simply by reforming the machinery, and whether the second was possible without further reorganization.

British strategy in a future war hinged on air power—its independent use and its support of the Army and Navy. The Imperial General Staff (where General Sir Cyril Deverell replaced Massingberd as chief early in April) still held that, if Germany attacked Belgium or France, Britain should send a Field Force to the Continent. On 12 March, Duff Cooper told the House of Commons that Britain could not rule out sending an expeditionary force to the Continent, for the advent of air power had increased the strategic importance of the Low Countries, and Britain's allies could "take a stronger and a bolder line" at the outbreak of war if they knew British reinforcements were on the way. Prompted by the Rhineland crisis to say what the White Paper had evaded, Duff Cooper did not speak for the Cabinet as a whole. Siding with Chamberlain and Swinton, Simon thought air warfare made it foolish even to contemplate such action for the Army. Although General Dill reported that the French "expect us to play a part in the defence of the Low Countries and realise that an army is essential if we are to play that part effectively," Inskip asked Duff Cooper whether it made any sense to send troops to the Continent before Britain's air defense

---

pointment "would make things very difficult" for Eden (Chamberlain diary, 8 March), and Chamberlain thought the reoccupation "afforded an excellent reason for discarding both Winston and Sam since both had European reputations which might make it dangerous to add them to the Cabinet at a critical moment" (diary, 11 March). See also Amery, *Empire at Bay*, p. 409; Jones, *Diary*, p. 186; Middlemas and Barnes, *Baldwin*, pp. 912, 916–17. Baldwin would only tell Davidson that Inskip was "'a safe man,'" and gave no other explanation for his appointment; Rhodes James, *Davidson's Memoirs*, p. 410. Hoare attributed Baldwin's change of mind to criticism in the press of a speech that Hoare had made in the House of Commons on defense coordination; Templewood, *Nine Troubled Years*, pp. 200–201. On 13 March, Baldwin wrote Hoare that "after long consideration," he had decided to appoint Hoare First Lord of the Admiralty; Templewood Papers.

[65] The *Times*, 14 March 1936; for the reaction of Churchill and his admirers, see Gilbert, *Churchill*, pp. 714–16.

system was adequate to thwart an air attack, "a form of warfare of which we have no real experience."[66] Planners on the Air Staff had virtually abandoned the staff's earlier interest in using troops to deny Germany forward air bases in the Low Countries. Harris and others viewed the Army (and Navy) as of secondary importance for both deterring Germany and counterattacking after Germany's opening offensive; indeed, they reasoned, the Field Force would be useless unless British air power were sufficient to make a counterattack possible.[67]

In another quarter of Inskip's new jurisdiction, the First Lord of the Admiralty reopened the controversy over control of the Fleet Air Arm, calling it a problem that "shrieks for coordination." Swinton protested Eyres-Monsell's "really amazing" initiative, knowing that the Admiralty wanted to take full control and arguing that the prime minister had prohibited reopening the question. Baldwin and Weir backed Swinton. Inskip reassured Monsell that he would not overlook the Fleet Air Arm in the continuous review of strategic ideas that must proceed "in the light of strategic developments."[68]

Late in March, Inskip asked the Chiefs of Staff to keep him informed about German rearmament. If it accelerated rapidly, the Cabinet might have to revise or reverse its decision that British rearmament must not interfere with normal trade, and adopt "some form of war system" of production.[69] As chairman of the DPR (in the prime minister's absence) and the PSOC, Inskip became aware of frictions in the peacetime system—the role of labor, the slow pace of rearmament.

Ernest Brown—Baptist lay preacher, war service in Italy (Military

---

[66] 309 *HC Debates*, 12 March, cols. 2347–50; Simon to Baldwin, 25 March, PREM 1/194; Dill to Montgomery-Massingberd, 20 April, Dill Papers, 5/1/2 (LHCMA); Inskip to Duff Cooper, 29 May, CAB 64/3. During the Rhineland crisis, Duff Cooper had countered allegations of the Army's unpreparedness by stating that it could at least send two divisions (albeit underquipped) to the Continent; meeting of ministers, 30 March, CAB 27/603.

[67] Not yet a convinced opponent of the continental commitment, Ellington maintained that, in spite of the vulnerability of the Field Force to German air attack, Germany must not be allowed to conquer the Low Countries, which remained vital to British security; COS meeting, 13 May, CAB 53/6. For the RAF's dilemma of planning for different German strategies, see Smith, *British Air Strategy*, pp. 103–5, and chap. 9. The choice was between intercepting a German advance in Western Europe and defending against a German knockout air strike. In the first case, defense and counterattack would require combined operations. In the second, which the Air Staff thought the more likely, the RAF would play virtually an independent role.

[68] Monsell to Inskip, 21 April; Swinton to Inskip, 28 April; Inskip to Monsell, 30 April; this and related correspondence in CAB 64/23. Weir to Baldwin, 20 May, PREM 1/282. Chatfield warmly thanked Churchill for his advocacy of Admiralty control; letter of 5 May, Chatfield Papers. On friction between the Air Ministry and Admiralty (also over the "bombs versus ships" controversy), see Bond, *Chief of Staff*, pp. 107–9; Roskill, *Hankey*, 3:252–53, and *Naval Policy*, pp. 393–94; Till, *Air Power and Royal Navy*, pp. 50–51.

[69] COS meetings, 16 and 25 March, CAB 53/5.

Cross), National Liberal since 1931, Minister of Labour since June 1935—thought the DPR(DR) had given too little recognition to the part that his ministry would play in the industrial side of rearmament. He told the Cabinet that the training programs of the Ministry of Labour could not provide skilled workers, the shortage of which had been noted by the ministerial committee. And Brown resented the allegation of both the DRC and DPR(DR) that his ministry did not cooperate with other departments, especially in recruiting men for the Services. In fact, he would like to give the Service departments "every possible assistance."[70] Duff Cooper blamed low troop morale, public apathy, and "pacifist agitation" for the inability of the voluntary system of recruiting to meet the needs of the Army. Brown agreed that the Services should be brought up to strength, but he warned against upsetting civilian industry and relations between the trade unions and employers. The Cabinet and DPR instructed the Service departments and Labour Ministry to establish an interdepartmental committee to examine these problems.[71]

Sir Arthur Robinson, chairman of the Supply Board, described the Principal Supply Officers Committee as something "of a recording angel" for work actually done by the Supply Board and other groups.[72] Unimpressed by either the PSOC or Inskip, Churchill told Hankey that the Government must "create a Ministry of Supply or Ministry of Munitions at once," although he was "rather shaken" when Hankey reminded him of his own important role in the Government's abandoning the Ministry of Munitions after the war. Churchill also chided Lord Weir for "lending all your reputation to keeping this country in a state of comfortable peace routine."[73] Weir assured Churchill that, if he thought the Government must organize the entire life of the nation for war, he would "advise it and push it hard."[74] Robinson and Weir

---

[70] Brown to Baldwin, 14 February, PREM 1/192; Brown memorandum, 21 February, CP 57(36), CAB 24/260, considered by the Cabinet on 25 February along with the report of the DPR(DR). See also Roskill, *Hankey*, 3:198–99; and Shay, *British Rearmament*, pp. 125–26.

[71] Duff Cooper memorandum, 2 April, CP 92(36), and Brown memoranda, 26 March and 2 April, CP 96 and 102(36), CAB 24/261; Cab 28(36), 8 April, Cab 23/83; DPR meeting, 7 May, CAB 16/136; Dennis, *Decision by Default*, pp. 75–76.

[72] Robinson to Hankey, 5 March, CAB 21/424.

[73] Hankey note of conversation with Churchill at Chartwell (they were neighbors in the country), 21 April, CAB 21/435, copies sent to Inskip and Baldwin; Churchill to Weir, 6 May, Weir Papers, 19/12; Gilbert, *Churchill*, pp. 723, 726–27, 736; Roskill, *Hankey*, 3:230. Like Churchill, J. L. Garvin thought the Minister for Coordination did not have enough authority and that a Ministry of Supply was needed: editorials in the *Observer* (e.g., 8 March); notes of 18 May; Garvin Papers.

[74] Weir to Churchill, 13 May, Weir Papers, 19/12. Reader quotes this exchange of letters in *Architect*, pp. 243–44; see also Gilbert, *Churchill*, pp. 729, 736.

agreed that the supply organization in the War Office was deficient. So did a growing number of ministers, officials, and influential people outside the Government, some of whom blamed Duff Cooper for indolence. If a separate department were not created in the War Office to handle supply, Weir wrote to Duff Cooper, the Army's supply program would remain slow "and the clamant appeal for an independent Ministry of Munitions will only gain in strength if this much wiser alternative be not proceeded with now."[75]

After the Cabinet's decisions of February, Robinson and the Supply Board had responsibility for allocating shadow firms to the Service departments and determining questions of priority among the Services. In working through their hypotheses for war against Germany or Japan in 1939, the board also had to wrestle with the problem of war potential. Would the approved shadow program produce what the Services considered sufficient reserves of supply for the first year of war or adequate industrial capacity for increasing production during war? Robinson was sure it would not, yet Weir continued to distinguish between remedying deficiencies and creating a war potential, which he told the DPR should be "considered afterwards."[76]

Whether the reorganized machinery of coordination could produce a common strategic doctrine, a lofty expectation of critics of the system so recently modified, remained to be seen. Nor did reorganization guarantee that Britain could solve problems of production and priority of supplies, especially if Germany rearmed even faster than British defense policy presupposed. Without an agreement on military strategy, lacking a "war system" of production, and equivocating between the DRC and Chamberlain strategies of deterrence, the Government had to prepare a convincing deterrent for the future—by a date that remained uncertain, for not altogether compatible purposes that ranged from general diplomatic sway to ensuring victory in a war of self-defense, with no clear notion of where to draw a line for Hitler or

[75] Robinson to Weir, 22 January, and Weir to Duff Cooper, 2 June, Weir Papers, 18/4, 17/8. On criticisms of and problems in the War Office: Bond, *British Military Policy,* pp. 177–78, and *Chief of Staff,* p. 111; B. H. Liddell Hart, *The Defence of Britain* (New York, 1939), pp. 340–42; Middlemas and Barnes, *Baldwin,* pp. 941–42; Postan, *British War Production,* pp. 41–42; Sir John Slessor, *The Central Blue: The Autobiography of Sir John Slessor, Marshal of the RAF* (New York, 1957), p. 95; Garvin notes, May 1936, Garvin Papers.

[76] DPR meeting, 7 May, CAB 16/136. On supply organization and the question of war potential after Inskip's appointment, see Ehrman, *Cabinet Government,* pp. 113–14; G. A. H. Gordon, *British Seapower and Procurement between the Wars: A Reappraisal of Rearmament* (London, 1988), pp. 148, 165, and chap. 20; Hurstfield, *Control of Raw Materials,* pp. 36, 425–32; Postan, *British War Production,* pp. 35–52; Scott and Hughes, *Administration of War Production,* pp. 57–58, 64–65.

how to punish Germany if he overstepped it. Germany's remilitarization of the Rhineland, an ominous backdrop for the Cabinet's efforts to
accelerate rearmament and reorganize machinery, showed how undeterred Hitler was by British policy in the present, and how fitfully
the British system of decisionmaking dealt with the German question.

[5]

Buying Time

Hitler's Rhineland coup easily subverted London's supposition that, rearming as a diplomatic broker, Britain could attach particular stipulations to the appeasement of Germany. In December 1935, shortly after the Defence Requirements Committee had submitted its report, Sir Samuel Hoare advised the Cabinet that accelerating British rearmament must accompany and, as far as possible, precede negotiations with Germany.[1] Hoare's formulation of Vansittart's notion of general deterrence required an unspecified amount of time before it could succeed, yet it also implied a willingness to take the diplomatic initiative and specify conditions before Hitler could take unilateral actions. While the DRC Third Report awaited Cabinet approval, Vansittart revised this idea as evidence grew that Germany would remilitarize the Rhineland before either country was ready to discuss a general settlement: recognizing that appeasement must be a dynamic policy, Britain could begin now, during the "interval" of rearming, to negotiate mutual and particular concessions, which would reduce the likelihood of confrontation and prepare the way for a general settlement later.

In practice, this amended principle of negotiating with advantage during rearmament was linked to several attitudes that vitiated whatever value Vansittart thought it might contain for the general or extended deterrence of Germany. The demilitarized zone of the Rhineland was not worth Britain's fighting for, unless Germany went on to attack Belgium and France. The particulars to negotiate with Germany, perhaps without French involvement, might include German economic

---

[1] See chapter 3. For background to the Rhineland question, see James T. Emmerson, *The Rhineland Crisis 7 March 1936: A Study in Multilateral Diplomacy* (London, 1977), chaps. 1, 2.

expansion in Eastern Europe to the detriment of French security. Britain should support the oil sanction against Italy and maintain military readiness in the Mediterranean, although this policy, which Eden thought would check Germany, continued to damage relations with France and Italy. Finally, British rearmament should be couched in public language that did not offend Germany too much.

Vansittart's formula degenerated further when, undeterred by Britain's show of force in the Mediterranean, Germany reoccupied the demilitarized zone before Britain could manage the "interval" to obtain some German concession in return. Britain endeavored to prevent the Rhineland crisis from escalating into war, not to roll back Hitler's advance. Duff Cooper alone argued that Britain would not gain on Germany in the next few years and should resist Germany's action, a sense of timing that Whitehall had barely examined before the crisis and the Cabinet now rejected. Having reduced the rather vague idea of a general settlement to specific parts that might soon be negotiated separately, the British theory of giving Germany something in return for something else moved closer to the practice of something for nothing, and all that this implied for future stability.

Rattled by the Rhineland, mesmerized by the Mediterranean, and importuned by the Services to provide political guidelines for defense policy, the Government established the Foreign Policy Committee (FPC) to reexamine Britain's "major policy." Vital questions affecting time and deterrence depended on the outcome of such a reassessment. In view of increasing tension, was it still correct to base rearmament on the doctrine of maintaining normal peacetime trade? How long must Britain sustain unusually high levels of force in the Mediterranean and at the same time consider Italy an unlikely enemy? Were collective and regional security dead? Should British deterrence continue to cover Belgium and France with plans that included dispatching the Field Force, or should deterrence be drawn in closer to self-defense? What particular concessions could Britain make to Germany, on whose terms, when, and with what implications for British prestige and European security down the road? Would Mussolini and Hitler join forces? The Rhineland crisis increased Whitehall's disarray over these questions and its desire to reduce Britain's international commitments. Decisions were needed that made some connection between Britain's immediate predicament and the long-term aim of preventing or winning a war, while taking into account actual failures to deter Mussolini and Hitler.

For reassessing policy, as well as for rearmament, reorganization, and dealing with Germany, the machinery of policy caused delay, inconsistency, and indecision. The machinery functioned effectively during the crisis itself, thanks to broad interdepartmental agreement against being drawn into war. But the committee system failed in important ways before and after the crisis. The Foreign Office, Cabinet, and short-lived Cabinet Committee on Germany did not produce a timely plan for using the Rhineland as a bargaining chip before Hitler could remove it from the board. Committees treated foreign policy and rearmament as separate issues, left conflicting strategies of deterrence unresolved, reacted to parliamentary outbursts and international crises as momentary annoyances, and postponed consideration of the long-term implications of urgent matters. The DRC never met again after completing its report, the ministerial FPC dawdled, and no committee resumed the originally comprehensive terms of reference of the DPR, whose agenda changed from managing the Mediterranean crisis to overseeing the Services' programs.

Although usually harmonious over calming the Rhineland crisis, interdepartmental relations deteriorated over rearmament and reappraising major policy. Ministerial amendments of the DRC report and criticisms of the defense machinery sparked mutual resentment. Experts blamed ministers for subverting military considerations with "purely political" ones, and similar language marked declining relations between the Services and Foreign Office. Such bureaucratic distinctions became increasingly deceptive and disabling as the meaning of policy broadened.

Departments tried to expand peacetime jurisdictions into planning for war, their idiosyncratic agendas predisposing departmental attitudes toward time and deterrence. The Foreign Office paid more heed than the Treasury or Services to the possibility of war with Germany before 1939, and also had more regard for Britain's commitments and reputation abroad. But the Foreign Office was also more impaired by internal disputes and temporizing. Officials there debated whether time might now be on Germany's side against Britain, and on Britain's against Italy. Vansittart's obsession with Germany annoyed many colleagues, including Eden, and his prestige ebbed inside and outside the Office, where buying time had become symptomatic of uncertainty. While the Foreign Office stumbled, the Treasury improved its status in interdepartmental bargaining. Chamberlain's preeminence in the Cabinet and his artful use of procedures helped increase the Treasury's leverage for limiting the strategies and supplies that Chamberlain thought Britain would need for deterrence from 1939 onward. In his opinion, Britain had more time than the Foreign Office feared and could build an effective deterrent more quickly than the Services bargained for. Although the new Treasury Inter-Service Committee would assist Treasury control over expenditure while the Government adhered to normal trade, the Treasury still entertained doubts about the cost and calendar of rearmament. Inter-Service coordination improved. So did the confidence of military experts who disparaged the Foreign Office for not reducing commitments and ensuring a peaceful period for rearming. Inskip got down to work, ably voicing the Services' collective concerns about strategic overreach now and material undersupply in case of war. The reorganization of the machinery of defense, aided by close collaboration between Inskip and Hankey, did not guarantee the development of a common strategy or the provision of adequate reserves in case of war.

As long as strategy, supply, foreign policy, and time remained in doubt, so did the uses and costs of deterrence. As long as this sort of disorder endured, the Services would give the Foreign Office some of the blame for Britain's strategic dilemma. And Chamberlain would be dissatisfied with the incremental system of policymaking that prevented the Government from solving it by unreservedly adopting his strategy of deterrence.

RHINELAND AND REASSESSMENT

Early in 1935, the Cabinet had instructed British diplomats to avoid any redefinition of Britain's specific obligations under the Treaty of Locarno. They must neither state that the demilitarization of the Rhineland was a vital British interest nor give any indication of what Britain "would do in a particular hypothetical case."[2] On 16 December 1935, Ralph Wigram noted with dismay that neither the Foreign Office nor the Chiefs of Staff had "given serious consideration" to the value to Britain of maintaining the demilitarized zone. Hitler had raised "the Russian bogey"—the Franco-Soviet mutual assistance treaty of May 1935, which France was now about to ratify and which, Berlin argued, undermined the Locarno Pact. Wigram presumed that "the great political argument against" the disappearance of the zone was "the removal of one of the few remaining serious checks on German action in Central and Eastern Europe," and warned that "at any moment we may well be faced with some serious German infringement of it."[3] Wigram's minute set in motion an examination of the Rhineland by various departments and committees, but before this process culminated in a final report Hitler sent German troops into the Rhineland in March.

---

[2] Cabs 3, 20, 21(35), 14 January and 8 April, CAB 23/81.
[3] Wigram minute on wires from Phipps (Berlin), C8329/55/18, FO 371/18852; other comments in *DBFP*, 15, no. 382.

Having failed to prevent this diplomatic confrontation, Britain sought to keep it from escalating into armed conflict. This response was implicit in several British considerations before the crisis: the strategic and political importance to Britain of the demilitarized zone; the legal interpretation of Britain's obligations under the Treaty of Locarno; longstanding readiness to negotiate with Berlin in the interests of European peace; continued tension with Italy in the Mediterranean; reluctance to support France.

In January 1936, Vansittart asked Hankey to have the Committee of Imperial Defence (CID) consider the strategic value of the demilitarized zone.[4] The General Staff viewed the zone as an advantage to Britain, because "of the additional security it provides to France, Belgium and Holland," and as a disadvantage to Germany in the event of war either in the west or in the east. The Air Staff considered maintaining the zone "a matter of negligible defensive value from the air point of view to France, Belgium or Great Britain," since Germany did not require this territory for air operations against any of these countries. On the other hand, keeping the zone demilitarized might force Germany to reduce its offensive air forces in proportion to the planes it would need to defend against attack by land.[5] The CID postponed discussion of these reports. Meanwhile, Lord Stanhope, who, as Parliamentary Under-Secretary of State for Foreign Affairs, represented Eden at the CID meeting on 30 January, gathered that the strategic value of retaining the demilitarized zone was not "of critical importance" for Britain.[6]

Orme Sargent (who had headed the central department from 1928 to 1933) and Wigram saw that the disappearance of the zone would "not merely change local military values" but also "lead to far-reaching political repercussions of a kind which will further weaken France's influence in Eastern and Central Europe," for German fortification of the zone would make it more difficult for France to support its eastern allies. Thus, it might well be to Britain's "ultimate advantage . . . to decide to resist Germany on this matter." On the other hand, Wigram thought that, since the zone was bound to disappear, "the important thing is to arrange that it disappear peacefully."[7] But London had always viewed the Locarno Treaty as a means for reducing European tension, not taking military action. With this in mind, Sir William Mal-

---

[4] Vansittart to Hankey, 8 January, C8329/55/18, FO 371/18852, and impatient reminder to Hankey on 18 January, C291/4/18, FO 371/19883.

[5] CIGS note, 27 January, CAB 4/24 (*DBFP*, 15, no. 483); Air Staff note, 24 January, CAB 4/24 (*DBFP*, 15, no. 482); Gibbs, *Rearmament*, pp. 230–33.

[6] CID meeting, CAB 2/6; also Foreign Office minutes, 29 and 30 January, C584/4/18, FO 371/19884.

[7] Sargent minute and memorandum (prepared with Wigram), 10 February, C796/4/18, FO 371/19884; Wigram minute of 9 January, C151/4/18, FO 371/19883.

kin, chief legal adviser in the Foreign Office (from 1929 to his disappearance in a flight over the Atlantic in July 1945), outlined legal and
procedural grounds for not defending the integrity of the demilitarized
zone by force. If Germany remilitarized the zone and gave no indication of an intention to attack France or Belgium, then even if Germany's
move "constituted an unprovoked act of aggression," Britain could
argue that it was not required to take immediate action and could
propose that the issue be settled by arbitration. Britain could provide
"something less than *military* assistance" to France until and unless the
League Council instructed otherwise.[8] Summing up, Eden advised
against adopting a position that would require Britain either "to fight
for the Zone" or to surrender it without negotiating for something in
return from Germany.[9]

The Foreign Office struggled over how to deal with Germany's resurgence. In a long memorandum of 21 November on "Britain, France,
and Germany," Sargent and Wigram had rejected two options: a policy
of drift; or encircling Germany by reverting to the prewar system of
alliances. Instead, they advocated continuing the policy of "coming to
terms with Germany," in collaboration with France. If Britain did not
do this soon, it would lose the chance to prevent German rapprochement with the Soviet Union and Japan, to "influence German designs"
in Central and Eastern Europe (a war starting there could lead to German occupation of northern France and Belgium), and to defuse the
dangerous issue of the Rhineland. Commenting on this paper, Lawrence Collier (head of the northern department in the Foreign Office)
rejected its conclusions as "a reversal of our previous policy," which
was to try to satisfy Germany's legitimate claims (e.g., disarmament) as
they arose, but not to discuss her illegitimate ones, especially territorial
designs on Eastern Europe. Vansittart warned against bargaining with
Germany until Britain had at least made quick and strong progress on
implementing the DRC report. Britain must not try to negotiate with
Germany "and fail, being still weak." Indeed, Britain must be "already

[8] Malkin memorandum, 14 February, given by Eden to the Cabinet Committee on
Germany on the same day, in CAB 27/599 (also enclosed in *DBFP*, 15, no. 521); also
Malkin memorandum of 30 January, cited in Sargent's memo of 10 February (see preceding note). The complex problem of interpreting the Locarno Pact was implicit in the pact
itself in 1925, when each signatory knew that its actions would be determined ultimately
by its own national interests. See Jon Jacobson, *Locarno Diplomacy: Germany and the West,
1925–1929* (Princeton, 1972); Gaines Post, Jr., *The Civil-Military Fabric of Weimar Foreign
Policy* (Princeton, 1973), pp. 64–65.

[9] Eden to Cabinet Committee on Germany, 14 February, CAB 27/599 (also in *DBFP*, 15,
no. 521). Eden's memorandum was drafted by Sargent, who simply repeated his memorandum of 10 February (cited in note 7 above). Barnett contemns Eden's paper as "just
another of those escapist documents to which British diplomacy was so prone"; *Collapse*,
p. 408.

strong or running into strength" in the not unlikely event of failure to reach a settlement. Yet Vansittart also agreed with Sargent and Wigram that reaching "an early agreement" with Germany might be wise because of the volatility of the Rhineland question.[10]

Early in 1936, Wigram called attention to the implicit contradiction between these two positions. Britain should establish better relations with Germany, "yet it seems impossible to make any move. We are told we must wait for our rearmament. But does our rearmament make any real progress?"[11] Vansittart thought that, before Germany violated the demilitarized zone, Britain would have a useful "interval"—"primarily for rearmament, but also and concurrently for making up our minds whether any agreement with Germany is possible." Eden agreed, urging the Cabinet to hasten rearmament so as to "be ready for all eventualities" and, while rearming, to consider the possibility of reaching an understanding with Hitler's Germany.[12]

Vansittart's attitude toward the "interval" of rearming did not solve Wigram's problem of how Britain could soon "make any move." The solution lay in the policy that Vansittart proposed in a memorandum of 3 February, which Eden circulated to the Cabinet on the eleventh. While waiting until stronger to open the question of a general settlement with Germany, and in order "to keep Germany in play" in the meantime, Britain "could fill in the interval by the approach to the particular." Germany would "be ready for aggression long before we and the League can be ready for defence," and indeed Germany might not wait until ready. Therefore, the League should be "dynamic" and the status quo "elastic." Britain must "gain time, hoping against hope that there may be some change of heart or system in Germany, or— with better ground—that we and our League associates may within a respite of x years, with energy, virility and much propaganda, grow to a position where defence can make attack too hopeless to be worth while." The "gap in time" between German and British readiness must be "bridged" with particular concessions to Germany that were consistent with reaching a general settlement. Recent reports from Germany argued against postponing negotiations altogether: some of Hitler's advisers thought that "time is on *their* side" and that Germany's position would only grow stronger. Eden added a strong "home front"

[10] Sargent/Wigram memorandum, 21 November, *DBFP*, 15, appx. Ia. Collier and Vansittart comments on Sargent/Wigram memorandum, 22 November and 1 December 1935, *DBFP*, 15, appx. Ib, Ic.

[11] Wigram minute, 10 January 1936, ibid., no. 436n; also Wigram minute, 9 January, C151/4/18, FO 371/19883; Rose, *Vansittart*, pp. 189–90.

[12] Vansittart minute, 10 January, C151/4/18, FO 371/19883; Eden memorandum, 17 January, CP 13(36), CAB 24/259 (also in *DBFP*, 15, no. 460); Cabs 3, 4(36), 29 January and 5 February, CAB 23/83.

argument: the British public would want the Government to seek agreement with Germany if they were expected "to foot a formidable bill" for rearmament.[13]

Knowing that Germany would challenge the demilitarized status of the Rhineland, and concluding that the zone would probably disappear, the Foreign Office hoped to "get some little benefit in return for its disappearance."[14] Officials in the Foreign Office concurred in viewing the zone as a bargaining chip, but disagreed over where to make other concessions on what Vansittart called "the particular." He himself advocated some restitution of Germany's former colonies in Africa rather than permit German expansion in Eastern Europe, which might lead to war or—just as dangerous—to reconciliation between Nazi Germany and Soviet Russia. F. T. A. Ashton-Gwatkin, head of the economic relations section of the League of Nations and western department, thought that, by allowing Germany to expand its export markets in Central and Southeastern Europe, Britain could help release the internal economic pressure that would otherwise cause Germany to set off "a general European war in the near future." Although unwilling to help Germany without being sure of getting something in return, other officials supported the idea of letting Germany take the predominant economic position in Central and Southeastern Europe— William Strang (central department), E. H. Carr and Owen St. Clair O'Malley (both in the southern department), Lord Stanhope, and Lord Cranborne (Parliamentary Under-Secretary).[15]

Phipps opposed economic concessions; these would not decrease the chances of a "fortuitous war" arising from a political incident, and would only increase Germany's capability for launching a "deliberate war of aggression" in the manner of Bismarck. Collier warned that economic expansion in Southeastern Europe "must mean political pen-

[13] Vansittart memorandum, 3 February, and Eden memorandum, 11 February, CP 42(36), CAB 24/260 (also in *DBFP*, 15, appx. IVb and no. 509). See also Andrew J. Crozier, "Prelude to Munich: British Foreign Policy and Germany, 1935–8," *European Studies Review* 6 (1976), 361–62; Rose, *Vansittart*, p. 191. Schmidt may overstate the contradictions in Vansittart's notions of time; *England in der Krise*, pp. 216–17, 392. In a thoughtful analysis of the relationship between rearmament and appeasement, pointing out that rearmament could hinder British action, Schmidt does not examine Vansittart's argument about using the "interval"; pp. 422–25.

[14] Wigram memorandum, 16 January, *DBFP*, 15, no. 455.

[15] Vansittart memoranda, 1 December (appx. Ic), 3 February (appx. IVb); Ashton-Gwatkin notes and memoranda, 21 November (appx. Ia), 31 January (with H. M. G. Jebb, member of the economic relations section, appx. IVa); Strang, Carr, Stanhope, and Cranborne minutes, 30 January–4 March (no. 490); *DBFP*, 15; Schmidt, *England in der Krise*, pp. 521–22, 526–27 (also chap. 3); Wendt, *Economic Appeasement*, pp. 290, 321–22; Andrew J. Crozier, *Appeasement and Germany's Last Bid for Colonies* (London, 1988), chap. 5; David E. Kaiser, *Economic Diplomacy and the Origins of the Second World War: Germany, Britain, France, and Eastern Europe, 1930–1939* (Princeton, 1980), pp. 171–74, 188–89.

etration as well." Vansittart objected to seeking an economic settlement except as part of a political settlement.[16] Sargent and Wigram would cede the demilitarized zone in return for Germany's participation in an air limitation agreement (in conjunction with an air pact to replace the Treaty of Locarno) and Germany's "most binding assurances and guarantees in respect of Central and Eastern Europe," but they did not propose that Britain commit itself to preventing German hegemony there.[17]

Supporting a settlement but averse to colonial concessions, Eden summarized the various options for the Cabinet and the Cabinet Committee on Germany, which Baldwin appointed on 14 February to consider how to approach Hitler. Any concessions, Eden emphasized, "must only be offered as part of a final settlement which includes some further arms limitation and Germany's return to the League." Without remarking on the paradoxical implications for deterrence, Foreign Office officials advised Eden to keep in mind that, if the Cabinet wished to seek a settlement with Germany, then "care must be taken" in the forthcoming debate on defense policy "not to give the Germans an excuse for alleging that we are defending our rearmament on the ground of the supposed hostile intentions which we attribute to them."[18] On 17 February, at its first and only meeting, the Cabinet committee agreed that negotiations could begin before the Italo-Ethiopian war ended (in spite of Hitler's wish to wait for that moment), on the subject of an air pact rather than the demilitarized zone. The committee held that "some diplomatic approach to Germany would greatly assist" the Government's White Paper on Defence.[19] Hankey did not want the White Paper to be "too beastly to the Germans," and Eden told him that the Office was "very divided on the subject."[20]

---

[16] Phipps to Eden, 19 February (no. 530); Collier minute, 30 January (no. 490n); Vansittart memorandum, 3 February (appx. IVb); *DBFP*, 15.

[17] Sargent (and Wigram) memorandum, 10 February, C796/4/18, FO 371/19884. On the question of an air limitation treaty, see also Wigram, Sargent, and Eden minutes, 28 February and 1 March, C1352/C1353/4/18, FO 371/19887.

[18] Eden memoranda, 11 February (covering Vansittart memorandum of 3 February), CP 42(36), CAB 24/260 (also in *DBFP*, 15, no. 509 and appx. IVb), and 14 February (see note 9 above); Foreign Office memorandum, 15 February, for Eden's use at 17 February meeting of the Cabinet Committee on Germany, *DBFP*, 15, no. 522. On the "spiral model" of international conflict, in which deterrence can provoke an insecure adversary, see Jervis, *Perception and Misperception*, chap. 3.

[19] Committee meeting of 17 February, CAB 27/599 (also in *DBFP*, 15, no. 524); Eden to Phipps, 24 February, *DBFP*, 15, no. 541. Members of the Cabinet Committee on Germany: Baldwin, R. MacDonald, Chamberlain, Eden, Halifax (Lord Privy Seal), Simon, J. H. Thomas (Colonial Secretary), and Runciman. On this meeting, see also Emmerson, *Rhineland Crisis*, pp. 66–67; Medlicott, *Britain and Germany*, pp. 20–22; Rose, *Vansittart*, pp. 191–92; Schmidt, *England in der Krise*, pp. 66–68.

[20] Hankey to Phipps, 14 February, Phipps Papers (Churchill College, Cambridge), 3/3, agreeing with the ambassador on avoiding beastliness.

Hankey's view prevailed, and the White Paper mentioned Germany as one of several nations increasing their armaments.

In spite of the Government's embarrassment over the Hoare-Laval plan and Baldwin's appointment of Eden as Foreign Secretary, Britain continued to pursue a dual policy toward Italy, supporting sanctions as a principal member of the League of Nations, while hoping for better relations with Italy. The question of sanctions continued to divide the Cabinet. The firmest support came from Eden, who disliked Italy more than he did Germany, and the strongest opposition from the Board of Trade and the Services.[21] Eyres-Monsell opposed prolonging the Mediterranean emergency, for the Navy had tasks elsewhere, and Britain "could not afford to overlook Japan." Indeed, he had warned the French that a Japanese move in the Far East "would be of greater concern to [Britain] with its vast interests in the Far East than German action in Eastern Europe." Swinton in effect spoke for all the Services when he warned the Cabinet that the emergency measures "threatened to handicap" the air force expansion. On 26 February, however, the Cabinet voted (Runciman and Monsell dissenting) in favor of the oil sanction, afraid that not doing so would discredit both the League and the Government, yet knowing that the French would not welcome this move.[22]

This Cabinet decision contradicted the assumption in defense policy of a tranquil Mediterranean, and disguised Whitehall's reservations about collective security. Early in January, Hankey observed that British public opinion still supported the League; so did the Government, "especially with Anthony at the Foreign Office." Lord Stanhope told the DPR(DR) that the Foreign Office wanted "to stand by" collective security "until something else could be worked out," and Thomas Jones thought Sir Alexander Cadogan's return from China to the Office would "strengthen the League position" there.[23] Yet Vansittart doubted that a League victory against Italy would impress Hitler unless "the strength and readiness of the component parts of the League" were much greater than was now the case; meanwhile, it had become "even more doubtful than before" that Italy would help other Euro-

[21] CP 54 and 70(36), 20 February and 5 March, CAB 24/260; Cab 11(36), 26 February, CAB 23/83.
[22] Cabs 3, 4, 7, 11(36), 29 January, 5, 17, 26 February, CAB 23/83; Monsell to Baldwin, 4 January, PREM 1/200; Admiralty memorandum, 5 February, CAB 16/140 (also in *DBFP*, 15, no. 496). Colonel Paget in Military Intelligence thought Germany might "make an agreement with Japan to counteract the Franco-Soviet treaty," adding that such a development "would be much worse for us than a German-Russian rapprochement." Paget to Hotblack (Berlin), 1 February, WO 19/384, also War Office (CIGS) memorandum, 17 January, CP 12(36), CAB 24/259.
[23] Hankey to Phipps, 2 January, Phipps Papers, 3/3; DPR(DR) meeting, 20 January, CAB 16/123; Jones, *Diary*, p. 176.

pean powers check German expansion. Chatfield blamed collective security for increasing Britain's liabilities, and Hankey thought every major case of collective security had really meant "collective insecurity."[24] Eden himself advised the Government to proceed cautiously, declaring its willingness to participate in the oil sanction only if the other members of the Committee of Eighteen at Geneva were willing to do so.[25]

The Cabinet's decision of 26 February rested in part on evidence that the threat of war in the Mediterranean had abated. The Foreign Office wanted the Admiralty to maintain its readiness in the Mediterranean until the political situation had cleared. Still, Eden thought it unlikely that increasing sanctions would cause Mussolini to retaliate. Drummond agreed, unless Mussolini faced defeat in Ethiopia and decided to precipitate "a general European conflict *in which Germany would join*," but Phipps discounted rumors of a "political engagement between Germany and Italy."[26]

British policies toward Rome and Berlin intersected in Paris, where the French had balked during the Mediterranean crisis and now might drag Britain into a conflict over the Rhineland or into commitments in Eastern Europe should the Locarno system of western security collapse. Unless Italy attacked Britain in the Mediterranean area, now an unlikely contingency, Britain's dependence on France for military assistance had become a diplomatic liability. In mid-January, Chatfield warned that the more Britain asked of France in the Mediterranean, "the more likely would [France] be to use her cooperation as an argument for similar aid on our part in the event of French difficulties with Germany at some future date."[27] Furthermore, Eden reported to the Cabinet that the German Government was questioning the compatibility between Anglo-French staff conversations and the Locarno Pact. Sargent and Wigram thought Hitler might use their alleged in-

[24] Vansittart memorandum, 3 February, *DBFP*, 15, appx. IVb; Chatfield at DPR(DR), 20 January, CAB 16/123; G. H. Thompson (Foreign Office) to Hankey, 13 February, and Hankey to Thompson, 14 February, CAB 21/450.

[25] Eden to Cabinet, 22 February, CP 53(36), CAB 24/260. Eden agreed with his Cabinet colleagues that he should "avoid taking the lead in this matter at Geneva"; Cab 11(36), 26 February, CAB 23/83. See also Eden's memorandum of 9 January, CP 5(36), CAB 24/259 (also in *DBFP*, 15, no. 442), and Baer, *Test Case*, pp. 208–9. The Committee of Eighteen represented the leading states among those League members who applied sanctions.

[26] DPR meetings, 14 January and 3 March, CAB 16/136; Cab 11(36), 26 February, CAB 23/83; Drummond to Eden, 25 January (no. 480) and 21 February (no. 534); Phipps to Eden, 29 February (no. 556); *DBFP*, 15.

[27] COS meeting, 13 January, CAB 53/5. Next day the DPR instructed the Services not to resume military and air talks with the French, but to continue the naval conversations then in progress; CAB 16/136. On the latter, see Marder, "Royal Navy," pp. 1350–51; Baer, *Test Case*, pp. 190–91.

compatibility as reason to denounce the pact and remilitarize the Rhineland; he would at the same time "take advantage of France and ourselves being involved in trouble in the Mediterranean."[28]

Eden and Vansittart thought Britain must take the lead in eventually reaching a general settlement with Germany, and this required bringing French policy into line. This task was made difficult from the start by the French tendency to view the League, the Locarno Pact, the Stresa Front, and their alliances in Eastern Europe as means for encircling Germany. And how could Britain accomplish this task if, as Sargent observed, the Government could not "safely and honorably allow to pass unnoticed and unanswered" the French Foreign Minister's remark that "the French government would have to treat an infraction by Germany of the demilitarized zone as a *casus foederis*"?[29]

When Pierre Etienne Flandin, who in January replaced Laval in the new coalition cabinet under Albert Sarraut, asked what Britain would do if Germany remilitarized the Rhineland, Eden did not want to make "any general statement regarding either policy or treaty interpretation." He suspected that the French "would probably like us to make up their minds for them, and then excuse themselves for not fighting for the Zone on the ground that we would not join them." And Sargent and Wigram guessed that, if Britain decided to open negotiations with Germany to replace the demilitarized zone with a revised Treaty of Locarno, France would acquiesce. Indeed, because of the difficulty of bringing French policy into line, the Foreign Office suggested that Britain might *"privately and quietly"* ascertain Hitler's willingness to negotiate a settlement.[30]

The French Chamber of Deputies ratified the Franco-Soviet pact on 27 February, Eden announced in Geneva on 2 March that Britain supported an oil embargo, and the interrelationship of British, French, Italian, and German interests drew closer than ever before at the Cabinet meeting of 5 March. Eden told his colleagues about Flandin's apprehensions. Italy had warned France that imposition of an oil sanction would force Italy to withdraw from the League, nullify the Franco-

[28] DPR meeting, 14 January, CAB 16/136; Cabs 1, 3(36), 15 and 29 January, CAB 23/83; Sargent (and Wigram) memorandum, 10 February, C796/4/18, FO 371/19884; see also Eden memorandum to Cabinet Committee on Germany, 14 February (note 9 above).

[29] Eden memorandum, 17 January, CP 13(36), CAB 24/259 (*DBFP*, 15, no. 460); Cabs 3, 4(36), 29 January and 5 February, CAB 23/83; Vansittart and Eden memoranda, 3 and 11 February, CP 42(36), CAB 24/260 (*DBFP*, 15, appx. IVb and no. 509); Sargent minute, 10 February, C796/4/18, FO371/19884; Clerk (Paris) to Eden, 7 February, *DBFP*, 15, no. 500.

[30] Eden memorandum to Cabinet Committee on Germany, 14 February (note 9 above); Sargent (and Wigram) memorandum, 10 February, C796/4/18, FO 371/19884; Foreign Office memorandum, 15 February, preparing Eden for meeting of Cabinet Committee on Germany, *DBFP*, 15, no. 522; Eden to Phipps, 24 February, no. 541.

Italian military agreement of 1935, and withdraw from the Locarno Pact. These threats, "together with the possibility of an Italian *rapprochement* with Germany and of German action in the demilitarized zone created a grave situation for France." France counted on British support in "concerting common action" in accordance with the Treaty of Locarno even if Italy refused to act. Flandin wanted to know whether the British Government agreed on these points before France could decide whether to support the oil embargo. The Foreign Office, Eden continued, considered German-Italian coalescence unlikely, partly because Italy wanted to maintain Austrian independence, "and partly owing to the well-known unreliability of Italian policy, of which Herr Hitler was well aware." Nor had Italy ever hinted to Britain that "she would disinterest herself from the Locarno Treaty," Eden asserted, unaware that very broad hints had reached Berlin during the past few weeks.[31]

After discussing treaty words such as "flagrant" and "assistance," the Cabinet agreed to refer to a small committee the complex legal questions that would have to be answered before the Government could reply in detail to Flandin. Meanwhile, because Eden "could not delay indefinitely" a reply to Flandin, the Foreign Secretary was instructed to discuss the Rhineland problem with Flandin in what Baldwin and Chamberlain called a "realistic spirit." In fact, "neither France nor England was really in a position to take military action against Germany in the event of a violation of the Treaty of Locarno." Finally, Eden should reopen bilateral negotiations with Germany concerning an air pact; perhaps France could be brought into these talks in which the question of the demilitarized zone might be settled amicably. Eden himself had recommended this course as "one way to get round the difficulty" of being drawn by France into a commitment if Germany breached the Treaty of Locarno.[32]

[31] Cab 15(36), CAB 23/83; also Edmond (Geneva) to Foreign Office, 4 March, *DBFP*, 16, nos. 11, 12, 20; O'Malley minute, 4 March, no. 18 (the Franco-Italian military agreements have helped tie France "to the chariot wheels of Italy at Geneva"); Baer, *Test Case*, pp. 222–27; Emmerson, *Rhineland Crisis*, pp. 69–70; Middlemas and Barnes, *Baldwin*, pp. 913–14; Parker, "Ethiopian Crisis," pp. 327–28. For signs that Mussolini was indeed disengaging Italy from Locarno, and that Italy and Germany were drawing closer together, see Baer, *Test Case*, pp. 229–31; Emmerson, *Rhineland Crisis*, pp. 84–87; Funke, *Sanktionen*, chaps. 5, 6; Petersen, *Hitler-Mussolini*, chaps. 12, 13; Esmonde M. Robertson, "Hitler and Sanctions: Mussolini and the Rhineland," *European Studies Review* 7 (1977); Weinberg, *Foreign Policy of Hitler's Germany*, chap. 10; Robert H. Whealey, "Mussolini's Ideological Diplomacy: An Unpublished Document," *Journal of Modern History* 39 (1967), 435–36.

[32] Cab 15(36), 5 March, CAB 23/83. On 6 March, Eden told German Ambassador Leopold von Hoesch that Britain wished to begin negotiations for an air pact; *DBFP*, 16, no. 29.

Knowing that the Mediterranean crisis prevented a united front among the other Locarno signatories, Hitler staged his Rhineland coup on 7 March, sooner than the British Foreign Office and Government had expected, four days after the publication of the White Paper on Defence, before the British were strong enough to negotiate a general settlement, and before they could use the demilitarized zone as a bargaining chip in negotiating any particular concessions preceding the general. To demonstrate his peaceful intentions, Hitler offered to rejoin the League of Nations and to replace the Locarno Pact with a number of agreements, including nonaggression pacts with France, Belgium, and Germany's neighbors to the east. In the diplomatic crisis that followed Germany's action, which was clearly "flagrant" in the terms of the Locarno Treaty, London pondered how to negotiate with Germany, limited the scope of any commitment to France and Belgium, considered the strategic implications of maintaining military forces in the Mediterranean, and began to reassess its policy.

On 8 March, Eden wrote that he would now be at a disadvantage in negotiations with Germany. Britain had lost the demilitarized zone as a "bargaining counter," and would find it difficult to persuade other European powers to seek new agreements that relied "on Germany's promises." Still, knowing that Hitler might repudiate any agreement when circumstances allowed, Britain must conclude "as far reaching and enduring a settlement as possible whilst Herr Hitler is still in the mood to do so." Meanwhile, the Locarno signatories should not tell Germany to evacuate the Rhineland unless "prepared to enforce it by military action." Britain should deplore the "manner" of Germany's action, not the "result." France could "hold us to our Locarno obligation and call upon us to join with her in turning German forces out of the Rhineland." Britain must not commit to assist the French if they so requested, an unlikely event because France was "not in the mood for a military adventure of this sort." Britain must discourage France from either taking military action against Germany or adopting a "policy of sulking and passive obstruction."[33]

The Cabinet and emergency meetings of a small number of ministers approved Eden's recommended line of policy. Britain deprecated Germany's unilateral repudiation of the Locarno Pact and would stand by its obligation to come to the assistance of France and Belgium if they were actually attacked by Germany. (Even in this event, however, Eden recommended against accepting a "heavier commitment" to intervene automatically "at a time when we found difficulty in carrying out an

[33] CP 73(36), CAB 24/261 (*DBFP*, 16, no. 48). Vansittart approved Eden's memorandum "enthusiastically"; Avon, *Dictators*, p. 388.

existing commitment.") Still, Britain had "a reasonable regard for the position into which Germany had got herself," and welcomed Hitler's "constructive proposals" for a new European settlement.[34]

Most ministers and experts agreed on two key points: the City and public opinion sympathized more with Germany than with France and would not support British economic or military action; it would be foolish to risk war. The notable exception was Duff Cooper, who argued that Britain would not be in a "relatively better position" against Germany three years hence, and that buying time would only allow Germany to dominate Europe and perhaps eventually the world. Baldwin recalled his campaign pledge never to undertake "sanctions again until our armaments were sufficient," and resented the French putting Britain on the spot. They should be told that strong action against Germany now would unleash "another great war in Europe" and that, if France and Russia defeated Germany, this war "would probably only result in Germany going Bolshevik," an indication of the view widely held in London that Hitler was preferable to Stalin.[35]

Members of the Foreign Office remained at odds over the kinds of concessions that might be offered to Germany. Ashton-Gwatkin, who wrote novels under a pen name, reiterated his opinion that economic assistance to Germany would help prevent war. Lord Cranborne, known as "Bobbety," agreed, adding that such assistance might include giving Germany "a freer hand" in Central and Eastern Europe. Lord Stanhope, Sargent, and Eden emphasized the need for a political settlement as a prior condition for economic assistance. Characteristically, Vansittart was more skeptical than the others about a German change of heart and less willing to consider abetting Germany's economic hegemony in the east. Britain must not "fatten" Germany prematurely, but test German intentions, meanwhile rearming and refusing to hand over Central Europe "to German penetration."[36]

[34] Cabs 16, 18, 19(36), 9, 11, 12 March; CAB 23/83; meetings of ministers, 13 and 14 March, CAB 27/603; Avon, *Dictators*, pp. 387–88; Emmerson, *Rhineland Crisis*, chap. 5. The Cabinet minutes of 11 March are printed in full in Éva Haraszti, *The Invaders: Hitler Occupies the Rhineland* (Budapest, 1983), appx. 2.

[35] Cab 18(36), 11 March, CAB 23/83. The Subcommittee on Economic Pressure (of the CID's Advisory Committee on Trade Questions in Time of War) advised that it was impossible to estimate how effective League sanctions might be; provisional report, 12 March (given to the Cabinet on 19 March), CP 85(36), CAB 24/261; examined in detail by Wendt, *Economic Appeasement*, pp. 317–20. On British opinion: Franklin Reid Gannon, *The British Press and Germany, 1936–1939* (Oxford, 1971), chap. 3; *History of the Times*, pp. 899–905; Jones, *Diary*, p. 181; Macmillan, *Winds of Change*, pp. 423–31; Nicolson, *Diaries*, pp. 248–50; Thompson, *Anti-Appeasers*, chap. 5.

[36] Minutes of 16–27 March, C1906/4/18, FO 371/19892, and C2086/4/18, FO 371/19894, some of which are in *DBFP*, 16, nos. 122, 135; Vansittart to Hankey, 16 April, C2842/4/18, FO 371/19902. See also Wendt, *Economic Appeasement*, pp. 325–30.

Vansittart thought that the Germans probably did want peace in Western Europe for the near future, but did "not ultimately desire peace in Central and Eastern Europe. And that affects us directly unless we intend to abandon the League and its principles, a possibility which I exclude." Sharing Vansittart's pessimism, Ambassador Phipps rejected the thesis that remedying Germany's economic distress would eliminate the Nazi movement: "Hitlerism is no longer the symptom but the disease itself." The ambassador called attention to the views of the German General Staff, which indicated that "the steadying action of the German army is one of time rather than of principle." Hitler would make war either before his Army was completely ready or when it "gives the word to go." The British military attaché in Berlin reported that the German Army did not want to risk war in the west, but considered eastern expansion inevitable and Germany's right.[37]

A settlement with Germany would have to wait. Neither the French nor the Germans wanted soon to enter such negotiation, and Vansittart agreed with Sargent that Britain must not rush things. Britain's immediate objective, to resolve the Rhineland question peacefully through diplomatic brokerage, guided its policy toward France and Belgium before and during staff talks among the three countries. By the time these were held in London on 15–16 April, their scope for Britain had been predetermined by the policy of conciliating Germany, by reluctance to spell out British obligations, and by fears that staff talks might entail a British commitment on the Continent.[38]

Baldwin, Ramsay MacDonald, and others advocated establishing closer contact with Hitler. Eyres-Monsell wanted a bilateral naval treaty with Germany to accompany the multilateral London Naval Treaty that was about to be signed.[39] Although Chamberlain thought staff talks would show Hitler that Britain meant business, he did not mean belligerence. Chamberlain told Flandin that Britain could not accept "as a reliable estimate of a mad dictator's reactions" the French Foreign Min-

---

[37] Vansittart minute, 17 March, and Phipps to Eden, 7 March, *DBFP*, 16, nos. 121, 43. Gladwyn Jebb (economic relations section of the League of Nations and western department) disagreed with Phipps; it was possible to remove the cancer of Nazism with "the radioactive treatment of increased world trade" (no. 43n). On the German Army: Phipps to Eden, 9 April, enclosing a memorandum from Colonel Hotblack on the German General Staff, *DBFP*, 16, no. 228.

[38] Sargent and Vansittart minutes, 17 March, *DBFP*, 16, no. 114n; Cabs 20, 21, 23, 26(36); 16, 18, 19 March, 1 April; CAB 23/83; meeting of ministers, 16 March, CAB 27/603.

[39] Cab 20(36), 16 March, CAB 23/83. Eden opposed signing a treaty with Germany at such an inappropriate moment; the Cabinet authorized the First Lord "to continue negotiations with Germany" but not to conclude a treaty "at the present time." On the London Naval Treaty (signed on 25 March by Britain, the United States, France, Canada, Australia, New Zealand, and India), see Gibbs, *Rearmament*, pp. 328–32, Roskill, *Naval Policy*, chap. 10, and Trotter, *Britain and East Asia*, pp. 170–77.

ister's opinion that Hitler would "yield without war" if France and Britain stood firm together. Chamberlain was glad not to have Churchill in the Cabinet. Churchill was "in the usual excited condition that comes on him when he smells war," and if he were in the Cabinet "we should be spending all our time in holding him down instead of getting on with our business." Chamberlain and Baldwin thought becoming involved in a war now "would very likely throw back the whole process" of rearmament. It could be stated to the French, Chamberlain said, that "our own Air Forces were so weak today that we could not do Germany much harm, but that in two years' time we should be able to hit her fairly hard."[40]

Some ministers echoed the warning of the Chiefs of Staff that staff talks with France and Belgium would make it virtually impossible to include Germany in later negotiations about a new system of security to replace the Treaty of Locarno. The COS reiterated the argument used by military experts and Hankey since the First World War: the disclosure of war plans was absurd since Britain could not be sure "as to the side on which we might be fighting."[41] These and other reservations underlay the CID's recommendations, which the Cabinet approved on 8 April. Staff conversations must be confined to Britain's "existing obligations under the Locarno Treaty" to intervene in case of an unprovoked German attack across the frontier; Germany's building fortifications in the Rhineland would not constitute "aggression" so defined. Talks must not include the question of British guarantees to France and Belgium in the event that conciliation failed, for "the effort of conciliation has not failed." British military representatives should discuss only "technical matters" (the forces and facilities available), not political questions such as whether Britain might withdraw forces from the Mediterranean or should increase its armaments.[42]

In Cabinet meetings, Eden sometimes expressed the concern of the Foreign Office that the Cabinet did not appreciate the real anxieties of the French Government. The Foreign Office did not agree with Flandin that this was "the best moment at which to accept the German chal-

---

[40] Simon to Baldwin, 25 March, PREM 1/194; Chamberlain diary, 12 March, and letter to Ida, 14 March, Chamberlain Papers, NC 2/23a, 18/1/951; meeting of ministers, 30 March, CAB 27/603.

[41] COS meeting, 31 March, CAB 53/5; COS memorandum (COS 452), 1 April, in CP 105(36), CAB 24/261 (also in *DBFP*, 16, no. 194); JPC report (JP 136), 1 April, CAB 53/27; Bond, *Chief of Staff*, p. 107. In its peace plan of 31 March, the German Government made the same point about the inconsistency between Anglo-French staff talks and future discussions of new security pacts.

[42] CID meeting, 3 April, in CP 105(36), CAB 24/261; Cab 28(36), 8 April, CAB 23/83. On these talks: Avon, *Dictators*, pp. 406–7, 417–18; Bond, *British Military Policy*, pp. 227–28; Gibbs, *Rearmament*, pp. 249–50, 608–11; Roskill, *Hankey*, 3:226–27.

lenge," and Eden suspected that the Frenchman's tough talk may have been meant to impress French public opinion rather than Hitler. Still, Flandin struck a sympathetic chord in the Foreign Office by emphasizing that, although French security was not immediately threatened and France would not act alone, the sanctity of treaties must be maintained and the Locarno powers had "a clear obligation to render military assistance."[43] General Maurice Gamelin, the French Chief of General Staff, told the British military attaché that, although Germany probably did not now intend to attack France, the German action would eventually increase French vulnerability to an "attaque brusquée" and block any immediate French assistance to their eastern allies or Austria.[44] Eden disagreed with Simon's argument that staff talks would end the prospect "of any serious proposals from Germany." Germany, Eden reminded colleagues, had broken the Locarno Treaty and "weakened French security, and, in the circumstances, Herr Hitler had no right to complain if conversations took place."[45]

On the other hand, Eden and his advisers were as determined as the Cabinet not to let France drag Britain into a dangerous confrontation with Germany, whether in Western or Eastern Europe. Vansittart thought Flandin would prove "movable by suasion" if the Locarno Treaty were replaced by some kind of security agreement.[46] Malkin restated legal grounds for Britain not to intervene militarily. Britain could interpret the phrase "in case of unprovoked aggression" so as to limit its response if, for example, Germany decided to make war in Eastern Europe and attacked France first in order to prevent France

[43] Clerk (Paris) to Foreign Office, 10 and 17 March, *DBFP*, 16, nos. 61, 120; Wigram memorandum, 12 March, no. 78; record of talks by representatives of the Locarno Pact powers, 10 March, no. 63. See Young, *In Command of France*, pp. 119–29, where the author laments that we may never know "what really went on within French official quarters" in the fortnight following the reoccupation (p. 120); also Anthony Adamthwaite, *France and the Coming of the Second World War, 1936–1939* (London, 1977), pp. 37–41; Avon, *Dictators*, pp. 386–89; Bond, *Chief of Staff*, pp. 103–8; Emmerson, *Rhineland Crisis*, chap. 4; Gibbs, *Rearmament*, pp. 241–44; W. F. Knapp, "The Rhineland Crisis of March 1936," in James Joll, ed., *The Decline of the Third Republic* (London, 1959); Warner, *Pierre Laval*, chap. 4. Stephen A. Schuker argues that Flandin knew Britain would not intervene, that he had no intention of confronting Germany alone, and that he used strong language in order to limit the damage done to Anglo-French relations by Hitler's action; "France and the Remilitarization of the Rhineland, 1936," *French Historical Studies* 14 (1985–86).

[44] Reports of Colonel F. Beumont-Nesbitt of conversations with Gamelin and Commandant Petibon, 12, 14, 20 March, C1838/C1912/C2203/4/18, FO 371/19891–92, 19896; also Military Intelligence note, 24 March, WO 190/409. Sargent called Gamelin's argument "not altogether sincere," for Flandin had the previous autumn intimated that France would never dare attack Germany in order to defend Russia, Poland, Czechoslovakia, or Austria; minute of 18 March in C1912/4/18.

[45] Meeting of ministers, 30 March, CAB 27/603.

[46] Vansittart minutes, 11 and 19 March, C1940/4/18, FO 371/19892, and C2048/4/18, FO 371/19894 (the first of these, redated 12 March, also in *DBFP*, 16, no. 78n).

from implementing its guarantees to Russia, Czechoslovakia, or Poland.[47]

Flandin and his colleagues were depressed by Britain's tendency to treat France and Belgium like Germany, an "unjust assimilation of guilt and innocence" in British proposals for conciliation. The French thought it "better to know at once that Locarno did not exist and that the British Government would do nothing."[48] Eden testily observed that "it is not for France to lecture us" on treaty obligations. He agreed with Vansittart that, in staff talks, Britain should adopt the same line as the French had a few months earlier regarding the Mediterranean crisis: Britain was reequipping its forces and therefore could not presently "undertake any commitments which are not in accordance with our factual capacities."[49] London parried French and Italian suggestions to lift sanctions so that Italy could help reconstruct the Stresa Front and cooperate fully with the Locarno powers concerning the Rhineland.[50] The British Government would not abandon the League or Ethiopia, and saw no inconsistency between participating in sanctions against Italy and refusing to do so against Germany if Germany fortified the Rhineland.[51]

In coordinating Western responses, London sought to reassure and restrain Paris, conciliate Berlin, and avoid undertaking any commitment to safeguard Eastern European countries. On 19 March, Britain, France, Belgium, and Italy together issued a statement that they would consider Germany's proposals of 7 March, discuss joint action, and begin preparing mutual assistance pacts to replace the Treaty of Locarno. A week later, Eden told the House of Commons that the Government wanted to avoid war and work for the "appeasement of Europe," that preserving the territorial integrity of France and Belgium was a

[47] Malkin minute of 14 March, C1994/4/18, FO 371/19893; Sargent-Malkin exchange of notes, 20 and 21 March, C2824/4/18, FO 371/19901. Malkin attended the meeting of ministers on 16 March to point out the legal implications of any British statement of policy on the Rhineland; CAB 27/603. See also George Sakwa, "The Franco-Polish Alliance and the Remilitarization of the Rhineland," *Historical Journal* 16 (1973), 140–41.

[48] Eden to Clerk and Wigram minute, both 17 March, *DBFP*, 16, nos. 119, 123.

[49] Eden note on Vansittart minute, 13 March, *DBFP*, 16, no. 88; Vansittart to Eden, and Eden note, both 31 March, no. 189.

[50] Eden at meeting of ministers, 13 March, CAB 27/603; Drummond to Eden, 28 and 30 March, 7 April, *DBFP*, 16, nos. 171, 176, 182, 212; Vansittart minute of discussion with French ambassador, 16 April, no. 243 (see also no. 251). Vansittart thought Italy might reduce its aims in Ethiopia if shown that restoring the Stresa Front could check the German threat to Austria.

[51] Cabs 23 and 27(36), 19 March and 6 April, CAB 23/83; Cabinet discussion of wire from Eden in Paris, 8 April, Cab 28(36), CAB 23/83. Vansittart advised against increasing sanctions against Italy because the League was "too weak, too vacillating and too divided." Yet he believed there was still "a possibility of preserving the credit and the authority of the League." Minutes of 10 and 16 April, *DBFP*, 16, nos. 235, 243.

vital British interest, and that he would not dishonor his country's signature at Locarno. Germany countered on 31 March with an elaboration of its peace plan of the seventh, proposing a cooling-off period of four months before concluding nonaggression pacts. On 1 April, Britain pledged to assist France and Belgium against unprovoked aggression and to establish or continue staff talks, should the effort of conciliation through a new security pact fail. In turn, Belgium and France (which had mutually revoked their 1920 alliance on 6 March) subscribed to the British position that efforts to conciliate had not failed. Not at all convinced this was true, the French wanted to know explicitly whether Germany recognized the existing political and territorial settlement in Europe. On 10 April, France reluctantly agreed to have Britain convey this and other queries to the German Government.[52] On 30 April, the British Cabinet instructed the Foreign Office to tone down the draft questionnaire so as to acknowledge, as Chamberlain put it, "the fact that the Germans were not menacing in the West" (although he conceded it was not clear what Germany's intentions were in the east). The revised questionnaire, weaker than Vansittart and Wigram desired but still unusually firm for such a document, was at last dispatched to Phipps in Berlin on 6 May.[53]

Although determined to avoid conflict, and sure that Germany did not intend to invade Belgium or France,[54] the British Government examined its strategic situation in case war broke out. Hankey told ministers the views of the Chiefs of Staff on 13 March. Britain must mobilize if its contribution were to have any value, and must also recall forces from the Mediterranean, where all "efficient war material" was positioned. Further study by the joint planners reinforced the advice of the COS, that Britain could not provide both home defense and security in the Mediterranean. Even if mobilization were ordered and forces withdrawn from the Mediterranean, the Army would need two months to prepare a Field Force of two divisions. And the RAF, after three or four months, would have insufficient strength at home "for security against air attack or to prosecute successfully an air offensive against Germany." Britain's main contribution would be economic warfare at sea, but should also be prepared to send light bomber squadrons to the

---

[52] *DBFP*, 16, pp. 227–28 and nos. 144, 199, 231, 236; also Cmd. 5134, 5149, 5175. On Eden's speech: Avon, *Dictators*, pp. 407–13; *DBFP*, 16, no. 186 (Nigel Law to Sargent, reporting that the City, profoundly affected by the speech, had not become pro-French but "pro-British"). Litvinov told Eden that the Soviet Government was perturbed at the failure of the Locarno signatories to include Eastern Europe in their proposals of 19 March; Eden to Viscount Chilston (Moscow), *DBFP*, 16, no. 169.

[53] *DBFP*, 16, nos. 269, 277, 283, 299, 304, 306, 307, appx. I; Cab 32(36), 30 April, CAB 23/84; Avon, *Dictators*, pp. 418–19; Emmerson, *Rhineland Crisis*, pp. 222–25.

[54] Military Intelligence memoranda, 19 and 30 March, WO 190/402 and 410.

Continent to assist the allied counteroffensive and protect Britain against air attack, and political considerations might require dispatching the Field Force.[55]

These appraisals gave London reason to turn the tables on Paris. Just as the French had said in the autumn that they could not help Britain in the Mediterranean for some months, now Britain could tell the French that, so long as the Mediterranean situation continued, British forces available for a European war would be severely limited.[56] The strategic situation, as an official in the Foreign Office succinctly put it, hardly warranted "any great risks in foreign policy." Nor did the Foreign Office look to the United States for help. The Neutrality Act, signed by President Franklin D. Roosevelt on 29 February, negated feelers from Washington about exchanging naval intelligence, details of armament programs, and ideas for a defensive war against Germany.[57]

Military advisers, Hankey, and Fisher were readier than the Foreign Office and Cabinet to recognize that the juxtaposition of the Mediterranean and Rhineland crises demanded a major reevaluation of British policy. The Chiefs of Staff advised that "so long as our Mediterranean commitments are maintained, our position in Northern Europe was a very weak one, even to the point of our being dependent on the French Navy for the protection of our coasts." Chatfield referred to "the extraordinary step the Foreign Office took of asking Italy, the Geneva criminal, to assist in the coercion of Germany."[58] Hankey wished that

[55] Meeting of ministers, 13 March, CAB 27/603; COS meeting, 12 March, CAB 53/5; JPC report, 16 March, COS memoranda 18 March and 1 April, and CID meeting, 3 April, all in CP 105(36), CAB 24/261 (the JPC report and COS cover note are also in *DBFP*, 16, no. 134); COS meetings, 17 and 31 March, CAB 53/5; Cab 25(36), 1 April, CAB 23/83; Air and Naval Staff notes in AIR 9/73; JPC appreciation of the case of unprovoked aggression in the near future, 29 April, CAB 53/27, approved by the COS on 4 May (COS 460), CAB 53/6; Gibbs, *Rearmament*, pp. 246–52. See also Bond, *Chief of Staff*, pp. 105–6, and *British Military Policy*, pp. 225–27; Dunbabin, "British Military Establishment," pp. 183–84. The COS had no contingency plan on file for military action in the Rhineland; see James Leasor and General Sir Leslie Hollis, *The Clock with Four Hands* (New York, 1959), p. 30.

[56] CID meeting, 3 April, in CP 105(36), CAB 24/261. The Cabinet and COS considered Chamberlain's proposal that Britain contribute a "symbolic" contingent to an international force that would be stationed on both sides of Germany's frontier with France and Belgium. Cabs 20, 21, 16 and 18 March, CAB 23/83; COS meeting, 16 March, CAB 53/5, and report, 17 March, CP 81(36), CAB 24/261. The COS viewed this as risky because it would further reduce British resources to meet emergencies that might arise in the empire. Fisher correctly guessed that "this whole idea will prove academic," minute of 24 March, T 161/718; Germany and France rejected it in any case.

[57] Foreign Office minute, early April, C2608/4/18, FO 371/19899; on American inquiries, Harrison, "Testing the Water," pp. 217–19.

[58] Inskip at Cab 25(36), 1 April, CAB 23/83; COS memorandum, 18 March, in CP 105(36), CAB 24/261; Chatfield to Admiral Sir Roger Backhouse (Commander in Chief, Home Fleet), 27 March, Chatfield Papers. Ellington did not see how Britain could maintain sanctions against Italy and at the same time ask Italy to cooperate over the Rhineland; Ellington to Brooke-Popham, 20 March, Brooke-Popham Papers, II/5 (LHCMA).

he could see "a real policy emerging," and regretted that Britain would "have to stick to the Covenant, as long as it lasts, because public opinion here will only face rearmament *as part of a League policy.*" The Mediterranean situation "mucked up" European politics, and Britain could not risk prolonged "antagonism with Italy, situated as she is at one of the bottle-necks of our long line of main communication" between Europe and the Far East. Fisher deplored that "'our parade of force in the Eastern Mediterranean, so far from impressing others, has merely made a laughing-stock of ourselves.'" Vice Admiral William M. James, Deputy Chief of Naval Staff, saw little correspondence between military readiness in the Mediterranean and the situation in Europe. The Cabinet was "blown hither and thither by winds beyond their control," its foreign policy having been "rudely shaken."[59]

This sort of criticism soon led to ministerial discussion of the failure and future of British policy, just as a year earlier the Chiefs of Staff had prodded the Government to reappraise defense policy and coordinate it with foreign policy. At the Cabinet meeting of 22 April, Eden questioned the future of collective security; Mussolini and Hitler had been successful, and separate governments were more concerned about their particular relations with the two dictators than about the principle of collective security against aggression. Baldwin announced that he would ask the Cabinet to consider establishing a committee to discuss this question, and reminded his colleagues that the rearmament program must proceed "as rapidly as possible."[60]

On 29 April, Eden wrote that "the determination of a policy at this time is a matter of the gravest difficulty and importance," and the Cabinet discussed foreign policy far more comprehensively than usual. Eden warned that Italy's imminent victory over Ethiopia (which, he failed to add, the Foreign Office had not expected to be so quick) was putting pressure on the Sudan and impressing opinion in Egypt, at a time when negotiations were under way in Cairo for an Anglo-Egyptian treaty. The Foreign Office had previously assumed that Mussolini's African adventure "would tend to check untoward developments in Central Europe, e.g. in Austria." But now Hitler seemed to be contemplating a move against Austria while Mussolini was preoccupied elsewhere. In that event, however, Mussolini would likely "support Austria and would expect France to assist him." A new align-

[59] Hankey to Dick Casey (Australia's Federal Treasurer), 20 April, CAB 63/51; Roskill, *Hankey*, 3:239; Fisher to Vansittart, 21 April, in Pratt, *East of Malta*, p. 35; James minute, 22 April, ADM 116/3042 (sent by Chatfield to Eyres-Monsell on 27 April).

[60] Cab 30(36), 22 April, CAB 23/84. Eden told Hankey that collective security had become an illusion after failing in the "perfect case of Italy" and would not work against Germany; Pownall diary, 23 April, in Bond, *Chief of Staff*, p. 110.

ment was probably evolving, with Germany and Yugoslavia coming together on one side and France and Italy on the other.[61]

The Cabinet soon turned to a general review of foreign policy, having concluded—more explicitly than at any previous Cabinet meeting—that "the general question of our policy in regard to the Italo-Abyssinian dispute formed part of the general question of major foreign policy." Eden raised questions about the League and British policy toward Germany. Eden thought the League Council would be divided in the future; while one group of nations watched Germany, and another group watched Italy, Britain alone was "compelled to watch both." He wanted the Cabinet to consider a possible détente with Germany, although he recognized that this put him on "rather controversial ground."

In the discussion that followed Eden's presentation, Inskip raised what the Services considered the most germane point of all: whether "the assumption of 'peace conditions' on which our present [rearmament] preparations were based, was compatible with the growing anxieties of the international situation." Inskip quoted Eden on the need to accelerate rearmament, and warned that he might soon have to ask the Cabinet for authority to see that manufacturers gave priority to orders connected with rearmament. Chamberlain thought Inskip's question, which involved a departure from the policy of rearming without harm to civil and export trade, "should be reserved until after decisions had been reached on the major policy of the Government." The Cabinet agreed, and approved the establishment of the Cabinet Committee on Foreign Policy (FPC), which was instructed to "consider and report to the Cabinet on the foreign policy to be adopted by the Government in the present international situation."

Both the Cabinet and the new Cabinet committee met the next day, 30 April. In the Cabinet's discussion of the draft questionnaire for Hitler, Duff Cooper rejected the idea of reaching détente with Germany "in order to gain time." Instead, Britain should support peace-loving nations—"all of which it so happened were members of the League of Nations"—to hold Germany in check. But neither the Cabinet nor the FPC (of which he was not a member) followed up on this argument. Chaired by the prime minister, the committee also included Ramsay MacDonald (Lord President), Chamberlain, Hailsham (Lord Chancellor), Simon, Eden, Halifax (Lord Privy Seal since November), and Inskip. The committee agreed that collective security had failed, the League must be reformed, and the Government should consider what

---

[61] For Eden's comments and the Cabinet's responses, see Eden minute, 29 April, *DBFP*, 16, no. 276n; Cab 31(36), CAB 23/84.

international repercussions might be caused by Britain's releasing itself from Article 16 of the Covenant.[62] Having asked Eden to prepare guidelines for future discussions, the FPC adjourned, not to meet again until mid-July. Soon Mussolini declared victory over Ethiopia and proclaimed an Italian empire (9 May), and the League, unwilling to declare its policy a failure, postponed discussion of sanctions from 11 May until 16 June.

Confusion and delay in both London and Geneva prolonged Britain's military concentration in the Mediterranean. On 4 May, an impatient First Sea Lord wrote bluntly to Vansittart. "What," Chatfield asked, "are the intentions of the Foreign Office?" In the Abyssinian department at the Foreign Office, G. H. Thompson thought Chatfield's question reflected "very clearly the growing impatience of the Service Departments over the confused situation which has endured so long." Vansittart and others sympathized with the Navy, but the Foreign Office could not yet tell when the political situation would clear up enough to permit a withdrawal of forces from the Mediterranean.[63] Eden opposed any major withdrawal from the Mediterranean because of the bad impression this would make on world opinion. Chatfield wanted assurances from Eden that, if the current state of "instant readiness for action" be relaxed to a state of "diplomatic tension," no subsequent diplomatic move would incite Italy to attack those reduced naval forces that would remain. This, Eden remarked, was asking him "to calculate the incalculable, for these matters were incalculable where a Dictator was concerned."[64]

In fact, the Foreign Office was sharply divided over the Mediterranean calculus and thus unable to clarify its intentions to Chatfield or the Cabinet. O'Malley, Maurice Peterson (Abyssinian department), and Strang advocated closing the Suez Canal to Italy. Even if this step did not prevent Mussolini from conquering Ethiopia, which now was on the verge of collapse, it would demonstrate Britain's and the League's determination to deny him "the full fruits of aggression." This action would not necessarily push Italy and Germany together, lead to war in the Mediterranean, or weaken Britain militarily. Vansittart disagreed. He did not want to risk igniting "the powder barrel of Europe," although Britain must "look forward to the utmost trouble with Italy in Africa even if not in Europe." The League's prestige would be

---

[62] Cab 32(36), CAB 23/84; committee meeting of 30 April, CAB 27/622.

[63] Chatfield to Vansittart, 4 May, Thompson minute, 6 May, Vansittart to Chatfield, 11 May, and other minutes in J3859/1000/1, FO 371/20191 (some of these in DBFP, 16, no. 317). See also Roskill, Naval Policy, pp. 268–69.

[64] Cab 37(36), 18 May, CAB 23/84; meeting of Cabinet Committee on the Mediterranean Fleet, 19 May, CAB 27/606.

damaged more by a conflagration following closure of the Suez Canal than by failing to save Ethiopia. Agreeing with Vansittart were Sir Lancelot Oliphant (Assistant Under-Secretary), Sargent, Wigram, Sir Victor Wellesley (Deputy Under-Secretary), and Reginald Leeper (head of the news department). Britain could restore its own prestige best by rapidly rearming, and must not propose action that could lead to an Italo-German combination, a breach with France, or war.[65]

There was more at stake than the future of the League, for Mussolini's triumph over Ethiopia might encourage him to challenge the British Empire. J. H. U. Lambert, a member of the Abyssinian department in the Foreign Office, thought that the characteristics of fascism would drive Mussolini to do just that. Thus, Britain must now choose whether "to take time by the forelock, and conjure or eliminate the evil—or take the fence only when it comes, although so many additions will have been made to it that by that time it will be of astronomical height." Eden regarded Lambert's paper a "most interesting" antidote for the pessimistic temptation "to think that we *cannot* deal with Italy now in a military sense. . . . I doubt myself whether we shall ever be in a better military position to meet an Italian challenge than we are today, for though we shall be stronger two years hence, so will Germany." But Wigram rejected the idea of using force now to check Italy's imperialistic ambitions as "quite impracticable and most dangerous." So did Thompson. Vansittart thought Lambert was "probably right" about an eventual clash between Britain and Italy, but believed that "time is rather on our side than on Italy's. Indeed we need time badly."[66]

Leon Blum, leader of the Popular Front that triumphed in the French elections of late April and early May, was convinced that Mussolini and Hitler would eventually coalesce. In Berlin, Phipps cautioned that "the French Socialist dog [might] be wagged by the Communist tail." If

[65] Memoranda and minutes, 24 April–4 May, in *DBFP*, 16, no. 273. See also Baer, *Test Case*, pp. 258–61; Parker, "Ethiopian Crisis," pp. 328–29. On 2 April, O'Malley suggested that perhaps "Mussolini never in his maddest moments contemplated what we generally call 'a mad dog act'"; *DBFP*, 16, no. 172n. General Dill doubted that Italy would chance war with Britain now, for the Italians would not want to risk losing the gains of "one of the biggest gambles in military history"; Dill to Major General G. W. Howard (Egypt), 3 May, Dill Papers, 5/1/2 (LHCMA).

[66] Lambert memorandum, 27 April (with Wigram and Eden minutes), *DBFP*, 16, no. 276; Thompson minute (with Vansittart comment), 28 May, no. 345. Other minutes on the Lambert memorandum can be found in R3335/226/22, FO 371/20411: e.g., Vansittart, 28 April; Peterson, 28 April ("Italy is a more real and a more imminent threat to us than is Germany"); Oliphant, 28 April ("the time is not yet"). Lord Rothermere thought Italy would easily beat Britain in a single-handed war because of its large air force; letter to J. L. Garvin, 13 April, Garvin Papers.

Blum should be "run by Moscow . . . and if Anglo-Italian relations do not soon improve, events will indeed be playing into the hands of Herr Hitler." Wigram could not view "negotiation with Germany as a serious proposition" so long as Anglo-Italian enmity continued, and Vansittart thought Phipps's report confirmed his own case for lifting sanctions. "All this may be true," Eden conceded, but neither he nor the British public was "prepared to sit round the table on friendly terms with the aggressor for many a long day." Cadogan advocated removing sanctions against Italy and revising both the Versailles settlement and the League Covenant.[67]

While members of the Foreign Office argued among themselves, military experts and Cabinet ministers grew more restless. Chatfield asserted that the Government's policy of collective security was out of step with its defense policy, and that "regional pacts would be only one stage less dangerous than collective security." If the Government decided to leave a strong fleet in the Mediterranean to thwart Italian hegemony even after sanctions were lifted, the Services would have to reexamine the military position in the Mediterranean, for the Defence Requirements Committee had based its recommendations on the assumption "that normal relations with Italy would be reestablished before long." Group Captain Harris and other members of the expanded Joint Planning Committee were preparing a strategic review of Europe and plans for war with Germany, but, now that collective security seemed dead, Britain was in a "transition period" and the Services did not know on what policy assumptions they should base long-term strategic planning.[68]

Colonel Pownall reckoned that Vansittart's prediction of a German war in the next two years would come true if Britain tied itself to France and did not "come to an arrangement with Germany." Baldwin told Eden he had "'no idea'" how to improve relations with Germany— "'that is your job.'" In the Cabinet on 20 May, someone warned that Mussolini and Hitler would come together if the League decided to maintain sanctions against Italy, and that Hitler was probably waiting for this decision before replying to the British questionnaire about his proposals of 7 and 31 March. The Cabinet was advised not to annoy Hitler, but to act soon, for public opinion was criticizing the Government's policy as "vague and inconsistent." This admittedly accurate

[67] Eden to Clerk, 15 May (no. 330), and Phipps to Eden, 27 May (no. 343; with minutes by Wigram, Vansittart, Eden, Stanhope, and Cranborne, the latter the only one concurring with Eden), *DBFP*, 16. Cadogan to Eden, 13 May, and to Vansittart, 16 May, Cadogan Papers (Churchill College, Cambridge), 4/1.
[68] COS meetings, 13, 26 May, CAB 53/6; Harris memorandum, early May, CAB 21/441.

description "was probably due to the fact that the policy was decided by the Cabinet and was apt to result in a compromise."[69]

At Cabinet meetings on 27 and 29 May, Eden recommended continuing the existing sanctions, so long as France cooperated. This would show respect for international law, and, because Italy might have designs on the eastern Mediterranean, Britain could press Mussolini for concessions (such as a declaration of his peaceful intentions) in return for lifting the sanctions, which were hurting Italy. Swinton, Inskip, and Hailsham wanted to end sanctions so as to keep Mussolini and Hitler apart. Duff Cooper agreed with Inskip that Britain should concentrate on Western Europe. In Inskip's judgment, Britain should "return to the balance of power in Europe," which was reemerging as a balance between Germany and Italy "over Austria." On the contrary, Walter Elliot, Minister of Agriculture and one of Eden's allies among the younger Cabinet members, asserted that Britain must maintain its presence in the eastern Mediterranean; to leave would be to repeat the mistake of "supporters of the Western Front Theory" in the Great War. And Chamberlain, who hoped that Mussolini might rejoin the League or "a united front against Germany" in return for an end to sanctions, also wanted Britain to demonstrate its determination not to play "second-fiddle" in the Mediterranean. Baldwin would negotiate with France and Italy to lift sanctions as soon as possible so long as the Government could save face.[70]

The Cabinet postponed further discussion until after the Parliament recess. Eden was instructed to see Italian Ambassador Dino Grandi about the possibility of a conciliatory gesture from Mussolini, and to do this before—not after, as Eden would have preferred—the League Council reconvened in June. The Cabinet also asked Eden to convey to Berlin how difficult it was to be kept in suspense by Germany's delay in responding to the questionnaire. Meanwhile, Eden did not want to give Germany cause to "break off" attempts at conciliation. Thus, he would not yet enter new staff talks with Belgium as Premier Paul Van Zeeland had suggested to him in Geneva on 15 May, playing upon the common interest of Britain and France in defending the Low Countries.[71]

The Cabinet did not distill these discussions to two essential ques-

[69] Pownall diary, 25 May, in Bond, *Chief of Staff*, p. 113; Rhodes James, *Anthony Eden*, p. 163; Cab 38(36), CAB 23/84.

[70] Cabs 39 and 40(36), CAB 23/84.

[71] Cab 40(36), 29 May, CAB 23/84; Eden and Cadogan minutes, 28 May (with earlier minutes by Wigram and Vansittart), C3689/4/18, FO 371/19905; also similar notes of late April and early May in C3103/C3422/4/18, FO 371/19903–904. On Belgian policy and staff talks after the reoccupation of the Rhineland, see David O. Kieft, *Belgium's Return to Neutrality* (Oxford, 1972), pp. 64–77.

tions linking foreign policy and defense. First, how could Britain simultaneously conciliate Mussolini and play first-fiddle in the Mediterranean? Britain played its fiddle for anyone interested in collective security, imperial security, and checking Italy. But folly might follow the fiddling: an unreconciled Italy could increase Britain's burden of imperial security, and could become a third major enemy in case of war with Germany or Japan. Second, what was the relationship among British policies toward Italy, Germany, and the League? Applying pressure on Mussolini jeopardized Anglo-French solidarity, European reconciliation, and British planning for a war with Germany. Appeasing him weakened the League without assuring that he would become docile in the Mediterranean or helpful in Europe. Both of these questions needed clear thinking about time and deterrence.

The conjunction of rearmament, reorganization, the Mediterranean emergency, and the Rhineland crisis elicited frequent references in Whitehall to uncertainties of time. No one knew when Germany would be militarily prepared for war, or whether Hitler intended to move before that date. There were several possible timetables according to which Britain could rearm its Services and accelerate the production of supplies. There must be an appropriate moment to seek a settlement with Germany, or to declare collective security a success or failure. Britain needed time to grow strong enough to deter Germany, but might already be able to meet the Italian challenge.[72] Italy would soon return its attention to Europe and have to choose sides.

Even before the Mediterranean crisis, most of these concerns had prompted Vansittart to advocate a policy he described as "cunctation"—delay a showdown with Germany, buy time for Britain to rearm, and keep Germany guessing about British intentions but be prepared to negotiate. The Cabinet subscribed to this policy without accepting Vansittart's hypothesis that a military conflict was probably inevitable.

Agreeing on the long-term goal of preventing war through military strength, the Government was befuddled over what short-term steps to take for both deterrence and appeasement during what Vansittart had in January 1936 called the "interval" of rearming. By seizing the moment, Germany's remilitarization of the Rhineland flouted the British policy of preventing crises and seeking a general settlement through a combination of rearmament and mutual undertakings. Brit-

---

[72] Mussolini told the French ambassador that he expected Britain "would be in a position of paramount strength" in two-to-three years and in the meantime would try "to avoid every kind of adventure or commitment which would retard the process." Drummond to Eden, 28 March, *DBFP*, 16, no. 176.

ain controlled neither the timing nor the extent of this concession, and could not ensure that Germany would make genuine concessions in return. If Britain could not prevent such German actions or use their proximity to bargain for concrete German commitments before the fact, how many particulars would the British be willing to concede? What would cause Britain to abandon its policy that efforts of conciliation had not failed, or to stipulate vital interests beyond the territorial integrity of France and the Low Countries? Would Britain allow particular concessions to become so major or numerous that they consolidated Germany's position to wage war without having satisfied Hitler or appeased Europe? Would this point be reached before or after Britain decided to threaten force over an immediate German challenge to a friendly nation rather than concede enough to prevent its escalation into armed conflict? Would London base that decision largely on considerations of geography and strategy, on commitments to other countries, or on measurements of Britain's military strength and war potential? Would the grounds for and military implications of this decision be conveyed to Germany far enough in advance to constitute a possible deterrent? Would the decision come before the British felt strong enough to prevent or win a war against Germany?

In the month since the Cabinet established the Foreign Policy Committee, the Government had scarcely touched on these questions, and its policy drifted. To some degree, open questions and inaction can be attributed to the fact that the Cabinet and Foreign Office condoned ambiguity as an inescapable reality of politics. With more or less resiliency, they left some room for adapting to changes in the international situation while Britain rearmed, and for Britain to keep the dictators guessing. This tolerance for uncertainty helps explain why, early in 1936, the Government tacitly accepted four different perceptions of the interrelationship of diplomacy, time, and deterrence. Two of these coexisted in the DRC strategy: Vansittart wanted to reassure France and deter Germany while Britain prepared for a war (perhaps before 1939) it probably could not avoid; the Chiefs of Staff and Hankey opposed coercive diplomacy and commitments to France until Britain was militarily ready for war (probably after 1939). Chamberlain would rely on completing an offensive air force by 1939 to prevent Germany from starting a war in Western Europe that could be averted. All three views had come under enormous pressure from Germany's move into the Rhineland, and so had Eden's persistent notion of impressing Mussolini, Hitler, and the League with a show of force in the Mediterranean.

The Mediterranean and Rhineland crises daunted British efforts to define deterrence comprehensively: using economic sanctions and military muscle in the Mediterranean; accelerating rearmament as an accompaniment to negotiating with Germany; impressing friendly and hostile nations with a combination of firmness and conciliation. The twin successes of Mussolini and Hitler underscored the contrast between Britain's long-term vision of deterrence through military strength in association with allies, and its immediate failures from a position of weakness and interdependence. By June 1936, the Government's state of indecision over policy and anxiety about time exceeded levels that might reasonably have accompanied even this unsettling situation, thanks in some measure to fragmentation, confusion, procrastination, and evasion in the machinery of policy.

THE MACHINERY OF CUNCTATION

While working on the White Paper, Hankey complained that democracy was not leaving him "time for much serious business at the moment!" He and his colleagues presumed that democracies needed much more time to form policy and educate public opinion than did dictatorships, whose leaders could act without being held accountable to electorates and could, in J. L. Garvin's words, "distract the credulous and imaginative democracies with peaceful assurances."[73] This presumption can be found in the DRC report of November 1935, in Vansittart's efforts to mount a campaign of public education in rearmament and foreign policy, and in postwar memoirs blaming public opinion—particularly the Labour party—for shortsighted opposition to rearmament.[74]

If the public needed educating, the Government used a fraudulent method of teaching. The White Paper did not reveal misgivings about the adequacy of its proposals for rearmament and the machinery of supply. The Government stood by collective security and used it to justify rearmament, yet also questioned the League's future and viewed defense through more traditional lenses of imperial security and European power politics. Not being beastly to Germany might win parliamentary votes for the White Paper and expedite reaching a settlement with Germany, but diplomatic gentility masked Whitehall's fear that Hitler would rearm faster than expected and, being nasty himself, overturn the status quo before Britain and the League could prevent it.

[73] Hankey to Hodsoll, 25 February, CAB 21/424; Garvin notes, March/April, Garvin Papers.

[74] On Vansittart: Gilbert, *Churchill*, pp. 724–26; Rose, *Vansittart*, pp. 188–89; Schmidt, *England in der Krise*, p. 125. For a particularly strong condemnation of parliamentary opposition, see Viscount Simon, *Retrospect* (London, 1952), pp. 179–81.

Supporting the League and conciliating Germany remained official policy while the Cabinet admitted to itself that "the general question of major foreign policy" must be reconsidered.

This sort of dissembling arose partly from the apprehension that giving out the truth about international politics might baffle the public at home or offend governments abroad. In this case, official statements tried to disguise the deepening bafflement of the Government itself. Historians have related this state of mind to politics in the Conservative party: the fear that rapid rearmament might polarize British society and lead to social revolution; the emergence of two groups critical of Baldwin's declining leadership and his Government's policy, one of them wishing to check Hitler by strengthening collective security and linking it to balance of power politics, the other rejecting collective security, wanting to restore realism and empire to the center of British policy, and more willing to conciliate Hitler.[75]

Little attention has been given to how the Government's bewilderment resulted from inadequacies in the system of policymaking.[76] Strained by rearmament and international crises, the machinery of policy both manifested and magnified Whitehall's inability to impose order on its own perception of things—to determine the best use of the time the British wanted to buy. The committee system wavered, the stakes and intensity of bureaucratic bargaining increased, and no reassessment of major policy occurred.

Reorganization and rearmament dominated the agenda of ministers from January to 7 March. During this period, the Cabinet or ministerial committees discussed these issues on sixteen occasions: nine meetings of the DPR(DR) in January; five Cabinet meetings in February and early March; two meetings of the Cabinet Committee on Coordination in mid-February. By contrast, ministers took up Italy and Germany in some detail at only seven meetings: Italy on 14 January (DPR), 17 and 26 February (Cabinet), and 5 March (Cabinet); Germany on 29 January

---

[75] Cowling, *Impact of Hitler*, pp. 117–38; Kennedy, *Realities*, pp. 285–86; Keith Middlemas, *Diplomacy of Illusion: The British Government and Germany, 1937–39* (London, 1972), pp. 95–104; Schmidt, *England in der Krise*, pp. 43–45, 448–49, 503–4; Thompson, *Anti-Appeasers*, chap. 5; Amery to Garvin, 21 and 23 March, Garvin Papers. Baldwin "devitalizes the Cabinet," Garvin complained, and preferred "mediocrities" to people like Churchill and Austen Chamberlain; notes of May and June.

[76] Barnett refers to the "ponderousness and torpor" of the machinery, in *Collapse*, pp. 415–16. Williamson Murray praises the logical bureaucratic system and blames its slowness on "those who ran it"; *The Change in the European Balance of Power, 1938–1939: The Path to Ruin* (Princeton, 1984), pp. 55–57. Kennedy argues that British leaders, already pressured by economic, social and imperial issues, "were themselves, psychologically and culturally, inclined to delay decisions"; *Realities*, p. 281. Going into more detail than these other authors, Schmidt cites the failure of the machinery "to coordinate viewpoints and clarify alternatives"; *England in der Krise*, pp. 529–30.

(Cabinet), 17 February (Cabinet Committee on Germany), and 5 March (Cabinet). On 30 January, the Committee of Imperial Defence decided to postpone consideration of the Rhineland's strategic value until Eden could consult Ambassador Phipps; nearly two months later, the CID took note of the fact that the Cabinet was now dealing with the crisis that had arisen in the meantime.[77] The Cabinet Committee on Germany met on 17 February, planned to reconvene after interdepartmental memoranda had been prepared, but never met again. From 17 February to 5 March, neither the Cabinet nor a ministerial committee discussed the German question.

Together, the Cabinet's completion of the White Paper on Defence on 2 March and Germany's remilitarization of the Rhineland on the seventh dramatically changed the content and pace of Cabinet business. After Hitler's "Saturday surprise," the Cabinet dealt substantially with the Rhineland and the Locarno Pact at eight meetings in March, of which five were specially called. In addition, as Baldwin informed the Cabinet on 16 March, "a small group of Ministers" was keeping the Rhineland situation "under continuous observation." Five such meetings were held in March, either at No. 10 Downing Street or in the prime minister's room at the House of Commons, regularly attended by seven Cabinet members: Baldwin, Ramsay MacDonald, Hailsham, Eden, Chamberlain, Simon, and Halifax (these same seven plus Inskip subsequently constituted the Foreign Policy Committee). The three Service ministers were apparently asked to attend, individually or severally, when the agenda included specific military questions.[78] These meetings neither alarmed nor offended the Cabinet as a whole, and both groups pursued the same lines of policy, although the smaller one seems to have been the more hesitant to support France and offend Germany. At no time during the height of the crisis did the Cabinet delegate executive authority to a committee as it had done in August 1935 for the Mediterranean emergency. The CID played a minor role; it established the "Plymouth" Subcommittee to consider the possibility of colonial concessions to Germany,[79] and it recommended guidelines for staff talks with France and Belgium.

During March, neither the Cabinet nor meetings of ministers dwelled long on relations with Italy, except for acknowledging that the concentration of forces in the Mediterranean weakened Britain's posi-

---

[77] CID meetings, 30 January and 26 March, CAB 2/6.

[78] Cab 20(36), 16 March, CAB 23/83; record of meetings of ministers in CAB 27/603, which began, Hankey informed the Foreign Office, "as such meetings often do, rather informally"; Hankey to Harvey, 17 March, C1996/4/18, FO 371/19893.

[79] Baldwin appointed this committee on 9 March, chaired by Lord Plymouth, Parliamentary Under-Secretary for Colonies.

tion if war broke out in Europe. The DPR stopped discussing the Mediterranean situation at its last meeting (3 March) before the reorganization of the machinery of defense. At its next (7 May) and subsequent meetings, the DPR handled rearmament, not foreign policy.

As international tension abated in April and May, so did the number of Cabinet and ministerial meetings dealing primarily with Germany (about six in April and four in May). The Cabinet returned to the problem of sanctions and collective security in April, now giving more heed to the interrelationship of Mediterranean and European politics than it had the previous month. The Cabinet Committee on Foreign Policy, established on 29 April to discuss this linkage, met on the thirtieth. In May, pressed by the Services to reduce military forces in the Mediterranean, the Cabinet continued to interweave policies toward Italy and Germany, culminating in the long discussions of the twenty-seventh and twenty-ninth.

This chronology of ministerial agendas suggests several peculiarities. First, the Cabinet badly misjudged Britain's European adversaries. British military, economic, and diplomatic intelligence did not foresee how soon Germany would march into the Rhineland and how quickly Italy would conquer Ethiopia.[80] Second, major questions of policy were separated from each other. Before Germany's move into the Rhineland, ministers normally segregated rearmament from foreign policy and discussed the latter infrequently. Moreover, they tended to view Italy and Germany as distinctive issues. To be sure, they used the Mediterranean situation to parry French requests for a firm stand against Germany, and they were aware that maintaining sanctions against Mussolini might push him into Hitler's camp. By and large, however, the Cabinet's agenda dealt separately with sanctions in the Mediterranean and a settlement with Germany. Only on 5 March did the Cabinet earnestly consider how the two problems intersected, and this seems to have been largely in response to Flandin's request for British statements dealing with Italy and Germany together.

Disjunction also continued to impair broad terms of reference. In July 1935, the DPR had been instructed "to ensure that our defensive arrangements and our foreign policy are in line." This comprehensive charter narrowed during the Mediterranean crisis, resurfaced in the DPR(DR), and disappeared in February 1936, when the DPR(DR) and Cabinet assigned to the DPR oversight of the defense programs. After the reorganization and the Rhineland episode, no committee took the

---

[80] Hitler made his decision only two weeks before the event, a timing that magnified the difficulty of prediction. Late on Friday night, 6 March, Christie telephoned Vansittart to report Germany's plan to act the next day; Wark, *Ultimate Enemy*, p. 52.

place of the DPR as it had been originally envisaged. By establishing the Foreign Policy Committee, the Cabinet made a promising start toward an integrated reexamination of policy. Although the FPC's membership excluded the Service ministers and its terms of reference did not mention defense policy, its creation—and Inskip's appointment to the committee—recognized that armaments and foreign policy should be brought into step. Except for agreeing that the League needed reform, the FPC accomplished nothing at its first meeting on 30 April and did not reconvene until 15 July. Marking time in the absence of any reassessment, the Cabinet maintained sanctions against Italy, sought concessions from Mussolini, rearmed against Germany, wanted a settlement with Hitler, and continued the policy of not allowing rearmament to interfere with normal trade.

Finally, ministers spent most of their committee time reacting to exigencies of the moment, and postponed discussion of the larger and longer-term context of events. The storm over reorganization, which strained Colonel Pownall's belief that "surely there must be some problems which are *not* urgent,"[81] delayed the Cabinet's discussion of rearmament and thus the White Paper on Defence. The Cabinet Committee on Germany was appointed in mid-February when the Government assumed it had time to decide—without fully informing France—how to use the Rhineland as a bargaining chip for some German concession toward a general settlement. Having lost this chip to Hitler's *fait accompli*, the Government concentrated on ending the crisis peacefully and quickly. Hitler captured the initiative in proposing the contents of a settlement, and he manipulated time by showing he was in no hurry to start negotiations. The Cabinet Committee on Germany faded away without meeting again or issuing a report. The Foreign Policy Committee did not consider policy toward Germany at its meeting on 30 April, and did not return to its task—recommending what foreign policy the Government should adopt—for two-and-a-half months. At the end of May, the Cabinet still awaited Hitler's reply to its questionnaire, annoyed that its own tactic for opening discussions with Hitler—on policies not yet determined by the Cabinet—was going nowhere.

Relationships between ministers and officials, which had been generally harmonious during the Ethiopian crisis in the autumn of 1935, deteriorated early in 1936 when the DPR(DR) amended the report of the Defence Requirements Committee, and when Swinton and Chamberlain criticized the existing machinery of policy. With more than usual animosity, officials and ministers referred to distinctions between

[81] Pownall diary, 3 February, in Bond, *Chief of Staff*, p. 100.

political and military considerations, and between the responsibility of ministers for taking political decisions and that of officials for giving expert advice.

Chatfield feared that the ministerial committee, which had already committed "a travesty of sound administration" by calling in Lord Weir, would not consider the DRC's report on its merits. Chamberlain faulted the DRC for not presenting a truly joint plan, and for under-estimating requirements for the Air Force in 1934 and again in 1935. Concerning the air program, he insisted, ministerial committees had based their amendments "on military rather than political considerations"—that is, on the expansion of the Luftwaffe and the threat of an air offensive against Britain.[82] Hankey blamed ministers for postponing most of the DRC's recommendations of 1934 for the Army and Navy programs, thus increasing Britain's military vul-nerability during the Ethiopian crisis. Massingberd charged that minis-terial committees were swayed by political and economic matters. Chatfield was "outraged" by Chamberlain's memorandum, frustrated at being "constitutionally tongue-tied," and offended by Swinton's "entire lack of confidence in the Chiefs of Staff as at present con-stituted." The chancellor was preoccupied with "financial dangers" to Britain, and in fact the DRC "had thoroughly played up" to Cham-berlain by not asking for more than was "absolutely essential." At Hankey's request, Fisher asked Chamberlain to reconsider his detrac-tion of the DRC, since experts and ministers really agreed on the need to expand all three Services, and ministers themselves were not irre-proachable when they postponed a decision concerning the Territorial Army.[83]

Hankey, Fisher, Chatfield, and Massingberd objected to the superim-position of a minister on the Chiefs of Staff because ministers did not direct planning in the separate Service departments, and therefore should not direct joint planning.[84] Having challenged this line of rea-soning by creating the new position, the Cabinet followed it by de-fining the duties of the new minister so as to preserve the right of the COS to discuss plans and initiate investigations on their own. Baldwin

[82] Chatfield to Hankey, 14 January, CAB 21/422A, describing Weir's attitude at the DPR(DR)'s first meeting as "defeatist . . . which is unlike him"; Chamberlain memoran-dum on defense coordination, 11 February, CP 38(36), CAB 24/260; also diary, 11 Febru-ary, Chamberlain Papers, NC 2/23a.

[83] Hankey to Fisher, 13 February; Massingberd note, 11 February, and letter to Hankey, 17 February; Chatfield to Hankey, 17 February; Fisher to Chamberlain, 15 February, CAB 21/424.

[84] Hankey memorandum, 7 February, CP 30(36), CAB 24/259; COS paper, 10 February, CP 36(36), CAB 24/260, and meetings of 13 and 24 January, CAB 53/5; Chatfield to Hankey, 17 February, CAB 21/424; Fisher to Baldwin, 13 January, PREM 1/196.

wanted the chiefs to be able to give "purely military reports direct without . . . being subjected to pressure from Ministers." Still, Chatfield remained suspicious of any suggestion that a "political" minister regularly attend meetings of the COS (he might "be away shooting or attending a race meeting"), and he continued to defend the "complete military right [of the COS] to give military advice unhampered by any purely political consideration."[85]

Procedural language reminded Whitehall of jurisdictions and connections in the machinery of policy.[86] Yet when ministers and experts used such phrases as "purely military reports" and "purely political consideration," they underestimated how purity was becoming a myth as military, political, and financial considerations commingled in the work of departments and committees. The increasing and emphatic use of such language early in 1936 marked the turbulence where complex issues foretelling war converged with simple rules belonging to peacetime routine. Caught in these same straits, the Foreign Office floundered, the Treasury tried to pilot accelerated rearmament according to normal trade and Treasury control, the Services wanted calm for the preparation of plans and supplies for war, and Inskip began to navigate between Hankey's idea of coordination and Chamberlain's aspiration for coherence.

According to his memoirs, Anthony Eden knew that some Cabinet "elders" resented his appointment, that he could not rely on Baldwin's support, that many Cabinet ministers believed that they should have his job, and that it was common practice for "a multiplicity of Ministers [to take] a hand at drafting a despatch."[87] In spite of these restraints and the Foreign Office's loss of face in the Hoare-Laval affair, Eden and the Office had wide margins for shaping foreign policy. In January and February, the Cabinet normally followed Eden's lead regarding Italy, collective security, and Germany. In the nervous weeks that followed Germany's remilitarization of the Rhineland, the Cabinet tightened the reins. Eden's colleagues imposed limits on what he and other ministers might say to French and Belgian representatives, and revised some of Eden's proposed statements to make them less offensive to Germany. As the crisis subsided, the Cabinet discussed procedures for negotiating with Hitler. Baldwin suggested that "there would be advantages" in having a minister convey the Government's questions to Hitler since "the ordinary diplomatic channels hardly seemed to function in dealing with dictators." Several ministers stated that "the general policy

85 Cab 9(36), 24 February, CAB 23/83; Chatfield to Hankey, 28 February, CAB 21/424.
86 On how "rules of the game" influence the decisionmaking process while leaving "flexibility for participants to maneuver," see Halperin, *Bureaucratic Politics*, pp. 104–15.
87 Avon, *Dictators*, p. 357; also Rhodes James, *Anthony Eden*, p. 163.

ought to be settled before the means by which it was to be carried out were discussed." Unconvinced of this, the Cabinet agreed to send the questionnaire for the German government through Ambassador Phipps, who would tell the Germans that, if they so desired, Britain would gladly send a minister "in order to facilitate negotiations."[88]

Mediterranean policy was the chief source of discord in Eden's relations with the Cabinet. By the end of May, many members were ready to lift sanctions against Italy and withdraw forces from the Mediterranean. Although Eden doubted that sanctions could be continued much longer, he remained convinced that Britain must keep a strong military position in that region. He did so against the objections of ministers who favored a major shift toward the problem of Germany, and of his detractors in London who, like J. L. Garvin, now considered him a "disastrous failure."[89]

Eden was not the picture of confidence or consistency. He thought some of his colleagues should have worried less about German reactions to staff talks and more about Germany's undermining the Treaty of Locarno and French security. Yet he resented French lectures on British obligations and did not feel bound to keep the French informed in detail of British dealings with Germany. He would not be too friendly to France or too unkind to Germany, attitudes that would offend the Cabinet and British opinion, call into question Britain's status as a guarantor of the Treaty of Locarno, and forfeit Britain's position of brokerage in negotiating a future settlement with Germany. Eden regretted the Cabinet's slowness in agreeing to the language of the questionnaire, and had reservations about sending a minister to talk with Hitler. But he himself had asked the Cabinet to consider this latter procedure, and he thought the Government's offer to do so would impress British public opinion and "make it more difficult for Herr Hitler to take refuge in evasion."[90]

While the Government awaited replies from Hitler and recommendations from the FPC, the Foreign Office was even more divided than the Cabinet and hardly ready to give confident advice. Foreign Office papers, Eden's memoranda, and Cabinet minutes show clear signs of Vansittart's ideas: negotiating "particulars" with Germany while buying time to rearm; seeking a way out of the confrontation with Italy because of its repercussions on European politics; questioning the

---

[88] Cabs 31, 33, 34(36), 29 April, 4 and 6 May, CAB 23/84; Wigram minute, 2 May, *DBFP*, 16, no. 291.

[89] Garvin notes, May–June, Garvin Papers. Garvin diagnosed Eden as suffering from "hereditary infirmities of rashness, provocativeness, anger, obstinacy."

[90] Eden minute, 18 May, C3677/4/18, FO 371/19905; Cab 30(36), 22 April, CAB 23/84. In his memoirs, Eden omits the issue of who should have given the questionnaire to Hitler; *Dictators*, p. 418.

effectiveness of collective security as currently practiced. Vansittart persevered in his forecast of the likelihood of a European war, but slid about in his directions for dealing with France, Italy, and Germany. Especially regarding the menace from Germany, Vansittart had allies in Wigram ("Wigs"), Sargent ("Moley"), and Phipps (Lady Vansittart's brother-in-law). Yet, although all of these men subscribed to the principle of general deterrence through military strength, none had drawn a clear line beyond which Britain must declare Germany's revising the status quo a cause for war. Differences arose even among this small group as Eden and officials in the Foreign Office weighed the content and timing of concessions to Germany, the degree of danger from Germany, the effect of economic sanctions and military strength in the Mediterranean, the future of collective security, and the relationship between Italian and German expansionism.

Perhaps this dissidence owed something to a decline in Vansittart's authority. In Hankey's view, Vansittart's position "was a bit shaken by the Hoare-Laval affair," and he had become "a bit disillusioned over his pro-French enthusiasms." When Cadogan arrived at the Foreign Office in February, soon to replace Sir Victor Wellesley as Deputy Under-Secretary, Cadogan and others correctly surmised that this move would lead to his succeeding Vansittart, although Vansittart spoke to Cadogan "as if he were staying on indefinitely."[91] Eden decided to retain Vansittart, but depended less on him than Hoare had done, and may have envied Vansittart's wealth, contacts, and knowledge of foreign affairs. Eden was glad to have Cadogan, a personal friend, back in the Office, and Chamberlain and Baldwin wanted to replace Vansittart, whom they now considered a liability for the Government. Not surprisingly, Vansittart felt more and more isolated from ministers.[92]

One of Vansittart's contemporaries complained to Tom Jones that the Foreign Office "has no organisation and is as much under-machined as the Cabinet Office is over-machined."[93] He had a point, for heads of department in the Foreign Office did not meet regularly to coordinate views, and the Permanent Under-Secretary was but one of many offi-

[91] Hankey to Casey, 20 April, CAB 63/51; Cadogan diary, 4 May, Cadogan Papers, 1/4; Dilks, *Cadogan*, p. 12. Colonel Pownall noted that Vansittart's "adhesion to France" was not liked by the Cabinet; Vansittart represented "an ever decreasing minority in the F.O., who were entirely split on the question." Bond, *Chief of Staff*, p. 104.

[92] Eden to King George V, 8 January, *DBFP*, 15, no. 437; Cowling, *Impact of Hitler*, p. 157; Middlemas and Barnes, *Baldwin*, p. 898. Apart from Duff Cooper, Vansittart later wrote, no one supported his views on Germany, and Churchill had become "an embarrassing ally" regarding German rearmament; *Mist*, pp. 496–97, 548–50, also 482–85 for his reaction to the criticisms of Tom Jones and Geoffrey Dawson. Eden's account of this period contains few references to Vansittart, *Dictators*, Book II, chaps. 2–4.

[93] Jones, *Diary*, p. 176. The same person said the Cabinet "breeds committees like rabbits," which only proved its "feebleness in reaching decisions."

cials who condensed information for the Foreign Secretary and advised him—so did the Parliamentary Under-Secretaries, Deputy Under-Secretary, and Assistant Under-Secretaries. With a tighter organization and a more effective Permanent Under-Secretary, the Foreign Office might have been able to strengthen Eden's hand in the Cabinet—either to support collective security or to reorient British policy. Yet, one wonders whether any structure or person could have achieved a solid consensus among officials in the Foreign Office on how to handle the extraordinary current of events around them. Playing for time was now more than a policy. It had become also an institutional habit of mind born of uncertainty and dissension, increasing the vulnerability of the Office to interventions from other departments.

Relations between the Foreign Office and Service departments were good regarding estimates of German forces in the Rhineland, and the contents of staff talks with France and Belgium.[94] On larger issues of European and Mediterranean policy, however, the Foreign Office and Services clashed. Air Vice Marshal Courtney considered "not unreasonable" Germany's fear of a Franco-Soviet combination and Germany's consequent need to expand its air force beyond parity with France if France ratified the Franco-Soviet pact. He thought Britain should try to block ratification, and he was struck by the "obvious sincerity" of the German air attaché's plea: if Britain prevented ratification of the pact, Germany would agree to limit its first-line strength to parity with France. Annoyed that Courtney had "talk[ed] international affairs" with the German, Eden thought it "no business of the Air Ministry to have [a] view about the Franco-Soviet pact." Vansittart, who already had a low opinion of British air intelligence, found it "quite astonishing . . . to see what the Air Ministry will believe of Germany."[95]

Shortly after the remilitarization of the Rhineland, the Chiefs of Staff urged that they be allowed to study in advance the "military aspects" of any treaty that might replace Locarno, "a course that was not fol-

[94] On German forces: documents of March in WO 190/391, 393–94, 402, 410; FO 371/19891–92, 19897–98. On staff talks: files C2748/C3422/C3456/C3712/4/18, FO 371/19901, 904–5; Pownall to Air Ministry, 8 April, AIR 9/74; Pownall to Hankey and Hankey note, 17 April, PREM 1/194; note from British representatives to Inskip, 17 April, CP 110(36), CAB 24/261 (also in *DBFP*, 16, no. 262); Cab 30(36), 22 April, CAB 23/84.

[95] Courtney to Wigram, 11 January, C213/4/18, FO 371/19883, with minutes by Eden, Vansittart, and others in the same file. In Military Intelligence, Colonel Paget could justify the remilitarization of the Rhineland "from the German point of view," for the Locarno Pact had "been seriously undermined by the Franco-Soviet treaty and the Franco-Italian military agreement." He hoped the Government would prevent the Foreign Office from doing "anything so detrimental to our interests" as upholding the status quo in Central and Eastern Europe. Paget to Hotblack (Berlin), 1 February, WO 190/384.

lowed in the framing of the Locarno agreement."[96] Preparing for staff talks showed that the Services had less sympathy for France and Eastern Europe and more for Germany than did the Foreign Office. After the talks concluded, Courtney asked the Foreign Office to try harder to dispel German suspicions about their scope; the Germans, he lamented, were withholding information from the British air attaché in Berlin because of the talks. Vansittart refused to amplify Britain's press communiqué; Germany was to blame for the talks in the first place, and Britain must not "crawl to the Germans by trying to explain the conversations away still further."[97]

The Mediterranean crisis aggravated negotiations for a treaty with Egypt, where Egyptian nationalism had increased along with the level of British forces and the dependency of Britain on Egypt for imperial security. Since the unsuccessful Anglo-Egyptian discussions of 1930, the military clauses of any settlement had become a more divisive issue both in London and in Cairo. Early in 1936, the Service staffs emphasized Britain's strategic interests in Egypt and the Suez Canal, and insisted that Britain's right to defend those interests should not be subject to time limits or the jurisdiction of the League of Nations. The Foreign Office—and Sir Miles Lampson, the High Commissioner in Cairo—did not want to jeopardize "friendly political relations with Egypt" by demanding military rights that were unacceptable to the Egyptians. Egypt refused to agree to terms acceptable to the Services, and Eden, declaring that Britain could not afford a collapse of negotiations at a time when Mussolini threatened its imperial interests, recommended that the Government go some way toward conciliating Egypt. Faced with conflicting military and political considerations, in May the Cabinet appointed a committee, chaired by Eden, to "put this complicated matter in the simplest possible language."[98]

---

[96] COS memorandum (COS 440), 17 March, in CAB 4/24. On 26 March, the CID agreed that the COS should be given this opportunity "before the conclusion of any general pact in the future"; CAB 2/6.

[97] Dill to Sargent, 30 March, with Sargent and Vansittart minutes, C2544/4/18, FO 371/19899; Vansittart minute on Courtney's telephone call to the Foreign Office, 17 April, C3062/4/18, FO 371/19903. One wonders how much the mutual respect and exchange of information between the Service staffs and their German counterparts shaped the political thinking of the British military establishment. In September 1935, Military Intelligence was pleased it knew more about German military planning than did the French, thanks to "the information given us in confidence by the Reichskriegsministerium, under the promise that we would not disclose it to any foreign power"; MI3b notes on French estimates of German strength, 14 September, WO 190/350.

[98] COS meetings and papers in CAB 53/5 and 53/27; JPC meetings, CAB 55/1; CID meetings, 6 February, 26 March, 27 April, CAB 2/6; Cabs 1, 5, 6(36), CAB 23/83, and Cabs 25, 31, 34, 35, 38(36), CAB 23/84; Eden memoranda, 29 April and 1 May, CP 112 and 126(36), CAB 24/262 (the first also in *DBFP*, 16, no. 274); minutes and papers of Anglo-

The Foreign Office—Eden with more conviction than Vansittart—contended that the political situation did not yet permit a major withdrawal of forces from the Mediterranean. The Chiefs of Staff viewed sanctions a failure from the start and warned that prolonging the military concentration in the Mediterranean interfered with rearming for contingencies of war against Germany and Japan, the political foundations for defense policy. G. H. Thompson noted the "tendency in Service circles to regard this department as rather a grim joke, and to feel that Foreign Office appreciations of the Italo-Abyssinian problem have been singularly wrong," just as the Foreign Office was inclined to blame the War Office "for having led us astray about the military prospects of the Italians." Thompson tacitly admitted that the Foreign Office and the Cabinet had exaggerated the effectiveness of sanctions.[99]

Uncertain about how the Ethiopian case would affect the future of collective security, the Foreign Office provided little guidance to the Service staffs. Vice Admiral James predicted that Britain's foreign policy would be "subjected to greater shocks ere the summer is through"; the Government "might even welcome suggestions from the Services" to help it out of its difficulties. Colonel R. F. Adam proposed that the Joint Planning Committee use its pending strategic review of Europe "to force the Foreign Office into giving us a proper foreign policy." Group Captain Harris, Adam's air colleague on the JPC, disagreed with this tactic, which was "putting the cart before the horse." The JPC's review and strategic plans "must be more largely governed by Foreign Office policy than vice versa," and thus the JPC should not study strategic questions until it received policy guidelines from the Foreign Office and Government.[100]

Whether the joint planners took the initiative or waited for the Foreign Office, the need to correlate foreign policy and military planning was very much on the minds of the Service staffs. The JPC and Chiefs of Staff had weathered two international crises which demanded most of their time and illuminated the risks of making commitments to potential allies or threats to likely enemies before Britain was prepared for war. Now, with an unrealistically low tolerance of uncertainty, they expected the Foreign Office to minimize political ambiguities. They

---

Egyptian Conversations Committee in CAB 27/607, some of these in CP 129, 131, 136(36), CAB 24/262; Pratt, *East of Malta*, pp. 122–24.

[99] Thompson minute, 6 May, *DBFP*, 16, no. 317n. Earlier in the year, Duff Cooper had advised the Cabinet that the rainy season and other problems made an Italian victory look "long and difficult" at best; memoranda of 17 January and 24 February, CP 10 and 52(36), CAB 24/259–60.

[100] James minute, 22 April, ADM 116/3042; Adam-Harris correspondence, 9 and 11 May, CAB 21/441.

wanted the Foreign Office and Cabinet to provide a calm interval for the preparation of war plans and capabilities. The Service staffs were as unperturbed by the paradox in this wishful thinking as the Foreign Office was unable to guarantee either the time or the political bases for completing plans.[101]

Neville Chamberlain's political ascendancy moved the Cabinet closer to his own opinions and strengthened the Treasury's influence on Government policy. Chamberlain claimed and deserved credit for ensuring that the Cabinet's decisions on rearmament embraced the strategy of deterrence through air power. He presented air deterrence as a coherent alternative to the DRC's "aggregate" of the views of the Services, and criticized the machinery for defense coordination. On the latter issue, unswayed by Fisher's defense of the existing system, Chamberlain again saw himself as the most thoughtful and effective agent for change, and he viewed Hankey as "a terrible reactionary on the subject," one who, as secretary of the DPR(DR), did "not scruple to put down as conclusions . . . what he would like us to decide instead of what we have decided."[102] Chamberlain's unwavering sense of his own importance in deliberations on foreign policy exceeded the facts, but not by a large margin. He was, "as usual," asked to take part in conversations with the French during the Rhineland crisis. He had "supplied most of the ideas and taken the lead all through" meetings which, to the Cabinet's pleasant surprise, brought a result that "rather limited than extended our commitments under Locarno."[103]

In April and May, because foreign affairs remained "anxious and obscure" and the Cabinet needed to make up its mind on how to keep the peace, Chamberlain "prodded" Baldwin to set up the Foreign Policy Committee. He convinced the Cabinet to postpone Inskip's question about peacetime supply until, having heard recommendations from this committee, the Cabinet decided what policy to follow. Chamberlain was apparently surprised by "the striking successes of the Italians," who were "arrogant, abusive of us and determined not to dis-

---

[101] Robert Jervis observes that planning staffs are more likely to question established policies and weigh contradictory evidence if they are freed from day-to-day problems; *Perception and Misperception*, p. 201. This holds true for the COS and JPC during the Mediterranean and Rhineland crises, yet at the same time these immediate tasks helped convince the Service staffs of the weaknesses of Government policy.

[102] Chamberlain to Hilda and Ida, 9 and 16 February, and diary, 19 January and 16 February, Chamberlain Papers, NC 18/1/949, 2/23a; Cowling, *Impact of Hitler*, pp. 152–53. More recently, Richard Crossman made the same point about the Cabinet Secretariat: "They prefer to record what should have been said. They are Platonists, not Aristotelians." *The Myths of Cabinet Government* (Cambridge, Mass., 1972), pp. 41–42.

[103] Chamberlain to Ida and Hilda, 14, 21, 28 March, and diary entries for 12 March and following, Chamberlain Papers, NC 18/1/951, 953–54, 2/23a. Eden acknowledged Chamberlain's support, "not least by seeing and guiding the press"; *Dictators*, p. 404.

cuss peace till they have got their enemies under their feet." Over lunch with Eden on 27 April, he called the League of Nations a failure in the Ethiopian case. Since the League could not be relied upon for security in the future, Britain should work toward regional pacts under the aegis of the League—agreements, that is, in Western Europe and the Far East where British interests were "directly concerned," not in Eastern Europe, where security should be left to others. Early in May, Chamberlain noted that events and opinion were moving in the direction he had sketched to Eden.[104] In the Cabinet on 27 May, Chamberlain backed Eden's argument that sanctions against Italy should be continued as an incentive for Mussolini to offer peaceful assurances. But at this and the next Cabinet two days later, Chamberlain signaled his growing impatience with the dual policy when he put more emphasis on approaching Mussolini than on maintaining sanctions. In this regard, he echoed the sentiments of most of his Cabinet colleagues; of Samuel Hoare, whom Baldwin had asked to rejoin the Cabinet as First Lord of the Admiralty; and of Treasury officials who scoffed at the Foreign Office's contention that sanctions were hurting Italy and would undermine that country by the end of the year.[105]

Chamberlain and his subordinates defended the principle of Treasury control apprehensively as the estimated costs came together for the defense requirements already approved, for the continuation of emergency measures in the Mediterranean, and for the long-term rearmament program under consideration early in 1936. In spite of the relatively more internal harmony than existed in the Foreign Office, however, the Treasury had its own uncertainties about estimates, timetables, priorities, and funding. Confusion over these issues contributed to doubts among Treasury officials that the genie of rearmament could be kept in the bottle of Treasury control and normal trade.

The rearmament program approved by the House of Commons on 10 March presented the Government and Parliament with a set of "special circumstances," as Sir Richard Hopkins observed a few days later. The new program, which would soon begin "in advance of Parliamentary authority," put the Treasury in an unusual position—"because the Chancellor has settled the total only in vague and general terms, because the expenditure is abnormal and not subjected to preliminary Parliamentary control, and because it involves many commitments of long duration."[106]

---

[104] Chamberlain to Ida and Hilda, 25 April and 2 May, and diary, 24 and 27 April, Chamberlain Papers, NC 18/1/958–59, 2/23a.
[105] Cabs 39 and 40(36), 27 and 29 May, CAB 23/84; Treasury minutes of 28 May and following, T 160/622; Cowling, *Impact of Hitler*, pp. 139–41.
[106] Hopkins minute, 13 March, T 161/718.

The Treasury had to reassure Parliament while harboring doubts. The White Paper stated that Treasury control would be maintained, and, shortly after the debate on defense, the Treasury assured the House of Commons that the House had not lost control over expenditure. At the end of the month, while preparing for the presentation of the supplementary estimates required by rearmament, Hopkins called his colleagues' attention to the difficulty he had finding "precedents for committing Parliament to heavy long-term commitments without the authority of a Vote."[107] Chamberlain thought Parliament should be given more information on "what we are contemplating," and Hopkins agreed. "Hoppy," as colleagues called this former classics scholar from Emmanuel College, Cambridge, advised the chancellor to state that "additional sources of supply must be established and these sources will in turn constitute a reserve source of supply in the event of emergency." Government control over the necessary long-term contracts would be exercised through "a carefully considered break clause." Chamberlain followed this advice *verbatim* in reply to a question in the House of Commons on 9 April, noting that it would be necessary to enter at once into "contracts of considerable duration, which may amount to three years."[108]

When Chamberlain presented his 1936 budget to the House of Commons on 21 April, he reiterated the original Service Estimates of £158 million and stated that another £20 million in supplementaries would be needed for implementing the White Paper. In order to raise additional revenue, the Government would increase taxes: the income tax by three pence in the pound (1.25 percent); certain indirect taxes, including the duty on tea by two pence per pound. Although attacked by Labour for substantially increasing the defense budget, contributing to a dangerous arms race, opening the doors wider to profiteers, and raising indirect taxes, the Government held its majority and the budget passed.[109]

Chamberlain told the House that the Government might borrow in the future. Unaccustomed to funding expanded defense programs of long duration during peacetime, the Treasury had, for more than a year, considered whether to resort to borrowing. During the "air panic" of early 1935, Fisher and Hopkins had seen reports that Germany

---

[107] W. S. Morrison (Financial Secretary to the Treasury) reply to a question in the Commons, 12 March, 309 *HC Debates*, cols. 2314–15; Hopkins minute, 31 March, T 161/718.

[108] Hopkins minutes and Chamberlain notes, 25 and 31 March, T 161/718; 310 *HC Debates*, 9 April, cols. 2936–37. For the repercussions of supplementary estimates on the Treasury's traditional means of limiting expenditure, see Peden, *British Rearmament and Treasury*, pp. 38–41.

[109] 311 *HC Debates*, 21 April, cols. 37–59; Shay, *British Rearmament*, pp. 77–78, 84–86.

was increasing its internal floating debt to pay for rearmament, and that Italy also was raising large amounts of money without immediate damage to the budget. Although distancing themselves from such unsound practices, by early 1936 Treasury officials accepted the principle of borrowing to meet what they considered extraordinary costs. Fisher came to this conclusion more easily than his colleagues, for he thought the German menace was near, advocated greater expenditure on rearmament than they did, and feared that increasing taxes would antagonize the British public at a time when unity and action were essential.[110]

Treasury experts agreed that borrowing must not entail bypassing Parliament, but must follow both "constitutional decency [and] constitutional practice" (Hopkins) by proceeding through parliamentary approval. Chamberlain concurred, having shown an interest in a defense loan as early as January 1935. As he readied his budget in April 1936, he assumed he would have to announce that the Government contemplated borrowing in the future "for the bulk of the [rearmament] programme," and he did not want to "create alarm and depression at the prospect of further and heavier taxation." Fisher advised Chamberlain: "The real argument for the present is that (a) the safety of the state is the supreme law and (b) the rearmament methods of our potential enemies—indeed the whole world—leave us no alternative." Although Chamberlain was not as alarmed as Fisher and eschewed the Roman legal principle about the safety of the state in his address on the budget, he recognized that these were "not ordinary times." Barring international agreement on disarmament, costs would "rise swiftly during the next few years to a peak, and after that . . . begin to descend" (although not to the old levels). The Government would not pay the whole bill by raising taxes; part of the costs "may properly be met out of loan."[111]

Chamberlain did not disclose the magnitude of the Treasury's quandary over control. The Treasury Emergency Expenditure Committee (TEEC) had been established in September 1935 to help the Services by expediting Treasury control over expenditure on supplies needed for the Mediterranean crisis. How to provide similar machinery for the rearmament program was the subject of an interdepartmental meeting

---

110 Fisher note, 2 December; Hopkins minutes, 7 October and 2 December; Phillips notes, 29 November; T 160/688; Meyers, *Britische Sicherheitspolitik*, pp. 408–9; O'Halpin, *Head of the Civil Service*, p. 292; Peden, *British Rearmament and Treasury*, pp. 73–76; Shay, *British Rearmament*, pp. 74–77.

111 Hopkins to Fergusson, 9 January, to Fisher and Fergusson, 28 February and 3 April, and to Chamberlain, 8 March; Chamberlain and Fisher notes on Hopkins's note of 3 April; T 171/324; 311 HC Debates, 21 April, cols. 52–55.

at the Treasury on 6 February, chaired by Fisher. He, Hankey, Robinson and others considered Lord Weir's recommendation to the DPR(DR) that an interdepartmental committee should have strong authority to sanction supply orders. It was agreed at this meeting that the TEEC should set up a subcommittee, chaired by Sir Arthur Robinson and with representatives from the Treasury and Service ministries. The TEEC then decided that its hitherto informal status should be regularized under the title Treasury Inter-Service Committee (TISC), and that Parliament be "informed of its existence."[112]

The metamorphosis from TEEC to TISC signaled the emergence of the problem of supply from an immediate international crisis to a longer season of building up domestic "war potential." The new committee did not eliminate interdepartmental mix-ups about time or allay the Treasury's fear that the demands of the Services would exceed the nation's peacetime capacity to produce and pay.

On 10 March, Duff Cooper informed Chamberlain that he assumed the Cabinet had authorized the completion of the Regular Field Force by 1939, the five-year program recommended by the DPR(DR) having "dated from 1934." He also asked whether the War Office had authority to begin negotiating with contractors to place orders for periods of three or more years. Sir Edward Bridges and Hopkins were sure that the DPR(DR) and Cabinet meant for the Field Force to be reconstituted over five years beginning in 1936, although they saw several references to a three-year period in the report of the DPR(DR) and wondered whether there might have been "an informal understanding" on this committee "to compress the five-year programme into three years." Hopkins notified the War Office that the chancellor did not wish to delay reequipping the Army, even though no inference could be drawn from the Cabinet's decisions that it intended to compress the five-year program into three years. Concerning long-term contracts, Bridges, Hopkins and J. A. N. Barlow agreed with the War Office that the development of a "war potential" depended on placing orders as soon as possible. But they insisted that proposals for entering into such contracts be submitted first to the TISC. Hopkins, who had chaired the TEEC and would chair the TISC, declared that Treasury control should not and need not cause "serious delay," and that the TISC was "ready to receive business at once."[113]

---

112 Meeting of 6 February, CAB 21/422A; Cmd. 5114, 4 March; Peden, *British Rearmament and Treasury*, p. 37; Roseveare, *Treasury*, p. 255.

113 Duff Cooper to Chamberlain, 10 March, and minutes by Bridges, Barlow, and Hopkins, 11–13 March; minutes of TISC meetings and correspondence with Sir Herbert Creedy (War Office); T 161/718. On contract procedures, see Peden, *British Rearmament and Treasury*, p. 38; Shay, *British Rearmament*, pp. 99–101.

Echoing Robinson's objections to treating the deficiency program and preparations for war as separate problems, Hankey hoped the machinery for handling long-term contracts would not break up in three years when most such contracts would probably end. This, he warned, would be a disastrous blow to building up "war potential."[114] Hankey's implicit question—how long would the shadow scheme last—was left open by the DPR(DR)'s ambiguous reference to supplies needed for the "3–5 years' programmes," and by the provisional nature of the Cabinet's approval of the committee's report. He could not have been comforted by signs that the Government would not fund the shadow scheme with enough money or over a long enough period to develop what he and the Services considered sufficient reserve capacity. The Cabinet distinguished between peacetime deficiencies and war potential, and approved a reduction in the DRC's recommended expenditures for the last two years of the new programs (1939–40) without ensuring that adequate reserves would be prepared by 1939. Chamberlain and the Treasury regarded three years as a long term for contracts, and their forecasts of annual costs for maintaining the new defense requirements did not envisage building a war potential of the kind recommended by the DRC.

The Services' definition of war potential threatened Treasury control. Late in March, Hopkins estimated that the War Office and Air Ministry soon planned to place long-term contracts for a combined total of about £200 million. And Hopkins viewed the request from the War Office to speed up reconstitution of the Field Force as "a forerunner" of future proposals from the Service departments to increase expenditure.[115] To the Treasury, the likelihood of losing control over such expenditure seemed far greater than the possibility that control would delay rearmament. Sir Warren Fisher, the Treasury's foremost advocate of rearmament, told members of the DPR that "Treasury sanction is required for expenditure flowing from Cabinet decisions of policy and that it is not admissable, as a means of evading this necessity, to seek after the event a quite meaningless 'covering' sanction from the Treasury."[116]

Rearmament gave the Treasury more cause than usual to regard its work as political and to influence national policy broadly defined. Cabinet decisions carried more than their usual significance for Treasury control. The Cabinet's approval of the DPR(DR) report "generally and provisionally" could be turned against the Treasury by a department or committee strong enough to convince the Cabinet that "the

---

[114] Minutes of meeting of 6 February (see note 112 above).
[115] Hopkins memoranda, 25 March and 2 April, T 161/718. For contract procedures and the TISC: Peden, *Rearmament and Treasury,* pp. 44–52; Shay, pp. 101–102.
[116] Fisher minute, 2 April, T 160/630.

international situation and other factors" dictated a change in policy. Similarly, the Treasury could employ these "qualifications" (as Hopkins called them) for its own purposes, particularly if it could show how a departure from approved policy affected the budget or national economy.

Chamberlain was more skillful and methodical than his ministerial colleagues in using the agenda and current policy as procedural devices to stop or steer discussion that might otherwise have led to decisions inconsistent with his comprehensive view of policy. He did this in meetings of the DPR(DR) and Cabinet in order to postpone decisions on the Territorial Army and the new naval standard, to prevent the shadow arms industry from interfering with normal trade, and to delay Cabinet discussion of the latter question until "decisions had been reached on . . . major policy."[117]

By the end of May, Chamberlain was readier than the Foreign Office to overhaul "major policy," more reluctant than the Services and Hankey to let any reassessment of policy upset peacetime commerce, and disgruntled with all of these constituent parts of the machinery. The double policy of coercing and conciliating Mussolini had failed. Britain should abandon the first half of that policy, but without playing second fiddle in the Mediterranean, and without including Eastern Europe in regional pacts that might replace collective security. Britain had more time to rearm than Vansittart, Eden, Fisher, or the French guessed, so long as what Inskip called "the growing anxieties of the international situation" were reduced by conciliatory diplomacy toward Germany, Japan, and Italy. Britain needed less time, supplies, and money to build an effective deterrent than the DRC presumed in its more balanced scheme of rearmament with a full shadow industrial scheme ensuring the production of large reserves for war. The international potential for war might be so limited over the next three years that the national war potential could be held within a thin and short shadow. With Inskip's help, the disparate strategic views of the Services could be resolved and defense policy reconciled with foreign policy in a coherent plan based on the Treasury's calculations of cost, industrial capacity, and time.

Inter-Service coordination improved thanks to reforms in the machinery. On the reconstituted Joint Planning Committee, which held its first meeting on 1 April, the senior members (Colonel Adam, Captain Tom Phillips, and Group Captain Harris) were joined by a junior representative from each Service (Colonel R. H. Dewing, War Office; Captain C. S. Daniel, Admiralty; Wing Commander H. H. Fraser, Air Min-

---

[117] Cab 31(36), 29 April, CAB 23/84.

istry). The new members convened frequently as a subcommittee in the CID offices at No. 2 Whitehall Gardens, and attended the meetings of the whole committee, which now occurred at least once weekly: fourteen in April and May (compared to seventeen in all of 1935, and six in the first three months of 1936). This increase in size and activity boosted the JPC's confidence. The committee wanted to start "a lot of hares," as Colonel Adam, its chairman, told B. H. Liddell Hart, and to press for "a clear statement of foreign policy, which is an urgent need for all planning." Adam found "the new coordinating system" quite promising, particularly the appointment of a new minister who could represent the Services' "joint view" to the Cabinet, correcting bias from the Foreign Office.[118]

During the winter and early spring, the JPC had spent almost all of its time preparing reports on the immediate military implications of the Mediterranean and Rhineland crises. On 22 May, the JPC agreed on its agenda for the near future. In addition to the pending strategic review of Europe and a study of trade defense and food supply, the committee would work on two plans for war: the "German Appreciation (1939)" (the year 1939 having been chosen in 1934 and still not reflecting the Services' estimate of a later date for Germany's military readiness), and the "Far East Appreciation." After completing these plans, the JPC would prepare one for a war in Europe and the Far East simultaneously. The JPC did not treat the Italian threat in the Mediterranean as a subject for long-term war planning, but reported—as requested by Inskip through the COS—on the military situation that would exist there and in North Africa following Italy's victory over Ethiopia.[119]

When the members of the JPC celebrated the committee's 100th meeting on 29 May "in a suitable manner,"[120] their high spirits owed something to the expectation that they could get on with long-term plans for war. Because of international crises, the JPC's progress on the German war plan had been delayed since its provisional report (1 August 1935) came before the COS (29 October), and the committee had not yet begun drafting the plan for war with Japan. To the Service

[118] Liddell Hart notes of talk with Adam and Colonel Paget at the Athenaeum Club, 15 May, Liddell Hart Papers, 11/1936/64 (LHCMA). In a letter to the author, 30 June 1974, General Adam recalled that the members of the JPC "got on together very well in spite of occasional inter-service jealousy." Major Leslie Hollis (Royal Marines) was appointed secretary to the JPC's new subcommittee; on his first impressions of the JPC and Hankey's anger with him for not initially following protocol for the circulation of documents, see Leasor and Hollis, *Clock*, pp. 29–32.

[119] JPC reports, 29 April, CAB 53/27, and 11 May (on the Mediterranean), CAB 55/7; meeting, 22 May, CAB 55/1; Inskip to Hankey, 4 May, CAB 21/436; COS meeting, 4 May, CAB 53/6; Pratt, *East of Malta*, pp. 117–18.

[120] JPC meeting, CAB 55/1. The JPC later learned that Hankey "was not greatly amused" by this party; Adam Papers, XI/1 (LHCMA).

staffs, planning for war presupposed a period of relative international calm and a redefinition of policy by the Foreign Office and Cabinet. Even if these wishes came true, the JPC would have to make assumptions about Germany's political intentions and strategic plans, and use these as bases for recommending courses of action for each Service. Would the result be a disjointed "aggregate of three Service plans," as Chamberlain had described the DRC report of November 1935? Or would the members of the JPC be able to reconcile inter-Service differences over German strategy and the form of a war in Western Europe?

We have seen, in the previous chapter, that the reorganized machinery of coordination did not resolve these differences, which centered around air power, the role of the Army and thus the nature of Britain's commitment to protect the Low Countries and France, and guesses about German military planning. At the same time, however, the appointment of Inskip invigorated interdepartmental debate and increased the visibility of military considerations among ministers.

Sir Thomas Inskip had been educated at Clifton and King's College, Cambridge, and left his barrister's practice to serve in Naval Intelligence during the Great War. A Conservative MP for most of the period since the war, he was no stranger to Parliament when he assumed his duties as Minister for Coordination of Defence. Although he had no executive authority and a minuscule staff (housed at Whitehall Gardens with the CID Secretariat), he soon impressed officers and civilians alike with his tact, his sense of the urgency and importance of his task, and his attention to the forest as well as the trees of defense policy. He chaired meetings of the Principal Supply Officers Committee and DPR. The latter, now responsible for supervising industrial production and rearmament, met twice in May—to discuss the first of the monthly reports from the Service departments and Ministry of Labour, along with the problems of recruiting skilled labor and negotiating with shadow industries.[121] Inskip usually chaired the CID, including the meeting of 3 April that determined instructions for British military representatives at staff talks with France and Belgium. He also chaired the CID's ad hoc subcommittees on Air Defence Research and Vulnerability of Capital Ships (to air attack), and sat on the Cabinet's Foreign Policy Committee as the single spokesman for the Service departments.

Three days before attending his first Cabinet meeting, Inskip met the Chiefs of Staff formally for the first time on 16 March in order "to make contact" with them. Later in the month he exercised his authority to convene the COS and asked the chiefs to help him anticipate sudden

---

[121] DPR meetings, 7 and 25 May, CAB 16/136.

requests for reports in an unstable international situation. The COS should be ready "at very short notice" to inform him on strategic matters, such as whether to withdraw forces from the Mediterranean in case of a European crisis. He and the COS agreed that the chiefs could, on their own initiative, continue to submit "their collective views to Ministers when they thought the situation necessary." On 13 May, Inskip called a meeting of the COS to discuss the strategic situation in the eastern Mediterranean, North Africa, and Europe; collective security; and the possibility of a German air attack against a British expeditionary force to the Continent "during the stages of embarkation, passage and landing." In addition, Chatfield volunteered that security in the Far East required adopting the new naval standard proposed by the DRC.[122]

Inskip improved coordination among departments, between them and the Supply Board, and among the Services, Cabinet, and Dominions. He kept Baldwin informed on major issues, and adapted to the administrative procedures that Hankey had developed. Above all, he heightened ministerial awareness of two major issues: the disparity between international tension and the "peace conditions" that guided the pace of rearmament; the contradiction between maintaining the military buildup in the Mediterranean and rearming for war in Europe and the Far East. He himself had begun to think that industrial production must be accelerated. He advocated leaving the Mediterranean, and, in the event of war with Germany, he questioned the wisdom of dispatching the Field Force so long as Britain's air defenses were weak.

At the time of Inskip's appointment, Chamberlain thought him not "the ideal man, but he is strong and sound and will make no friction with either the Chiefs of Staff or the Service Ministers."[123] Chamberlain supposed that the new man, who was not beholden to a single Service, would help him push the strategic and budgetary case for air power. Simon hoped Inskip would restrain Eden from promising land forces to France and Belgium in a war with Germany.[124] Inskip shared his two colleagues' appreciation of air power and its implications for deterrence and diplomacy, and they expected him to side with them on the Foreign Policy Committee. He would be all the more useful an ally there because of the absence of the Service ministers from the committee, and on the Cabinet because Baldwin could be persuaded to accept the counsel of his own deputy without appearing to affront the Services.

---

[122] COS meetings, 16 and 25 March, 13 May, CAB 53/5–6.
[123] Chamberlain to Ida, 14 March, Chamberlain Papers, NC 18/1/951.
[124] Simon to Baldwin, 25 March, PREM 1/194. Chamberlain, Inskip, and Simon rejected Eden's proposal to hold a special Cabinet meeting on 6 April to enable staff talks to begin on 8 March instead of a week later; Hankey to Baldwin, 3 April, CAB 21/472.

On the other hand, Inskip assured Eyres-Monsell that he would not prematurely "frame or advance" his views on strategic matters, about which "no one holding this office could contemplate a rigid status quo or finality." The documentary record sustains this self-appraisal of a man who, upon taking office, was more open-minded than Chamberlain and might conceivably make friction in the future with the chancellor's strategy of deterrence.[125]

Even before the campaign for reorganization built up a head of steam, Hankey had envisioned strengthening the JPC and creating an inter-Service intelligence committee to work in association with the JPC.[126] And in January he began to arrange for Colonel H. L. Ismay to become Deputy Secretary to the CID the following August—"much earlier than [Hankey] originally intended," according to Ismay,[127] who had served in the Somaliland during the war and was military secretary to the Viceroy of India from 1931 to 1933.

These modifications alone would not have settled inter-Service disputes, partly because, as Hankey's biographer writes, he "had become more rigid in his outlook and fixed in his ways; . . . still subject to the influence of his naval upbringing and training."[128] Yet Hankey adjusted to the reformed machinery better than might have been expected of one who had strongly resisted major reorganization in the first place. He and Inskip began to develop a relationship of mutual respect through committee meetings and daily traffic in the close quarters at Whitehall Gardens. As Secretary to the Cabinet, CID, DPR, and COS, Hankey soon learned that Inskip did not intend to usurp powers belonging, in Hankey's view, to the Secretariat, interdepartmental committees, or individual ministers.

Hankey knew that Inskip had Chamberlain's ear and could be a useful advocate for increasing the pace of rearmament. He suggested

---

[125] Inskip to Monsell, 30 April, CAB 64/23. For a wide array of appraisals of Inskip, see Bond, *Chief of Staff*, pp. 95, 112; Chatfield, *Navy and Defence*, p. 97; Gibbs, *Rearmament*, p. 772; Ismay, *Memoirs*, p. 75; Johnson, *Defence by Committee*, pp. 234–37, 249–51; Meyers, *Britische Sicherheitspolitik*, pp. 401–2; Macmillan, *Winds of Change*, p. 432; Roskill, *Hankey*, 3:207–8; Shay, *British Rearmament*, pp. 214–16; Lord Astor to J. L. Garvin, 17 March 1936, Garvin Papers. In a lecture to the Imperial Defence College in October 1949, Ismay called attention to the new minister's lack of executive authority, but said the position had been a "step in the right direction"; Ismay Papers, 3/4/12 (LHCMA).

[126] The idea of such an intelligence committee had come from the War Office in July 1935, and Hankey must not have been enthusiastic about it, for, although approved by the CID on 30 January, the new committee remained inactive until reconstituted in July 1936 as the Joint Intelligence Committee. See chap. 3, note 99, and chap. 4, note 37; Hinsley, *British Intelligence*, pp. 34–36; Roskill, *Hankey*, 3:212.

[127] Ismay to Major General W. L. O. Twiss (Army HQ, India), 29 January, Ismay Papers, 1/1/34 (LHCMA); also letter to Twiss of 21 August 1935, 1/1/32, when Hankey first approached him about filling such a new position.

[128] Roskill, *Hankey*, 3:210–11.

to Inskip that the DPR's receiving monthly progress reports from the Services "would provide an opportunity to 'ginger up' the War Office a bit." He complained to Inskip about delays in implementing the DRC Third Report, urging that "we ought administratively to speed up almost to war conditions." Whether to follow this with "more heroic measures, such as constituting a Ministry of Supply or taking powers for control of industry, can come later." Already dubious about the assumption of peace conditions, Inskip conveyed Hankey's concerns to the DPR on 25 May, warning the committee to be prepared to discuss an acceleration of defense programs after the Whitsun recess.[129] The DPR(DR) and Cabinet had authorized the DRC to settle inter-Service arguments over priority of supply if this could not be done through the Principal Supply Officers organization. Willing to let the Supply Board, PSOC, and DPR cope with this issue, Hankey and Inskip allowed the DRC to disappear without fanfare, although Hankey regretted that it was not given the chance to hasten rearmament.[130]

Hankey anticipated a few years "of increasing international confusion," during which Britain must "stave off war and . . . strengthen ourselves in case one day we can stave it off no longer." Meanwhile, Britain was pursuing "the proper policy" of trying to bring Germany and France together, and "the Huns" had made more plausible proposals for replacing the Treaty of Locarno than had the French.[131] There was general agreement among Hankey, Inskip, and the Chiefs of Staff that the remilitarization of the Rhineland was neither the issue nor the time for resisting Germany, that Britain should limit its obligation to assist France in this crisis and in any agreement that might replace the Locarno Treaty, and that collective security and general deterrence carried too many political risks and strategic diversions. Maintaining a reinforced military presence in the Mediterranean weakened British security in case of an immediate emergency with Germany or Japan, and delayed long-term rearmament for war with those most likely enemies. By conciliating Germany and reconciling Europe, not by encircling Germany, diplomacy should buy time for the Services to prepare strategic plans and supplies for war. The reorganization of the machinery of defense increased the potential weight of this military advice by strengthening the JPC and giving the Services a common ministerial spokesman.

This system of decisionmaking compares with a recent description of how British foreign policy has been made since the Second World War:

[129] Hankey to Inskip, 21 April and 22 May, CAB 21/573 and 702; DPR meeting, 25 May, CAB 16/136.

[130] Roskill, *Hankey*, 3:319.

[131] Hankey to Casey, 20 April, CAB 63/51; Schmidt, *England in der Krise*, pp. 195–208.

"Debate is purposely restricted, clashes of principle blurred, and the acceptable, rather than the best, solution selected."[132] The Cabinet and Foreign Policy Committee postponed the task of reassessing foreign policy, and the DPR no longer was responsible for aligning that policy with defense programs. The Foreign Office played for time to allow Britain to rearm, but also to await developments in Berlin and Rome, and to decide what policy Eden should recommend to the Cabinet. Thus, while Eden and Vansittart pressed for an acceleration of rearmament during what they presumed might be only a short interval of peace, they did not reconcile contrary views of how that time might be filled with conciliating the dictators or displaying British military strength, and they did not specify limits beyond which Britain must forcibly resist German expansion in Central and Southeastern Europe. The Treasury was willing to expedite work on the approved Service programs, but also determined to avoid the costs, interference with normal trade, and longer period that would have accompanied wholesale adoption of the shadow scheme for building up war potential. In order to concentrate on supply and war plans, the Services wanted a longer interval than the Foreign Office thought likely and a state of international repose that the Foreign Office could not furnish.

Separately, each of these constituents of the machinery of cunctation voiced reservations about the effectiveness of immediate or general deterrence while Britain rearmed. Singular agendas determined their respective positions. So did the Mediterranean and Rhineland crises, which upset hopeful premises about showing force to Mussolini and negotiating conditional concessions to Hitler, and which encumbered procedures and timetables for long-term rearmament.

The machinery reached tenuous compromises that perpetuated inconsistencies among these different positions, a result of Hankey's axiom of policymaking by committee: the coordination of disparate judgments of expert advisers and their well-briefed ministers. Because of the bargaining required by this system of mutual adjustment, decisionmaking was hampered by delay, heterogeneity, and indecision. In spite of shocks in the Mediterranean and Rhineland, these characteristics preserved a variety of options for the Cabinet to weigh as circumstances unfolded, including taking risks and showing force for purposes other than self-defense. These traits could also prompt impatient members of the Government to reduce incoherence in policymaking and minimize the alternatives for deterrence.[133]

[132] Zara Steiner, "Decision-making in American and British Foreign Policy: An Open and Shut Case," *Review of International Studies* 13 (1987), 6.

[133] Braybrooke and Lindblom implicitly endorse Hankey's method when they maintain that systems of mutual adjustment and incremental change can preserve "a rich variety of impressions and insights that are liable to be 'coordinated' out of sight by hasty and inappropriate demands for a common plan of attack." *Strategy of Decision*, p. 106.

Hankey's axiom, along with both its susceptibility to confusion and its retention of alternatives, was being challenged in the Cabinet as political leadership there shifted more and more from Baldwin to Chamberlain. Chamberlain's private papers reveal both satisfaction and frustration at serving as prime minister designate. He welcomed Baldwin's frequently deferring to him on questions of policy, but lost patience when unable to cure the prime minister of irresolution. Chamberlain thought Baldwin asked too many people for advice and was then "left in the air having no opinion of his own."[134] Chamberlain's opinion was clear. By steps he deemed logical, and by refuting experts when their advice disagreed with that reasoning, the Government could solve Britain's strategic dilemma by agreeing upon a homogeneous architecture of foreign policy, strategic doctrine, supply, finance, time, and deterrence.[135] If the reorganized machinery of defense did not help produce this result, which would eliminate all of the alternative schemes for deterrence except Chamberlain's during the interval of rearmament, Whitehall would be caught between incremental and rational styles of decisionmaking as Chamberlain forced the Cabinet to make up military and diplomatic minds along with its own.

---

[134] Chamberlain to Ida, 29 February, and diary, 1 March, Chamberlain Papers, NC 18/1/950, 2/23a.

[135] On politicians' challenging or choosing expert advice, see Halperin, *Bureaucratic Politics,* pp. 146–50. Chamberlain fought against what some political scientists view as realities of decisionmaking: consistency and coherence are impossible for complex issues; individuals and organizations do not integrate considerations when confronting many goals and ambiguous information; "cybernetic" planning, which tends to separate questions of policy, is more common that "analytic," which tries to integrate them. See Lindblom, *Intelligence of Democracy,* chap. 11; Jervis, *Perception and Misperception,* pp. 24–28; Steinbruner, *Cybernetic Theory of Decision,* pp. 85–86.

PART IV

THE SEARCH FOR COHERENCE, JUNE 1936–MAY 1937

[6]

Foreign Policy at Risk

In the last twelve months of Baldwin's premiership, British policy went through its fourth stage since the Defence Requirements Committee issued its first report early in 1934. During this period, June 1936 to May 1937, both the content and the machinery of policy reached an impasse. The Spanish Civil War barged in on the already crowded agenda of the Foreign Policy Committee, the Defence Plans (Policy) Committee was established to discuss plans for war, and a vigorous Chamberlain prepared to succeed an ailing Baldwin. British reflections on deterrence underwent several changes in emphasis. The problem of defining Britain's vital interests became more explicit as Italy intervened in Spain and Germany turned its attention to Austria and Czechoslovakia. Examination of major strategic papers entailed listing Britain's extensive commitments alongside its limited resources. The many references to connotations of the word "policy" showed how much deterrence embraced competing departmental jurisdictions. Together, these circumstances increased pressure on British foreign policy by exposing its faults and diminishing its relative importance as one element of national policy; on deterrence by emphasizing strategic liabilities and financial constraints; on the Foreign Office by expecting it to manufacture time until 1942; and on policymaking in the manner of Baldwin and Hankey.

In the summer and autumn of 1936, British foreign policy continued along familiar paths. Although Germany did not answer the British questionnaire of early May, London maintained that efforts of conciliation had not failed, took the lead in unsuccessful negotiations for replacing the Treaty of Locarno, and postponed any offer of particular concessions to Germany. Days after the League of Nations lifted sanctions against Italy in July, the outbreak of the Spanish Civil War regenerated the Mediterranean crisis, threatened to align Britain's three potential enemies in one ideological bloc, kept the British Government somewhere between resisting and conciliating Mussolini, and multiplied irresolution in the machinery of policy. London struggled over its deteriorating strategic position, applied new intelligence to planning for war against Germany, and guessed about Hitler's next move. Friction increased between military and diplomatic experts over the reduction of commitments and dangers while Britain rearmed. By December, the reassessment of Britain's "major policy" was still in limbo. No one in the Government could say that it had made much progress toward reconciling foreign policy, rearmament, time, and deterrence, and the blame for this was assigned largely to the Foreign Office. The Office might snub and thwart dictators while also trying to appease them, and Eden persistently advocated defending—and perhaps augmenting—Britain's vital interests in the Mediterranean so as to deter both Mussolini and Hitler. The Chiefs of Staff warned against stalling conciliation and threatening force so long as Britain lacked the requisite military strength to win a war. The Spanish Civil War pushed the Cabinet still further toward the latter counsel, which meant limiting commitments, taking fewer risks, holding fewer trumps for coercive diplomacy until 1942, and negotiating with Germany from what was not yet a general position of strength.

After the New Year, the pressure for change intensified, partly because of continuing risks abroad but also because of coincidental events in London. Vansittart's formula of a year earlier for negotiating particulars with Germany had bogged down. Making Germany guess about British intentions also kept London guessing about how to play for time. Among the possibilities considered were concessions in Central and Eastern Europe, where Britain might sell Germany some "lumber." Because of Italy's escalating intervention in Spain, the so-called Gentleman's Agreement (in early 1937) with Mussolini was soon followed by the Cabinet's decision to regard Italy as neither a "reliable friend" nor a "probable enemy," and providing security in the Mediterranean conflicted with British strategy for security in the Far East. British policy divided neither the Rome-Berlin Axis nor the German-Japanese Anti-Comintern Pact (both of which were announced in November 1936) and did not close the rift between the Axis and the rest of Europe.

As time progressed further into the interval that the Government presumed it had to prepare for war, foreign policy lost ground to strategy, strategy to finance, and European deterrence to self-defense. British foreign policy became entangled with strategic plans, the controversy over the Army's mission in a European war, news that the RAF would not finish Scheme F by 1939 under conditions of normal trade, a dramatic increase in the defense budget, and the prospect of Chamberlain's succession. Partly by accidents of timing, these issues converged so as to alter the very meaning of policy, amplify the risks of foreign policy at home, and heighten the magical thinking about the year 1942. In interdepartmental bargaining, a divided Foreign Office stumbled before a determined Chiefs of Staff, who, with Hankey's help, downplayed intelligence from their own staffs indicating that the Wehrmacht might be ready for war before 1942. Chamberlain and the Treasury virtually abandoned 1939 as a target date for rearmament and became Whitehall's strongest advocates of 1942 as a goal. They delayed proposals from the War Office and Admiralty, and proposed a five-year plan for funding defense. These confrontations—along with the Treasury's resounding triumph in bureaucratic politics—weakened the old DRC coalition, discouraged interventionist ideas about assisting allies or accumulating vital interests abroad, and reduced the flexibility for planning contingencies of deterrence while rearming. The Government showed no interest in risking war in Europe before Germany completed its rearmament or attacked Britain, the Low Countries, or France. The term "policy" was understood more and more inclusively, foreshadowing war while counting on peace. Its usage blurred the lines between foreign policy and strategy, revealed the inequality between international dangers and domestic resources, challenged the idea of a major continental commitment for the Army, and underscored the Treasury's case for economic stability and the target date of 1942.

The confusion and semantic changes in policy illuminated Britain's strategic quandary and engendered a twofold plan of escape from it. First, time could be bought until 1942 through conciliation without firm reciprocal guarantees from the dictators or threats of force from London. Second, the committee system required new leadership to overcome the indecision now held partly responsible for Britain's unremitting predicament. Chamberlain was determined to maintain Britain's peacetime economy, decrease its international liabilities, concentrate on the air deterrent, and bring order to national policy. These intentions raised the expectations of a growing number of British citizens who would have welcomed coherence no matter who succeeded Baldwin.

COMMITMENTS AND DANGERS, JUNE–DECEMBER 1936

On 6 July, having recently returned from Geneva, Eden told the Cabinet how depressing the situation had become. The League, France, and smaller powers were all weak. Britain's defenses were inadequate, its foreign policy hesitant, its interests in the Far East vulnerable. "Impressed by the gravity" of this situation, the Cabinet and Foreign Policy Committee agreed that he should arrange for Anglo-French-Belgian talks to be held in London on 23 July. The three governments recognized the now irreversible fact of Germany's remilitarization of the Rhineland. They invited Germany and Italy to participate in a five-power conference to draw up new security agreements for Western Europe and, if possible, to discuss other questions regarding European peace.[1]

During the next few months, London prepared for this conference—which never took place—with the knowledge that Belgian policy was in the process of drastic revision. Alarmed by electoral gains by both political extremes in Belgium, Paul Van Zeeland and new Foreign Minister Paul-Henri Spaak decided to end their country's close relationship with France, keep Belgium from becoming a guarantor in any new security pact, and concentrate on programs of national unity and national defense.

The implications of Belgium's apparent move toward neutrality lay at the center of arguments between the British Services and Foreign Office over the dimensions of the proposed five-power conference.[2] The Chiefs of Staff discounted the French argument that Belgium's new policy would have "grave consequences" for British interests. The military experts advised that Belgian neutrality would be to Britain's advantage, that Belgium was right to wish "to avoid the risks of being drawn into war as a result of French commitments in Central and Eastern Europe," and that staff talks with any power were impractical because Britain could not be sure on whose side it might have to fight.[3] Eden agreed with Vansittart that it was "useless and therefore unwise" to force an unwilling Belgium to guarantee France as the French wished. Still, they and the central department in the Foreign Office showed more sympathy for France than did the military advisers, and less inclination to accede to Germany and Italy on points that might cause them to abandon their acceptance, in principle, of the invitation to attend a five-power conference. Eden warned the Cabinet on 9 December that the military's proposed line of policy was too risky, and he

[1] Foreign Policy Committee, 15 July, CAB 27/622; Cabs 50 and 53(36), 6 and 16 July, CAB 23/85; *DBFP*, 16, nos. 476, 477.

[2] *DBFP*, 17, passim; Kieft, *Belgium's Return*, chaps. 4, 5; Gibbs, *Rearmament*, pp. 611–22; Young, *In Command of France*, pp. 151–54.

[3] JPC meetings, 24–27 August, CAB 55/2, and report, 28 August, CAB 55/8; COS meetings, 31 August, 20 and 30 October, CAB 53/6; COS reports, 1 September, CP 218(36), CAB 24/263 (also *DBFP*, 17, no. 156), 26 October, CP 296(36), and 9 November, CP 302(36) (also *DBFP*, 17, no. 361), CAB 24/265; DCOS draft report, 24 November, and COS report, 25 November, CAB 53/29.

recommended continuing "the policy of cooperation with Belgium which France, and to a less extent His Majesty's Government, have followed since the war."[4]

The Chiefs of Staff opposed the Foreign Office's view that a five-power conference should also consider problems of security in Central and Eastern Europe. The COS would object to any agreement that might carry an Eastern European war into Western Europe or oblige Britain to assist France in such a conflict, even if Germany attacked France. Although an Eastern European war might recoil "ultimately on our heads," the chiefs believed that "appeasement in Western Europe," a necessity for British security, would be improbable if France and Britain gave too much consideration to "Russian interests."[5] The Foreign Office did not want France to ruin negotiations for a new Locarno agreement "by maintaining impossible demands in the East." Many in London thought that Leon Blum's Government might do this because the Spanish Civil War reinforced the ideological affinity between the Popular Front and the Soviet Union. Nevertheless, the Foreign Office argued, a western pact by itself, "unaccompanied by any general settlement, would be merely a poultice applied to one of the few parts of Europe which at present are not inflamed," and could even be "dangerous, since it would create in the West a false sense of security, while giving to Russia and to the lesser powers of the East and Centre the feeling that they had been abandoned to their fate." Thus, Britain should "decline to disinterest [itself] in the East" and should "insist on the need for a general settlement."[6]

Sir Thomas Inskip called attention to the emphasis the COS put on "the desirability from the military point of view of reducing our commitments to the minimum and of keeping our hands as free as possible."[7] The Cabinet's conclusions regarding a five-power conference usually occupied ground somewhere between this advice and that of the Foreign Office. Belgium should not be asked to guarantee Britain or France. Britain should try to procure guarantees from France and Germany, but should not increase its commitments "by reason of the

[4] Vansittart, Sargent, and Eden minutes, 27 and 29 October, C7631/4/18, FO 371/19914; Wigram minute, 9 November, C8049/4/18, FO 371/19915 (see also *DBFP*, 17, no. 361n); Sargent to Vice Admiral James, 25 November, Wigram memorandum, 25 November, and Vansittart minute, 1 December, C8479/C8744/C8819/270/4, FO 371/19851; Eden memorandum, 5 December, CP 332(36), CAB 24/265; Cab 73(36), 9 December, CAB 23/86. The major papers from Eden and the Foreign Office on the five-power conference: *DBFP*, 17, nos. 114, 206, 321, 349, 389, 433.

[5] COS report, 1 September, CP 218(36), CAB 24/263 (also *DBFP*, 17, no. 156).

[6] Foreign Office memorandum, 19 August, CP 220(36), CAB 24/263 (also *DBFP*, 17, no. 114).

[7] Cab 56(36), 2 September, CAB 23/85.

Franco-Soviet treaty," or risk blocking a western agreement by making other European questions part of a five-power conference. Eden should ask Van Zeeland to define Belgian policy so as to include resisting violation "of Belgian air by German aircraft," but should not (as Eden had proposed) urge the Belgians "to remove the present uncertainty as regards their attitude toward cooperation with the French."[8]

Vansittart accused the Cabinet of making "watery amendments" in the recommendations of the Foreign Office, all in pursuit of starting conversations with the Germans. This, he wrote, was "a perversion. The essential object is to get a good, durable, defensible treaty with the Germans. And we shall only get that by firmness." Nor did Vansittart appreciate allegations from the War Office and Chiefs of Staff that rebuffs had discouraged Germany from seeking Britain's friendship.[9]

Like the Chiefs of Staff, the Cabinet was less willing than the Foreign Office to reassure France and more eager to conciliate Germany. The COS suspected that the Foreign Office really wanted an alliance with France rather than a multilateral security pact.[10] The COS thought recent events "raised a shadow of apprehension" about the future. Britain could not rely on French support in a war against Germany "irrespective of the causes of the quarrel," and indeed might one day "have to face the contingency of French hostility." The Joint Planning Committee considered "the value of France as an ally to be an unreliable quantity." The Chiefs of Staff resented the French for assuming "without justification" that Britain would send troops to France at the start of a war in Western Europe. "If we were *not* going to do that we should very soon be isolated in Europe," Vansittart commented, adding that General Deverell had stressed this point himself in a meeting earlier that day regarding the Army's role.[11]

Because of all the conditions being raised by the five governments, Vansittart, Wigram, and Phipps viewed an emasculated western pact as "a complete phantom and perhaps a dangerous phantom" (Wigram) which would not contribute to the period of peace needed to rearm.[12]

[8] Ibid.; also Cabs 60, 62, 64–66, 73 (36); 28 October; 4, 11, 13, 18 November; 9 December; CAB 23/86; CID meeting, 29 October, in CP 296(36), CAB 24/265; Eden memoranda, 3 December, *DBFP*, 17, no. 433, and 5 December, CP 332(36), CAB 24/265 (both of them drafted by Wigram and Sargent).

[9] Vansittart minutes, 19 November, *DBFP*, 17, no. 389n, and 17 November, Vansittart Papers, 2/29; Wark, *Ultimate Enemy*, pp. 88–89.

[10] Chatfield at CID meeting, 10 December, CAB 2/6.

[11] COS reports of 1 September and 26 October (see note 3 above); JPC "strategic appreciation" for a war with Germany (JP 155), 26 October, CAB 53/29; Vansittart minute, 27 October, C7631/4/18, FO 371/19914; minutes of meeting with Inskip and others, same day, CAB 64/35.

[12] Wigram to Phipps, 29 October, Phipps Papers, 2/25; Wigram minute, 9 November, C8049/4/18, FO 371/19915; Vansittart paper, 10 September, *DBFP*, 17, appx. I.

How, then, could Britain keep Germany in play during the interval before British rearmament would help achieve a general and durable settlement, and how much time was left before Hitler might precipitate war?

Neither the Foreign Office nor the Cabinet thought it was time for particular concessions to Germany. Eden and others in the Office doubted the wisdom of opening the colonial question; so did the Plymouth Subcommittee, Foreign Policy Committee, and Cabinet, although the door was left slightly ajar because, as Chamberlain argued, closing it would contradict the policy of keeping Germany in play. Vansittart would play the colonial card only if Britain could be "sure of getting something very real and tangible in return," for he agreed with Phipps that restoring African colonies would whet Germany's appetite in Europe.[13]

There was stronger support in the Foreign Office and Cabinet for financial or commercial concessions. In July, Eden thought these might reduce the drift toward autarky that could cause Germany to make war to capture sources of raw materials. In the Cabinet, Inskip was not alone in thinking that if Britain worked "for the appeasement of Germany's economic conditions he would feel that we had a policy for which there was some hope." Chamberlain questioned the motives of Dr. Hjalmar Schacht, who, as president of the Reichsbank and as Economics Minister, was Berlin's most ardent suitor for colonial and economic appeasement. Runciman opposed tariff concessions as a reversal of the policy of imperial preference. In November, having read a report from Phipps on Germany's Four Year Plan for economic self-sufficiency, Eden agreed "emphatically" with Vansittart that Germany be given "*nothing* except she change her political ways." Economic assistance "without political return" would only improve Germany's capacity to rearm and to expand into Central and Southeastern Europe.[14] And here the matter rested into December while the Cabinet concentrated on the five-power conference.

[13] Vansittart paper, 10 September, appx. I; Vansittart to Eden, 21 September (no. 220); Phipps to Eden, 22 and 30 October (nos. 318, 342); *DBFP*, 17; Vansittart to Swinton, 22 September, FO 800/394. Also FPC meetings, 21 and 27 July, CAB 27/622, to discuss the report of the Plymouth Subcommittee of the CID (report of 9 June in CAB 27/622 and *DBFP*, 16, appx. III); Cab 62(36), 4 November, CAB 23/86; Crozier, *Appeasement and Germany's Last Bid*, chap. 6; Rose, *Vansittart*, pp. 194–96.

[14] Eden to Runciman, 17 July, and Runciman to Eden, 23 July, *DBFP*, 16, nos. 463, 478; Cab 62(36), 4 November, CAB 23/86; Vansittart minute, 3 September, *DBFP*, 17, no. 135n; Jebb memorandum, September, ibid., no. 250; Chamberlain minute, 5 October, T 188/168; Phipps to Eden, 4 November, with minutes by Vansittart, Eden, and Ashton-Gwatkin, *DBFP*, 17, no. 350; Wendt, *Economic Appeasement*, pp. 336–41, 449–50. On Schacht's activities, see Crozier, *Appeasement and Germany's Last Bid*, chap. 7.

In the absence of particular initiatives, and certain by early December that a five-power conference suitable to Germany and Italy would bring neither a general settlement nor a desirable limited one, Vansittart did not want to rush five-power negotiations. "We are surely interested in gaining time," he wrote, "or not preventing others from wasting it."[15] Vansittart's obsession with time had increased since his conversation with German leaders during his "busman's holiday" in Berlin in August. He returned to London with at least a faint hope for a lasting settlement through a combination of negotiations and rearmament. "We might succeed with Time, if we do not kill Time by premature disarmament." If Britain "could hold [Germany] for a while by a combination of reasonableness and honest-to-God strength, we could still turn the corner."[16] How to delay Germany and for how long was yet another contentious issue between the Foreign Office and Chiefs of Staff.

Vansittart, Eden, Sargent, and Wigram believed that British rearmament had begun to impress Berlin and other European capitals, but would not soon reach a sufficient level to prevent or turn back Germany's next "forward move." In June, aware that remilitarizing the Rhineland had strengthened Germany's position for expansion to the south and east, Vansittart warned the DPR that this move might come (against Czechoslovakia) as early as 1937 or perhaps even by the end of 1936. In November Eden told the Cabinet to expect "some challenge" from spring 1937 onward.[17] These estimates rested on the unpredictability of the Nazi leadership, the implications of Germany's economic policy of autarky, and new evidence about German rearmament.

Hitler was a "chameleon," Ribbentrop "dangerous," and "Goering and the lunatics" might exploit economic difficulties and use "mass propaganda" to force Hitler's hand.[18] In July, the War Office and Industrial Intelligence Centre (IIC) reported that the Wehrmacht would probably reach its peacetime strength of thirty-six divisions by November 1936 (not by April 1937 as previously reckoned). In August, Germany announced that it was lengthening the term of compulsory service in the armed forces to two years; a month later, that the Army's peacetime strength would be increased to thirty-nine divisions. Military Intelligence began to subscribe to the IIC's judgment that further expansion

---

[15] Vansittart minute, 7 December, *DBFP*, 17, no. 488n; Eden, however, wanted the Foreign Office to prod other governments for replies to London's latest communiqué.

[16] Vansittart paper, 10 September, *DBFP*, 17, appx. I; on his visit to Berlin, see Rose, *Vansittart*, pp. 196–99.

[17] DPR meeting, 11 June, CAB 16/136; Cab 63(36), 4 November, CAB 23/86.

[18] Vansittart paper, 10 September (appx. I); Vansittart and Sargent minutes, 16 November (no. 345n); *DBFP*, 17.

of the German Army was inevitable, and it decided that statements from the German War Ministry could no longer be trusted. The IIC and Naval Intelligence reported that, although Germany adhered to the Anglo-German Naval Agreement of 1935 (the Admiralty wanted to believe this), German industrial capacity was sufficient to complete and indeed exceed by 1940 the level of strength allowed by that pact. Various sources, including the Air Staff's intelligence directorate, now predicted that the Luftwaffe would number 2,500 first-line machines by April 1939, whereas Scheme F for the RAF aimed at a first-line strength of about 1,700 aircraft by the same date. All of this news depressed Wigram and Vansittart, who viewed the shadow industry as incomparable to Germany's more dramatic rearmament. Britain's "inadequate measures," Wigram somberly predicted, may well "expose us in quite a near future to the most terrible demands which we shall not be strong enough to resist."[19]

Speaking for the Chiefs of Staff to the CID in early December, Chatfield expressed dismay over Eden's statement about a challenge from Germany as early as next spring. Britain could not be prepared for war until 1939 at the earliest, and the COS emphasized the objective of staying out of war. Thus, the Chiefs of Staff supported Belgian neutrality and a five-power agreement on terms acceptable to Germany and Italy as means to this end. For the same reasons, Hankey "never despaired of coming to terms with Germany one day." The more he examined the possibility of a war with Germany, "the more silly a business" it seemed to him. Although the Germans "could knock us about most frightfully" in the first few months, Hankey thought Britain would "wear them down" as the war went on, and both countries would be "so exhausted by the end that we should probably become a prey to Bolshevism—the very thing Hitler most fears."[20]

Ironically, the expansion of the Joint Planning Committee (JPC), which Hankey had advocated early in 1936, led to a major clash between him and the joint planners. In its provisional report (26 October)

---

[19] War Office/IIC memorandum, July 1936, circulated to the CID on 24 July, CAB 4/24 (this and Air Ministry/IIC reports on German air strength also in CAB 48/4); Newton (Berlin) to Eden, 25 August and 23 September, *DBFP*, 17, nos. 132, 231; central department memorandum on German air strength, 18 November (no. 386), and Wigram minute, 19 November (no. 390), *DBFP*, 17. See also Wark, *Ultimate Enemy*, pp. 55–57, 89–91, 139–41; Smith, *British Air Strategy*, pp. 167–68. According to Hinsley, there was no systematic assessment of Germany's Four Year Plan; *British Intelligence*, p. 33. Wark shows that this plan confirmed the IIC's view that Germany was preparing for total war; the IIC downplayed reports of German shortages in vital raw materials late in 1936 and early in 1937; *Ultimate Enemy*, pp. 175–76, 231.

[20] CID meeting, 10 December, CAB 2/6; COS report, 9 November, CP 302(36), CAB 24/265; Ismay to Inskip, 9 December, CAB 53/6; Hankey to Phipps, 9 October, Phipps Papers, 3/3.

for the contingency of war against Germany in 1939, the JPC underlined the inadequacies of British defense programs, in contrast to Germany's totalitarian preparation of a "war effort" that might enable her to knock out Britain from the air and defeat the West in a quick war.[21] Hankey assured Baldwin, who had been alarmed by an earlier draft of the JPC report, that there was "'no magic in the year 1939'" and "'no cause for panic'" if Britain did not complete its defenses by then. Hankey did not mention Colonel Ismay's warning of September that Hitler would not necessarily wait until 1942 to make war, and that Britain should not count on "too generous a time margin." When the Deputy Chiefs of Staff (DCOS) discussed the JPC paper in December, Hankey, its chairman, labeled those portions dealing with German military and industrial power as "worst case" and "defeatist," and he saw to it that they were either amended or eliminated.[22]

Group Captain Arthur Harris, the Air Staff's senior member on the JPC, reacted angrily to the revised draft in a letter to his deputy chief. The JPC had based its statements "upon the investigations and conclusions reached by the Intelligence Departments of all three Services and supported by Morton's Industrial Intelligence organisation," and Hankey's depiction of Germany's "parlous condition" scarcely corresponded to Germany's truculence toward Russia "or anyone else who has or might have crossed her path during the past 2 years."[23] In fact, the IIC was drawing the JPC and Foreign Office together in assessing the German threat.[24] The JPC's draft report and the Foreign Office's warnings about 1937 carried this common message: the approved programs for rearmament with deadlines extending beyond 1939 would not adequately prepare Britain for the possibility that Germany's political intentions and military capacities might converge for a lightning war against the West by 1939, if not before.

While the JPC implicitly supported the Foreign Office's charge that progress on rearmament was much too slow, its "strategical review" of July substantiated the political conclusion firmly held by the Chiefs of Staff. The "danger of simultaneous tension" with Germany, Italy, and Japan "dictates a policy directed towards an understanding with Ger-

[21] JPC provisional report (JP 155), 26 October, CAB 53/29.

[22] Ismay paper on home defense, September 1936, CAB 64/3; DCOS meetings, 12, 19, 24, 30 November, CAB 54/1; Wark, *Ultimate Enemy*, pp. 195–200 (including Hankey's note to Baldwin of 9 October); Roskill, *Hankey*, 3:236–37; Bialer, *Shadow*, pp. 129–31. Wark views the JPC's report as evidence of "the revolution in outlook" in Army and Air intelligence, and characteristic of the "pessimistic" phase in British intelligence about Germany that began in the autumn of 1936.

[23] Harris to Courtney, 25 November, AIR 2/1406.

[24] Ashton-Gwatkin noted that the IIC had been useful to the Foreign Office, and "we should welcome its being strengthened"; 28 July, W6990/160/50, FO 371/20456.

many and a consequent postponement of the danger of German aggression against any vital interest of ours."[25] The Service staffs and Hankey believed that Eden and the Foreign Office threatened to preclude appeasement and bring danger nearer by bad diplomacy—that is, by rebuffing German overtures, by stalling in five-power negotiations, by tying Britain to France and Central and Eastern Europe, and by using rearmament as a diplomatic weapon before its political beastliness could be matched by its military effectiveness. To Eden, Vansittart, Wigram, and Sargent, appeasement required something in return from Germany, Britain's vital interests were connected to the security of France and Central Europe, and military strength—or at least "running into strength"—was an instrument for deterrence even before Britain was ready for war. The antithesis between these two correlations of diplomacy, time, and military power had grown sharper by December 1936, not merely because of the German question but also as a result of developments in the Mediterranean.

In a speech to the 1900 Club on 10 June, Chamberlain declared that it would be mad to continue the policy of sanctions which had failed to save Ethiopia from Italian aggression. Collective security needed to be replaced by League-sponsored regional agreements that actually reflected the vital interests of the signatories. Chamberlain's speech hastened the Cabinet toward a decision that Eden himself now supported, although he had hoped the Cabinet would wait until Mussolini gave reassurances to the League. On 17 June, the Cabinet agreed to raise sanctions against Italy, and instructed Eden "to take the initiative" in Geneva. The Government survived a storm of protest in the House of Commons, the League followed Britain, and in early July the League Assembly voted to end sanctions.[26] The sigh of relief along Whitehall was muffled by continued debate over policy in the Mediterranean and silenced by the Spanish Civil War.

In the Cabinet on 17 June, Eden underscored the need to maintain Britain's "prestige and power" in the Mediterranean after sanctions ended and to "deter" further Italian expansion. Chatfield and the Chiefs of Staff resisted any increase in Britain's Mediterranean commitments and reiterated their year-old advice: friendly relations with Italy must be restored so that Britain could withdraw forces from the Mediterranean and "return to a state of normal distribution which will permit us to be more ready to defend our interests at Home or in the Far

[25] JPC "Strategical Review," 3 July (approved by the COS on 13 July), CAB 53/28.
[26] Eden memoranda, 11 June, CP 159 and 165(36), CAB 24/262 (also in *DBFP*, 16, nos. 360, 361); Cabs 41 and 42(36), 10 and 17 June, CAB 23/84; Avon, *Dictators*, pp. 436–37; Baer, *Test Case*, pp. 294–95; Fuchser, *Neville Chamberlain and Appeasement*, pp. 56–58; Middlemas and Barnes, *Baldwin*, pp. 939–40; Parker, "Ethiopian Crisis," pp. 330–31.

East."[27] The JPC, however, expressed more interest than the COS in improving Britain's strategic position in the eastern Mediterranean—notably, by constructing a military, naval, and air base on Cyprus if an Anglo-Italian rapprochement did not materialize. At the Foreign Office, Sargent and Cadogan emphasized reconciliation with Italy, whereas O'Malley, Thompson, and Eden thought Britain would need a base on Cyprus "whatever the future orientation of our policy, or that of others, in the Eastern Mediterranean" (Eden).[28]

Differences between the Foreign Office and Services concerning Egypt diminished as the Chiefs of Staff and Inskip accepted compromises rather than risk the greater damage to imperial security that a collapse of negotiations would bring. (In the same spirit, the British Government signed the Montreux Convention of 20 July, which permitted Turkey to fortify the Black Sea Straits.) By the terms of the Anglo-Egyptian Treaty of Alliance, signed on 26 August, Britain would withdraw its garrison from Cairo but could station land and air forces in the Canal Zone for the next twenty years, keep forces at Alexandria for up to eight years, and, in emergencies, count on Egyptian assistance.[29] A member of the eastern department viewed solving the Palestine question as "almost as important a pre-condition of consolidating our position in the Eastern Mediterranean as the success of treaty negotiations with Egypt." The outbreak of an Arab revolt in Palestine in April, and Italy's proven ability to exploit Anglo-Arabian differences, underlined "the necessity of keeping on the right side of the Arabs" in the Middle East and securing British communications through the "corridor" Palestine-Transjordan-Iraq.[30] Weakening Britain's future military position in Egypt drew all the more attention to the value of a base at Cyprus.

[27] Cab 42(36), 17 June, CAB 23/84; COS memorandum, 18 June, CP 174(36), CAB 24/263; COS meetings, 16 and 25 June, CAB 53/6; War Office note, 16 June, WO 106/282; Chatfield to Hankey, 24 June, CAB 21/436. On differences between the Foreign Office and COS, see also Gibbs, *Rearmament*, pp. 384–85, and Pratt, *East of Malta*, pp. 35–39.

[28] JPC report, 21 July, and COS memorandum, 29 July, CP 211(36), CAB 24/263; Foreign Office minutes on CP 211, 5–18 August, R4650/294/67, FO 371/20383.

[29] Eden memoranda, 8 and 19 June, CP 156, 160, 177(36), CAB 24/262; COS meetings, 8 and 25 June, 6 July, CAB 53/6; meetings of Cabinet Committee on Anglo-Egyptian Conversations, June–July, CAB 27/607; Cabs 41 and 43(36), 10 and 23 June, CAB 23/84; Avon, *Dictators*, pp. 442–43; DBFP, 16, nos. 354 (CP 156), 483, appx. V.

[30] Minute of 8 August, R4650/294/67, FO 371/20383. On War Office and Colonial Office fears of a "serious Moslem outbreak" and Arab-Jewish conflict in the Middle East: Cab 36(36), 13 May, CAB 23/84; meeting of Directors in War Office, 11 June, WO 106/281; Ormsby-Gore memoranda to Cabinet, 4 July and 26 August, CP 190 and 225(36), CAB 24/263; Cab 51(36), 9 July, CAB 23/85. For interdepartmental squabbling over the Palestine question, see Michael J. Cohen, "Direction of Policy in Palestine, 1936–45," *Middle Eastern Studies* 11 (1975).

The dual policy of coercing and conciliating Italy survived the end of sanctions and continued to divide Whitehall because of Anglo-Italian rivalry in the eastern Mediterranean. It more than regained its former grip on the Government because Spain was "blowing up," as Sir Warren Fisher observed in August, "and, if we don't look out, may blow up Europe too."[31]

By the end of August, the Service staffs, Foreign Office, and Cabinet agreed on certain principles regarding the Spanish Civil War and its strategic repercussions. Britain would adhere to a policy of nonintervention and should maintain friendly relations with whatever government Spain might have in the future. The naval base at Gibraltar (soon to become an air base as well) must be protected for imperial communications, no matter whether Britain elected to hold the Mediterranean or use the "Cape" route in a future war. The territorial integrity of Spanish Morocco was of "vital importance" because of its close proximity to Gibraltar. Italian occupation of the Balearic or Canary Islands would affect British strategic interests, although "not vitally." Britain should work closely with France to prevent other powers—especially Italy and the Soviet Union—from intervening and causing the war to escalate. Fortunately for British policy, Leon Blum and his Foreign Minister, Yvon Delbos, pursued nonintervention against the wishes of most of the French left, and French strategic interests coincided with British (as they had not done during the Ethiopian crisis), for French plans for a European war assumed a peaceful frontier with Spain and open routes of passage across the Mediterranean for troops stationed in North Africa. London informed Rome that "any alterations of the status quo in the Western Mediterranean must be a matter of the closest concern" to the British Government.[32]

The question of belligerent rights soon divided the Cabinet, however. Hoare (and the Naval Staff) wanted the Government to confer

---

[31] Fisher note, 19 August, T 160/683.

[32] Foreign Office (O'Malley) memorandum, 19 August, *DBFP*, 17, no. 115; COS report, 24 August (amending JPC report of 20 August in CAB 55/8), CP 234(36), CAB 24/264 (also in *DBFP*, 17, no. 126); Chatfield to Hoare, 4 August, *DBFP*, 17, no. 56; Foreign Office minutes, 28–31 August, W9708/62/41, FO 371/20535, and W10452/9549/41, FO 371/20574; FPC meeting, 25 August, CAB 27/622; Cab 56(36), 2 September, CAB 23/85; Eden to Ingram (Rome), 3 September, and Ingram to Eden, 12 September, *DBFP*, 17, nos. 159 and 188; Avon, *Dictators*, pp. 451–52. For secondary accounts: Jill Edwards, *The British Government and the Spanish Civil War, 1936–1939* (London, 1979); Willard C. Frank, Jr., "The Spanish Civil War and the Coming of the Second World War," *International History Review* 9 (1987); John F. Coverdale, *Italian Intervention in the Spanish Civil War* (Princeton, 1975); Adamthwaite, *France and the Coming of War*, pp. 42–46; Geoffrey Warner, "France and Non-Intervention in Spain, July–August 1936," *International Affairs* 38 (1962); Young, *In Command of France*, chaps. 6, 7.

belligerent rights on both sides in Spain, partly out of sympathy for General Francisco Franco, but largely because this would release the Admiralty from having to protect ships under British registry that might be carrying war materials. The Cabinet backed Eden's recommendation to make belligerent rights and recognition of Franco hinge on Franco's capture of Madrid.[33]

Belligerent rights formed a new part of the ongoing dispute in London over military power in the Mediterranean. This debate grew more explicit and ominous regarding the possibility of an ideological alliance that would threaten Britain on three fronts. The German-Austrian agreement of 11 July (reestablishing friendly relations and recognizing Austrian sovereignty as a "German state") had improved relations between Germany and Italy. The Joint Planning Committee feared that the Spanish Civil War might lead to a European conflict between "the forces of Fascism on one side and the forces of Bolshevism on the other—with Great Britain in the latter camp."[34] Military Intelligence viewed the communist ideal of world revolution as the greatest threat to the British Empire. Hankey wondered whether "before long it would pay us to throw in our lot with Germany and Italy," since bolshevism already threatened France and Spain.[35] Alluding to German-Japanese conversations that led to the signing of the Anti-Comintern Pact on 25 November, the Admiralty thought Italy might join, making this an "anti-Russian bloc" which Britain must not antagonize by becoming "involved in hostilities on the side of Russia."[36]

The prospect of a world dividing along ideological lines reinforced the counsel of Hankey and the Chiefs of Staff for appeasement without belligerence or temporization. British foreign policy, Hankey had urged early in June, must "avert any possibility that the three menaces, or any two of them, shall mature simultaneously," and must buy time for completing rearmament. These aims required reducing existing entanglements and incurring no new commitments, allowing Germany to realize any ambitions it might have in Eastern and Central Europe,

---

[33] Cabs 57 (14 October), 58 (21 October), 60 (28 October), 62 (4 November), 64 (11 November), 66 (18 November), 67 (25 November), 69 (2 December), CAB 23/85–86; meeting of ministers and Chatfield, 22 November, with appendixes, CP 312(36), CAB 24/265. On the Admiralty and Foreign Office: Avon, *Dictators*, pp. 464–65; Chatfield, *Navy and Defence*, p. 92; Edwards, *British Government and Spanish Civil War*, chaps. 3, 4; Pratt, *East of Malta*, pp. 40–48; Roskill, *Naval Policy*, pp. 374–76.

[34] JPC report, 20 August (see note 32 above).

[35] MI3 appreciation, 20 August, WO 190/452; Hankey memorandum, 20 July, CAB 63/51. The General Staff considered a German-Italian alliance possible; they might then "seek alliance with Japan so as to embarrass Russia and England": MI3(?) note, 8 June, WO 190/436; Deverell minute, 16 June, CAB 64/14.

[36] Phillips (Admiralty) to Foreign Office, 21 November, R6974/226/22, FO 371/20412.

and reestablishing "cordial relations with Italy."[37] The Chiefs of Staff cited the Ethiopian crisis as evidence that, if Mussolini wanted to exploit the Spanish Civil War, he would "not be deterred by threats [but] only by the certainty that force, and adequate force, will be employed against him." Britain "should take no action which we are not prepared to back up by all the force at our command," or else the action would fail and "further . . . alienate Italy." Effective action would probably cause war with Italy, which is "the only power whose forces are fully mobilised and available for immediate operations." Rapprochement with Italy was a strategic necessity.[38]

The Foreign Office was neither blind to these ideological and strategic concerns nor united in its attitudes toward Italy and the Mediterranean. In August, G. H. Thompson foresaw a weakening of Britain's Mediterranean position no matter which side won in Spain: "Do not let us be too confident about holding both ends of the Mediterranean in comfort." Cadogan wanted to "do nothing to offend Italy" so long as there was any chance of securing a five-power agreement. This chance, Sargent warned, would virtually disappear if Europe divided into two ideological blocs. In order to prevent this division, perhaps Britain should keep France from "going Bolshevik" (which both Italy and Germany feared) and free Italy "from the feeling of isolation and vulnerability which the Abyssinian affair has left her with." Although meant to help convince Mussolini that Britain would oppose changes in the status quo in the western Mediterranean, the statement proposed by the Foreign Office, supported by the COS, and approved by the Cabinet was couched in a "vague formula" and would be delivered privately so as to give Italy "no legitimate cause of complaint or offence."[39] In September and October, London assured Rome that Britain wanted to restore friendly relations, and that neither its rearmament nor its strong naval position in the Mediterranean was directed at any particular power.[40]

On 25 October, Germany recognized the Italian annexation of Ethiopia. Reports of Italian collusion with Germany were more dramatically substantiated on 1 November when Mussolini announced the formation of the Rome-Berlin Axis, invited peace-loving nations to co-

[37] Hankey memorandum, "Foreign Policy and Imperial Defence," 8 June, circulated to Baldwin, Eden, and Inskip, CAB 63/51.

[38] COS report, 24 August (see note 32 above); JPC report, 16 October, CAB 53/29, revised by the COS on 20 October, CAB 53/6.

[39] Thompson and Cadogan minutes, 10 and 14 August, R4650/294/67, FO 371/20383; Sargent minute, 12 August, *DBFP*, 17, no. 84; Foreign Office memorandum, 19 August, ibid., no. 115.

[40] Hoare to the press, 22 September (no. 226n); Drummond to Foreign Office, 7 October (no. 271); Eden to Drummond, 13 October (no. 291): *DBFP*, 17.

operate around it, and called for Anglo-Italian reconciliation. A few days later, Vansittart, the Chiefs of Staff, Inskip, and Hankey discussed Eden's request for a comparison of European military forces as of May 1937. It was agreed that, for this study, the COS should assume Germany and Italy against Britain, France, and Belgium, with Russia either neutral or cooperating with the West.[41]

Could an Anglo-Italian understanding prevent the Axis from maturing into a military alliance, reduce the possibility of a sudden Italian attack against British interests, and give Britain security in the Mediterranean in case of war with Germany or Japan? Those were paramount and realistic objectives according to the Services and Hankey, and, although more skeptical than the military experts, Vansittart and others in the Foreign Office still hoped that Italy might be disengaged from Germany. But Eden would not trust Italy to keep a Mediterranean agreement; the Chiefs of Staff were naive to state that Britain would not need a base at Cyprus "if we improve relations with Italy," for Mussolini would agree only to what suited him at the moment. Similarly, Lawrence Collier thought the Admiralty—and Drummond in Rome—were deluded "to suppose that any agreement with Signor Mussolini will prevent him from aggression against us, if he thinks it will pay, or detach him from his natural alliance with other aggressors."[42]

In the regular Cabinet meeting on 4 November, Inskip reminded Eden that the COS stressed the importance of an understanding with Italy. Unlike Germany, which always demanded more when Britain offered any concession, Italy probably did desire "good relations" with Britain. Hoare and Duff Cooper strongly supported Inskip. At a special Cabinet meeting late that afternoon, Hoare thought "it would be necessary to assume for a long time that we should be unprepared," and that the first priority of foreign policy should be "to get Italy out of the list of countries with whom we had to reckon." Eden warned that Hoare's attitude "might be mistaken for flabbiness." He agreed that relations should be improved, but this would be difficult because of "Italian psychology. In suspecting us of designs in the Mediterranean, they were treating us as though we were Italians and thinking of what they would do in our place." The Cabinet and Eden agreed that, in his speech to the House of Commons on the next day, he would both affirm Britain's vital interest in free communication through the Mediterranean and refer to Italy in friendly terms. Tilting toward the conciliatory side of this dual message, however, the Cabinet concluded

[41] Inskip minute, 6 November, and meeting of 9 November, CAB 53/29.
[42] Eden minute (critical of a memorandum by Sargent), 5 November, *DBFP*, 17, no. 352; Collier note of 4 December on Admiralty paper (see note 36 above).

that Eden "should in the light of the discussion adopt a policy of improving relations with Italy."[43]

A week later, Eden told the Cabinet he "had not realized . . . that a decision of policy was being taken" at the special meeting on 4 November. Reconciliation with Italy would probably never reach "such a point as to justify a lessening of our armaments in the Mediterranean," and Italy would surely continue its anti-British propaganda in the Middle East. Eden did not ask the Cabinet to reverse its decision, however, and on the eighteenth he informed the Cabinet that Anglo-Italian conversations were proceeding smoothly toward a "Gentleman's Agreement" to observe the status quo in the Mediterranean. Mussolini preferred this to a formal pact, and both governments fancied a bilateral agreement over the French proposal for a multilateral one.[44]

Yet Eden also wanted to "show a tooth." Italy and Germany recognized Franco's insurgent government on 18 November. Although Hitler decided not to commit large forces to a conflict he regarded as a useful diversion of European attention away from Germany, Italy increased its aid to Franco and its military activity in the western Mediterranean, where Mussolini charged that the Soviet Union posed the real threat to the status quo by supporting the Spanish Republic. The Italian military buildup on Majorca was so dangerous that Eden asked the Cabinet to consider "how grave would be the risk to our position in the Mediterranean if Italy were permitted with impunity to make another move such as the establishment of Italian control in the Balearic Islands." It was a "vital interest" for Britain not "to abdicate the responsibilities of a Great Power." The Government must decide whether "to resist or to acquiesce." A decision that Britain had a "vital political interest" in preventing Italian domination of these islands would require a "demonstration of adequate military strength" and an unambiguous warning of what would cause Britain to use that force. Germany might exploit a Mediterranean war (and even attack first toward the west), but "the probability of a considerable accession of strength to Germany resulting from war in which Great Britain and France were engaged against Italy is not unequally balanced" by the likelihood that future relations with Germany could be "conducted with very much greater advantage to ourselves if we had demonstrated beyond all possibility of doubt that in the Mediterranean there is a point beyond which the United Kingdom cannot be driven . . . , and that where a vital interest is threatened, the English will be found, for all we speak so often and so smoothly of compromise and conciliation, not to be at

---

[43] Cabs 62 and 63(36), 4 November, CAB 23/86.
[44] Cabs 64 and 66(36), 11 and 18 November, CAB 23/86.

heart a meek nor in action a timid people at all." Negotiations for the Gentleman's Agreement should continue, meanwhile, as a "useful test" of Italy's good faith.[45]

The Cabinet—and Eden himself—decided not to take any action before the Chiefs of Staff reported their views on the strategic significance of an Italian occupation of Majorca or Italian use of facilities there or in the Balearic Islands generally.[46] The Cabinet sidestepped this fundamental question: was it about time to reduce expectations for reconciliation and adopt an explicit policy of deterrence? In Eden's view, such a policy would have included a substantial show of force in the Mediterranean above normal levels, strong French support, trip wires east of Gibraltar and Spanish Morocco, and willingness to consider appeasing Italy so long as those interests were respected.

No evidence suggests that the Cabinet might soon have decided to use force in Europe or the Mediterranean unless Germany attacked Britain, the Low Countries, or France, or unless Italy assaulted British possessions or seized Spanish Morocco. Avoiding war and buying time for rearmament were general aims of foreign policy on which ministers, military advisers, and most officials in the Foreign Office concurred. Yet disagreement over how to achieve these objectives and how much time remained to do so had grown stronger since the previous spring, when the Cabinet established the Foreign Policy Committee to reassess policy and postponed the question of accelerating the shadow scheme until decisions had been reached on "major policy."

In June, Hankey supposed that if Britain could "keep the peace we hold the balance of power—in our present weakness a precarious balance, but as we grow stronger it may become decisive." Inskip asked the DPR whether the date for completing the defense programs should be moved up to less than three to five years. Vansittart warned that European peace might not last as long as three years, and agreed with Hoare that the Government should advertise rearmament so as to have "a steadying effect in Europe." Weir wondered whether "everything possible was being done to prevent the steady growth of inevitability of war," and contended that the economic consequences of taking full powers to accelerate production would probably "make war certain." Chamberlain emphasized the grave industrial and financial effects of such action, asked whether installing emergency powers now would

[45] Eden memorandum (drafted by O'Malley and substantially revised by Vansittart), 14 December, CP 335(36), CAB 24/265 (also in *DBFP*, 17, no. 471); Avon, *Dictators*, pp. 465, 470; Edwards, *British Government and Spanish Civil War*, pp. 138–42 (who incorrectly credits Eden with drafting this paper and thus implicitly distances Vansittart from its strong case for deterrence). For Italian designs on Majorca, see Coverdale, *Italian Intervention*, chap. 5.

[46] Cab 75(36), 16 December, CAB 23/86.

prepare Britain for a German "forward move" by 1937, and thought "Germany's next forward step might not necessarily lead us into war." The committee decided to continue working on the authorized policy of "a maximum achievement within the next three years," but to keep the matter under review.[47]

After the Cabinet decided to lift sanctions against Italy, Chatfield thought there was need for "a long view in foreign policy," rather than taking decisions "only in the light of immediate expediency." He would seek a settlement with Japan and make no military commitments beyond maintaining British security in the Mediterranean and the territorial status quo in Western Europe. In the Cabinet, ministers urged the Government to "make up its mind" on major questions of policy, and several recommended that British policy exclude the possibility of defending Eastern Europe. In the CID Secretariat, Pownall blamed the gloomy European situation on "the Vansittart policy." Chamberlain was very concerned that "we have no policy." As the Government began negotiations for a five-power conference on European security, Wigram challenged three assumptions made by the JPC and COS in their strategic review: that "democracies will not fight except in the event of a direct threat to their own security"; that Germany "will inevitably absorb a large part of Central and Southeastern Europe into her orbit"; and that Britain had "no immediate strategic interests" in intervening in a war in or around Austria. Wigram thought it impossible to "foretell in advance the exact circumstances in which even democracies will fight, and no one can say what is inevitable and what is not"; intervention in Central Europe might become a "political necessity."[48]

The Services, Foreign Office, and Cabinet agreed that the League of Nations should be reformed so as to preserve its machinery for conciliation while limiting the obligations of member states to use economic sanctions or military force unless their vital national interests were threatened or their commitments to regional pacts required such action.[49] As collective security continued its decline, Cadogan, sounding very much like Chatfield, complained that British policy had not been

---

[47] Hankey memorandum (see note 37 above); DPR meeting, 11 June, CAB 16/136.

[48] COS meeting, 25 June, CAB 53/6; Cab 50(36), 6 July, CAB 23/85; Pownall diary, 6 July, in Bond, *Chief of Staff*, p. 115; Chamberlain diary, 11 July, Chamberlain Papers, NC 2/23a; Wigram minute on JPC's strategic review (see note 25 above), 24 July, C5356/4/18, FO 371/19910. For Chatfield's views, see also Pratt, *East of Malta*, pp. 38–39.

[49] Hankey memorandum, 20 July, CAB 63/51; memoranda by Hoare, Admiralty, and Inskip, 10, 17, 20 August, CP 213, 214, 223(36), CAB 24/263; Chamberlain and Swinton memoranda, 11 August, W11340/79/98, FO 371/20475; FPC meeting, 25 August, CAB 27/622; Eden draft speech for British delegate at forthcoming meeting of the League Assembly, 28 August, CP 228(36), CAB 24/264; Cab 56(36), 2 September, CAB 23/85.

successful so far. "In fact we haven't *got* a policy; we merely wait and see what will happen to us next." This charge certainly seemed to apply to the Far East as well, where British policy toward Japan remained ambivalent, cautious, and unchanged either by the September report of Sir Frederick Leith-Ross (Chief Economic Adviser to the Government) or by the German-Japanese Anti-Comintern Pact of November.[50]

Eden exhorted the Cabinet to improve the nation's defenses so that it could "speak with the fullest authority" in any crisis. Hankey protested that, although the Chiefs of Staff had been "directed to sharpen their swords," they had received no guidance about the circumstances in which Britain might enter a war. Inskip found it difficult "to know what our policy was and what kind of possibility our defensive preparations were intended to meet. Collective security had disappeared and nothing had been substituted for it." Vansittart criticized the Chiefs of Staff for not having "agitated in the past a lot more" to rectify Britain's weakness; had they not left this agitation largely to the Foreign Office, they would have been less inclined now to dub him "an alarmist."[51]

As 1936 drew to a close, Chatfield wrote to the First Lord that, if there was a risk of war before 1939, instructions to the Services "ought to be changed and the whole manner in which we are carrying out our rearmament ought to be immediately stiffened up." The Services still needed answers to this question: "Is our military unreadiness going to dominate our foreign policy, as we feel it should, or is our foreign policy going to carry us into war when we are not ready for it?"[52]

As usual, Chatfield's statement of alternatives was clear, simple, and unambiguous, the first of them implicitly isolationist and the second interventionist. He, the other Service chiefs, and Hankey had concluded that, if war came sooner than in three to five years, the fault would probably lie more with the British Foreign Office than with the dictators. The prerequisite for holding the balance of power was keeping the peace. Peace required appeasing Hitler and Mussolini without any of the following: deferring or rebuffing their offers of conciliation; showing political firmness or military force before Britain had what the Services considered sufficient strength to back it up; disrupting long-

[50] Cadogan diary, 25 September, Cadogan Papers, 1/5. On the Leith-Ross report and British policy toward China and Japan, see Louis, *British Strategy in the Far East*, pp. 231–33; Trotter, *Britain and East Asia*, pp. 185–98.

[51] Eden at Cab 57(36), 14 October, CAB 23/85; Hankey at COS meeting, 20 October, CAB 53/6; Inskip at Cab 62(36), 4 November, CAB 23/86; Vansittart minute, 17 November, Vansittart Papers, 2/29.

[52] Chatfield to Hoare, 11 December, Chatfield Papers. On the isolationist implications of the COS advice, see Schmidt, *England in der Krise*, pp. 474–78.

term planning and risking the escalation of international conflict by making commitments to other nations and intervening when Britain's vital interests were not directly threatened; stretching the definition of those interests to include Central and Eastern Europe or Mediterranean territories (except Spanish Morocco) that were not part of the British Empire. By limiting Britain's obligations and postponing threats of force until Britain was militarily prepared for war, the military experts would narrowly circumscribe the meaning of deterrence and restrict the Government's options in foreign policy.

Eden and Vansittart offered a different diagnosis of instability and prescription for treating it. War would be caused by irreconcilable dictators, not by a Foreign Office whose policy recommendations were unfortunately hampered but not necessarily dictated by military weakness. The prerequisite for keeping the peace was holding the balance of power. Holding the balance demanded willingness to accompany appeasement with the same list of corollaries that Hankey and the Chiefs of Staff would have excluded. By keeping open the possibilities of increasing Britain's obligations and threatening force before prepared for war, the Foreign Office would provide the Government with a flexible set of options. Reassuring likely allies; exacting something from Hitler in return for giving him something else; competing with Mussolini for head of the Mediterranean: if friendly nations and the British public saw these as "good deeds in a naughty world," Britain might still be able to combine moral suasion, political brokerage, and military strength to limit the dictators' gains and prevent a European war.

Neither the Cabinet nor any of its committees had reconciled these two designs of policy or chosen to follow one of them, and Britain's "major policy" had not changed much since April. Still, the more that conflicts between these two analyses surfaced, the more the Cabinet, CID, Foreign Policy Committee, and DPR showed a ministerial bent toward that of the military experts. The impetus for change accelerated early in 1937 as foreign policy encountered the unprecedented coincidence of strategic plans, quarrels over the Army's mission, and Chamberlain's warm-up for the premiership.

THE ASCENT OF STRATEGY AND FINANCE,
DECEMBER 1936–MAY 1937

When Chatfield posed his question about military readiness, he gave a traditional, Clausewitzean definition of the relationship between strategy and foreign policy: "Strategy should, of course, wait on policy; that is to say, your policy should be decided on for general international and political reasons, and you should be prepared to back up your policy strategically by force if necessary. Alternatively, policy must depend on strategy, or rather, upon military strength, because it is no good deciding on a policy which you cannot defend if it is challenged." Like Chatfield, the Chiefs of Staff had frequently invoked this theorem, occasionally adding that some questions were "politico-strategical," in which it was "impossible to draw any hard and fast rule as to where policy ends and strategy begins." (No such ambiguity appeared in a 1936 publication of the Command and General Staff School in the United States, which emphasized that "politics and strategy are radically and fundamentally things apart. Strategy begins where politics ends.")[53] In disputes between the COS and Foreign Office, both sides exploited the vague line between foreign policy and strategy—the COS by stressing military liabilities and preparedness, the Foreign Office by treating defense as subordinate to external policy.

From December 1936 onward, the line between policy and strategy grew even more difficult to draw, to the disadvantage of the Foreign Office and extended deterrence, when war plans and the debate over the Army's role in a continental war surfaced at the highest levels of policymaking. The word "policy" was variously used: sometimes inclusive of foreign policy, strategy, war plans, supply, and finance; sometimes restricted to one or more of these issues. A hybrid term even during peace, "policy" acquired increasing overtones of war and a new ministerial committee responsible for discussing its connotations—the Defence Plans (Policy) Committee. By the time of Baldwin's resignation, the bargaining power of the COS against the Foreign Office had increased, strategy matched the "international and political reasons" of the Foreign Office as bases for deterrence, and finance was the supreme constituent of national policy.

Correspondence among Vansittart, Hankey, and Chatfield reiterated the argument in Whitehall over how to reduce the risks of war on as many as three fronts. In a long paper of December titled "The World Situation and British Rearmament," Vansittart warned that Germany intended to build "an international anti-Bolshevik front" with Japan and Italy and use it as a means for expansion. The German drive for hegemony in Central and Southeastern Europe could be turned at any time against Britain. Ultimately, Britain would have to rely on force, *"the only argument in which Germany believes,"* for Hitler could not be trusted to honor any treaty. Meanwhile, Britain must try to separate

---

[53] Chatfield to Hoare (see preceding note); Ismay to Inskip on the COS view of Belgium and five-power negotiations, 9 December, CAB 53/6; CID meeting, 10 December, CAB 2/6; the American publication quoted in Samuel P. Huntington, *The Soldier and the State: The Theory and Politics of Civil-Military Relations* (Cambridge, Mass., 1957), p. 308.

Italy and Germany; be ready to make concessions so long as these did not strengthen Germany dangerously (such as expansion to the south and east) and Germany offered something reliable in return; avoid any harsh action that would rally German moderates to the side of the Nazi leadership; neither pander to France nor underrate her strength; and hope to find a way around America's neutrality laws (perhaps possible with "Franklin Roosevelt the Second"), which made Britain all the more dependent on its own sources of supply.

Britain, Vansittart continued, had to prepare "for a date that is not ours," and it was the task of the Foreign Office to provide the "material commodity" of time at least until 1939. Doing so would depend less on Britain's ability to defend itself than on *a really impressive display of strength on our part*," much more than the rearmament already under way. It might be "cheaper to face [the attendant difficulties] now;" bridging the "time-lag of at least one year in our preparations compared with those of Germany" could be done "without over-great damage to our export trade." Without an acceleration of rearmament the Foreign Office would probably not "be able—it certainly *cannot undertake*—to manufacture the quota of time assigned to it."[54]

Vansittart's former colleagues on the Defence Requirements Committee still disagreed with him over how to avoid war. Hankey had little faith in France as an ally, and he gave Germany's internal problems more weight than did Vansittart as "deterrents to war." A more conciliatory policy was necessary until Britain was so strong that Hitler would "hesitate to attack." While Hankey urged that rearmament be expanded, he would avoid serious damage to trade, which provided the wealth that was Britain's long-run advantage over the dictators. Chatfield concurred with Hankey's criticisms of Vansittart's paper, which offered only a continuation of the drift and "ad hoc decisions" that would force Britain's hand "not by our interests but from some general undertaking that we have made or may make . . . of a collective nature in Europe." Let Germany expand southeastward, for this would in fact weaken her world position. Britain must reach an understanding with Japan as soon as possible, for only then would Britain be strong enough "to sit on the fence in Europe." Vansittart replied that, although Britain should not reveal to France its "limited liabilities or

---

[54] Vansittart comments here and preceding are from Vansittart draft memorandum, 16 December, W18355/18355/50, FO 371/20467, printed on 31 December, *DBFP*, 17, appx. II. On Vansittart's optimistic attitude toward "Roosevelt the Second" and the possibility of exchanging defense information with the United States, see Richard A. Harrison, "A Presidential *Démarche*: Franklin D. Roosevelt's Personal Diplomacy and Great Britain, 1936–37," *Diplomatic History* 5 (1981), and also "Testing the Water," pp. 224–27. On 27 October, Swinton told the Cabinet that the DPR had authorized him to find out whether the Air Ministry might purchase aircraft from the United States; Cab 59(36), CAB 23/85.

intentions" in Central and Eastern Europe, it should "keep Germany guessing" about those areas. Unwilling to jeopardize the possibility of improving relations with the United States, Vansittart doubted that an agreement with Japan was feasible. Even if Britain could "neutralise Japan at least till we are safer in Europe," a European war would, as Chatfield himself pointed out, inevitably lead to war in the Far East.[55]

Ostensibly, British policy toward Germany did not undergo major revision. Negotiations for a western pact continued to falter, chiefly because of German (and Italian) objections to a French and German guarantee of Britain, and to a strengthening of collective action. On 24 March, the Cabinet approved Eden's recommendations. Britain (and France) would accede to the Belgian request to be released from the agreement of March 1936 that the Locarno Treaty would remain provisionally in effect. The British and French Governments would maintain that agreement, implying that "the provisional period was still running and that the 'effort of conciliation' had not failed." The Anglo-French declaration of 24 April released Belgium from its guarantee of France under the Locarno Pact, and noted Belgium's intention to defend itself against aggression. The faint possibility of a five-power pact remained alive, more so for Eden than for Vansittart, who thought that this "pretence" would soon have to be abandoned because "the Germans do not mean to have any settlement in Europe." Also alive was the equally small chance of starting trilateral staff talks to "outbid Hitler," who on 30 January had offered to guarantee Belgian neutrality.[56]

The idea of particular concessions to Germany made little progress, in spite of conversations between Leith-Ross and Schacht. The Foreign Office rejected Leith-Ross's recommendation—supported by its own economic section—to offer Germany economic aid or colonial restitution without requiring specific political guarantees from Germany. The Foreign Policy Committee agreed with Eden that concessions (whether in Europe or Africa) could be proposed only if Germany pledged something concrete in return through a general and political settlement. On the prospect of such a settlement, the credibility of German pledges, and Britain's willingness to offer concessions, Chamberlain, Hoare, and Inskip were more optimistic than Eden, still more than Vansittart

---

[55] Hankey memorandum, 21 December, CAB 63/51; Chatfield to Vansittart, 29 December, and Vansittart to Chatfield, 1 January 1937, FO 800/394–95; Chatfield notes, 5 January, sent to Hankey, Deverell, and Ellington, Chatfield Papers; Roskill, *Hankey*, 3:237–38, and *Naval Policy*, pp. 323–24.

[56] Cabs 13 and 19(37), 24 March and 28 April, CAB 23/88; FPC meetings, 10 March, 6 April, and 19 May, CAB 27/622; Vansittart (2 April) and other minutes on staff talks, February and April, C1142/C1634/C2937/271/18, FO 371/20738; *DBFP*, 18, nos. 101, 166, 259, 266, 280, 281, 327, 380, 388, 421, 431; Kieft, *Belgium's Return*, chap. 6; John Harvey, ed., *The Diplomatic Diaries of Oliver Harvey, 1937–1940* (London, 1970), pp. 15–16.

and Sargent. Across the Channel, meanwhile, Delbos was " 'at his wit's end' " about devising a successful policy, and Blum saw no way " 'to take the initiative out of the hands of Germany.' "[57]

The issue of German designs on Central and Eastern Europe remained controversial, a major source of doubt over the policy of cunctation. Eden observed that Italy's distractions in Ethiopia and Spain had "advantages for German policy in Central Europe," but also disadvantages because Germany had to "face the world with only a weakened and untrustworthy Italy as an ally." Germany aimed to dominate Czechoslovakia "as the first step towards German penetration into the Danube Basin," by force if necessary. In his remarks of 19 May to the delegates at the Imperial Conference, Eden did not include this area among Britain's "vital interests" in Europe (which he limited to the prevention of any hostile power from occupying the Low Countries or northern France). He described the Government's policy in these terms: "Without undertaking any military commitment we should make it clear that we were interested in events in Central Europe." In the Foreign Office, Strang, Cadogan, and O'Malley thought Britain should disinterest itself in Central and Eastern Europe more than Vansittart and Sargent thought prudent. O'Malley advised selling some of the "lumber of Versailles" (British interest in Austria and Czechoslovakia) while this "would still fetch a price" (improved relations with Germany). Vansittart objected. Surrendering Eastern Europe to Germany, he wrote, was "quite incompatible with our interests. We fought the last war largely to prevent this." If Britain assisted German designs there (as Lord Lothian recommended after a private visit to Berlin), it would be "going dead against the democratic tide, *and the effect on the USA would be catastrophic.*"[58]

In the Gentleman's Agreement of 2 January 1937, Britain and Italy pledged to uphold the territorial status quo in the Mediterranean area, and "to respect the rights and interests" of all the Mediterranean

---

[57] FPC meetings, 18 March, 6 April, and 10 May, CAB 27/622; Leith-Ross and Sargent correspondence, January, T 188/168; *DBFP*, 18, nos. 86, 92, 118, 129, 148, 163, 210, 296, 307, 315, 379, 483, 485; Crozier, *Appeasement and Germany's Last Bid*, pp. 194–205; Wendt, *Economic Appeasement*, pp. 437–39, 450–52; Middlemas, *Diplomacy of Illusion*, pp. 112–15; Adamthwaite, *France and the Coming of War*, pp. 56–57.

[58] FPC meeting, 10 March, CAB 27/622. Eden to Hadow (Prague), 23 February (no. 200); Eden minute, 24 April (no. 399n); Eden at Imperial Conference, 19 May (no. 510); O'Malley and Sargent minutes, 4, 8 May (no. 479n); Vansittart minutes, late May (no. 480n); also nos. 135, 162, 566: *DBFP*, 18. See also Rhodes James, *Anthony Eden*, p. 170; Dilks, *Cadogan*, pp. 14–15; Kaiser, *Economic Diplomacy*, pp. 188–91. For the Foreign Office's assessment of the impact of American neutrality legislation: *DBFP*, 18, nos. 332, 333. On Anglo-American relations in general: C. A. MacDonald, *The United States, Britain and Appeasement, 1936–1939* (New York, 1981), and William R. Rock, *Chamberlain and Roosevelt: British Foreign Policy and the United States, 1937–1940* (Columbus, Ohio, 1988).

powers. Transit through the Mediterranean was a "vital interest" to both Italy and the British Empire, and these interests were "in no way inconsistent with each other." At the time of its announcement, Eden, Vansittart, and Sargent regarded this agreement as a success for Britain: it was "a sudden turn to Italy's previous policy," although Britain should not suggest publicly that its aim was "to 'detach' Italy from Germany" (Sargent); exploiting this success would "automatically loosen the Italo-German tie," leaving Britain "a more reasonable, or anyhow tamer, Germany to deal with" (Vansittart); a détente from which Italy "has at least as much to gain" as Britain (Eden).[59] Two days later, Eden learned that large numbers of Italian volunteers had landed in Spain, an ungentlemanly violation of the agreement. He warned ministers on 8 January that, because Italian and German intervention had become serious, the Spanish Civil War was turning into an international ideological struggle in which Hitler and Mussolini might "conquer Spain." Unless Hitler were checked now, the voices of restraint in Berlin would be silenced once again, and the Führer would probably raise trouble in Czechoslovakia, Memel, or Danzig. Standing up to the Nazi dictator now would help "avoid a European war." Eden recommended that Britain encourage and participate in an enforcement of nonintervention by a kind of international blockade of Spanish ports, but most of Eden's colleagues strongly opposed such action.[60]

For the next few months, Hoare and the Admiralty resisted any suggestion from the Foreign Office for a greater show of naval force off Spain to deter Italy and Germany, for the result might be war with both dictatorships, a warning with which the other Service ministers, Inskip, and Chamberlain agreed. The Cabinet and the Foreign Policy Committee maintained the policy of 1936: no belligerent rights; no recognition of Franco's government; no threatening military confrontation with Italy, but support of the efforts of the Non-Intervention Committee, which included representatives from Italy and Germany.[61]

At a COS meeting late in January, Chatfield said that the Gentleman's Agreement had changed the Mediterranean situation, and that "it would be a matter of Foreign Office policy . . . as to whether we

[59] Anglo-Italian declaration, 2 January, and exchange of notes, 31 December, *DBFP*, 17, no. 530 (also Cmd. 5348); Sargent, Vansittart, and Eden minutes, 1, 2 January, ibid., no. 527.

[60] Eden memorandum, 8 January, CP 6(37), CAB 24/267, and meeting of ministers, 8 January, CAB 23/87 (also in *DBFP*, 18, nos. 32 and 33); Avon, *Dictators*, pp. 486–87.

[61] Eden memorandum, 1 March, and Naval Staff note, 3 March, CP 80 and 82(37), CAB 24/268; Cab 10(37), 3 March, CAB 23/87. On British responses to Franco's blockade of Bilbao: Cabs 14–19(37), April, CAB 23/88; FPC meetings, 30 April and 10 May, CAB 27/622; Hoare and Chatfield notes, 26 April, CP 122(37), CAB 24/269; Avon, *Dictators*, pp. 498–99.

should ever again be placed in the position of contemplating hostilities against a power with whom it was in our vital interest to keep friend- ly." A few days earlier, the Chiefs of Staff had reported that, although Italy had established "military air stations" in the Balearic Islands, Italian control of the islands would not "vitally affect British strategical interests." British prestige would decline, but this "would not have really serious consequences, unless we had tried, and failed, to thwart the Italian project."[62] The implication of the COS was clear: if Britain tried, responsibility would fall upon the Foreign Office, and success would require more military force than Britain could risk using.

In February, the CID and Cabinet concluded that the Gentleman's Agreement was not firm enough to justify maintaining any longer the Cabinet's decision of 1934 that "no expenditure need be incurred on measures of defence required to provide exclusively against attack by Italy." Future consideration of expenditures on Mediterranean and Red Sea ports should assume that "Italy cannot be counted on as a reliable friend, but in present circumstances need not be regarded as a probable enemy." This change in policy, to an equivocal and fuzzy mean be- tween the reliable friendship and probable enmity of Italy, scarcely corresponded to the situation described by Eden to other ministers in April: British "relations with Italy were far from satisfactory, and there appeared to be a greater danger to peace from some incident created by Italy . . . than from similar action by Germany." Officials in the Foreign Office disagreed over the seriousness of the Italian threat and how to deal with the Axis. Cadogan recommended de jure recognition of the Italian conquest of Ethiopia so as to reduce Britain's anxieties in the Mediterranean and "prevent the cleavage between the Dictator States and the rest of Europe becoming too irreparable." O'Malley doubted that this gesture would have any calming effect; instead, he argued, better Anglo-German relations would make the Italians "more tract- able." Eden concurred with O'Malley; Anglo-German reconciliation, not the Gentleman's Agreement, would divide the Axis. Sargent took a less gloomy view toward Italy, while Vansittart warned against being "bluffed into a *bad* agreement with Germany through fear of Italy."[63]

---

[62] COS meeting, 22 January, CAB 53/6; COS memorandum on the Balearic Islands, 19 January, CP 10(37), CAB 24/267, taken note of by the Cabinet on 20 January, Cab 2(37), CAB 23/87.

[63] CID meeting, 11 February, discussing a memorandum of 5 February by the Joint Oversea and Home Defence Subcommittee, all in CP 65(37), CAB 24/268; CID conclu- sions approved by the Cabinet on 24 February, Cab 9(37), CAB 23/87; Eden at Defence Plans (Policy) Committee meeting, 19 April, CAB 16/181; Cadogan memorandum, 10 May, with minutes by O'Malley, Sargent, and Eden (no. 479), and Vansittart minute, 3 June, on O'Malley's minute of 2 June (no. 566), *DBFP*, 18 (see also nos. 246, 365). On Eden, see Pratt, *East of Malta*, pp. 71–73.

Britain's European and Mediterranean policies contained assumptions about time and deterrence that were more hopeful than demonstrable. Eden viewed time as "our one essential"; Britain grew a little stronger each day, and "in this sense time is on our side." Britain should continue "firmness against aggression but encouragement to good behavior." British rearmament had helped cause "recent German quietude," reassured small nations, and steadied the situation in Europe. British strength in the Mediterranean had impressed Mussolini. Vansittart thought that everybody except Belgium was "playing for time." He and Cadogan advised against mentioning arms limitation in discussions about a general settlement lest Germany suspect that the Government did not intend to complete its rearmament program. Although Germany had not challenged the status quo as Vansittart and Eden had predicted the previous summer and fall, Vansittart did not trust Hitler's assurance that Germany would create no more diplomatic surprises. "The era of surprises is *not* over . . . . Most of the really unpleasant surprises are still in posse." Cadogan warned that Britain may "have reached a point where we should grasp at anything" that might strengthen the moderates in Berlin and deny extremists an excuse to explode. Phipps regarded delays as working in London's favor; British rearmament, along with German doubts about Britain's attitude toward aggression in Eastern Europe, had helped prevent Germany from opening up the issue of eastward expansion. Strang would "make it clear beyond doubt what we will fight for" and, "for the rest, neither say that we will fight nor that we won't." Drummond believed that British rearmament had shocked Italy, showing that "England is less decadent than some ambitious Italians had calculated." In Chamberlain's opinion, rearmament had been welcomed "with a sigh of relief" by many European nations and had "reinforced" the arguments of moderates in both Germany and Italy. Britain must seize any opportunity to reach "a general *détente,* whereas a policy of drift may lead to general war."[64]

In fact, the British Government was guessing at least as much as some of its members hoped the Germans and Italians were. Britain had

[64] Documents in *DBFP*, 18: Eden minutes, 10 and 13 January, 20 and 24 April, 20 May, nos. 8n, 59n, 399n, 404n, 479n; Eden at Imperial Conference, 19 May, no. 510; Vansittart minutes, 16 and 25 February, 19 April, nos. 166n, 167n, 404n; Cadogan minute, 25 February, no. 167n; Phipps to Sargent, 11 January, no. 53, and to Eden, 13 April, no. 399; Strang minute, 1 February, no. 135; Drummond to Eden, 25 March, no. 348; Chamberlain draft letter to Henry Morgenthau (U.S. Secretary of the Treasury), 11 March, nos. 268, 290, and memorandum of 2 April, no. 366; Cadogan minute of 28 April quoted in David Dilks, "'We Must Hope for the Best and Prepare for the Worst': The Prime Minister, the Cabinet and Hitler's Germany, 1937–1939," *Proceedings of the British Academy* 73 (1987), p. 316.

not reconciled Mussolini, nor deterred him by showing force or soliciting Germany. Britain had not dissolved the Axis or the Anti-Comintern Pact, both of which played upon British fears of bolshevism. British policy toward Germany, the common partner in these ideologically congenial pairs, had neither abandoned efforts of conciliation nor explicitly disinterested Britain if Germany should attempt to expand in Central or Eastern Europe.

Beneath the surface of continuity, British policy toward Germany had become more volatile than ever, its willingness to make concessions resting on unstable and contradictory premises. Concessions could—or should not—precede a general settlement, and they need not—or must—depend on something more palpable in return than German promises of good behavior. In the indefinite interval before Hitler's next major move, finding particulars was—or was not—a matter of urgency, for this was—or was not—the right time to counterbalance rearmament with conciliation and reduce Berlin's guesswork as to British intentions. It was the right time because British rearmament had helped quiet Germany, or because Britain's military weakness simply required it to take some initiatives toward détente. Moderates in the Nazi regime could or could not leash the party's extremists. The era of surprises might be or was not over. Germany did or did not have a legitimate claim to exercise hegemony over Central and Eastern Europe. Britain could preempt German designs on Austria and Czechoslovakia by using these countries as Versailles "lumber," large bargaining chips for a settlement with Germany. Or Britain could offer other chips to bargain for the security of Central and Eastern Europe, which would be an explicit or implied trip wire for British military intervention. Granting particular concessions might reduce diplomatic confrontations and prevent war indefinitely, or might buy time for Britain to prepare for the explosion that German ambitions would inevitably set off.

These premises clustered around two contrasting ratios of appeasement and military strength. One position looked at Britain and sought limits—to Britain's dependence on allies, its support of the European status quo, its reasons for using force, and its use of deterrence as a peacetime policy to prevent or limit international crises. The other looked at Europe and sought reliance—on Britain's potential allies, its commitment to European stability, its willingness to use force if that stability were threatened, and its deterrent capacity to prevent forcible German actions. Although London still followed a course somewhere between these two positions, the mood along Whitehall continued to swing toward the first.

Chatfield and the Chiefs of Staff were not alone in deducing from political commitments and strategic dangers that their own Foreign Office was largely to blame. This attitude showed itself increasingly in meetings of the Cabinet and ministerial committees, where a formidable coalition among Service ministers, Minister for Coordination, chancellor, Home Secretary, and prime minister opposed Eden's call for a more aggressive policy toward Mussolini. Minus Duff Cooper, this same combination had grown dissatisfied with the evident lack of progress in negotiating with Germany.

Privately, some accusations were scathing. Hoare wrote to Chamberlain that the Foreign Office was so inclined toward making agreements with France and "so much biased against Germany (and Italy and Japan) that unconsciously and almost continuously they are making impossible any European reconciliation." In the Foreign Office itself, Cadogan thought Britain must talk with the Germans, not hide "our heads in the sand." If British rearmament was backward as Vansittart admitted, "we must have time. We must *do* something. It's no good, as Van does, framing no policy and merely saying 'Rearm.'"[65]

Hoare assumed that Chamberlain's imminent move to No. 10 Downing Street would make it "possible greatly to change the European atmosphere." Hoare had in mind improvements in personnel, efficiency, and ideas about foreign policy in the Cabinet. The Germans also looked forward to changes in London. As Phipps reported from Berlin, they preferred Chamberlain to Baldwin and hoped Eden and Duff Cooper would leave their positions "and that then everything in the garden will be lovely."[66]

Hoare may not have recognized how much Chamberlain had already begun to exploit the divisions and channel the momentum generated by ministerial consideration of the Army's role and several major strategic studies. Discussions of these subjects referred to "military policy," "war strategy," "general plans for war," and "general policy." These terms, most of which encompassed supply as well as operations, loosened the close association that Whitehall had normally made between "policy" in general and foreign policy in particular. In this unsettled semantic climate, strategy and finance gained at the expense of foreign policy, with consequent narrowing of Britain's options for deterrence.

In October and November 1936, the controversy over the Army's

[65] Hoare to Chamberlain, 17 March (also notes of January on foreign policy), Templewood Papers; Cadogan diary, 26 and 28 April, 24 May, Cadogan Papers, 1/6. Cadogan did not expect help from the Americans, who were "more woolly headed than any other race on earth"; diary, 25 March, ibid.
[66] Hoare to Chamberlain, 17 March, Templewood Papers; Phipps to Strang, 16 March, *DBFP*, 18, no. 302.

part in a European war heated up. The Supply Board's annual report cited figures from the War Office and Air Ministry revealing serious gaps of up to 50 percent between the war potential that would "be created by 1939 under the Deficiency Programmes, and that required for the first year of the war." As Inskip pointed out to the CID, the War Office assumed mobilization of Territorial Divisions to reinforce the Regular Field Force; the Cabinet had not approved this hypothesis and the Treasury would not fund it. At the Treasury, Bridges understood the Services' desire to expand their programs "to provide a greater means of insurance," but warned against proceeding so fast as to injure export trade, disrupt wages and prices, and slow down the major projects of rearmament itself.[67]

Inskip obtained the Services' concurrence with his own judgment about the priority of air defense over an expeditionary force,[68] but this did not settle the issue of the Army's role. Hankey, Pownall, Ismay, and the General Staff all doubted that air power would stop or replace armies in the next war, and rejected the doctrine of "limited liability." Britain, they maintained, still had a vital interest in the territorial integrity of the Low Countries and France, and should be prepared to send a substantial force to the Continent.[69] Vansittart strongly opposed Inskip's suggestion—it was Chamberlain's idea—for the Government to inform France that Britain's contribution on land would be limited to the Regular Field Force. (Otherwise, Chamberlain argued, the French would not know to change their strategic plans so as to strengthen their left flank, and their "rear would be turned.") This would discourage France, Vansittart cautioned, and cause "a landslide" of eastern and southeastern European states toward Germany. Fisher emphasized air and naval power as Britain's "most effective contribution" in a European war, and regarded 600,000 men—the peacetime goal envisaged by the DRC—as the desirable maximum for the Army even while at war. Vansittart, Hankey, and Deverell rebutted. It might become necessary to mobilize a much larger Army, and the means could be found in the "residuum" of national resources that would remain after the needs of the Air Force and Navy had been met. America might relax its neutrality laws "given discreet diplomacy" (Vansittart), and its

[67] Supply Board annual report, 30 September 1936, CAB 60/16; PSOC meeting, 13 October, CAB 60/4; CID meeting, 19 November, CAB 2/6; Bridges memorandum, 20 October, T 161/841.

[68] Inskip to Service ministers, 28 September, and memorandum, 7 October, CAB 64/3; CID meeting, 29 October, CAB 2/6.

[69] Pownall paper, June 1936, CAB 21/509 (Hankey sent copies to Inskip, Dill, and Fisher); Deverell note, 16 June, CAB 64/14; Third Interim Report of the Field Force Committee, July, WO 33/1434; Western Plan, by command of the Army Council, 11 November, WO 33/1446.

supplies "might again make the difference between victory and defeat, as in the last war" (Hankey). Britain "could not enter a war with any limitation of liability," and removing the Territorial Army's liability "for foreign service would kill the movement" (Deverell).[70]

Inskip could not, he informed Chamberlain early in December, refute the "emphatic opinions" held by Vansittart and Deverell, and he had reluctantly come to the conclusion that there was "no hope of limiting in advance of the occasion the size of the army we will send to France." Chamberlain told the DPR that this matter of supply raised important political questions, and thus should be referred to the Cabinet.[71] The controversy came to a head in December in the Cabinet and CID when Duff Cooper and Chamberlain presented cases for and against a sizable continental commitment. For the next several months, the War Office, Chiefs of Staff, Hankey, and Vansittart reconstructed the DRC coalition less Fisher, and Chamberlain capitalized on weaknesses in that group as he restated his own case for deterrence through air power.[72]

Duff Cooper argued that the Cabinet was and should be "committed to the principle of a Field Force of 5 Regular and 12 Territorial Divisions," and that British "military policy" had since the turn of the century assumed the possibility of sending the Army to the Continent. The newly appointed Director General of Munitions Production (Vice Admiral Sir Harold Brown) reported that Britain's industrial situation would now permit a start on equipping the Territorial Army, and that doing so would, "by broadening the basis of supply, assist materially" in the production of war potential for a mobilized force. Thus, it was materially possible to end the Cabinet's three-year postponement (of February 1936) of a decision regarding the Territorial Army.[73]

Unimpressed with the opinion of "the interested Department," Chamberlain argued that approving Duff Cooper's apparent goal—mobilization of the Regular Field Force and all twelve Territorial Divi-

---

[70] Fisher-Hankey-Ismay correspondence, 23–27 October, and minutes of meeting of Inskip, Deverell, Vansittart and others, 27 October, CAB 64/35; Chamberlain diary, 25 October, Chamberlain Papers, NC 2/23a.

[71] Inskip to Chamberlain, 5 November, CAB 64/35; DPR meeting, 26 November, CAB 16/136; Inskip-Duff Cooper correspondence, 27, 30 November, CAB 64/35.

[72] For accounts of this controversy, including the problem of recruiting, see Bond, *British Military Policy*, pp. 233–43; John Charmley, *Duff Cooper: The Authorised Biography* (London, 1986), pp. 97–99; Dennis, *Decision by Default*, pp. 72–99; Gibbs, *Rearmament*, chap. 12; Howard, *Continental Commitment*, pp. 114–17; Lippincott, "Strategy of Appeasement," chap. 6; Meyers, *Britische Sicherheitspolitik*, pp. 174–89; Shay, *British Rearmament*, pp. 136–40.

[73] Duff Cooper memoranda, 3, 4, and 14 December, CP 325, 326, and 337(36), CAB 24/265; Brown "Reminiscences," chaps. 21, 22, in Papers of Sir George W. Turner and Vice Admiral Sir Harold Brown (LHCMA); also Postan, *British War Production*, pp. 43–44.

sions on or shortly after the outbreak of war—would not be "reaffirmation of a previous decision." The aim of British policy, "to deter war," could more readily be achieved by increasing air defense and the striking power of the Air Force than by equipping the Territorial Army for war on the Continent. The country's industrial capacity could not stand more than the reequipment of the Regular Field Force sanctioned by the Cabinet in February 1936. British public opinion was "strongly opposed to Continental adventures," and the French had no business dictating how Britain should distribute its forces. Britain should have a Regular Army of five divisions, with the Territorials assigned to home and air defense. On Chamberlain's recommendation, the Cabinet postponed a decision on equipping the Territorial Army and referred the question of the Army's role to Inskip and the Chiefs of Staff.[74]

Before the COS reported, Hankey and Vansittart reaffirmed the DRC's position. Hankey doubted that the Service programs had "absorbed full capacity of industry and manpower." Like some later critics of theories of nuclear deterrence, Vansittart rejected Chamberlain's claim for the "decisive importance" of air power, and called attention to "incontestable political facts"—if Britain limited its expeditionary force to five divisions, France would cease "to think us worth while" and Britain would become isolated. The controversy delayed Army planning and negated Eden's policy of trying "to arrest a landslide in favour of the dictators."[75]

In January, the Chiefs of Staff reendorsed the March 1936 White Paper's definition of the Army's role, supported the War Office, and repeated the DRC's emphasis on a balanced program of rearmament for all three Services. The COS parried Chamberlain's request for a comparison between the deterrent power of land and air forces at equivalent levels of expenditure. They argued that land and air forces could not be compared with each other, nor could their relative strategic values be precisely measured in financial terms. It was impossible "to say whether or no air forces could stop armies." Because totalitarian states could mobilize their peacetime activities for a major offensive at the outbreak of war, "the earlier that all our forces can intervene the greater their value, and the knowledge of this fact in foreign countries might have considerable value as a deterrent." Vansittart agreed, pointing out more forcefully than the Chiefs of Staff that air power could not

---

[74] Chamberlain memorandum, 11 December, CP 334(36), CAB 24/265; Weir notes on draft of this paper, Weir Papers, 17/10; Cab 75(36), 16 December, CAB 23/86; Chamberlain diary, 24 December, Chamberlain Papers, NC 2/24a.

[75] Hankey to Inskip, 17 December 1936 and 18 January 1937, CAB 64/35; Hankey paper, 18 January, CAB 21/509; Vansittart minutes, 14–30 December, C9094/C9095/C9096/6761/62, FO 371/29882, and 8 January 1937, C205/205/62, FO 371/20701.

stop the German Army, and that any British contribution on land must be immediate, for time no longer had "the same meaning" as in 1914. The political objective of British "military policy" was to prevent Germany from isolating and paralyzing France, thereby depriving Britain "of the French counterweight with which at present we hope to be able to resist German ambitions."[76]

Noting the COS emphasis on the "composite nature" of modern warfare, Inskip proposed a compromise. Instead of equipping twelve Territorial Divisions to be ready in the first four months of war (the "ultimate aim" recommended by the COS), a goal that he considered economically unfeasible, the Government should provide sufficient supplies to train these divisions. In an emergency, these supplies could be concentrated so as to prepare "one or more" divisions (Chamberlain would have preferred "one or two") to reinforce the Regular Army within four months. On 3 February, the Cabinet agreed in principle with Inskip's recommendation. Before a decision was taken, however, and although acknowledging that "national safety came before finance," Chamberlain wanted to know the cost of Inskip's plan and the time needed to complete it.[77]

The Cabinet would not return to this issue until late April 1937. Meanwhile, Chamberlain knew that the COS report masked disagreement in the War Office, where the General Staff did not wholeheartedly endorse a continental commitment, and among the Services. Chamberlain had expected the COS to advocate a continental commitment unless assisted by someone like Lord Trenchard, who would have made sure they took "an objective view." Chamberlain was amused to have been told by Hoare and Swinton "that *their* Chief of Staff really agreed with my views." Although he did not expect one Service dog to eat another, he was satisfied "to know that the sea dog and the air dog think the war dog ought to be eaten—by some other dog!"[78]

[76] COS meetings, January 1937, CAB 53/6, and report, "Role of the British Army" (COS 550), 28 January, CP 41(37), CAB 24/267 (based largely on CIGS memorandum attached to minutes of COS meeting of 19 January); Vansittart minutes and marginal comments on COS report, 1–3 February (for Eden's use at the Cabinet on 3 February), C928/928/18, FO 371/20746. See also Dennis, *Decision by Default*, pp. 93–95, and the full summary of the COS report in Gibbs, *Rearmament*, pp. 448–54.

[77] Inskip to Chamberlain, 1 February, CAB 64/35; Inskip memorandum, "The Role of the British Army," 2 February, CP 46(37), CAB 24/267; Cab 5(37), 3 February, CAB 23/87; Inskip to Duff Cooper, 5 February, CAB 64/35.

[78] Chamberlain to Inskip, 16 and 24 December, CAB 64/35; Chamberlain diary, 24 December and 7 February, Chamberlain Papers, NC 2/24a; Chamberlain to Ida, 6 February, NC 18/1/993. For ambivalence and vagueness in the War Office: Chamberlain diary, 24 December; Liddell Hart to Bullock (24 November), correspondence and conversations with Deverell (November and December), Liddell Hart Papers, 1/129, 1/232, and 11/1936/99 and 118 (LHCMA); Bond, *British Military Policy*, pp. 234–35; Dennis, *Decision by Default*, pp. 78, 82–84.

Inter-Service discord, along with differences between the COS and Vansittart on the one hand and Vansittart and Eden on the other, strengthened Chamberlain's hand against the old DRC coalition as he argued for a comprehensive definition of policy with emphasis on air deterrence and economic resources. He had good opportunity to do this even while the Army question remained in abeyance, for the Chiefs of Staff had agreed that their plans for a war against Germany must include the possibility of sending a force overseas, and this contingency appeared in another strategic study as well.

In February 1937, the Chiefs of Staff signed three major reports: "Planning for War with Germany"; "Review of Imperial Defence"; "Comparison of the Strength of Great Britain with that of Certain Other Nations as at May, 1937." These contained diverse meanings of policy, along with strategic contingencies for which Britain was militarily unprepared. Bridging strategy, foreign policy, and supply, these studies also enabled the Service staffs to test the political authority of the Foreign Office and the financial wisdom of the Treasury—with much more success in the first case than in the second.

The JPC's completion of the draft of the report on planning for war with Germany, delayed for many months by the Mediterranean and Rhineland crises, prompted Hankey, the DCOS, and the COS to distinguish between policy and plans. Policy was "the function of Government," plans "the function of the Chiefs of Staff." They recommended that, whether in peace or war, a small ministerial body should determine "war policy." The COS would prepare "general war plans" (or "war strategy") to "give effect to the Government's war policy" and submit them to the ministers for examination and approval. Once approved, these general plans would guide detailed planning by the military staffs.[79]

In the report on war with Germany, the COS and JPC used "policy," "general policy," "general conception," and broad strategic "plans" to indicate military courses of action (in alliance with France and Belgium) in a conflict with Germany in 1939. Assuming that Germany would be the aggressor, the military experts recommended preparing for a long war in which Britain and its allies could build up military resources for a successful counteroffensive. Their economic position would be jeopardized if the United States strictly applied an embargo on arms exports. British naval policy would be the same whether Germany tried to knock out Britain or France first: the security of sea communications,

[79] DCOS meetings and draft reports, November–December 1936, CAB 54/3; COS meeting, 11 January 1937, CAB 53/6; COS memorandum, "Higher Control of Operations in War" (COS 545), 22 January, CAB 4/25, approved by the CID in principle on 11 February, CAB 2/6.

and the application of economic pressure on Germany. Alternative policies would be necessary, however, for British forces on land and in the air. If Germany aimed its main assault against Britain, all resources must be used to defeat it: the RAF should be prepared to counterattack Germany's "air striking force and its maintenance organisation" (although the Government might decide "to retaliate in kind" if Germany bombed British cities indiscriminately); the Field Force "would probably not be sent to the Continent in the first stage of war, nor until the main enemy attack had been repulsed." If Germany attacked France, Britain must send forces "to the Continent at the earliest possible moment," and start "an immediate air offensive from this country in support of France" (the targets would depend on whether the greater danger came from German land or air forces). If Italy and Japan remained neutral, Soviet intervention—or the threat thereof—would help make possible an allied counteroffensive. But the military advisers recommended preparing precautionary plans in case of Italian or Japanese intervention, against which British naval strategy "would have to be largely defensive, until the issue with Germany had been settled." If confronted with the hostility of Japan and Italy in a German war, "the naval forces of France and Great Britain would be faced with a most formidable task."[80]

The object of this report, the first of its kind for Britain in the 1930s, was to obtain the Government's earliest possible approval of the "general policy" for a war with Germany. The Services could then prepare detailed (or "subsidiary") plans, which would "provide the basis of a national plan of defence"—indeed of an allied plan, for the COS attached "importance to the initiation of joint plans with our Allies at the beginning of the war." A landmark in planning for war, the report is also noteworthy for what it omitted or glossed over. First, on the advice of Hankey and the deputy chiefs, the COS did not attach those portions of the JPC draft that stressed Germany's great economic and military potential. Second, the military staffs' accent on joint planning with France and Belgium belied their opposition to staff talks with those countries during peacetime because of alleged doubts over which side Britain might have to support in a future war. Third, the report mentioned the advantage that could come of Soviet intervention and recommended that detailed plans take into account what operations might be undertaken by "prospective allies" in Eastern Europe, but the experts did not add their strong misgivings about the reliability of

[80] COS report, "Planning for War with Germany" (COS 549), 15 February, CAB 53/30, covering those parts of the JPC's "Provisional Report" of 26 October (the entire JPC report in CAB 53/29) which the DCOS recommended be forwarded to ministers (DCOS report, 5 January, CAB 53/29). The COS amended the JPC draft on 12 January, CAB 53/6.

Russia or the disadvantages of France's eastern alliances for British security. Fourth, the report did not indicate how much the alternative plans for Britain's land and air forces already competed for resources: Fighter and Bomber Commands disagreed over how best to discourage or withstand a German knockout blow, while the War Office and Air Ministry disagreed over the likely roles of both the Luftwaffe and the British Army.[81]

Finally, the Chiefs of Staff did not reveal that the DCOS had not heeded their instruction to consult the Foreign Office as the DCOS reviewed and updated the JPC's draft report. Instead, the Deputy Chiefs of Staff recommended that the COS omit the JPC's section on "political factors"—the attitudes, military forces, and economic strengths of European powers in 1939. The JPC's assumptions for 1939 were "already out of date in certain respects," and any revised political appreciation prepared "with the Foreign Office would similarly be rendered obsolete by the rapid march of events."[82]

The Foreign Office had traditionally prepared separate political reviews for Imperial Conferences, and Hankey, the COS, and the Foreign Office agreed on a minor departure from this practice. For the Imperial Conference of May 1937, the Joint Planning Committee should include in its draft "Review of Imperial Defence" the views of the Foreign Office concerning political factors.[83] In the first two sections of the COS "Review," which incorporated the opinions of the Foreign Office on international liabilities and threats, "policy" meant foreign policy. In the third part ("Rearmament in the United Kingdom"), the term pertained to rearmament in general, minimum interference with peacetime industry, and each Service's program of rearmament. The terminology in the section on the strategic situation in cases of war was similar to that of the report on war with Germany. "Policy" referred to the preparation of measures for major courses of military action: two contingencies for a German war; in case of Japanese aggression, reinforcement of Singapore and dispatch of the fleet to the Far East (equal in strength to Japan's fleet if the new naval standard were imple-

[81] COS report, "Planning For War with Germany" (COS 549), 15 February, CAB 53/30. See also earlier discussion in this chapter and notes 22–25, above; Webster and Frankland, *Strategic Air Offensive*, pp. 86–92. Wark criticizes the COS—and gives a rather speculative explanation of their motives—for agreeing to purge the JPC's sections on German strength; *Ultimate Enemy*, pp. 200–202. On Army and Air intelligence regarding German rearmament and strategic planning: Inskip-Churchill correspondence, CAB 64/6; Hinsley, *British Intelligence*, pp. 76–80; Wark, pp. 59–64, 76–77, 93–94; Watt, "British Intelligence," pp. 267–68.

[82] COS meeting, 30 October, CAB 53/6; DCOS report, 5 January, CAB 53/29.

[83] COS meeting, 16 October 1936, CAB 53/6; meeting of ad hoc CID (Official) Subcommittee on the Imperial Conference, 16 October, CAB 16/153.

mented); stronger defenses in the Mediterranean in the unfortunate event that Britain could no longer count on "friendship with Italy and the weakness of Spain."[84]

Summarizing the liabilities for Britain and the Commonwealth, the Foreign Office began with Germany: a threat to the United Kingdom (and thus to the Commonwealth) if Germany conquered Western Europe; an "indirect threat" if Germany made war in Central or Eastern Europe, for a German victory there "would lead to the eclipse of France, unless she were supported in time by this country, . . . and might well lead to an eventual clash between the British and German Empires." Second, in a war with Japan, the security of Australia, New Zealand, and India would depend on retaining Singapore as a naval station and sending the fleet to the Far East; Soviet military assistance to Britain "might be of considerable value." Third, the preservation of British possessions and influence in the Mediterranean (where Britain could no longer count "on a friendly and submissive Italy") was important for imperial communications. Finally, the security of India was "essential for the maintenance of the Commonwealth."[85]

The JPC and Chiefs of Staff adopted this list in the same order of importance for national and imperial security, adding as first priority the "security of our imperial communications throughout the world." They also raised the possibility of a "world war" against an ideological combination of Germany, Japan, and Italy. In this event, which they expected diplomacy to avoid, Britain would have to place the defense of the United Kingdom and Singapore above the security of communications in the Mediterranean, and shipping to the Middle East and Far East "would have to be diverted to the Cape route."

When the COS discussed the JPC's draft review containing the appraisal of the Foreign Office, Chatfield found that it "suffered from a preponderantly political bias." He disputed the indirect threat to Britain if Germany expanded eastward. Britain needed a "clear policy" that it would only guarantee the security of France and the Low Countries against aggression and would not intervene if France attacked Germany in support of Czechoslovakia. The COS amended the draft report so as to lessen the potential threat to the United Kingdom of a war in Central or Eastern Europe, emphasize the danger of being drawn into it, and tone down Britain's interest in supporting France in such a conflict.[86]

In their comparison of European military strengths as of May 1937,

---

[84] COS "Review of Imperial Defence" (COS 560), 22 February, as amended by the CID on 25 February, in CP 73(37), CAB 24/268; JPC drafts in CAB 53/30.

[85] Sargent to Ismay (revising a JPC draft), 15 January, CAB 55/9.

[86] COS meeting, 5 February, CAB 53/6, and review (see note 84 above); summary of this report in Gibbs, *Rearmament*, pp. 409–15.

the JPC and COS considered policy implicitly: the possible political intentions of European powers; the military strategies that they might adopt in war. With the Soviet Union neutral, Britain and France (and Belgium) would be markedly superior to Germany and Italy in naval power, enabling the Western allies "to exercise decisive economic pressure in a prolonged war." Germany and Italy would have numerical superiority on land, but the German General Staff would probably not advise undertaking an offensive because of French and Belgian frontier defenses. Only in air power would the enemy have "an advantage sufficient to offer any chance of a quick success" in 1937. In long-range bombers, "of particular value for exploiting the initiative in warfare," this advantage would be "exceptional": Germany 800, Italy 232, for a total of 1,032; Britain 48, France 256, Belgium 9, total 313. In spite of this superiority, Germany was unlikely to go to war in 1937, for "German military opinion as a whole" did not believe that air power alone could win a war, and had little faith in "wholehearted" Italian cooperation. The military value of Soviet intervention on the side of the West would be "doubtful, especially if it is likely to be accompanied by Japanese hostility," in which case "the forces required for our Home and Far Eastern Fleets would leave nothing available for the Mediterranean." Russian neutrality would be preferable from the British naval point of view, and the mere threat of Russian intervention constituted "a powerful moral deterrent against Germany going to war."[87]

At the Foreign Office, Oliver Harvey, Eden's Principal Private Secretary, noted the discrepancy between the figures in this report and the more favorable comparison of British and German forces that Swinton gave the Cabinet early in February. Vansittart saw the COS report as an alarming and understated admission of Britain's military weakness, "despite all the warnings put out by the F.O. for years past." He had repeatedly warned that Germany might gamble on an all-out air offensive against Britain, "but the Chiefs of Staff have never been willing to admit it" until now. Everything depended "on how much time we get." Fortunately, the Government's recently published White Paper on Defence (16 February, forecasting the expenditure of £1,500 million over the next five years) had "put us on the map again all over Europe." On the other hand, Europe was also aware that there was "a long gap between promise and performance."[88]

Ministerial examination of these reports did not settle arguments

[87] COS report, "Comparison of the Strength of Great Britain with that of Certain Other Nations as at May, 1937" (COS 551), 9 February, in CP 58(37), CAB 24/268; JPC draft report, 22 December 1936, CAB 55/9, slightly amended by the COS on 22 January, CAB 53/6. The origins of this report were discussed in the preceding section.

[88] Harvey minute, 15 February, and Vansittart minutes and marginal comments on the COS report, 14–19 February, C1406/205/62, FO 371/20701.

among experts, clarify the language of policy, or demarcate respective departmental jurisdictions over "politico-strategical" issues. When the CID considered the draft "Review of Imperial Defence" on 11 February, Vansittart (in Eden's absence) declared that the Chiefs of Staff had underestimated the difficulty of reaching agreements with Germany and Japan, as well as the danger to France if Germany attacked eastward. Chatfield replied that the COS had thought Britain might have "to give away less in negotiating agreements than we should sacrifice in the cost incurred in building up our defences." The COS needed advice on "the future trend of our foreign policy in general and our commitments under the League in particular." Chamberlain rejected the report's allegation that "orthodox financial policy" had placed strict limitations on the rearmament program; the problem was Britain's limited "power to expand." The revised paper made Chamberlain's point by stating that Britain had accelerated its rearmament "so far as is compatible with the minimum interference of the normal industrial activities of the country." The CID did not support Vansittart's bid to make a clear statement of Britain's interest in preventing Germany's conquest of Eastern Europe and isolation of France.[89]

Inskip acknowledged that, because of how the review was prepared, it contained "both the political and the military aspects of the position." Thus, Chatfield admitted, there were "certain discrepancies between the military and political outlooks." Hoare and Swinton did not want therefore to question the freedom of the Chiefs of Staff to express their own opinions in a review under their signatures. Hoare said that "the military aspect should not be subordinated to the political point of view." This did not suit Chamberlain, who stated that "if the Chiefs of Staff had assumed an incorrect political basis, it would then be necessary for the military aspects to be reexamined." The CID did not resolve the positions of Hoare and Chamberlain, or debate how autonomously the COS might construct the political bases for their military advice, but approved the amended COS report "as a military review applicable to the international situation as it exists today."[90]

In the Cabinet's discussion (24 February) of the COS report on European military strengths, Duff Cooper mentioned that more recent intelligence information indicated a faster expansion of the German Army

[89] CID meetings, 11, 25 February, CAB 2/6; Ismay-Vansittart correspondence, 12, 15 February, and COS meetings, 12, 18 February, CAB 53/7; Vansittart to Chatfield, 16 February, Chatfield Papers; COS review (see note 84 above); Gibbs, *Rearmament*, pp. 396–97.

[90] CID discussion on 11 February and approval of revised review on 25 February, CAB 2/6. Chamberlain thought the COS had exaggerated Britain's military obligations as a member of the League of Nations.

than suggested by this paper.[91] But the main topic was Germany's superiority in long-range bombers. Swinton asked his colleagues not to infer that the Air Ministry was failing to carry out its expansion program. The Cabinet knew about intelligence estimates of Germany's accelerating air rearmament, but refused to increase production by Government interference as Swinton recommended if the RAF hoped to complete Scheme F by April 1939. The Cabinet had agreed with his advice to avoid unrealistic attachments to "literal tests of numerical parity," and to use other measurements of air strength—types of aircraft, offensive power of bombers, and so on. On 19 February, the DPR had recommended approval of measures that must be taken now (recruiting pilots and skilled mechanics) if the Government should decide later to adopt the Air Ministry's latest plan for expansion (Scheme H): 2,500 first-line aircraft by April 1939 (Germany's apparent objective), including a "deterrent force" of 1,700 bombers, with reserves to be completed by 1941 (instead of by 1939 under Scheme F).

The Cabinet approved this recommendation on 24 February, and along with it the Air Ministry's novel techniques for reconditioning the policy of parity: reserves could count as front-line strength while Britain tried to catch up with Germany by 1939; long-range bombers with heavy warloads would enable Britain to achieve strategic deterrence if not numerical parity. (On the fourth, Hoare had told the DPR he supported shifting reserves to the front line, for "it was desirable to put more into the shop window which would act as a deterrent.") The report on strengths as of May 1937, Swinton pointed out, had based its British figures on the incorrect assumption that half of first-line strength could be transferred back to reserve, and had overlooked how British short-range bombers, based in France, "could be quite effective against important German objectives."[92]

On 11 February, the CID approved the recommendation of the Chiefs of Staff that a small ministerial committee be appointed in peacetime "to examine, from the point of view of Government policy, plans for a major war," and "to provide a possible nucleus of a War Committee or War Cabinet in the event of war." A few days later, Baldwin appointed the Defence Plans (Policy) Subcommittee of the

---

[91] Cab 9(37), 24 February, CAB 23/87. Duff Cooper probably had in mind the War Office/Industrial Intelligence Centre report of 13 January on the German Army (FCI 100), CAB 48/4, which Hankey distributed to the CID on 6 February.

[92] Cabs 4, 5, 9(37), 27 January, 3 and 24 February, CAB 23/87; Swinton memoranda, 14 (Scheme H) and 22 January, CP 18 and 27(37), CAB 24/267, and 11 February (modified Scheme H), CP 69(37), CAB 24/268; Swinton to Inskip, 28 January, CAB 64/6; DPR meetings, 4, 19 February, CAB 16/137; Smith, *British Air Strategy*, pp. 165–72; Gibbs, *Rearmament*, pp. 565–66; Peden, *British Rearmament and Treasury*, pp. 128–29.

CID: himself as chairman, Chamberlain, Simon, Eden, the Service ministers (Duff Cooper, Hoare, Swinton), and Inskip. The DP(P)'s terms of reference were identical to those recommended by the CID, except that "defence plans" was substituted for "plans for a major war."[93]

After a delay of two months, on 19 April the committee discussed the COS report "Planning for War with Germany." In spite of the omission of the JPC's gloomiest sections from the revised report, Swinton, Inskip, and Hoare still found the joint planners too pessimistic regarding Britain's vulnerability to air attack when compared to Germany's. Swinton agreed with Hoare that the industrial area of the Ruhr "presented a very formidable target"; its inhabitants "were the least pro-Hitler section of the German population and might prove very sensitive to intensive air bombing." Chamberlain asked whether the report implied that Britain would go to war without having held staff conversations with its allies. The Chiefs of Staff had been invited to attend this meeting (they had proposed close collaboration between the COS and a new ministerial body), and Chatfield replied that staff talks "presupposed a virtual alliance" and were incompatible "with the prospective conclusion of a Five-Power Pact." Chamberlain and the committee agreed to stipulate that the desirability of conversations with France and Belgium "should be kept in mind, with a view to their consideration if the international situation should deteriorate so seriously as to render them necessary."[94]

Chamberlain wanted to know "the precise meaning" of the report's phrase that, in case of a German assault against France and Belgium, "'our land forces must give immediate support on the Continent, with a view to ensuring cooperation between the French and the Belgians.'" Duff Cooper thought the French would probably defend only their own frontier if Britain did not send troops to the Continent. Simon, whose Home Office had responsibility for air raid precautions, suggested that the Germans might feint against France, inducing Britain to send the Field Force, and "then launch the whole weight of her air attack on this country." The Territorial Army, Duff Cooper replied, was more suitable for internal security than the Field Force, whose "speedy despatch" to help France and Belgium "would be essential." The committee neither adopted nor ruled out a continental commitment, concluding that "time is the essence" in assisting Britain's allies, and that the "aim should be to place ourselves in a position to release the Field Force at the earliest possible moment consistent with the situation at home."

[93] Above, note 79; composition and terms of reference, 15 February, CAB 16/182; Ehrman, *Cabinet Government*, pp. 117–18.
[94] DP(P) meeting, 19 April, CAB 16/181. Subsequent quotes are from this document.

Subject to its observations on staff talks and dispatching the Field Force, the DP(P) approved the two alternative cases to govern British planning and the COS recommendations for preparing detailed plans, and authorized the concerned departments and committees to put these recommendations into effect. Chatfield had explained the COS view of the need for Government approval of the "general policy" to pursue in a war with Germany, and he referred to the "policies" for each of the three armed forces in the two contingencies. Although the DP(P) did not discuss this terminology, the committee implicitly accepted the recommended procedure: Government approval of major contingencies and courses of action suggested by the COS; preparation of detailed plans by the Services based on these approved policies or broad plans.

In the DP(P) meeting, Eden observed that the report did not take into account "the possibility of Italian hostility . . . as a likely contingency." He thought that German exploitation of a Mediterranean conflict to further its interests was likelier than Italian intervention in a war between the West and Germany. At this moment, "trouble was more likely to arise in the Mediterranean than elsewhere in Europe." Hoare agreed that the atmosphere of Anglo-Italian relations was awful, but Swinton thought Italy's economic weakness would hold Mussolini back, and Duff Cooper considered Anglo-Italian differences "trivial" compared with Anglo-German disagreements. To Hankey and Chatfield, it seemed that Eden's remarks contradicted the recent conclusion of the CID and Cabinet that Italy was not presently a "probable enemy." The Chiefs of Staff, Chatfield stated, "would be glad of guidance as to whether our preparations for war against Italy were now to take priority over preparations against Germany."

Inskip reassured Eden and the DP(P) that studies regarding the Mediterranean and Far East were also being prepared.[95] In January, the JPC had proposed to examine the military situation in the Mediterranean, basing their study on the "extremely unlikely" assumption of a unilateral war with Italy in August 1937; any resultant plans could be modified to fit more likely contingencies of multilateral war.[96] The JPC postponed this appreciation until the summer. Meanwhile, at the request of the Chiefs of Staff, the joint planners revised their report of October 1936 on Cyprus, dutifully following the COS guidelines. For financial and strategic reasons, Cyprus should not become a major base; instead, docking facilities should be developed there and at Alex-

[95] Ibid. In March, Eden had concurred with O'Malley's criticism of the summary treatment of Italy by the COS in this report; *DBFP*, 18, no. 246.
[96] JPC's proposed terms of reference, 27 January, CAB 53/30; approved by the COS on 8 February, CAB 53/7.

andria. The COS still wondered what "political assumptions" should govern preparations for war against Italy. In view of Eden's remarks at the DP(P) meeting on the previous day, did the CID want to reconsider its conclusion of 11 February?[97]

At that CID meeting, Chamberlain had urged that "the cost of taking defensive measures" against Italy be ascertained "before making any decision to incur such cost."[98] Chamberlain and the issue of cost dominated ministerial discussions of the Army's role and the new naval standard in April and May.

On 28 April, the Cabinet considered Duff Cooper's estimate of costs for implementing Inskip's Army proposal approved in principle by the Cabinet on 3 February. Duff Cooper went further than Inskip's plan by also recommending the provision (by April 1941) of as much equipment as possible to ready the first contingent of four Territorial Divisions within four months of the outbreak of war; and investigation of the industrial capacity needed to mobilize the other two contingents by the seventh month of war. These recommendations reflected two concerns of the War Office—notably the Director General of Munitions Production—about supply: that equipping the Territorial Army for training would not create much war potential; that a slump might occur in placing orders when the deficiency program ended, unless the Army could show interested firms that it needed additional capacity for war reserves. Inskip supported the first of Duff Cooper's additional proposals, but Chamberlain replied—not entirely accurately—that Inskip and the Cabinet had previously decided on mobilizing only two Territorial Divisions when war broke out. The chancellor doubted that the country could afford to fund Duff Cooper's recommendations, the Admiralty was about to introduce a larger naval program, and he would soon "have to propose a fixed limit to which the Services would have to conform."[99]

On 5 May, Chamberlain agreed to Duff Cooper's first set of proposals based on Inskip's plan, subject to Treasury approval in detail of the expenditure involved. He suggested that the Cabinet consider the role

---

[97] COS meetings, 22 January, CAB 53/6, 5 March and 20 April, CAB 53/7; JPC meeting, 4 February, CAB 55/2, and report, 26 February, CAB 55/9; COS report, 28 April, CAB 53/31.

[98] CID meeting, 11 February, CAB 2/6.

[99] Duff Cooper memorandum, 23 April, CP 115(37), CAB 24/269; Cab 19(37), 28 April, CAB 23/88; Brown note, 22 February, and minutes of meeting in the War Office about supply, 4 March, Turner/Brown Papers, 14. Chamberlain's views had strong support in the Treasury; Peden, *British Rearmament and Treasury*, pp. 136–37. In March, Chamberlain had applauded Liddell Hart for his articles in the *Times* on limiting the continental role of the Army; letter to Liddell Hart, 8 March, Liddell Hart Papers, 1/159/1 (LHCMA); see also Mearsheimer, *Liddell Hart*, pp. 114–15.

of the Army later, "in comparative leisure." At that time, he hoped his colleagues would decide to limit Britain's contribution on land in a continental war. Unlike Inskip, Chamberlain "definitely did challenge the policy of [the Government's] military advisers" on an issue that was not "a purely military matter." Inskip said he "had no alternative but to accept what [Chamberlain] would agree to," but he cautioned the Cabinet not to assume that this decision could henceforward "be regarded as the limit of what our effort would be in time of war."[100]

Bitterly disappointed not to have a firm decision on the role of the Army, Duff Cooper lost his temper in one of what his friends called "Duff's veiners" because of the physiognomic effect of his outbursts. He declared that merely equipping the Territorial Army for training "was not a military policy," and he could only accept this interim decision "under protest and because he hoped that [it] would lead to a permanent decision." Although Eden did not think it possible now, "as a matter of practical politics," to supply the Territorial Army beyond the level acceptable to Chamberlain, he "would greatly regret any departure from the previous decision that 5 Divisions should be available to go abroad." The Cabinet approved the proposals to which Chamberlain had agreed, and referred the question of the Army's role to the DP(P).[101]

Chamberlain also placed cost at the nexus of planning for the Navy. In June 1936, the Joint Planning Committee had discussed the form that its Far East appreciation would take, but did not resume this task until March 1937, although the Admiralty continued to view Japan as the most dangerous long-term threat to British interests. During this long delay, the Anti-Comintern Pact and the deterioration of Britain's relations with Japan heightened the risk that a European war could spread to the Far East, particularly if the Soviet Union intervened against Germany. Thus, Hoare warned that Soviet intervention would be a disadvantage to Britain "from the naval point of view."[102] The JPC's appreciation of 7 May 1937 assumed a one-to-one war against Japan, pointing out that the guidelines for employing the armed forces in this improbable event could be applied or adapted to the more likely cases of war against Germany or Germany and Italy. In these latter contingencies, operations against Germany could delay for "a very

---

[100] Cab 20(37), 5 May, CAB 23/88.

[101] Ibid. Duff Cooper to Chamberlain, 4 May, pleading for "a military policy as soon as possible," copy in CAB 64/35; Bond, *British Military Policy*, pp. 240–41; Dennis, *Decision by Default*, pp. 96–99; Gibbs, *Rearmament*, pp. 456–58. On Duff Cooper's thin skin, see Charmley, *Duff Cooper*, pp. 88–89.

[102] DP(P) meeting to discuss the COS report on planning for a German war, 19 April, CAB 16/181; Hoare had made the same point regarding the COS report on European military strengths, Cab 9(37), 24 February, CAB 23/87.

considerable period" the dispatch of a fleet to Singapore, Britain's indispensable base of operations in a Pacific war. The adumbration that Singapore might fall prompted Hankey and the Chiefs of Staff to regard this study as confirmation of the need for friendly relations with Japan. At the same time, Hankey and the Admiralty tried to assure the Australian, New Zealand, and Indian delegations at the Imperial Conference that Britain would guarantee the security of Singapore even if at war with Germany and threatened by Italy in the Mediterranean.[103]

On 11 May, a week before the Chiefs of Staff discussed the JPC's draft appreciation, the DP(P) considered the Admiralty's proposal for a "new standard of naval strength." This paper reiterated the DRC's recommendation of November 1935—which the Cabinet had tabled— for a navy large enough to defend British interests against Germany and Japan together. Now the Admiralty wanted a decision in principle to adopt this new standard, for there was no guarantee that Britain could avoid war on two (or three) fronts. Without a clear decision on long-term naval strength, as Sir Samuel Hoare told the committee, it would be "almost impossible to make war plans." This uncertainty would in turn, the Admiralty argued, limit "the Navy's ability to implement our foreign policy."[104]

Eden stated that Britain might improve its relations with Japan (although an alliance was impossible because of American and Canadian opposition), and that the Foreign Office thought the proposed standard was "right." At Chamberlain's insistence, however, the DP(P) decided to postpone making "definite recommendations" to the Cabinet until the committee could work out the financial implications of the new standard, relate these to the other Service programs, and give a "complete picture" of the estimated costs of maintaining the approved deficiency programs after their completion. During the next few weeks, Eden and other British representatives at the Imperial Conference supported the Australian plan for a nonaggression pact in the Pacific, and expressed some optimism (Eden's more cautious than Chamberlain's) about reaching an Anglo-Japanese understanding. Such agreements had become all the more attractive because the British

---

[103] JPC meetings, 23 March–7 May, CAB 55/2; COS meeting, 18 May, approving the JPC's study as the basis for reports to send forward to the DP(P) and Australia, New Zealand, and India (for the Imperial Conference), CAB 53/7; COS "Appreciation of the Situation in the Far East" (COS 596), 14 June, CAB 16/182. On Britain's Far Eastern strategy and the Imperial Conference, see Gibbs, *Rearmament*, pp. 397–98, 415–19; Pratt, *East of Malta*, pp. 50–55; Roskill, *Hankey*, 3:271–78, and *Naval Policy*, pp. 347–53; Trotter, *Britain and East Asia*, pp. 199–202.

[104] Admiralty memorandum, "New Standard of Naval Strength," 29 April, CAB 16/182; DP(P) meeting, 11 May, CAB 16/181. The following quotations are from the DP(P) minutes.

could not fulfill their commitment to defend Singapore unless they reached the Admiralty's proposed new standard.

War plans, strategic studies, the Army's future role, the Navy's proposed new stàndard, the RAF's doctrine of a long-range offensive force—deliberation over these subjects accentuated the dilemmas, contradictions, and confusion surrounding British policy. Opinion in London divided over the appropriate mix of virtues for Britain's international reputation, the likelihood and proximity of war with Germany, how to avoid or postpone it, German and British strategy for war, the proper peacetime attitude toward France and her Eastern European allies, and the value of Soviet intervention. Italy was neither a reliable friend nor a probable enemy, and the British Navy should be seen in the Mediterranean but not heard. Britain might use the Gentleman's Agreement to separate Italy from Germany, yet Italy might be the greater threat at the moment and, at least in the Admiralty, the Anti-Comintern Pact was strategically more ominous than the Axis. The unthinkable contingency of a three-front war was contemplated.

The presumption that totalitarian regimes could mobilize for an all-out opening offensive inspired contrasting strategies for deterring or fighting them in the future: preparing all three Services to intervene quickly (Chiefs of Staff, Hankey, and Vansittart); concentrating on offensive air power and limiting the Army's role in a European war (Air Staff, Swinton, and Chamberlain). In the Air Ministry, the emphasis on bombers was questioned by those who, partly because of slowness in producing sufficient bombers for the RAF's needs, advocated using air defense and fighters to convince Germany to forgo the costs of a knockout offensive against Britain. Moreover, Scheme H for the RAF would dress Britain's "shop window" for deterrence without parity or reserves by 1939 (Hoare, Cabinet), or it would provide sufficient front-line forces and reserves for an offensive strategy in case of war against Germany after 1941 (Air Ministry).

During the interval of peace, rearmament and deterrence should conform to insular definitions of national interest (Admiralty, Air Ministry, Treasury), or they should reflect a wider conception of the interdependence of British and European security (War Office, Foreign Office). Committing an enlarged Field Force to the Continent was politically essential (Vansittart) or militarily unnecessary (Chamberlain) for deterrence. Checking Mussolini and Hitler now in Spain would help prevent war later in Europe (Eden), or would probably precipitate such a conflict (Admiralty and COS). Conciliation without coercion might prevent war on one or more fronts; commitments and guesswork should be reduced, vital interests explicitly confined to the security of British territory, the Low Countries and France, and staff talks even with those states withheld (COS and Hankey). Rearmament and foreign policy should reassure likely allies and at the same time keep Germany guessing about British reactions to German expansion in Central Europe (Foreign Office). The Chiefs of Staff and Joint Planning Committee wanted clear statements of long-term foreign policy on which they could base plans for war, and they regarded immediate dangers as symptoms of the inability of the Foreign Office to provide time or heed Britain's limited military resources. The Foreign Office doubted it could manufacture enough time unless Britain demonstrated greater military prowess in rearmament, used firmness to obtain concessions from Germany in a general settlement (Eden, Vansittart, and Sargent), and showed force in the Mediterranean (Eden, O'Malley).

None of these issues permitted an easy distinction between foreign policy and military planning as definitions of policy became more inclusive. The controversy over the Army's role hinged on military policy. The preparation of war plans introduced the war policy of the Government and the policies or plans recommended by the COS for employing the armed forces. These terms stood for different things to different constituencies. To the Services and Hankey, military policy and war policy meant chiefly supplies and strategic plans. The Foreign Office had in mind the encouraging and deterring effects of British preparations on other governments. Supply committees fixed upon building up necessary reserves, the Treasury upon industrial capacity, trade, and cost.

In April 1936, the Cabinet envisaged external affairs above all when it spoke of the need for decisions on "major policy." A year later, references to policy connoted the strategic roles of the Services and the economic resources of the nation as much as foreign policy. Policy now meant war in the future as well as diplomacy in the present. This change in meaning was a sign, if not a cause, of the increasing vulnerability of the Foreign Office—and of deterrence as a means of foreign policy—to pressures from other quarters.

The Service staffs viewed war as too serious a business for diplomats. They pressured the Foreign Office to redirect Britain's foreign policy, and at the same time they limited its influence on strategic planning. The Chiefs of Staff prevented the DP(P) from reading alarming evidence of the scale of German rearmament, intelligence which corroborated and drew upon that of the Foreign Office. By not consulting the Foreign Office for a new political section in the revised report on war with Germany, the Deputy Chiefs of Staff kept diplomatic experts from relating plans for a future war to the Office's political assumptions of the present.

[294]

To military experts, the present was an anachronism and ad hoc reporting a nuisance. Urgencies must be replaced by long-term planning, and foreign policy changed so as to reduce the current number of commitments and dangers. To diplomats, the present was reality, and strategic planners could not escape it by imagining wars at future dates that the Services presumed diplomacy would buy. Some diplomats doubted Britain could count on at least two more years of peace to plan for a European war. Others wondered why the Service staffs "waste their time in making plans against 'a war arising out of German aggression in 1939' when a war arising out of Italian action is a much more immediate if less dangerous possibility."[105]

By weakening the connection between war plans and the present international situation, the DCOS and COS reduced the deterrent potential of operational planning while Britain rearmed. In their view, both current weakness and future contingencies required Britain to avoid diplomatic confrontations and abjure threats of force. The outbreak of war during the interval of rearming to prevent it would mark the failure of foreign policy, not the fault of military planning. These attitudes impressed the Cabinet and increased the burden on the Foreign Office to buy time through conciliation, without demanding substantial concessions from the dictators in return, and without making deterrent threats backed by insufficient force to win a conflict.

The Spanish Civil War helped prolong instability in the Mediterranean, no new security pact replaced the Locarno Treaty in Western Europe, and British leaders privately admitted that their nation's foreign policy had reached a dead end with nothing to show for European reconciliation. Where would the next crisis occur, and how could Britain either prevent this or keep it from escalating? What fronts and dates should preface plans for war? What levels of strength should the Service programs attain in how many years? Was time on the side of Britain or its enemies? For examining these questions, the influence of the Service staffs drew at least even with that of the Foreign Office as ministers considered strategic studies and the Army's role from December 1936 to May 1937. The Foreign Office and the Services continued to dispute the boundary between their two estates, at times acting as if both the meaning and substance of policy depended largely on the outcome of bilateral contests between diplomatic and military points of view. Their interdepartmental rivalry intensified at the same time that Chamberlain knew he would soon succeed Baldwin.

[105] G. G. Fitzmaurice (legal adviser) minute on COS 549 (see note 80 above), 28 May, A3587/448/45, FO 371/20666.

Chamberlain had a coherent and "objective" scheme that would clarify the meaning of policy and eliminate inconsistencies among its component parts. As both foreign policy and strategy were subsumed under broader headings of policy, Chamberlain upheld financial premises against what he viewed as the "interested" biases of other departments. Because of Britain's limited resources, he would preserve the doctrine of normal trade, reduce the number of potential enemies through conciliation accompanied by sufficient rearmament to get their attention without provoking them, concentrate on air power, expect the Foreign Office to manufacture time past 1939, and use deterrence as an instrument of self-defense rather than coercive diplomacy or European security. How much could Britain pay for defense and by when? To Chamberlain, this was the essential "politico-strategical" question, and he was determined that the machinery of policy work toward his orderly answer.

[7]

From Baldwin to
Chamberlain

By the spring of 1937, the failures of decisionmaking by committee overshadowed its achievements. Foreign policy neither reduced the number of Britain's potential enemies nor guaranteed enough time for the nation to rearm. Rearmament programs and war plans did not reconcile strategy and cost or inter-Service differences. The preservation of various options for applying deterrence lacked a firm consensus on how to use them. To an increasing number of ministers and experts, these failures were the result of disorder in London as much as disquiet in world affairs. To them, unsolved puzzles of policy proved the inadequacies of coordination and summoned up the imagined virtues of coherence.

The problem of distinguishing between political and military points of view, habitually faced by experts in the Foreign Office and the Service departments, spread out into ministerial discussions. So did the use of inclusive terms such as "military policy," "war policy," "general policy," and "complete picture." The Cabinet and its committees did not channel this language into a comprehensive redefinition of policy or reconciliation of its major components. The demise of the Defence Requirements Committee ended the chance that this strong coalition of experts would have pressed the Government to do so. The Foreign Policy Committee concentrated on particular questions as they arose. The Defence Policy and Requirements Committee usually confined itself to the matter of supply, but now and then discussed broader subjects. The Committee of Imperial Defence, meeting more frequently than usual after Inskip took the chair, examined some strategic topics having repercussions on foreign policy. The Defence Plans (Policy) Committee, appointed in February, discussed the COS war plan for Germany, the Army's role, and the Admiralty's proposed new naval standard, all of which had implications for foreign policy and finance. Together, these committees correlated areas of policy more often than had normally been the case in long-term planning. Four committees, however, now covered the terms of reference originally given to the DPR alone in July 1935. Their overlapping agendas and delays caused confusion even as their language denoted coherence.

The equilibrium among departments and their respective agendas changed markedly in favor of the Treasury. Interdepartmental conflict increased, aggravated by international unrest, strategic risks, chronological worries, and financial constraints. The Foreign Office lost stature because of drift, internal discord, and Vansittart's declining influence even among his former colleagues on the DRC. In the eyes of Eden and others, Vansittart's dogmatic representation of one school of thought in the Foreign Office became a liability for the Office itself. The Chiefs of Staff were fed up with a foreign policy of guessing coupled with predictions of war no later than 1939. They outmaneuvered the Foreign Office in warning against risks, extended deterrence, and premature hunches about German intentions. Both constituencies blurred their traditional, bipolar distinction between political and military spheres of competence.

The emerging winner in the struggle over the meaning, substance, and tempo of policy was the Treasury. The escalating cost of rearmament prompted Chamberlain and the Treasury to conjure up great magic for the year 1942—with more powers over national policy than either the year or the Treasury had hitherto enjoyed. The Treasury launched a five-year program of borrowing for defense and extended the political boundaries of Treasury control while Chamberlain sought to integrate the subdivisions of policy around the central principle of finance. Rearmament, and thus also foreign policy and deterrence, must be limited by what military strength Britain could afford to produce before 1942 and to maintain thereafter. The Government should reduce Britain's international commitments, define its vital interests so as to avoid war over threats to other nations, and limit its military liability on the Continent. Britain should assume a peaceful interval of rearmament until 1942, and then bet on the combined deterrent capability of air power and economic stability. Britain would have more time than the Foreign Office expected, to prepare a more insular and less flexible strategy of deterrence than the DRC and War Office had proposed, at lower cost than the Services would request. Preventing the next war could be done more economically than preparing to fight it.

Chamberlain rode toward the premiership on a wave of anticipation caused as much by the unusual conjunction of problems of national policy early in 1937 as by the prospect of having an energetic new leader at No. 10 Downing Street. Unlike Baldwin, Chamberlain promised to impart both efficiency and order to British policy at a time when preparations for war threatened to draw the country farther away from peacetime habits of mind. He would require the Foreign Office to discard drift for conciliation and the Services to curb their profligacy. He would expect Inskip and Hankey to reconcile inter-Service conflicts over supply, strategy, and combined operations, still unremedied in spite of improvements in the coordinating machinery. In a committee system that tolerated contradictions, Chamberlain made progress on all of these issues by adroitly using the machinery, his authority as chancellor, his small group of ministerial allies, and his prerogatives as heir apparent. His personality, policies, and rational method of decisionmaking all portended a strong prime ministership that would institutionalize coherence, using conciliation to avoid war until 1942 while preparing enough military force to deter any remaining enemies after that date.

CABINET, FOREIGN OFFICE, AND SERVICES

In July 1936, at the urging of Chamberlain, Baldwin agreed to meet a delegation of Conservative critics of his Government, including Churchill, Austen Chamberlain, Leo Amery, and Lord Salisbury. Although Churchill did not "consider war with Germany inevitable," he thought concerted rearmament would make it "much less likely." Baldwin stated that public opinion in a democracy learned only "by butting their heads against a brick wall. " He was fully behind rearmament but agreed with his chancellor not to allow it to upset normal trade. His heart would not break if Hitler moved east, and if it came to fighting in Europe, he hoped "to see the Bolshies and Nazis doing it."[1]

Baldwin neither persuaded these critics to join a "united front" with the Government nor provided much leadership in the Cabinet. Chamberlain was "horrified" when Baldwin told him that the Cabinet would not have to take any decisions on policy in July because the League Assembly had adjourned. In October, Wigram thought the prime minister might have awakened from three months of dozing (the length of his convalescent absence from London), and indeed Baldwin saw the parliamentary delegation again in November.[2] His health was poor, his

[1] Correspondence and minutes of meetings (28 and 29 July), PREM 1/193, and CAB 21/437–38; also Cab 50(36), 6 July, CAB 23/85, and Chamberlain diary, 5 July, Chamberlain Papers, NC 2/23a.
[2] Chamberlain diary, 11 July, Chamberlain Papers, NC 2/23a; Wigram to Phipps, 29 October, Phipps Papers, 2/25; record of meeting of 23 November, PREM 1/193. Eden later

nerves frayed. The crisis over King Edward VIII's romance with Mrs. Simpson and his abdication (on 10–11 December) left Baldwin little time for international politics. "'I hope that you will not try to trouble me too much with foreign affairs just now,'" he told Eden in October during their first conversation in three months, and Eden "found this an astonishing doctrine."[3] Nor did Baldwin want to be bothered after the abdication, although he chaired the FPC and DP(P). Marking time until his retirement, he drew Hoare's reproof for blithe passivity, by which Hoare characterized more than the last few months of his premiership.[4]

German rearmament; the search for a new Locarno agreement; the failure of collective security in the Ethiopian war; the international and ideological repercussions of civil war in Spain; the role of the British Army in a European war: these issues caused the Cabinet (and a few informal meetings of small groups of ministers) to discuss general foreign policy and its relationship to defense more often than had been the case before the Rhineland crisis. Still, the Cabinet did not reconcile Eden's warning about a possible challenge from Germany in 1937, his argument for forcibly resisting Italy in the western Mediterranean, Inskip's reminder that the Services had been authorized early in 1936 to work on three-to-five-year programs, and Chamberlain's dictum that the tempo and goals of rearmament were fundamentally economic questions. The Cabinet relied on four major committees to make recommendations on these large questions of policy: the Cabinet Committee on Foreign Policy; the Defence Policy and Requirements Committee; the Committee of Imperial Defence; and the Defence Plans (Policy) Committee. None of these committees achieved the reconciliation of policy that eluded the Cabinet.

In July, the FPC was expanded from eight to twelve members with the addition of the Colonial Secretary (William Ormsby-Gore), president of the Board of Trade (Runciman), First Lord of the Admiralty (Hoare), and Dominions Secretary (Malcolm MacDonald). The FPC reconvened on 15 July, not to follow up on its discussion of collective

---

refuted the impression given by the press that Baldwin kept in close touch with him while absent from London; *Dictators*, pp. 454–55. On Baldwin's meetings of July and November with the delegation: Middlemas and Barnes, *Baldwin*, pp. 946–48, 955, 969; Gilbert, *Churchill*, chap. 38 and pp. 803–6; Leopold S. Amery, *My Political Life*, vol. 3: *The Unforgiving Years* (London, 1955), pp. 197–98; Dennis, *Decision by Default*, pp. 69–71. Before the November meeting, Amery talked with Hoare, "who entirely shares my view about the futility of talking about using our Army on the Continent"; diary, 23 November, in *Empire at Bay*, p. 430.

[3] Avon, *Dictators*, pp. 460–61.

[4] Hoare to Chamberlain, 17 March 1937, Templewood Papers. On Fisher's exasperation with Baldwin and the Cabinet, see O'Halpin, *Head of the Civil Service*, p. 218.

security on 30 April, but in response to recent Cabinet discussion of a proposed meeting of the Locarno powers. Including this meeting, the FPC sat ten times from July 1936 to May 1937, with a seven-month hiatus between the meetings of 25 August and 10 March 1937. The Cabinet followed the committee's advice on policy toward Germany, the proposed five-power conference, reform of the League of Nations, and the Spanish Civil War. The committee's agendas listed these issues separately. The FPC did not evaluate foreign policy as a whole, nor did it stretch its terms of reference to correlate external affairs, rearmament, and strategic plans.[5]

Chaired by Inskip as the prime minister's deputy, the DPR included nine other ministers, Lord Weir, and the COS as expert advisers.[6] Also present at most meetings after the reorganization of March 1936 were Vansittart, the chairman of the Supply Board (Sir Arthur Robinson), representatives of the supply divisions of the Service departments, and, starting in October, the Director General of Munitions Production (Vice Admiral Sir Harold Brown) in place of the Master General of Ordnance (Major General Sir Hugh Elles). The DPR met eighteen times from June 1936 to May 1937, adjourning for the months of August and September. Most of its work dealt with progress and priority regarding supply, industry, and labor. Occasionally, the DPR aired defense policy broadly, discussing, for example, the interconnection of foreign policy, deterrence, time, supply, and cost (11 June); the "political and priority issues" raised by the War Office's plans for the organization and equipment of the Army (26 November); and the RAF's new plan for expansion, Scheme H, in relation to assumptions about German air strength by 1939 (4 and 19 February 1937). At these meetings, the DPR reaffirmed the rearmament policy approved in March, referred the Army question to the Cabinet, and recommended Cabinet approval of a modified Scheme H.

Under Inskip's chairmanship, the CID held fifteen meetings during this period, with a holiday break from 30 July to 8 October. Judged by the number of meetings (there had been only five in all of 1935) and the topics covered, the CID was becoming more than a clearing house for

---

[5] In July, Hankey recommended the amalgamation of the FPC and Cabinet Committee on Germany (which had not met after 17 February). The Colonial Secretary and president of the Board of Trade had served on the latter; Monsell had not, but Hankey thought Hoare should join the FPC because of his having recently been Foreign Secretary; Hankey to Baldwin, 8 July, CAB 27/599; Cab 51(36), 9 July, CAB 23/85. M. MacDonald joined the FPC on 27 July.

[6] The other ministers on the DPR: Lord President (R. MacDonald), Home Secretary (Simon), Service ministers (Hoare, Duff Cooper, Swinton), Labour (Brown), chancellor (Chamberlain), Foreign Secretary (Eden), and president of the Board of Trade (Runciman).

its large network of subcommittees. The CID approved the planning assumption of a German knockout blow from the air at the start of war (29 October 1936); discussed supply for the Army in relation to peace-time finance and wartime use (19 November and 10 December); recommended a change in the policy toward Italy that governed defense expenditure in the Mediterranean (11 February); approved the COS recommendation for a small ministerial committee to examine war plans with regard to Government policy (11 February); and revised the COS "Review of Imperial Defence" (11 and 25 February). The debate over the Army's role moved up to the Cabinet. The change in Mediterranean policy, approved by the Cabinet, sought to reconcile the respective concerns of the Foreign Office, Services, and Treasury, but the vagueness of the new formula left uncertain the relative priority among these. Having compared the political and military aspects of the Imperial Defence Review, the CID adopted a procedural compromise that preserved both points of view without resolving them.

The establishment of the DP(P) in February 1937 had been foreshadowed in the original terms of reference of the DPR in July 1935 (the DPR should ensure that "the plans and preparations" of committees and departments were "consistent with our general defensive policy"), and in the DPR's evolution into a sort of "war committee" during the Mediterranean crisis.[7] Now, the DPR no longer had these tasks, the CID did not assimilate them, and the completion of the war plan for Germany by the Chiefs of Staff made the deliberations of the DP(P) seem both necessary and timely. Two months after its formation, the DP(P)—with the Chiefs of Staff attending as expert advisers—examined and approved this war plan in the context of foreign policy as well as military strategy. Consonant with its terms of reference, the DP(P)'s agenda soon expanded beyond war plans to include the rearmament programs of two of the Services. Whereas the DPR had handled new expansion plans for the RAF, the DP(P) assumed responsibility for debating the Army's role and the Admiralty's proposed new standard of naval strength. While the ministers of these two Services wanted Cabinet approval of military and naval policy so their staffs could proceed with plans, Chamberlain insisted that careful estimates of cost must precede such major political decisions.

In early 1937, four committees were doing the work that one (the DPR) had been assigned in July 1935. Eight ministers sat on all three defense committees—prime minister, Minister for Coordination, chancellor, Home Secretary, Foreign Secretary, and Service ministers; six of these (not the Secretaries of State for War and Air) were also members

---

[7] For discussion of the DPR, see chapter 1; for the DP(P), see chapter 6.

of the Foreign Policy Committee. Taken together, the agendas and discussions of these committees evidence increasing interaction among the major components of national policy, thanks partly to the simultaneity of these issues and partly to Chamberlain's demand that they be considered in relation to each other. On the other hand, the overlapping agendas of the DPR, CID, and DP(P) resulted as much from confusion and uncertainty of purpose as from coordination of effort. No one could say for sure whether the DPR was a subcommittee of the CID or the Cabinet. Referrals to and from committees traced irregular patterns. Quite apart from the perennial pause for recreation during August and September (interrupted only by one meeting of the Cabinet and one of the FPC), committees procrastinated, for reasons not always attributable to homework, departmental self-interest, or normal procedure. The FPC sometimes took a long-term view, but usually reacted to exigencies. No single committee looked regularly at the complete picture.

The Cabinet and FPC generally supported Eden's recommendations on Germany, although without strongly defending the Foreign Office against the Chiefs of Staff over staff talks, Belgium's place in a new Locarno agreement, and the fate of Central and Eastern Europe. The Cabinet and FPC were more willing than Eden—and Eden was readier than Vansittart—to concede on these issues, all of which helped chart the extent of British commitments and deterrence in Europe, if doing so might improve the chances of reaching a settlement with Germany.[8] Differences between Eden and his ministerial colleagues were more pronounced regarding the Mediterranean, with the Cabinet rejecting Eden's idea of checking Mussolini and Hitler with a more aggressive policy toward their intervention in the Spanish Civil War.

Some cabinet members—notably Hoare—agreed with Sir Warren Fisher that Eden was weak, and held the Foreign Secretary responsible for drift, risk, and failure in British foreign policy. They did not know how much Eden's private life depressed him, nor how much he regretted that three other members of the FPC—MacDonald, Simon, and Hoare—had been Foreign Secretaries. One of these, Hoare, told Chamberlain that he "found it difficult to listen to others talking on subjects on which he felt he knew more than they did." Chamberlain and Eden were, in Eden's words, "closer to each other than to any

---

[8] Vansittart thought that support for a "good and lasting" agreement with Germany was potentially greater in the Cabinet than in Cabinet committees. He regretted that his memorandum of December 1936 (see chapter 6, note 54) was not circulated to the Cabinet "and therefore did not reach some at least of your colleagues . . . who might have benefited by it to your advantage in dealing with them." Vansittart to Eden, 3 July 1937, Vansittart Papers, 2/14.

other member of the Government." Although surprised by Chamberlain's speech of June 1936 regarding sanctions against Italy, Eden welcomed the chancellor's determination of the following spring to "take more interest in foreign policy" than Baldwin had done, and "looked forward to working with a Prime Minister who would give his Foreign Secretary energetic backing." To Swinton and others on the Cabinet, however, Chamberlain had taken Eden's measure, challenged his authority, and shown a superior grasp of the interrelationship of foreign policy, defense, and economics.[9]

To Eden's vulnerabilities in the Cabinet must be added the deepening dissension in the Foreign Office. Officials there continued to disagree over timing, concessions, and conditions in negotiating with Germany, and over whether to conciliate or coerce Mussolini. The Foreign Office's position on Germany was especially susceptible to personality conflicts and changes in personnel. Vansittart wavered between hopes that German "moderates" would eventually persuade Hitler to negotiate a general and durable agreement, and fears that Germany would never want such a European settlement. He advocated a Field Force of at least seventeen divisions, but his idea of a major continental commitment was challenged by others inside the Office. Eden pointed out that the question was "how to make the best use of our resources," and he did not press for a settlement of the debate over the Army's role as energetically as Vansittart begged him to. Strang found Inskip's conclusion logical and probably inescapable: Britain could not afford to maintain a large peacetime Army as well as a powerful Navy and Air Force.[10]

Eden lacked confidence in Vansittart, whose nervousness and extreme views might make potential enemies " 'think the more of us as potential victims.' " Fisher and Chamberlain agreed with Eden that Vansittart must go, but they opposed Eden's choice of Cadogan to succeed him. Fisher thought Vansittart's trip to Berlin in August "must inevitably *postpone* the reform of the F.O." in any case, for Berlin would take a negative view of his departure so soon after he had gotten on good personal terms with Nazi leaders. No one remarked upon the

[9] Fisher to Chamberlain, 15 September 1936, and Chamberlain diary, 25 April 1937, Chamberlain Papers, NC 7/11/29/9, 2/24a. For Eden's depression over his private life, see Rhodes James, *Anthony Eden*, pp. 171–72. On Eden and the Cabinet: Avon, *Dictators*, pp. 433–35, 501–2; Carlton, *Eden*, pp. 84–86, 100–101; Swinton, *Sixty Years*, p. 166.

[10] Vansittart and Eden minutes, 18 and 29 December 1936, C9096/6761/62, FO 371/19882; Vansittart minute, 8 January 1937, C205/205/62, FO 371/20701. On 11 January (latter file), Eden noted that he was "as anxious as . . . Vansittart to see this controversy ended," but the minutes of the Cabinet and DP(P) indicate that Eden did not press hard for a solution or for a Field Force as large as Vansittart desired. Strang minute, 11 February, C1050/928/18, FO 371/20746.

contradiction between Eden's argument for removing Vansittart from the Foreign Office and Fisher's for at least temporarily keeping him there, nor did anyone comment upon the irony that this Germanophobe might have won admirers in the Reich Chancery. Vansittart refused Eden's offer of the ambassadorship in Paris and was determined to remain in London because, as he told Eden, he was "convinced that the next two years will be very difficult in Foreign Affairs in *internal* politics."[11]

Vansittart's effectiveness in these politics eroded further. Ralph Wigram's death late in December was a severe blow. Wigram had been Vansittart's close confederate, manipulating Foreign Office procedures so as to aggrandize business regarding Germany and underscore his own views. Hankey's son, who had worked under Wigram, praised him as "an incredible chief—slave-driving, exacting, generous to a degree over minor questions, absolutely reckless in the liberties he took with instructions he thought wrong (though I never knew him fail to pull it off!), unlimited guts in backing you up."[12] William Strang, the new head of the central department who had studied at University College London and the Sorbonne before the war, held a more orthodox view of administration and a more open mind on negotiating with Germany so as to reduce the amount of guessing left to Hitler. In April 1937, Phipps happily left Berlin for the ambassadorship that Vansittart had declined, and relations between the two men had cooled. Soon after Phipps's departure, Sir Nevile Henderson arrived at the Berlin Embassy, feeling that he "had been specially selected by Providence with the definite mission of . . . helping to preserve the peace of the world." Vansittart also had something to do with this selection, but soon regretted it.[13]

Cadogan's hostility toward Vansittart ranged from reasonable criticism to inordinate contempt. An Old Etonian (like Eden and Vansittart), Cadogan had read history at Balliol College, Oxford, entered the Diplomatic Service in 1908, and been described by Sir Eyre Crowe after the war as "the best man in the Office." Cadogan faulted Eden for

[11] Fisher to Chamberlain, 15 September 1936, Chamberlain Papers, NC 7/11/29/9; Eden to Baldwin, 27 December, Baldwin Papers; Harvey, *Diplomatic Diaries*, pp. 22, 44; Rhodes James, *Anthony Eden*, p. 159; Rose, *Vansittart*, pp. 200–201; Middlemas, *Diplomacy of Illusion*, pp. 77–78; O'Halpin, *Head of the Civil Service*, pp. 250–52.

[12] Robin Hankey (First Secretary at the British Embassy in Warsaw) to Strang, 21 January 1937, Strang Papers (Churchill College, Cambridge), 4/1. See also Jones, *Diary*, p. 299; Lawford, *Bound for Diplomacy*, pp. 256, 277–79.

[13] Sir Nevile Henderson, *Failure of a Mission: Berlin, 1937–1939* (New York, 1940), p. 3; Middlemas, *Diplomacy of Illusion*, pp. 73–74; Rose, *Vansittart*, pp. 202–3. Hankey put in a good word to Eden on Phipps's behalf; Hankey to Phipps, 23 December 1936, 2 and 21 January 1937, Phipps Papers, 3/3.

caring too much what the opposition press wrote, and he feared that the Foreign Secretary had "lost a bit of his nerve."[14] But Cadogan indicted Vansittart for the "bankrupt" policy that was "rushing us to disaster." Vansittart wanted to "keep Germany guessing," but "all the guessing that's been done for the past 3 years has been done by *us*," and Britain had "left the *whole* initiative" to Germany. The prospective visit of the Germanophile Lord Lothian to Berlin to interview Hitler made Vansittart "very blue," but Cadogan did not regard this sort of personal diplomacy as "worse than Van's policy of doing *nothing*." Vansittart danced "literary hornpipes" in his memoranda, "bring[ing] discredit on the Office." In October 1936, having officially succeeded Sir Victor Wellesley as Deputy Under-Secretary, Cadogan found the Foreign Office a "mess of destroyed causes and smug, complacent incompetence." In April 1937, he complained that Sargent carried on Wigram's work and "Van laps it up." Cadogan had decided that his loyalty to the Foreign Office was less important than his duty to show how Britain's present policy did not "point to any solution or appeasement."[15]

The external effects of these internal conflicts were twofold. First, although no one in the Foreign Office denied the advantage of negotiating from a position of military strength, Cadogan and Strang (and O'Malley) challenged Vansittart's thesis that Britain could manufacture time for rearmament by keeping Germany guessing. They thought Britain should bring Germany into negotiations for a settlement— sooner than Vansittart judged wise, and willing to offer particular concessions as part of a settlement that might not be as general as he had in mind. Second, the stature of the Foreign Office was in question. As played by Vansittart and Wigram, playing for time had become to Cadogan an embarrassing symptom of his department's ineptitude, and Whitehall knew that the Foreign Office was divided over policy toward both Germany and Italy. The Foreign Office had rarely been so exposed to mediation, intrusion, and contradiction by those outside it who considered foreign policy fair game among the subspecies of general policy.

The Service staffs, exasperated that foreign policy kept them guessing, launched a campaign to outflank the Foreign Office. Just as Colonel Adam had wished, the Joint Planning Committee used its "strategical review" of July 1936 to recommend appeasing Germany and

[14] Cadogan diary, 20 August 1936, Cadogan Papers, 1/4; family background and early career in Dilks, *Cadogan*, pp. 1–5.

[15] Cadogan diary, 11 and 24 September, 15 October, 3 November 1936, 26 and 28 April, 24 May 1937; Cadogan Papers, 1/5,6; some of these entries quoted in Dilks, *Cadogan*, pp. 13–14.

limiting Britain's liabilities.[16] Similarly, the JPC and COS took every opportunity to add matters of policy to their "military point of view" in papers regarding Germany and a new Locarno agreement, Italy, the Spanish Civil War, and the Mediterranean. The reactions of the Foreign Office to this challenge mixed genuine desire for cooperation with strong resentment of the Services' political suppositions and territorial presumptuousness.

Of the JPC's review, Wigram minuted that writing reports of this kind was "not really [the] business" of the Service staffs. Sargent recalled that the Foreign Office had originally asked for an answer to the "technical question" of European military strengths; instead, the JPC presented "an analysis of British policy, British interests, and British capacity of defence throughout the world."[17] In November, Wigram wished that the Chiefs of Staff would "keep to their proper functions" rather than give advice on political aspects of the proposed five-power conference, but Sargent doubted that the Foreign Office could keep the COS "from being more interested in politics than in strategy." Vansittart frowned upon this "muddle-headed incursion" of the military experts, but did not "want to warn these gentlemen off politics altogether," for he had often trod on their ground and would continue doing so.[18] When the Admiralty requested the Foreign Office's participation in an interdepartmental study of air warfare in the Spanish Civil War, Vansittart noted, "On general grounds I am anxious—and have always been—to keep the F.O. in close contact with defence measures or information and should be loath to discourage our collaboration with the Service Departments." The Foreign Office and Service departments arranged for the Foreign Office to revise and centralize the political sections of the Services' intelligence reports, just as the Industrial Intelligence Centre now did for the economic sections. The point, in Lawrence Collier's view, was to place the writing of such political papers into the hands "of our own people, who are alone really competent to do it." He saw "no logical reason why [the Service departments] should expect to be able to write accurately about foreign politics, any more than we can expect to write accurately about gunnery."[19]

[16] JPC review, 3 July, CAB 53/28. Adam: see chapter 5 and note 100 (Adam to Harris, 9 May 1936, CAB 21/441).

[17] Wigram and Sargent minutes, 24 and 31 July, C5356/4/18, FO 371/19910; Sargent to Hankey, 15 August, CAB 21/441.

[18] Wigram, Sargent, and Vansittart minutes, 27 November, FO 371/C8479/C8480/270/4. The COS countered that they were "surely in the best position to gauge the reactions of their opposite numbers in Germany" if Britain held staff talks with Belgium and France; Ismay to Inskip, 9 December, CAB 53/6.

[19] Vansittart minute, 1 April 1937, W5432/5432/41, FO 371/21398; Foreign Office minutes, June 1937 (including Collier's of 24 June), W5789/531/50, FO 371/21225. Ashton-

Both the Foreign Office and Service staffs recognized that the distinction between political and military (or technical) considerations could be misleading. Wigram thought British "military strategy" in a Central European war was "more or less equivalent to political necessity,"[20] and the Chiefs of Staff described some issues as "politico-strategical." In spite of these signs that the prospect of war obscured the line between policy and strategy, the Foreign Office and the Services continued to use "political" and "military" to demarcate their respective jurisdictions as they submitted their views independently on an expanding array of interdependent issues.

The core of conflict between the Services and Foreign Office was this dilemma: what policies and plans should be adopted now to give Britain the best chance of preventing or winning a war that might break out as early as 1937 or perhaps later than 1942? The Services wanted diplomacy to provide a peaceful period in which their staffs, untroubled by commitments and crises that jeopardized British security, could develop reserves and plans for war. The Foreign Office could not promise such a tranquil interval, particularly if British rearmament neither restrained the dictators nor reassured their potential victims.

The disparity between these two positions was implicit in the decision of Hankey and the DCOS to eliminate the political section from the JPC's draft paper on war with Germany and to ignore the Foreign Office in revising the paper because of the obsolescence of any current "political appreciation" regarding the future.[21] The assessment of intelligence and the preparation of war plans could adhere to either of these perceptions of time: Germany would not be ready for war by 1939, and Italy was not a probable enemy (COS); Hitler might upset the European status quo before 1939, and Mussolini might do so even earlier in the Mediterranean (Foreign Office).

Internally divided and unsure about how to conciliate and deter in the short run, the Foreign Office faltered as the Services disclosed cracks in existing policy and demanded new guidelines for long-term

---

Gwatkin praised the work of the IIC; Desmond Morton was "always in close touch with the F.O."; minute of 30 July, W14500/137/50, FO 371/21218 (see also chapter 6, note 24). Hinsley maintains that the FPC was hampered by the lack of "interdepartmental coordination of intelligence at the lower level"; *British Intelligence*, p. 74. This is an important point about a major Cabinet committee, but it may overstate both the FPC's interest in correlating intelligence and the lack of interdepartmental coordination.

[20] Wigram minute, 24 July, C5356/4/18, FO 371/19910.

[21] In his discussion of the "contribution of strategic planning to appeasement," Murray faults the JPC and COS for giving "worst case hypotheses" to ministers, and states that "there was almost no cooperation between the Foreign Office and the military services in the drawing up of strategic surveys"; *Change in the European Balance of Power*, pp. 62–63. The first of these indictments is generally correct, the second is exaggerated, and neither takes into account the problem of timing.

planning. Yet the Services and Foreign Office together were vulnerable to several charges of the kind that Chamberlain would certainly exploit. Coordination had not produced agreement about timetables and deterrence. Concurrence between the Foreign Office and COS on the Army's continental commitment was superficial, and their political and strategic assumptions were questionable. Finally, no matter how much the Foreign Office and Services might agree, their combined territory did not constitute the whole of "major policy," decisions on which required more than the reconciliation of their respective positions.

Treasury Control and the Coherence of Policy

Certain that war was too serious a business for generals and diplomats, Chamberlain and the Treasury regarded "military policy" and "politico-strategical" questions as parts of a larger domain in which economic considerations must clarify alternatives and determine choices. Exploiting the plural connotations of policy, the Treasury's notion of control encompassed strategy and foreign policy as well as expenditure, and pushed the Government closer toward Chamberlain's conceptions of limited deterrence and extended time.

In July 1936, Sir Edward Bridges warned that the total expenditure on defense over the next few years would be "many millions in excess of the figures contemplated when the D.R.C. report was approved by the Cabinet." J. A. N. Barlow complained that Treasury control was "rapidly becoming a mere form." Thanks to the prospect of a defense loan and "the assumption of the imminence of a war next month or next year," the Services had begun to believe that they could ask for money "in unlimited quantities." Proposals for increases in social services could also be expected, and "once adopted they are almost impossible to reduce or eliminate." Fisher declared that the Treasury Inter-Service Committee must not "be treated as a farce."[22]

The forecast grew even more frightening. In November, Chamberlain informed the Cabinet that costs were "mounting at a giddy rate" far beyond the estimate of £400 million for programs approved by the Cabinet the previous February. Bridges observed that defense policy had entered a "new stage," and the Government might soon have "to revise the priorities and coordination of the whole scheme, by reference to two basic facts. (1) Our fundamental defence needs. (2) What can be achieved in the next few years, having regard to our

---

[22] Bridges, Barlow, and Fisher minutes, 22–27 July, and Bridges minute, 20 October, T 161/841.

resources in labour, materials and industrial organisation." The situation, Bridges wrote in January 1937, was "highly abnormal." The Service departments had requested £289.5 million in their original estimates for 1937, compared to expenditures of about £190 million in 1936 (this latter sum included supplementary estimates and exceeded the figures of £158 million in original estimates plus £20 million in supplementaries in Chamberlain's budget of April 1936). Although the Treasury and chancellor had customary means of regulating both original and supplementary estimates, "control over most Defence expenditure is extremely slight."[23]

Recognizing that annual routines were no longer adequate, yet haunted by nightmares of where long-term financing might lead, Treasury officials and Chamberlain devised means to increase both spending and Treasury control. Since revenue alone would not cover the authorized Service programs (raising taxes to that degree was out of the question), the Treasury prepared a five-year plan for borrowing £400 million at £80 million annually. In February 1937, Hopkins described the forthcoming Defence Loans Bill as "extremely important and quite unprecedented in this country." The Cabinet approved Chamberlain's recommendation that disclosing in the White Paper on Defence the total sum needed over the next five years—£1,500 million—would wake up the country to the necessary costs and show Europe "how determined we were to recondition our armaments."[24] In the House of Commons, the Government easily overcame Clement Attlee's accusation from the left that the country was being organized " 'permanently on a war basis.' "[25]

Reaction from the right to financing the loan proved more troublesome. Having failed to win the Bank of England's support for a large loan that would alarm the City unless accompanied by some reduction of financial risk, Chamberlain proposed the National Defence Con-

---

[23] Chamberlain at Cab 63(36), 4 November, CAB 23/86. Bridges minute, 14 January, T 161/783. On the Service Estimates for 1937, see also minutes by Bridges (27 November), Hopkins (7 December), and others in early 1937, T 171/332; Shay, *British Rearmament*, pp. 142–43.

[24] Hopkins minute, 4 February, T 160/688; Cab 7(37), 10 February, CAB 23/87. Other sources on borrowing: minutes by Phillips (27 November 1936) and Hopkins (9 January, 28 February, 8 March 1937), T 160/688; by Hopkins and Chamberlain (5 February 1937), T 172/1853; Peden, *British Rearmament and Treasury*, pp. 78–79; Shay, *British Rearmament*, pp. 144–47; Hancock and Gowing, *War Economy*, pp. 68–69; Meyers, *Britische Sicherheitspolitik*, pp. 409–10. On the views of the Committee on Economic Information (a subcommittee of the Economic Advisory Council) and its ties with the Treasury, see Susan Howson and Donald Winch, *The Economic Advisory Council, 1930–1939* (Cambridge, 1977), pp. 108–9, 141–45, 351.

[25] Middlemas and Barnes, *Baldwin*, pp. 1029–33.

tribution (NDC). As he explained to Churchill, profits on manufacturing arms were not a vice (unless the armaments were used "for aggressive purposes"); the NDC presumed that *"increases* of profits in industry . . . are the fairest source from which to look for our requirements."[26] But the combined pressure of the City, industry, and his own party's Finance Committee forced a disappointed Chamberlain to withdraw his version of the NDC shortly after moving to No. 10 Downing Street.[27] Late in June, a revised NDC that simply taxed profits rather than their increase won the approval of business and the Government's parliamentary majority.

The Treasury was willing to lose innocence through borrowing if it could preserve self-respect by limiting expenditure. Chamberlain saw borrowing not merely as an unfortunate necessity; it was also a salutary opportunity to "curb the present enthusiasm" of the Services for extravagant proposals and teach them that "there are limits to the amount of money at their disposal."[28] How to enforce this lesson was the subject of extensive study in the Treasury from January to June 1937. Treasury officials proceeded, in Hopkins's words, "on the assumption that we shall not, and cannot afford to, allow ourselves to slip quietly into American or French budgetary methods but shall strive, at any rate till disaster overwhelms us, to keep within the limits of decent finance."[29]

Their work culminated in the paper of 25 June, "Defence Expenditure," by Sir John Simon, Chamberlain's successor at the Treasury. If trade and prosperity did not suffer setbacks, the sum of £1,500 million could be available for defense over the next five years (1937/38 to 1941/42), £400 million in borrowed money and the rest in revenue. He anticipated "staggering" costs to maintain the force levels already approved. Since Cabinet and Treasury control were in jeopardy, he recommended that the Service departments and Minister for Coordination estimate costs for completing and maintaining the authorized programs. The Treasury should examine these estimates and indicate how much money it thought could be spent. The DPR should then "determine priorities between conflicting claims and recommend to the Cabinet maxima for the expenditure by each Department year by year

---

[26] Chamberlain to Churchill, 6 May, Chamberlain Papers, NC 7/9/1937. On the NDC, see Peden, *British Rearmament and Treasury,* pp. 87–88; Shay, *British Rearmament,* pp. 147–55.

[27] Chamberlain diary, 21, 29 April, 27 May 1937, Chamberlain Papers, NC 2/24a.

[28] Chamberlain minute, 5 February 1937, T 172/1853; Chamberlain to Hilda, 25 April, Chamberlain Papers, NC 18/1/1003.

[29] Hopkins minute, 14 May, T 161/783.

during the period of the programme, such maxima not to be exceeded except by further authority." While this review was under way, "decisions on new projects of major importance should be postponed."[30]

A powerful maneuver to increase Treasury control, Simon's memorandum combined financial assumptions and political tactics in three rules for rationing defense spending. First, the five-year total of expenditure must conform to industrial and financial resources, normal trade, and the needs of consumers, or the nation would face economic collapse. The Treasury was the best judge of such figures and the most important agent in restoring a process which, Simon wrote, was "rapidly breaking down"—that is, "correlating the rising total burden of Defence liabilities to the whole of our available resources."[31] Second, the Treasury's figure of £400 million to be borrowed for rearmament was based on its estimate of what the country could afford to pay from revenue—without unbalancing the budget, raising taxes to intolerable levels, or drastically cutting social expenditure—for annual maintenance of the Services at their established footing after the five-year period of building and borrowing was over.[32] Third, the chancellor's normal means of limiting expenditure by cutting the annual Service Estimates must be buttressed by giving him the power to ration each Service department's total spending over the next five years.

In his last six months as chancellor, Chamberlain anticipated Simon's precepts. He insisted that the calculation of cost must precede the contemplation of decisions to strengthen Mediterranean defenses, adopt the Admiralty's proposed new naval standard, equip the Territorial Army for a continental war, or build war potential beyond the authorized peacetime levels, even if this procedure might delay the approval of all of the war policies and plans recommended by the Services. Chamberlain upheld normal trade with reasoning that gave this doctrine the powers of both admonition and salvation: rearmament must stay within the limit of resources that normal trade permitted because "any additional strain [on these resources] might put our present Programmes in jeopardy."[33] He acted upon these principles with a

[30] Simon memorandum, 25 June, CP 165(37), CAB 24/270, approved by the Cabinet on 30 June, Cab 27(37), CAB 23/89. On rationing: Peden, *British Rearmament and Treasury*, pp. 38–44, 80–87; Shay, *British Rearmament*, pp. 159–63; Gibbs, *Rearmament*, pp. 279–81.
[31] Simon memorandum (see preceding note).
[32] Hopkins minute, 25 July 1936, T 161/841, and memorandum of 14 May 1937, T 161/783; Peden, *British Rearmament and Treasury*, pp. 88–89; Shay, *British Rearmament*, p. 162.
[33] Chamberlain commenting on Inskip's memorandum of 1 February, "Progress in Defence Requirements," CP 40(37), CAB 24/267, at Cab 5(37), 3 February, CAB 23/87; see also Bridges's minute on Inskip's paper, 2 February, T 161/778.

tenacious consistency that could only be inspired by faith—that war would not come to pass.

Chamberlain deftly used the machinery of policy to postpone decisions that might change authorized policy from what he and the Treasury thought acceptable. On the question of the Army's role, his interventions were pivotal at every stage: referrals among DPR, CID, COS, Cabinet, and DP(P); terms of reference for the COS and DP(P) to examine the Army's role in conjunction with that of the other Services; instructions for the War Office to relate its requirements to costs. Repeatedly delayed by Chamberlain, by the end of May 1937 a Cabinet decision on the Army ostensibly awaited recommendations from the DP(P). Before the committee took up this question, however, the Cabinet decided in June not to decide until it knew more about costs and inter-Service priorities, and the Army's fate was caught up in the general review of defense requirements and expenditure. Meanwhile, Chamberlain could agree to the DP(P)'s conclusion of 19 April concerning plans for war with Germany—to be able "to release the Field Force at the earliest possible moment consistent with the situation at home"—without supposing that the committee had sanctioned the preparation of a major or automatic continental commitment.[34]

Chamberlain expected to win such arguments. In October 1936, he noted "a general acceptance of my position as heir apparent and acting P.M. and I am sending for people and endeavoring to conduct business as if I were in fact P.M." Knowing that his position meant power and patronage, he was sure he deserved it for having long been the Cabinet's prime mover and best thinker. While preparing his speech for the 1900 Club in June 1936, and without having first consulted Baldwin or Eden, Chamberlain "felt that the party and the country needed a lead, and an indication that the Government was not wavering and drifting without a policy."[35] The 1937 budget was "all my own idea," and "I did most of the work" on the White Paper on Defence. In December 1936, "I got the Cabinet to agree to an enquiry into the role of the Army," and in February, "I have at last got a decision about the Army and it practically gives me all I want."[36]

After the Second World War, Duff Cooper, one of Chamberlain's

[34] Chamberlain to Inskip (with draft terms of reference for COS), 16 December, CAB 64/35, and regarding draft terms of reference for DP(P), 13 May, CAB 21/509; Cab 27(37), 30 June, CAB 23/89; DP(P) meetings, 19 April and 13 July, CAB 16/181; Shay, *British Rearmament*, p. 164.

[35] Chamberlain diary, 17 June and 7 October 1936, Chamberlain Papers, NC 2/23a.

[36] Chamberlain to Ida, 6, 20 February 1937, NC 18/1/993, 995, and diary, 24 December 1936, NC 2/24a; Chamberlain Papers.

most irascible antagonists, wrote that Chamberlain "lacked experience of the world, and . . . also the imagination which can fill the gaps of inexperience."[37] Chamberlain's colleagues were not looking for Duff Cooper's sort of worldliness or creativity. Fisher wrote expectantly to Chamberlain: "'There is reform and positive action required in almost every direction; and even matters which superficially might be accounted small may turn the scale in this ill-poised world. These as well as more obvious things need clear thinking, courage, and decision. And it is these qualities that we are now going to have in action.'" Sir Samuel Hoare, one of Chamberlain's most deferential supporters, urged him to make his premiership as great a contrast to Baldwin's as possible: "Make your motive force evident as 'efficiency' . . . [and] make a small inner Cabinet the outward sign of this new efficiency chapter."[38]

Chamberlain had already begun to do this, confident that he was a distinctively modern leader who could overcome the inertia of inter-departmental bickering and bureaucratic red tape. He counted on the support of a small group of ministers: Hoare, Simon, and Inskip on the FPC, DPR, and DP(P); Halifax (FPC); Swinton (DPR and DP[P]); with Weir another ally on the DPR. They easily outweighed what Chamberlain contemptuously called the "Boys Brigade" of ministers (Ormsby-Gore, Elliot, Oliver Stanley, W. S. Morrison, M. MacDonald) who often defended Eden. Like Chamberlain, his confederates mistrusted Britain's strongest potential allies in Europe (France) and the Pacific (the United States), and they believed that understandings with Germany and Japan required more conciliation and less procrastination than the Foreign Office seemed willing to provide. They rejected Eden's argument that toughness in the Mediterranean would deter Mussolini and impress Hitler, and advised conciliating Mussolini or isolating him through a settlement with Germany. They gave home defense and the RAF's offensive striking force greater financial and strategic value than a substantial continental commitment for the Army, and they doubted Duff Cooper's ability to lead the War Office. They were receptive to Chamberlain's claims that the strategic roles of the Services were matters of policy, that policy must be viewed comprehensively, and that he could bring order to its interlocking parts.

[37] Duff Cooper, *Old Men*, p. 200.

[38] Fisher quoted in O'Halpin, *Head of the Civil Service*, p. 218; Hoare to Chamberlain, 17 March, Templewood Papers. For Leo Amery's similar advice to Chamberlain, see *Empire at Bay*, pp. 426–27, 439, also Amery-Garvin correspondence, 15–16 November 1936, Garvin Papers. Chamberlain intended to use "'a sort of inner Cabinet on policy'" (Middlemas, *Diplomacy of Illusion*, p. 61), but he declined Amery's offer to be a member of a "small policy Cabinet" free of departmental duties.

Unlike Eden, Chamberlain had strong departmental backing. It has been stated that the Treasury's plan to ration expenditure "had an exclusively financial origin," and that, at least until the defense review of the summer and fall of 1937, Treasury officials viewed rationing "as a means of re-establishing Treasury control of expenditure rather than of influencing the direction of defence policy."[39] The origins and goal of rationing were not so limited as this. By late 1936 questions of policy and time easily crossed bureaucratic boundaries. Troubled by the inability of either the Services or the Foreign Office to make up their minds, sure that finance was a universal principle governing any definition of national policy, the Treasury sought to control more than expenditure.

Fisher's views on strategy were closer to Chamberlain's than to those endorsed collectively by the DRC in 1935. Fisher thought it necessary "to determine the size of our war-time army before defining the part it is to play," even if this looked like "putting the cart before the horse." Like Chamberlain, he would inform the French "in no uncertain terms" that Britain had no intention of sending troops to the Continent "on the scale of the last war, and that we ourselves must decide how our army can be most usefully employed."[40] Bridges attributed the sharp increase in the War Office's projected expenditure for 1937 partly to "the Foreign Office . . . always commenting on the deterioration of the general situation and the need for greater preparedness." When Chamberlain stated that Britain "cannot afford to miss any opportunity of reducing the international tension,"[41] he had in mind the financial implications as well as the political effects of appeasement. By offsetting rearmament with wholehearted efforts for conciliation, Britain could bring about a general pacification that would validate the Treasury's limiting the costs and prolonging the time for building an effective deterrent.

Chamberlain and Treasury officials did not consider the Foreign Office the best judge of how to measure or use time. In February 1937, Chamberlain called the Cabinet's attention to the apparent "alleviation in the international situation and [to] the dangers of overloading the [defence] programmes beyond the material capacity of the country." With reference to the "time factor," he asked "was it really necessary to

---

[39] Peden, *British Rearmament and Treasury,* p. 41.

[40] Fisher notes on the Army, 23 October 1936, CAB 64/35. Although Fisher thought the ultimate goal for the Army should be seventeen divisions, he conceded to Chamberlain that " 'air strength should be an *absolute priority,* accompanied by naval development' "; Peden, *British Rearmament and Treasury,* p. 127.

[41] Bridges memorandum, 31 December 1936, T 161/754; Chamberlain memorandum to FPC on Anglo-German relations, 2 April 1937, *DBFP,* 18, no. 366.

stick rigidly to a date in 1939 for completion of our programmes?" He, Fisher, and Hopkins all feared disastrous consequences if Britain re-armed too rapidly, abandoning "decent finance" (Hopkins) and "un-dermining ourselves before the Boche feel it desirable to move" (Fish-er). They had begun to formulate the doctrine that inspired the defense review undertaken after Chamberlain became prime minister. Particu-larly because Britain could hope to win only a long war, economic stability was the "fourth arm" of defense, a peacetime deterrent more significant than military strength and one that would be lost if other countries detected "signs of strain" in Britain.[42]

These imperatives prompted Chamberlain and the Treasury to im-pose two kinds of delay on rearmament. First, decisions to change the programs for the Army and Navy must await completion of the review of defense expenditure. Second, the Treasury's five-year plan of expen-diture, to begin in 1937, envisaged virtual completion of the authorized programs by March 1942. This timetable overshadowed 1939—the original goal of the DRC, the date by which Vansittart still feared Ger-many would start a European war, and the year in which Chamberlain and the Cabinet had (early in 1936) expected the completion of Scheme F to give Britain air parity with Germany and an effective deterrent. This new five-year plan also prolonged to six years the three-to-five-year program (to begin in 1936) approved by the Cabinet early in 1936. Concerned with the production of commodities that were more mate-rial than time, the Treasury would extend at least until 1942 the amount of time the Foreign Office was expected to produce. Meanwhile, the calendar and deterrent potential of the Treasury's doctrine of economic stability could be challenged: by enemies whose economic instability might cause them to launch attacks for quick victories before 1942; by supply experts who doubted that Britain would have sufficient re-serves for the early stages of combat in 1942; by military experts who expected German military advisers to measure British deterrence ac-cording to military forces more than economic policies; by diplomatic officials who wanted Britain to have greater military power for man-ufacturing time with general, immediate, and extended deterrence while rearming; and by allies who wondered whether Britain, without committing substantial military forces to the Continent, would avoid conflict at their peril.

The Cabinet's decision of February 1936 had not been binding with respect to force levels or dates of completion, and it left in place a

[42] Cab 5(37), 3 February, CAB 23/87; Hopkins minute and Fisher note, 14 May 1937, T 161/783; Inskip "Interim Report on Defence Expenditure" (drafted by the Treasury), 15 December 1937, CP 316(37), CAB 24/273.

political equilibrium in which the Foreign Office, Service departments, and Treasury could recommend changes. Seizing the day, capitalizing on uncertainties in and disputes between the other departments, Chamberlain and the Treasury upset that balance by pressing for a harmonious correlation among foreign policy, rearmament, time, deterrence, and finance. The authorized programs, perhaps with some revision and acceleration, must suffice until 1942 because Britain could not afford to build even larger regular units and war reserves before then or to maintain these additions afterwards. These programs would suffice: until 1942, because conciliation could decrease the number of Britain's enemies and avert war with those that remained; after 1942, because Britain would then be strong enough—particularly in the air—to deter them indefinitely and keep the peace without having to continue expanding its armed forces.

Chamberlain and the Treasury presupposed that, the faster the pace of rearmament and the higher the cost, the greater the risk would be of economic instability and loss of international influence. The slower the pace and lower the cost, the more reason the Government had to restrict deterrence. Britain must limit its commitments abroad, concentrate on air power to deter or defeat an attack against British territory, reduce the number of potential enemies by taking every opportunity to conciliate them, and not regard their next "forward moves" as causes for war.

The Foreign Office did not embrace this grand design. Vansittart and some others continued to argue that it was unreasonable to count on dictators to behave in conformity with British schedules, unwise to conciliate them without firm reciprocal guarantees, imprudent to disinterest Britain in Central Europe and to narrow deterrence to defense of the United Kingdom, and impolitic to limit in advance the size of an expeditionary force for a European war. The persuasiveness of these attitudes among Cabinet ministers, however, had been eroded by intradepartmental differences, by pressure from the Services against courting danger, and by the force of Chamberlain's logic.

COORDINATION AND DISCORDANCE

The Services concurred with Chamberlain regarding conciliation, but did not subscribe to his axioms about supply or strategy. The authorized reserves of supply would not provide adequate potential in case of war. Air power had not yet prevented or won wars. Yet, in spite of improved coordination, the Services did not offer an alternative defense policy free of the discordant clutter that Chamberlain resolved to clean up. They pursued separate courses in strategy, combined operations, and supply, and the sum of their goals for rearmament gainsaid the Government's doctrine of normal peacetime trade.

Notwithstanding the expansion of the Joint Planning Committee in the spring of 1936, strategic planning continued to lag. In July, Hankey observed that an "undue number of ad hoc questions" had been referred to the JPC and "caused interference with the primary item of long range planning." He recommended that the JPC be made freer to concentrate on preparing contingency plans for war against Germany and in the Far East. Until these studies were completed, the JPC would not be able "to take in hand the preparation of war plans for the event of hostilities in the Far East accompanied by a war in Europe or the Mediterranean."[43] Further delays occurred, however, as the JPC had to work on exigencies that Hankey and the Services thought diplomacy should have spared them. By mid-March 1937, the JPC had finished only one of the three appreciations for war (Germany). Even that study had been slowed by the "incubus of a series of ad hoc problems," and also by "certain unresolved questions of major defence policy, e.g., the role of the British army." The decision to augment the JPC had proven a valuable boost to joint planning, in the opinion of its members, but had not prevented delays in the preparation of strategic appreciations and "detailed war plans."[44]

The Deputy Chief of the Air Staff, Air Vice Marshal Courtney, complimented the JPC's German appreciation for containing "many concepts which have never been put down on paper before." He criticized the JPC for preserving, since 1934, an assumption which no longer corresponded to "realistic political conditions"—"that the Low Countries are vital to our security and that in order to secure them the Army must be got overseas as early as possible." Moreover, the JPC's discussions had been "acrimonious at times." Still, their talks had also been "immensely valuable," each member of the JPC had had to compromise "in order to produce an agreed report at all," and the committee deserved to be congratulated for "a most admirable piece of work."[45]

The Joint Intelligence Committee (JIC) played only a minor role in strategic planning in the winter of 1936–37. In June 1936, the COS agreed to expand the functions of the JIC, the new name for the inter-Service intelligence committee that apparently had never met. The JIC

[43] Hankey at two meetings on 27 July 1936: COS, CAB 53/6; Inskip and CID secretaries, CAB 21/473.

[44] JPC meeting, 17 March, CAB 55/2; also JPC report on its agenda, 27 January, CAB 53/30.

[45] Courtney to CAS, 30 October 1936, AIR 2/1406.

should "assist the JPC when the latter required coordinated intelligence" and requested such information. On 7 July, at its first meeting, the JIC expressed interest in receiving copies of all JPC papers, but Colonel Pownall told the JIC's secretary, Major Leslie Hollis, that he strongly opposed "increasing the distribution of Joint Planning Papers." The JPC consulted the JIC in preparing the report on European military strengths and the Far Eastern strategic appreciation. Yet the JPC acknowledged such assistance only grudgingly, if at all, and relied largely on information obtained directly from the Industrial Intelligence Centre (which usually sent a representative to meetings of the JIC) and the intelligence directorates of the Service departments. The IIC had achieved preeminence among these sources regarding German rearmament: in the War Office, MI3 noted "we must agree" when the IIC gave estimates of German strength and equipment. Indeed, it appeared to Mr. Ashton-Gwatkin in the Foreign Office that the IIC was "developing away from its original conception as a secret cell for industrial intelligence into an embryo official staff" for a Ministry of Defence. The IIC, JPC, and Foreign Office all coordinated intelligence, frequently combining industrial, military, and political information, but the assessment of intelligence was still virtually anyone's game and guess. It remained to be seen whether the JIC would bring order to this muddle of jurisdictions and have a major impact on strategic planning.[46]

Chaired by Hankey and meeting more frequently than before the reorganization of March 1936, the Deputy Chiefs of Staff (DCOS) had a major impact on plans and the organization of command. They couched their criticism of the JPC's provisional report on war with Germany in procedural language. The JPC had gone "beyond the work of planning" and considered subjects—notably defects in Britain's preparations for war—that fell outside its "terms of reference" for this appreciation. The DCOS did not, however, attempt to undo the compromise that the JPC had agonizingly reached among the Services' views of their strategic roles in a European war.[47]

The DCOS recommendation to establish a peacetime ministerial committee for determining "war policy" originated in a letter of July 1936 from General Deverell to Hankey. The CIGS cited difficulties in

---

[46] COS meeting, 16 June, CAB 53/6; JIC report, "Revised Functions and Working Arrangements of the Joint Intelligence Subcommittee," 14 July, CAB 54/3; Hollis to JPC, 7 July, CAB 21/441; JPC minutes, CAB 55/2; MI3 note, 10 December 1936, WO 190/497; Ashton-Gwatkin minute, 30 July 1937, W14500/137/50, FO 371/21218; Hinsley, *British Intelligence*, pp. 31–33, 36–39.

[47] DCOS report to COS, 5 January 1937, CAB 53/29. The DCOS met twelve times from July 1936 to June 1937.

issuing instructions to field commanders during the Ethiopian crisis as evidence of backwardness in preparing for the "higher direction of war." In modern war, orders must be issued quickly, and "practically every plan or operation will involve more than one service." When the Chiefs of Staff discussed this letter in October, Chatfield stressed that "in most cases nowadays, all three Services were concerned in operations. Operations often became a national question rather than one affecting a single Department only." Major issues would need "ministerial concurrence" such as the DPR had given during the Ethiopian crisis. The COS agreed to Hankey's suggestion that the DCOS examine this question of command.[48]

The COS considered the DCOS report in January 1937. Pointing out that the DCOS had proposed a ministerial body to control policy during war, Chatfield urged his colleagues to recommend the establishment of such an executive in peace as well to approve "important basic questions of war strategy." The COS recommended measures for "higher control of operations in war," seeking a mean between departmental autonomy and unified command. After the Ministerial Controlling Body determined "war policy" and approved "general plans," the Service departments remained "constitutionally . . . responsible for the transmission of instructions to the Commanders of their respective forces in the field, but in cases where more than one Department is concerned, these will require coordination through the machinery of the Committee of Imperial Defence before they are issued." Instructions applying to more than one Service could be sent to each commander by his respective department, or could "by interdepartmental arrangement be sent by one Department to its commander in any particular theatre with instructions to him to transmit them to his colleagues in the other Services."[49]

These recommendations led to the establishment of the Defence Plans (Policy) Committee, which approved the COS/JPC report "Planning for War with Germany." The latter included provision for joint operations, instructed the RAF to prepare plans to assist the other two Services, and assigned to the JPC responsibility for coordinating the war plans of all three arms. Yet none of these documents or decisions stated in unambiguous terms exactly how the coordinating machinery would decide upon the relative importance of two or more Services in combined operations. Much was left to personalities and the adaptation of the COS and JPC to specific situations, with no imperative that

[48] Deverell to Hankey, 9 July, CAB 53/28; COS meetings, 16 and 20 October, CAB 53/6.
[49] COS meeting, 11 January 1937, CAB 53/6; COS memorandum, "Higher Control of Operations in War" (COS 545), 22 January, CAB 4/25.

differences among the Services must be resolved by their staffs, by the Minister for Coordination, or by the Ministerial Controlling Body.

This sort of administrative shapelessness, which might favor the older and larger Services as the Government weighed military policies and plans, was especially disquieting to the Air Ministry. Commenting on the COS report on war with Germany, Group Captain Harris, Deputy Director of Plans, argued that "until some decision has been reached as to the nature and extent of the system of coordination [of operational control] which is to be adopted, detailed planning for war cannot be undertaken." The RAF had to consider its role in support of naval operations and its "coordinating the action of the air striking force with . . . land operations at a critical stage in the campaign." Harris hoped that the Air Staff could "get down to planning the operational control of future campaigns in a manner permitting departmental detail to be settled in the light of overall policy rather than ad hoc guesswork."[50] The "departmental system of control," which Harris criticized as outmoded in modern warfare, stayed in fashion. As the Deputy Chiefs of Staff revised the Manual of Combined Operations, they compromised between the Admiralty's opinion that departmental control worked well and the Air Ministry's view (supported by the War Office) that the current system was "open to all the risks of divided command."[51]

In fact, the Services were in disarray over the tactics and command of combined operations. Relations between the Admiralty and Air Ministry deteriorated as they fought over which should control aircraft used to support naval operations or defend shipping. With help from the press and certain Members of Parliament, the Admiralty forced the Government to reopen the question of control of the Fleet Air Arm. Inskip saw no other way to resolve differences, and Baldwin concurred over Weir's objections.[52] Weir's sympathies lay with the RAF for reasons which he and Swinton did not regard as parochial. Swinton was afraid that "we are getting more and more into water-tight compartments, where each Service stakes out its own claims and assumes exclusive responsibility for everything concerned with the provision and use of its own arm." Weir warned that reopening the Fleet Air Arm

[50] Harris memorandum for Deputy Chief of the Air Staff (Vice Marshal R. E. C. Peirse), 8 March 1937, AIR 9/81.

[51] DCOS meetings, 16 July and 15 December 1936, 7 January, 2 February, 27 April 1937, CAB 54/1; related DCOS papers in CAB 54/3.

[52] Inskip to Baldwin, 5 November and 7 December 1936, and notes of conversation with Baldwin, 15 December, PREM 1/282; Inskip to Weir, 13 November, CAB 64/24. On this stage of the controversy: Cross, *Swinton*, pp. 181–88; Middlemas and Barnes, *Baldwin*, pp. 1019–22; Roskill, *Hankey*, 3:291–93, and *Naval Policy*, pp. 394–404; Till, *Air Power and Royal Navy*, pp. 51–54.

question would hinder "the development of that unity of Defence Service cooperation which is so nationally important." Chamberlain helped soothe tempers, promised Weir that such difficulties would not recur when he became prime minister, regretted that both the Admiralty and Air Ministry had become "embittered," and guessed correctly that the Admiralty would gain control over the Fleet Air Arm.[53]

Inskip's report of 21 July, approved by the Cabinet, gave this control to the Admiralty but kept shore-based aircraft under the jurisdiction of the Air Ministry. This compromise angered Swinton and only papered over the persistent argument regarding the uses and effectiveness of air power. The Air Staff, for example, opposed the use of convoys because they would be vulnerable to enemy air attack. On the JPC, Harris told Captain Tom Phillips, "When you are on the bridge of your flagship and you are struck by a bomb, you will say to your captain that was a bloody big mine we struck." Nor did the decision on the Fleet Air Arm settle the argument among the Chiefs of Staff about command of joint operations. Each chief acknowledged the value of unity of command so long as his Service was the dominant partner, but the Chief of the Air Staff insisted that cooperation under separate commands would be desirable in some circumstances. He failed to mention that, in his own Service, the establishment of separate Bomber and Fighter Commands inhibited the coordination of offensive and defensive operations, and reflected the growing debate between the merits of attack and defense as deterrents to enemy air strikes.[54]

In June 1936, the DPR discussed rearmament and supply organization in response to Baldwin's request for assurance "that everything reasonably possible is being done to get the things which the Services need without any avoidable delay." Churchill had advised Inskip to create "'the structure of war industry and its organisation,'" but Inskip joined Chamberlain and Hoare in agreeing with Weir's advice: the Services should continue to work within the authorized framework; a Ministry of Supply with emergency powers should not be established in peacetime.[55] On 1 July, the Cabinet approved the recommendations

[53] Swinton to Weir, 6 January 1937, Weir Papers, 19/1; Swinton to Baldwin, 17 February, Weir to Baldwin, 2 March, and other notes, PREM 1/282; Inskip-Baldwin-Weir correspondence, February–March, Weir Papers, 19/14; Chamberlain to Weir, 13 March, Weir Papers, 19/14; Chamberlain to Hilda, 13 March, Chamberlain Papers, NC 18/1/998.

[54] Inskip to Chamberlain, 21 July, PREM 1/282; Cab 33(37), 29 July, CAB 23/89; COS meetings on the Fleet Air Arm question, 9 April, 6 and 18 May, CAB 53/7; Webster and Frankland, *Strategic Air Offensive*, pp. 82–83. Harris quoted in General Sir Ronald Adam, letter to the author, 30 June 1974. Phillips went down with the *Prince of Wales* in December 1941 off Malaya following a Japanese air attack. The debate over the vulnerability of capital ships to air bombardment continued, unresolved by a CID subcommittee's report of 30 July 1936; CP 259(36), CAB 24/264; Roskill, *Hankey*, 3:252–53.

[55] Baldwin to Inskip, 10 June, CAB 64/31; Weir to DPR, 10 June, CAB 16/140; DPR meeting, 11 June, CAB 16/136; Reader, *Architect*, pp. 245–48; Shay, *British Rearmament*,

of the CID's ad hoc Subcommittee on War Office Production. A Director General of Munitions would be appointed as a new member of the Army Council, with unified control over the production and supply of munitions. This new position, which might form the nucleus of a Ministry of Munitions in case of war, would accelerate production and develop "reserve plant for emergency production" in accordance with the shadow industry scheme.[56]

The creation of this office, and the appointment on 23 July of the energetic Vice Admiral Brown as the first director general, strengthened the Cabinet's reply to the Conservative deputation at the end of July. Baldwin, Inskip, and Halifax assured these critics that rearmament was moving forward, with the air program at the top of the list of priorities and all possible peacetime measures for supply either under way or under consideration.[57] This vindication belied apprehensions and disputes along Whitehall about both production and organization in the ambiguous zone of time between peace and war.

Inskip informed the Cabinet about problems in recruiting, finding sufficient skilled labor for armaments industries, and producing tanks and antiaircraft guns. The Principal Supply Officers Committee and its subcommittees estimated "big gaps between War Potential arising directly from the reconditioning of the Services and the War Potential in case of war." Sir Arthur Robinson noted the Supply Board's dissatisfaction with arrangements (dating from 1927) for expanding the supply organization in war. A Ministry of Supply should be viewed as a necessity, not a last resort, and consideration should be given now to the powers and structure of such an institution.[58] In the autumn, the Supply Board's annual report emphasized the gap between the two classes of war potential; closing it would require expanding the shadow industry, Robinson told the Principal Supply Officers.[59]

On 4 November, Inskip told the Cabinet that the recent report of the Royal Commission on the Private Manufacture of and Trading in Arms could lend credence to the argument of Parliamentary critics in favor of

---

pp. 128–30. On the DPR, Duff Cooper did not want to vote at this time against creating a peacetime Ministry of Supply.

[56] Report of subcommittee, 19 June, approved by CID on 25 June, CP 187(36), CAB 24/263; Cab 49(36), 1 July, CAB 23/85. Sir Warren Fisher chaired the subcommittee; its draft report and minutes in CAB 16/148. See also Postan, *British War Production*, pp. 33, 36–37; Scott and Hughes, *Administration of War Production*, pp. 24–27.

[57] Records of meetings of 28–29 July, PREM 1/193, and CAB 21/437–38.

[58] Cabs 43 and 55(36), 23 June and 29 July 1936, CAB 23/84–85; meeting of Inskip, Hankey, and assistant secretaries, 27 July, CAB 21/473; Robinson memorandum, 28 July, CAB 60/16.

[59] Supply Board annual report, 30 September, CAB 60/16; PSOC meeting, 13 October, CAB 60/4. In July, Desmond Morton had issued the same warning in a memorandum to Churchill criticizing Inskip; Gilbert, *Churchill*, pp. 765–67.

a peacetime Ministry of Supply. Inskip warned that such a measure would mean "putting the country practically on a war basis." Swinton suggested increasing controls over industry, a sign of the Air Ministry's growing doubt that it could complete Scheme F by 1939 or catch up to Germany unless aircraft production were accelerated (the issue that eventually caused Chamberlain to request Swinton's resignation in May 1938). But the Cabinet approved the line Inskip proposed to take in the House of Commons: the existing system of supply, including the shadow industry plan, had recently been improved and further improvements would be made; any major reorganization of the machinery or "diversion of industry from peace to war production" would cause a "great loss of time" in the programs under way.[60] Sir Harold Brown would not have been welcome at this meeting. Because of the "present prohibition against interference with industry," he wrote to Robinson, and unless armaments were "given some degree of priority . . . , then any attempt to exercise priority will probably be a waste of time."[61]

On the same day that the Cabinet discussed how to fend off criticism in the House of Commons, the Joint Intelligence Committee defined mobilization as more than bringing military forces "up to war strength" and forming "additional units . . . according to a preconceived plan." Because modern warfare required "the utmost effort of the whole nation," mobilization must now involve the distribution of manpower and material among the Services, industry, and the public.[62] The Cabinet had moved some distance forward with supply, but its willingness to prepare the nation for "utmost effort" was restrained by two powerful peacetime biases: for maintaining normal civil and export trade; against creating new ministries that would increase government controls over private enterprise and centralize powers normally distributed among several departments.

Lord Weir's advice consistently embraced both of these predispositions, and he carried them also to meetings of the CID's ad hoc Subcommittee on Supply Organisation in War. Weir asserted that organiza-

---

[60] Inskip memorandum, 30 October, CP 297(36), CAB 24/265; Cab 63(36), 4 November, CAB 23/86; Gibbs, *Rearmament*, pp. 301–2; Gilbert, *Churchill*, pp. 795–98; Middlemas and Barnes, *Baldwin*, pp. 968–69; Shay, *British Rearmament*, pp. 130–32. The Labour party's Defence Committee advocated both a Ministry of Supply and a Ministry of Defence; Dalton, *Fateful Years*, pp. 90–91. On the report of the Royal Commission (Cmd. 5292), see Roskill, *Hankey*, 3:246–49; Scott and Hughes, *Administration of War Production*, pp. 70–71.

[61] Brown to Robinson, 21 November, CAB 21/673.

[62] JIC report, 4 November, CAB 55/8; the JIC expanded upon this paper on 11 February 1937, CAB 55/9. In May, the IIC had received what it viewed as conclusive proof that Germany considered economic preparations for war more important than military ones; Wark, *Ultimate Enemy*, pp. 168–69.

tion would depend on war plans, and he recommended this hypothesis: a preponderance of naval power over that of the enemy; an air striking force and air defense force as powerful as possible; a "relatively small and well equipped" Army. Robinson urged that plans be made at once for a central ministry to take over the supply and design sections of the Service departments; otherwise, Britain might enter "the next war, as we did the last, with a makeshift supply organisation." True to form, Weir opposed the peacetime courting of wartime conditions. Before taking a decision on the scale of a wartime ministry, which he himself would keep small, the Government should wait to see how much progress had been made by 1939 on the deficiency program. A month later, the PSOC noted how this progress had been jeopardized by the inability of the supply committees to complete their studies of requirements by April 1937 as originally planned, partly because of the Government's indecision over the Army's role.[63]

Disputes over strategy, joint operations, and supply were to be expected, given the special interests of the Service departments, uncertainties about the time and place of the next war, and the unproven yield of air forces. Rejecting the notion that a Ministry of Defence or Ministry of Supply could solve such problems, Inskip and Hankey collaborated in trying to strengthen the machinery of coordination. They sought compromises among the competing interests of the Services, and they magnified the expert advice of the Service staffs on issues that were political as well as military.

Inskip was more than a stand-in for the prime minister but lacked the power and staff of a minister of defense. He stood by Baldwin at the meetings of July and November with the parliamentary deputation of critics, among whom he considered Churchill a troublemaker; on the Air Defence Research Committee (which reported progress in experiments with radar), Churchill had offended Inskip and Swinton by raising wider issues of air policy and finding fault with the Air Ministry.[64] As chairman of the DPR and PSOC, Inskip apprised the Cabinet of progress and difficulties in supply, and he agreed with Chamberlain that the approved policy of upgrading the Services stretched British resources to the point where acceleration might disrupt rearmament.[65] In meetings of the Cabinet and FPC, Inskip's own convictions lent

[63] Inskip memorandum, 7 December, CAB 4/25; CID meeting, 10 December, CAB 2/6; meetings of subcommittee (Inskip, Robinson, and Weir), 29 January and 4 May, CAB 60/28; PSOC meeting, 28 June, CAB 60/4; Hurstfield, *Control of Raw Materials*, pp. 74–75.

[64] Cab 50(36), 6 July, CAB 23/85; correspondence among Inskip, Churchill, Swinton, Hankey, and Sir Henry Tizard, May–July 1936, CAB 21/426 and CAB 64/5; Cross, *Swinton*, pp. 176–77; Gilbert, *Churchill*, pp. 743–44, 750–59; Roskill, *Hankey*, 3:230–34.

[65] DPR meeting, 11 June 1936, CAB 16/136; Cab 5(37), 3 February 1937, CAB 23/87.

weight to the advice of the Chiefs of Staff concerning the proper aims of British foreign policy: reduce international tension by conciliating Italy and Germany; avoid political commitments having no direct bearing on British security; and steer clear of conflict in the Mediterranean, for the prospect of war with Germany—and perhaps Japan—was alarming enough.

Although Inskip fancied air forces, he dealt even-handedly with the three Service departments over controversial issues of strategy and joint operations, earning him a reputation for prudence and fairness. But his virtues could as easily be viewed as indecisiveness and other forms of weakness, particularly by contemporaries with strong opinions about the respective functions of the Services in the next war and the results that coordination should achieve. As Inskip told Baldwin, Chatfield would not "feel much confidence in my judgment alone" regarding the Fleet Air Arm. Swinton complained to Weir that "we seem to be getting right away from the conception the Cabinet had in appointing a Minister for Coordination, whose primary duty was to make the General Staffs of the three Services work together as a combined staff." Weir agreed that Inskip's handling of the dispute over providing aircraft for merchant ships was "a poor start in effective coordination." Liddell Hart was surprised at how little Inskip's principal secretary, H. G. Vincent, knew about naval strategy. "Since Vincent's ideas are presumably those of Inskip also," Liddell Hart's talk with the secretary "shook my confidence badly in the grasp that the coordinators of defence have of the fundamental problems of defence."[66]

In December 1936, Weir advised Chamberlain that it was Inskip's job—indeed his "major problem"—to deal with the Army's role. Chamberlain told the Cabinet that, although Inskip had been talking about the Army "from the point of view of supply," he had another task as well, "to oversee strategy." After the Cabinet requested a report from Inskip and the Chiefs of Staff, Chamberlain doubted that Inskip alone could "supply what is lacking" to ensure an objective report from the COS.[67]

No other issue so clearly demonstrated Inskip's unfortified position between Chamberlain and the Services. Without a ministry or a strong staff, he could be swayed by various forces. Inskip's predilection for air

---

[66] COS meetings, 9 April and 18 May 1937, CAB 53/7; Vincent minute to Inskip, 30 April, CAB 64/25; Inskip note of conversation with Baldwin, 15 December 1936, PREM 1/282; Swinton-Weir correspondence, 6 January 1937, Weir Papers, 19/1; Liddell Hart notes, 5 November 1936, Liddell Hart Papers, 11/1936/95, also notes of talk with Bullock, 25 June 1937, 11/1937/54 (LHCMA). Inskip apologized to Weir for "bungling" the Fleet Air Arm issue; letters of 17 February and 3 March, Weir Papers, 19/14.

[67] Weir notes for Chamberlain, December 1936, Weir Papers, 17/10; Cab 75(36), 16 December, CAB 23/86; Chamberlain to Inskip, 24 December, CAB 64/35.

defense, enlivened by Charles Lindbergh's remarks on air power during lunch at the House of Commons,[68] made him uneasy about a continental role for the Army. He corresponded and talked with Liddell Hart, who thought the Army's reluctance to admit that mechanization would improve its effectiveness without increasing its size arose from fear that politicians would "withhold the money thus saved for modernisation as soon as [the Army] had shown that the numbers could be reduced."[69] Inskip cautioned Duff Cooper not to create confusion between the deficiency program and the question of supplies for war. He lost patience with the War Secretary, who, by "hammering away about the 17 Divisions instead of getting on with the things that are urgent and that can be done now," gave Inskip reason to recommend that Chamberlain change the leadership at the War Office.[70]

All of these considerations, along with Inskip's intellectual partiality for consistency and efficiency, put him in Chamberlain's camp, but Inskip was not a camp follower. Unlike Chamberlain, Inskip did not wish to limit Britain's liability for fighting on European soil to, at most, the Field Force augmented by two Territorial Divisions. Unlike Chamberlain, he was willing to accept the unanimous recommendation of the military experts against such a decision, without thinking it necessary to consult Trenchard, whose passion for offensive bombing forces he did not share; indeed, Inskip was especially interested in the deterrent capability of Spitfire and Hurricane fighters, the first orders for which had been placed in June 1936. Inskip did not require the Chiefs of Staff to subscribe to a common strategic doctrine which deduced small land forces from principles about air power. He did not insist that costs be determined before new decisions were taken. He urged the Cabinet to take at least interim decisions on equipping the Territorial Army so that the Supply Organisation had "some basis to work upon," and he feared that the Treasury's plan for reviewing defense expenditure would slow down the programs already in progress.[71]

---

[68] Nicolson, *Diaries* (entry of 9 December 1936), p. 283.

[69] Inskip-Liddell Hart correspondence, February–June 1937, Liddell Hart Papers, 1/400, and Liddell Hart notes of talk on 24 February, 11/1937/8 (LHCMA).

[70] Inskip to Duff Cooper, 5 February 1937, CAB 64/35; Inskip to Chamberlain, 21 May, Chamberlain Papers, NC 8/24/3. On Chamberlain's removal of Duff Cooper from the War Office, see also Chamberlain diary, 23 May, and Chamberlain to Hilda, 30 May, Chamberlain Papers, NC 2/24a, 18/1/1006; Duff Cooper, *Old Men*, pp. 205–6 ("I acquired little credit at the War Office"); Charmley, *Duff Cooper*, pp. 90–91, 100–102.

[71] Inskip to Chamberlain, 1 February 1937, CAB 64/35; Cabs 19 and 20(37), 28 April and 5 May, CAB 23/88; DP(P) meeting, 13 July, CAB 16/181; Shay, *British Rearmament*, pp. 163–64. Sir Harold Brown later praised Inskip for his help in trying, with little success, to convince the Treasury that "the provision of orders for a long-term programme would ultimately lead to major economies"; "Reminiscences," p. 160, in Turner/Brown Papers (LHCMA).

Chamberlain seemed willing to tolerate such signs of independence, perhaps because he assumed that someone as reasonable and modest as Inskip must, when it really counted, side with him. But Chamberlain underestimated the strength of several attitudes that Inskip acquired as he gained experience in office. First, although Inskip acknowledged the bonds between financial stability and national security, he was readier than Chamberlain to make finance the more dependent side of that relationship and to test the validity of the doctrine of normal trade. Second, when the Chiefs of Staff mixed military and political considerations, Inskip reacted more sympathetically than Chamberlain and was far less inclined to be dogmatic or hierarchical about where wisdom lay for making political judgments. Finally, Inskip saw his job primarily as fostering cooperation among the Services, all three of which he served, not as resolving inter-Service conflicts.

To some degree, Inskip learned these attitudes from Hankey as the two men adapted the machinery to problems of supply, strategy, and command. Hankey favored the appointment of a Director General of Munitions, opposed creating a peacetime Ministry of Supply, and recommended that the Minister for Coordination should advise the Government when to put into motion the "priority machinery" for supply in case of war.[72] Enclosing a paper by Colonel "Pug" Ismay, who assumed his duties as Deputy Secretary to the CID in August 1936, Hankey informed Inskip that the War Office did not take seriously enough its responsibility for air defense, and advised him how to handle this issue without "bringing the Secretariat into conflict with the War Office." If anyone wished to put Chamberlain's case on the Army's role before the COS, he wrote to Inskip in December, it should be Chamberlain himself, for "I do not know anyone else who shares it with sufficient conviction to put it forward." In January and February 1937, Hankey urged Inskip to seek a Cabinet decision on the Army: preferably not by citing Hankey himself, whom Chamberlain probably regarded "as one of the 'old gang' [DRC] on this subject," nor by circulating to ministers a perseverant memorandum by Duff Cooper "which would have created friction." Yet Hankey, like Chamberlain and the Treasury, would not rearm so fast as to jeopardize the doctrine that "'trade is wealth, and money is the sinews of war.'"[73]

Because of sustained agitation by the Admiralty, Hankey reluctantly

---

[72] Hankey to CID, 26 September 1936, CAB 4/25, approved by the CID on 8 October, CAB 2/6. The president of the Board of Trade had previously had this responsibility.

[73] Hankey to Inskip, 21 September 1936, CAB 64/3; 17 December, CAB 21/509; 18 January and 8 February 1937, CAB 64/35; Hankey to his son (Robin), 22 December 1936, in Roskill, *Hankey*, 3:238. Ismay found the atmosphere at Whitehall Gardens grimmer than when he had left the CID Secretariat in 1930; *Memoirs*, pp. 76–77.

concluded that the question of control over the Fleet Air Arm must be reopened.[74] Hankey abhorred such conflicts. They not only wasted time, but also exposed the Chiefs of Staff to ministerial interventions, and could reduce the collective power of the COS to act "as a valuable 'steering' machine" for defense policy.[75] Hankey used his chairmanship of the DCOS to safeguard and amplify this power, by which strategy could shape foreign policy. Amending the JPC's draft appreciation of plans for war with Germany lessened the risk that some ministers might panic and blame the Services for underestimating the German threat. The preparation of war plans gave the COS a fulcrum for offering at least indirect advice on peacetime foreign policy and supply. Thus, Hankey regretted that the DP(P) waited so long to discuss the COS report on Germany.[76] Hankey opposed Deverell's suggestion that the Minister for Coordination sign orders to be issued by the Chiefs of Staff for combined operations, ostensibly because the minister did not head an "executive Department," but largely because Hankey did not want any new office to weaken either the authority of the Service departments or the direct link that he had forged between the COS and the War Cabinet in the Great War.[77]

With hindsight refracted by the Second World War, his private secretary wondered whether Hankey's skill at working out compromises was not misplaced in the 1930s. During his last few years in office, perhaps Hankey produced compromises between two sides in the Cabinet "when a definite decision either for or against would have been better for the country."[78] And perhaps Hankey had remained Secretary too long—twenty-five years at the CID when he celebrated his sixtieth birthday in April 1937. But compromise was the essence of defense by committee practiced by Hankey and preached to the Secretariat, where, shortly before leaving to command the School of Artillery, Pownall considered Hankey "far too valuable to dispense with prematurely."[79]

In March 1937, Hankey wrote to his son that "'we are incomparably better organised as a Government machine than before the war.'"[80] Especially when lacking a strong and opinionated prime minister, how-

---

[74] Hankey to Inskip, 28 November 1936, CAB 21/423, and 3 May 1937, CAB 64/25.
[75] Hankey's last meeting with the COS before his retirement, 25 July 1938, CAB 53/9.
[76] Hankey to COS, 19 March 1937, CAB 55/9.
[77] COS meeting, 16 October 1936, CAB 53/6.
[78] Burgis MS.
[79] Pownall diary, in Bond, *Chief of Staff*, p. 113. Hankey bade Pownall an unusually affectionate goodbye (p. 116).
[80] Letter of 7 March, in Roskill, *Hankey*, 3:277.

ever, the machinery was prone to indecision, inconsistency, and delay, all of which contributed to the disorder in British policy. It was a pragmatic system, better at responding to particular urgencies than looking at the whole picture, and more likely to condone than to quash contradictions.

As defense merged with foreign policy and finance under the genus of national policy, Inskip and Hankey felt growing pressure from Chamberlain, whose emphasis on finance they found increasingly persuasive, and whose ideal of coherent policy their practice of coordination failed to realize. The "old gang" of civilians on the DRC had disbanded. Hankey and Fisher no longer had much confidence in Vansittart. Hankey and Chamberlain tacitly agreed that there was no particular "magic" to the year 1939, and that Germany's next "forward move" need not draw Britain into war. Having helped strategy gain influence compared to foreign policy, Hankey had now begun to concede Chamberlain's argument for subjecting strategy to financial constraints. Hankey and Inskip accepted the fact that this latter process would increase ministerial scrutiny over defense policy.

Chamberlain had already put his personal stamp on policy by placing finance at the center of a comprehensive definition of policy, preventing or precipitating discussion, forming alliances on "inner Cabinets" such as the FPC and DP(P), and challenging the recommendations of interested departments or official committees. He had begun to reshape the machinery of policy by acting on Baldwin's behalf, manipulating its procedures, and preparing to ration defense spending. To most of Chamberlain's colleagues in the Cabinet and Conservative party, his objectives and his methods of decisionmaking were right for the times. They knew he intended to lead the Cabinet with forceful opinions of his own, a disputatious manner in meetings, and a determination to integrate the major components of national policy in a coherent plan.

Chamberlain offered fair promise that foreign policy would decrease risks and buy time until 1942, that rearmament would comply with economic stability at home and limited liability on the Continent, and that deterrence would compress to manageable dimensions of air power and self-defense. Changing the leadership and style of the system of decisionmaking would give order to policy and solve Britain's strategic dilemma. Few of his contemporaries would have guessed how illusory were these expectations.

Conclusion

Starting with the Defence Requirement Committee's (DRC) first report in February 1934, the British Government tried to solve fundamental problems of security during a period when dictatorships in Germany, Japan, and Italy showed an increasing disposition to war. The contradictions and delays in British policy resulted not merely from Britain's difficult strategic and economic situation, but also from indecision in the system of policymaking as it applied peacetime routines to warlike preparations. Among the members of the Cabinet, Chamberlain was the least inclined to drift in uncertainty, the most optimistic about preventing war, and the most critical of the administrative machinery under Baldwin and Hankey. By early 1937, three years of internal discord and international crisis had prepared Chamberlain to take charge with strong convictions about both policy and decisionmaking.

In 1934–35, British policymakers began to formulate a comprehensive strategy of deterrence. Completing the deficiency program for the Fighting Services would provide the best deterrent against the aggressive ambitions of any adversary. Meanwhile, "showing a tooth" in the Far East could impress Japan and demonstrating the will to become powerful in the air could deter Germany. The inclusiveness of this thinking owed much to inconsistent assumptions. Vansittart argued fatalistically that broad and rapid rearmament offered the only hope of bargaining effectively with Germany and, if war should come before 1939, winning it in concert with France. The Chiefs of Staff and Hankey replied temperately that Germany would not be ready for war before 1942, and warned the Foreign Office and Cabinet not to take risks or extend British deterrence to potential allies while Britain rearmed to sufficient levels of strength for victory in war. Chamberlain confidently held that rearming the RAF, combined with skillful diplomacy in Europe and the Far East, would enable Britain to prevent war without incurring the cost of rearming the other two Services or the liability of promising France a substantial expeditionary force.

Reconciling these three views of deterrence, or even elaborating each of them separately, required decisions about timing—whether Germany or Japan was the nearer threat, what balance should exist between conciliation and coercion, when Britain might be ready or willing to go to war, how much "magic" to assign to 1939 or 1942 for completing the Service programs, and what effect sudden changes in the international climate might have on long-term plans. The Defence Policy and Requirements Committee (DPR) was established, in the summer of 1935, to consider such questions. The committee's broad terms of reference instructed it to review "the defensive situation as a whole" and ensure that "defensive arrangements and foreign policy are in line."

Appointed sixteen months after the DRC completed its report, the DPR had a dubious patrimony. Administrative confusion and bureaucratic conflict had obscured the Government's vision of future security. The five-year deadline of 1939 for rectifying the worst deficiencies for all the Services had begun to slip, the Treasury had drawn a line between paper plans and material preparations for war, and the policy of air parity had not deterred Hitler from unilaterally upsetting the Versailles settlement. The DPR inherited contrasting modes of policymaking: the coordination and mutual adjustment of competing opinions without eliminating inconsistencies among them (MacDonald, Baldwin, and Hankey); the integration of policy in a coherent plan (Chamberlain). The first of these methods fostered disorder in British policy and preserved several alternatives for construing deterrence. The second promised order, a single doctrine of deterrence, and a solution to Britain's strategic predicament.

The Mediterranean crisis increased confusion in both the substance and the machinery of British policy. Britain followed a dual policy of conciliation and sanctions against Italy, a country hitherto excluded from the list of potential enemies but now causing trouble at an unexpected time and place. The coercive side of this policy included attributes that modern theorists associate with conventional and extended deterrence in situations that might lead to limited war, and Eden argued that showing force against Italy now would strengthen Britain's position for deterring Germany and Japan in the future. But the effectiveness of Britain's show of force was hampered by uncertainties about Mussolini, collective security, Germany, likely allies, and Britain's own international reputation. The use of coercive diplomacy made Italy a third potential enemy in all but official designation, jeopardized Anglo-French relations, and, by pushing Italy toward Germany while Italy looked toward Africa, increased the vulnerability of Central and Eastern Europe to German expansion.

The emergency disrupted the assumptions and procedures on which defense policy had rested since early 1934, raising new questions for the DPR to examine if it should return to the broad terms of reference that it set aside to concentrate on the crisis. The weight of expert advice increased because members of the DRC regularly attended meetings of the DPR, emphasizing how the crisis delayed long-term planning for defense. The Services criticized the Foreign Office for allowing collective security to increase Britain's insecurity, and their conception of appeasing Germany because of weakness differed from Vansittart's argument that negotiations with Germany must await at least "a strong and immediate beginning" on the new rearmament proposals of the DRC. Uneasy about the combined costs of the emergency and rearmament, the Treasury prevented the merging of these two categories of supply in the shadow scheme before the Cabinet could discuss the DRC's report of November. The Services agreed on the foolishness of showing force in circumstances they usually described in worst-case terms, but not on the relative value of sea and air power in a war with Italy. Hankey underscored the COS advice against taking risks, and resented the mounting criticisms of his machinery from people outside the Government who pointed out that coordination had not yet produced a coherent strategic doctrine for war in Europe or the Pacific.

The Mediterranean crisis unnerved British thinking about timing and deterrence. Alarmed by the disparity between present difficulties and future security, many ministers and expert advisers treated the crisis as an anomalous interruption in long-term planning that must be made to disappear as soon as possible, an attitude that weakened British deterrence in this test case. At the same time, the liabilities and frustrations of actually showing force and seeking French assistance seemed to validate this general rule of the Service staffs: in the hazardous region between peace and war, threatening force and making commitments to other nations before being ready for war would neither prevent dictators from taking what they wanted nor buy time for Britain to prepare for more dangerous confrontations ahead.

Hitler's remilitarization of the Rhineland redoubled London's disarray over policy and doubts about deterrence. Occurring while British forces were still tied up in the Mediterranean, the Rhineland crisis caused further interruptions in British planning, upset the Foreign Office's calculations for negotiating with Germany, and prompted the Government to renew the hitherto unsuccessful attempt to reassess foreign policy and its implications for defense.

The Cabinet's approval of new Service programs shortly before Hitler's action did not resolve different perceptions of time regarding the rate of German rearmament, the date of a European war, the schedules for completing the Services' respective programs, or the pace for implementing the shadow scheme to ensure adequate supplies for war. Nor did the Cabinet reconcile contrasting strategies of deterrence. Trying to incorporate the disparate views of its members, the DRC had disjointed plans for readying all three Services for various contingencies. Chamberlain rejected the "aggregate" thinking of the DRC and proposed a limited, efficient, more insular, and less expensive design based on air power. Chamberlain criticized Hankey's system of coordination for discouraging objectivity and coherence, and he welcomed the creation of the position of Minister for the Coordination of Defence. This new Cabinet post, and Inskip's appointment to it on 3 March without a ministry to back him up, were deemed acceptable by a Government that wished neither to stand still nor to run in its defense policy. Inskip soon learned that his two chief tasks—improving defense planning "as a whole" and increasing industrial capacity—defied quick solutions.

In the winter of 1935–36, Vansittart concluded that it might be necessary and possible to negotiate with Germany before Britain was strong enough to open discussions for a general settlement, which he doubted would guarantee peace in any case. During the "interval" of rearmament, Britain could play for time by offering "particular" concessions to Germany that were compatible with a general understanding to come later. Members of the Foreign Office disagreed over where to find these particulars, but hoped at least that they could use the demilitarized zone as a bargaining chip for gaining something concrete in return from Germany. Hitler moved first, however, seizing both the day and the chip. While Britain kept open the possibility of replacing the Locarno Treaty with a new security pact, the Services vented their distress over dangers and delays, Inskip asked whether the assumption of "peace conditions" underlying rearmament was consistent with the inhospitable international climate, and the Cabinet established the Foreign Policy Committee (FPC) to reexamine "major policy" in the light of the recent failures of collective and regional security.

By the end of May 1936, the disorder in British policy included profound misgivings about time and deterrence. The rush of events carried Britain farther away from conditions of peace, yet the deliberate pace of rearmament seemed to postpone the day when Britain could feel secure. Germany's Rhineland coup thwarted London's hopes for gaining solid reciprocal concessions from Germany at moments which Britain had some freedom to determine. The concentration of British forces in the Mediterranean neither prevented Mussolini from conquering Ethiopia nor warned Hitler away from unilaterally overthrowing the treaties of Versailles and Locarno. The success of the two dictators stifled British efforts to define deterrence comprehensively, combining conciliation with demonstrations of military force, the will to rearm, and international solidarity against aggression.

The Government's confusion can be attributed in part to irresolution in the machinery of policy, which generated more consensus for ending crises than for long-term planning. The Cabinet and its committees separated major questions of policy, reacted to urgencies as if they were discrete problems to be solved and put away, and either postponed or cursorily treated any broad reassessment of policy. The DPR's function was now limited to overseeing rearmament, no committee resumed the DPR's original terms of reference, and the FPC did not reconvene until mid-July after its inaugural meeting of 30 April. Divisions inside the Foreign Office widened, and the Service staffs grew more impatient with its failure to provide them with a tranquil interval for long-term planning.

Chamberlain dominated ministerial deliberations of defense policy. He pushed the Cabinet further toward his strategy of deterrence based on an air striking force, insisted on the survival of sound finance and normal peacetime commerce, believed that Britain had more time to rearm than the Foreign Office presumed, and guided the agenda according to his conception of "major policy." Chamberlain hoped Inskip would soon improve the system of defense by committee. The chancellor's patience with it was wearing thin. Because of Baldwin's neglect and Hankey's possessiveness, Chamberlain thought, the machinery unfortunately tolerated inconsistencies among the views of the Foreign Office, Treasury, and Services, preserved contradictory strategies for deterrence, and aroused anxiety in what he thought should be a confident period of carrying on business as usual.

The subsidence of the Rhineland crisis and end of sanctions against Italy did not lead to significant changes in British foreign policy or to the aligning of "defensive arrangements and foreign policy" that the DPR had set out to achieve in July 1935. The outbreak of the Spanish Civil War in July 1936 and the completion of major strategic studies early in 1937 amplified the disharmonies in British policy and in the system of decisionmaking. As the meaning of "policy" enlarged, Chamberlain expected soon to have the prime ministerial power to integrate its parts and remodel its administration.

The British Government took the lead in negotiations for a five-power conference to discuss a new security pact, but made little progress. Britain's dual policy toward Italy remained in place because of

Anglo-Italian rivalry in the eastern Mediterranean and the strategic consequences of the Spanish Civil War. By December 1936, the Cabinet did not know whether, as Chatfield put it, military unreadiness would "dominate our foreign policy" or foreign policy would "carry us into war when we are not ready for it." Specific disputes between the Foreign Office and COS reflected this general antithesis: the Foreign Office would, and the Chiefs of Staff would not, accompany conciliation with political firmness or demonstrations of force, international commitments, and implicitly broad definitions of British interests before Britain was prepared for war. The Cabinet inclined toward the COS, its willingness to take risks enervated by successive crises.

Early in 1937, British policy toward Germany appeared to be at an impasse, and the Cabinet decided, as if removing someone from the standard invitation list for a garden party, that from now on Italy was neither a "reliable friend" nor a "probable enemy." Britain was not deterring either dictator, let alone reconciling Germany, Italy, or Japan. The Foreign Office drew most of the blame for these failures, even from some of its own members, and sentiment along Whitehall grew for approaching Germany and Italy without further delay.

The mood for change arose also from debate over the Army's role in a European war, consideration of several strategic reports (including plans for war with Germany), and proposals for expanding the Air Force and Navy. These discussions merged foreign policy, strategy, war plans, supply, and finance under inclusive definitions of "policy," which obscured the line between foreign policy and strategy, gave the COS additional leverage against the Foreign Office, and enabled Chamberlain to place cost at the center of things. Although no consensus appeared regarding deterrence, the advantage continued to shift in favor of the COS against the Foreign Office as the Chiefs of Staff denounced confrontations, cunctation, and coercion. While the Services and Foreign Office continued to quarrel over how to manufacture time, Chamberlain and the Treasury consolidated their case for basing deterrence on cost, economic stability, and air power.

During Baldwin's last year in office, the machinery of policy showed signs of having both a weak prime minister and a strong heir presumptive, and the Treasury triumphed in the bureaucratic politics of deterrence. The Defence Plans (Policy) Committee, established in February 1937, examined war plans, the Army's role, and the Admiralty's proposed new naval standard. This committee and three others—CID, FPC, and DPR—now did the work that the DPR had initially been given before the Ethiopian crisis. Neither these committees nor the Cabinet defined "policy" in a clear and consistent manner as its multiple connotations entered ministerial discussions. Their agendas overlapped because of confusion as much as coordination, they often temporized, and they did not reconcile the various components of policy. The authority of the Foreign Office declined as critics blamed Eden and Vansittart for an ineffectual policy of drift. The Services exploited this weakness by regarding issues as "politico-strategical" and insisting on peace while they prepared for war, which they still believed was unlikely to occur as early as 1939.

Chamberlain and his Treasury advisers took a large view of "major policy," and treated economic stability as a defensive weapon with deterrent power. They rejected 1939 and targeted 1942 as the proper goal for expanding the Services, as much as safe borrowing would allow, to levels of force that regular budgeting could maintain afterward. Accordingly, the Treasury prepared a five-year plan for borrowing £400 million to help fund rearmament and for rationing expenditure among the Services, on whose list of priorities Chamberlain would place the needs of the Air Force at the top and those of the Territorial Army near the bottom. Chamberlain wanted to stretch time and restrict deterrence. He assumed that a conciliatory foreign policy would enable Britain to avoid war until 1942, and that then British military strength would suffice to deter any enemies who remained. He presupposed a degree of rationality among dictators and a span of time that Vansittart disbelieved, and he viewed deterrence in terms of self-defense that the Foreign Office considered too narrow. Although Inskip and Hankey did not try to force the Services to be as "objective" in their joint reports as Chamberlain wished, they acknowledged the force of his thesis binding time and deterrence to economic stability, and they knew that his leadership meant changes in policy and policy-making.

The Government's search for coherence since the Rhineland crisis had led to broad definitions of policy while uncovering confusion among its elements and inadequacies in its machinery. Chamberlain's accession to the premiership in May 1937 began a new stage of that search, for he was determined to ensure its success, confident that success depended on his leadership, and certain that coherence would prevent war. The period from May 1937 to the outbreak of war over two years later has its own dramatic unity, built around the fruition and collapse of Chamberlain's design.

Chamberlain's efforts to bring order to British policy prevailed in February 1938, when the Cabinet approved Inskip's recommendations for defense expenditure and Eden resigned. Inskip's proposals treated economic stability as the fourth arm of defense. They preserved the doctrine of normal trade and reiterated the Treasury's five-year plan for budgeting and rationing, policies which lent magic to 1942 as the goal for rearmament and presupposed that Britain's economic staying power in a long war would help deter Hitler. Inskip's report recognized the superior deterrent power of air forces (with emphasis on air defense) and relegated the Army to imperial and home defense, drastically limiting Britain's liability to send troops to the Continent. Inskip expected foreign policy to avoid making threats or taking risks. Deterrence was largely a matter of self-defense; extending British security to cover potential allies was the last of Britain's objectives.

Eden and Chamberlain concurred on the need to reduce the number of Britain's enemies, who were officially made three when the CID added Italy to the list in July 1937 (a few days before the Sino-Japanese conflict recommenced), and who drew ostensibly closer together when Italy joined the Anti-Comintern Pact in November. The two men also agreed on opening negotiations with Germany for colonial concessions and a general settlement, and on letting the Germans know that Britain would consider the possibility of peaceful changes in the borders of Central and Eastern Europe. In contrast to Chamberlain and the Chiefs of Staff, however, Eden did not want to open conversations also with Mussolini; he judged Britain's defenses strong enough to warrant some firmness and watchful waiting in diplomacy; he doubted that Britain's enemies would soon settle their own differences to threaten war on three fronts; he valued France as an ally; he welcomed signs from Washington that Roosevelt wanted to improve Anglo-American relations and help check the dictators; and he did not think the prime minister's legitimate interest in foreign affairs should include private correspondence with Mussolini without the knowledge of the Foreign Secretary.

Eden's resignation signaled a threefold victory for Chamberlain. First, foreign policy "must be, if not dictated, at least limited" by the state of Britain's defenses—and these by economic constraints—more than Eden would accept.[1] Second, fundamental incompatibilities of policy must not be perpetuated by bureaucratic politics, but resolved by the prime minister and Cabinet, if not by the FPC or CID. Finally, the prime minister must dominate the full Cabinet and any smaller "inner Cabinets." Dissent was illogical, cumbrous, and expendable to a leader with ideas and determination. The same principles were illustrated when Swinton resigned in May 1938, his advocacy of government interference in aircraft production a sore point with Chamberlain.

Chamberlain did not radically overhaul the machinery of policy, but simplified it and made it more efficient through his use of the FPC,

---

[1] Chamberlain marginal note on Eden's letter of 9 September 1937, PREM 1/210; Chamberlain diary, 19 February 1938, Chamberlain Papers, NC 2/24.

CID, and inner Cabinet. Starting in January 1938, Chamberlain convened the FPC much more frequently than it had met before. Several of its members also formed his inner Cabinet—Lord Halifax (who replaced Eden), Hoare, Simon, and Inskip. Chamberlain had welcomed the reorganization of defense committees in November 1937, when the CID incorporated the DPR and DP(P) so as to eliminate the "lop-sided and inconvenient arrangement" of having three committees exist "side by side . . . , all dealing with defence matters and all of equal authority."[2] Chamberlain took the chair when the CID, meeting as the DP(P), discussed defense policy and plans. Here, too, he could count on the support of the members of his inner Cabinet; and on the advice of the Chiefs of Staff against undertaking foreign commitments that might lead to war.

Chamberlain's triumph at home early in 1938 occurred after almost two years of relative German quietude in European affairs, but it coincided with actions in Berlin that would soon dismantle the order that he had given British policy. At the very moment when the Cabinet fastened to Chamberlain's solution for the problem of security, Hitler decided to shake up his own administration and Europe as well. He reorganized the German High Command and made Joachim von Ribbentrop his Foreign Minister before launching a policy of expansion in Central and Eastern Europe, defying his generals' longstanding advice—like that of their British counterparts—that they would not be ready for war in 1939. While Chamberlain's Government tried to keep Germany guessing about British intentions, Hitler correctly guessed that Britain would not intervene in that part of Europe. Germany's moves there, like the remilitarization of the Rhineland in 1936, preempted British attempts to negotiate a European settlement with tangible German concessions. From the *Anschluss* with Austria in March 1938 to the invasion of Poland on 1 September 1939, Hitler's sense of timing progressively destroyed Chamberlain's rational plans for preventing war with appeasement and rearmament until at least 1942; preventing it thereafter with forces built on a peacetime economy; and solving Britain's strategic dilemma through his own personal mastery over policy, machinery, and time.

After the *Anschluss*, the Foreign Policy Committee discussed how to avert German action against Czechoslovakia. Chamberlain doubted that, if Germany annexed the Sudetenland, Hitler would seize the rest of Czechoslovakia. Similarly, Halifax asked the FPC to distinguish be-

---

[2] Inskip note, 3 November 1937, covering Hankey's proposals for reorganizing the committees, approved by the CID on 18 November, CP 284(37), CAB 24/273. See also Roskill, *Hankey*, 3:288–89.

tween "Germany's racial efforts . . . and a lust for conquest on a Napoleonic scale." He disagreed with the argument that Britain should encircle Germany because Hitler would "pick a quarrel with France and ourselves" after having achieved hegemony in Central Europe. (Vansittart, recently replaced by Cadogan and "promoted" to the position of Chief Diplomatic Adviser to the Government, enjoyed more support for this thesis from Churchill than from the Foreign Office.) Halifax pointed out that Britain's general statements about peace in Central Europe "have no longer any deterrent effect." Only a "clear and unequivocal" commitment to Czechoslovakia might have such an effect, but it might also, because of France, bring war upon Britain "earlier rather than later."[3] During the next few months, the Cabinet, FPC, Foreign Office, and COS concurred that Britain should not guarantee Czechoslovakia.

During the Czech crisis of September, Chamberlain did not convene the FPC. He relied less on the Cabinet than on informal meetings of two groups of ministers: the inner Cabinet for major policy (sometimes without Inskip, often with Cadogan, Vansittart, and Sir Horace Wilson); the Service ministers and Inskip for defensive measures (with Inskip serving as liaison between the two groups).[4] Chamberlain's appeasement of Hitler during this crisis marked the culmination of coherence in British policy. This policy presumed ethnic limits to Hitler's demands and supposed that war was not inevitable. It treated deterrence as a long-term objective. The purpose of deterrence was to prevent a western war with a formidable air force and strong economy, not to trigger a preventive war in Eastern Europe when the RAF was unprepared and Germany could hurl a knockout attack against Britain. In fact, London's incorrect assumption that Germany was already prepared for such a strategy helped enable Hitler to deter Britain in September 1938.

Whitehall's second thoughts about this policy, which were expressed even in the inner Cabinet a few days before Chamberlain agreed to hand over the Sudetenland to Hitler at the Munich Conference, increased afterward as the rest of Czechoslovakia was dismembered.[5] An

[3] FPC meeting (and Halifax memorandum), 18 March 1938, CAB 27/623.
[4] Records of meetings in CAB 27/646 and CAB 16/189.
[5] For recent analyses of British policy and planning from Munich to the outbreak of war, see especially Robert J. Beck, "Munich's Lessons Reconsidered," *International Security* 14 (1989); Dilks, " 'We Must Hope for the Best' "; Christopher Hill, *Cabinet Decisions on Foreign Policy: The British Experience, October 1938–June 1941* (Cambridge, 1991); Murray, *Change in the European Balance of Power*, chaps. 6–9; G. C. Peden, "A Matter of Timing: The Economic Background to British Foreign Policy, 1937–1939," *History* 69 (1984); Wark, *Ultimate Enemy*, pp. 67–79, 110–23, 145–54, and chap. 8; Donald Cameron Watt, *How War Came: The Immediate Origins of the Second World War, 1938–1939* (New York, 1989). The

increasing number of ministers, including Halifax, thought that Hitler might indeed want nothing less than domination over Europe. Early in 1939, amid rumors that Germany planned to invade Holland, Halifax described the atmosphere as like that around a child, in which anything was possible and "there were no rational guiding rules."[6] It was no longer Chamberlain's milieu in London or abroad, although he himself did not recognize how much the times were changing.

Upon rational guiding rules Chamberlain had built an entire system of belief about preventing war and modernizing British government. Logic prescribed his scheme for deterrence, which he based on premises about the British economy, the role of air power, the behavior of Hitler, and the availability of time. Reason also guided Chamberlain's conception of decisionmaking, which entailed coherent plans and businesslike operation over the long term. He was, in some ways, like his nemesis. Both Chamberlain and Hitler had vision, both had grand designs, both viewed timing as an agent of policy, both scorned traditional bureaucratic and military thinking, both were convinced they were right. But Chamberlain's faith in preventing war was no match for Hitler's will to have one, his use of time was the antithesis of Hitler's, and his methodical decisiveness was a far cry from Hitler's *brutale Entschlossenheit*.

Whitehall recognized the likelihood that Napoleonic lust now drove Hitler, and that 1939 might have more magic than 1942 after all. The Government redefined deterrence in terms that Chamberlain had suppressed and about which he continued to have reservations. First, the Cabinet extended British deterrence—recognizing the security of Holland as a vital British interest, preparing to support France in any case of German aggression, and binding Britain to Eastern Europe. In response to Germany's seizure of Bohemia and Moravia in mid-March, the Anglo-French guarantee of Poland on 31 March established a trip wire in Eastern Europe. This guarantee either would deter Hitler or would mean war in the west if Hitler attacked Poland, although Chamberlain remained more willing than most of his colleagues to consider peaceful changes in Poland's boundaries, and more reluctant to include the Soviet Union in Britain's new eastern front. Second, the Government reverted to the "aggregate" strategies of the three Services, re-

---

problem of deterrence during this period is considered also by Alex Alexandroff and Richard Rosecrance, "Deterrence in 1939," *World Politics* 29 (1977); Mearsheimer, *Conventional Deterrence*, chap. 3; Smith, *British Air Strategy*, pp. 214–26. Two recent and contrasting studies of Chamberlain: John Charmley, *Chamberlain and the Lost Peace* (Chicago, 1989); Richard Cockett, *Twilight of Truth: Chamberlain, Appeasement, and the Manipulation of the Press* (New York, 1989).

[6] FPC meeting, 23 January 1939, CAB 27/624.

storing the Army's continental commitment and introducing conscription. (Meanwhile, giving priority to the construction of fighters for home defense clashed with both supporting the Field Force and building bombers for a counteroffensive.) Third, overcoming opposition from the Treasury, the Cabinet abandoned normal trade, approved additional and large-scale borrowing, and created a Ministry of Supply. Finally, the Cabinet decided that deterrence required risking war before Britain was prepared to win it, although Chamberlain still thought war could be prevented.

The machinery of British policy was affected by Hitler's compression of the time that Chamberlain had presumed Britain would have to rearm. The resignations of Duff Cooper (October 1938; he had moved from the War Office to the Admiralty in May 1937) and Inskip (January 1939) were symptomatic of a gradual dissolution of Chamberlain's grand scheme. So was the increasing authority of the Foreign Office under Halifax, and the Treasury's inability to uphold finance as the fourth arm of defense, indispensable for the long war that British planners had some hope of winning. The escalating pressure on approved programs and peacetime procedures caused a new rash of committees: the Cabinet Committee on Defence Programmes and Acceleration (October–November 1938); the Strategical Appreciation Subcommittee of the CID (March–April 1939); the Cabinet Committee on Defence Programmes and their Acceleration (March 1939); the Ministerial Priority Committee for supply (from July 1939); and the Defence Preparedness Committee (from 23 August to the outbreak of war).

What if British deterrence in 1938 had included an unequivocal pledge to France, trip wires in Eastern Europe, a continental commitment for an augmented Field Force, a full-scale shadow armament industry, a Ministry of Supply, and a willingness to fight while rearming? In one form or another, this counterfactual question about timing still preys upon accounts of British appeasement under Chamberlain. Together, these policies would have given Britain a flexible set of options for deterring or fighting Hitler, and they might have either prevented Hitler's seizure of Czech territory or caused war before Hitler had secured a strong economic and strategic base in Eastern Europe. On the other hand, these policies would have poured money into obsolescent weapons, particularly airplanes, instead of developing modern prototypes that might provide the necessary edge to repel a German offensive against Britain after 1939.

Britain's position during the Munich crisis has deep factual roots in decisions that the British Government made or avoided before Chamberlain became prime minister. From 1934 to 1937, Whitehall weighed alternative policies for their deterrent value. As chancellor, Chamberlain identified flexibility with disorder, and argued against it for economic, strategic, and political reasons. He found support for his views—if not for every detail of his design—in the Cabinet, Treasury, Foreign Office, Chiefs of Staff, and Secretariat, all of which had grown frustrated with difficulties that they blamed increasingly on inefficient policymaking and weak leadership at the top. These constituents built up powerful momentum and high hopes for a change in administration that would solve problems of policy. The search for a coherent strategy of deterrence was Whitehall's, not only Chamberlain's, and the policy of appeasing Germany without risking war was British, not simply personal.

Yet there remains a deeply personal and tragic thread in this story. The nation invested a great deal of confidence in Chamberlain's leadership, and Chamberlain equated his decisiveness with Britain's survival. The rational and personal paths had converged in 1937, but began to separate after the Munich Conference. Chamberlain never discarded completely the wishful thoughts he had held since Britain began rearming: there was no particular significance to the year 1939, Germany's next coup need not cause war, his own manner of administration would reduce confusion along Whitehall and solve Britain's strategic dilemma, and British deterrence would be credible in Berlin. Britain declared war against Germany on 3 September 1939, half a year later than the DRC's original guess in 1934, but only halfway into the five-year period of expenditure recommended by Chamberlain and the Treasury early in 1937. The shadowy period of peace ended with the failure of deterrence, and gave way to the uncertainty of victory in war.

Bibliography

UNPUBLISHED SOURCES

Government Documents

Official records consulted at the Public Record Office (PRO), London: CAB (Cabinet, committees, Secretariat); PREM (prime minister); FO (Foreign Office); T (Treasury); ADM (Admiralty); AIR (Air Ministry); WO (War Office).

Private Papers

General Sir Ronald Forbes Adam, Liddell Hart Archives, King's College London.
Stanley Baldwin, Lord Baldwin, Cambridge University Library.
Air Chief Marshal Sir Robert Brooke-Popham, Liddell Hart Archives, King's College London.
Vice Admiral Sir Harold A. Brown (and Sir George W. Turner), Liddell Hart Archives, King's College London.
Lawrence Burgis, Churchill College, Cambridge.
Sir Alexander Cadogan, Churchill College, Cambridge.
Neville Chamberlain, Birmingham University Library.
Admiral of the Fleet, Lord Chatfield, National Maritime Museum, London.
Field Marshal Sir John G. Dill, Liddell Hart Archives, King's College London.
James Louis Garvin, Harry Ransom Humanities Research Center, University of Texas at Austin.
Sir Maurice Hankey, Lord Hankey, Churchill College, Cambridge.
Sir Samuel Hoare, Lord Templewood, Cambridge University Library.
Sir Hastings Lionel Ismay, Lord Ismay, Liddell Hart Archives, King's College London.
Sir Basil Liddell Hart, Liddell Hart Archives, King's College London.
Field Marshal Sir Archibald Montgomery-Massingberd, Liddell Hart Archives, King's College London.
Sir Eric Phipps, Churchill College, Cambridge.
Sir William Strang, Lord Strang, Churchill College, Cambridge.
Sir Robert Vansittart, Lord Vansittart, Churchill College, Cambridge.
Sir William Douglas Weir, Lord Weir, Churchill College, Cambridge.

[345]

PUBLISHED SOURCES

Government Documents

Documents on British Foreign Policy, 1919–1939, Second Series, London 1947–84. (DBFP)
Parliamentary Debates, Commons, Fifth Series.
Parliamentary Debates, Lords, Fifth Series.
Parliamentary Papers.

Official Histories

Collier, Basil. *The Defence of the United Kingdom.* London, 1957.
Gibbs, N. H. *Grand Strategy*, vol. 1: *Rearmament Policy.* London, 1976.
Hancock, W. K., and M. M. Gowing. *British War Economy.* London, 1949.
Hinsley, F. H. *British Intelligence in the Second World War*, vol. 1. London, 1979.
Hurstfield, J. *The Control of Raw Materials.* London, 1953.
Postan, M. M. *British War Production*, rev. ed. London, 1975.
Scott, J. D., and R. Hughes. *The Administration of War Production.* London, 1955.
Webster, Sir Charles, and Noble Frankland. *The Strategic Air Offensive against Germany, 1939–1945*, vol. 1. London, 1961.

DIARIES, MEMOIRS, AND AUTOBIOGRAPHIES

Amery, Leopold S. *The Empire at Bay: The Leo Amery Diaries, 1929–1945*, ed. John Barnes and David Nicholson. London, 1988.
——. *My Political Life*, vol. 3: *The Unforgiving Years.* London, 1955.
Attlee, Clement R. *As It Happened.* London, 1954.
Avon, Lord (Anthony Eden). *Facing the Dictators.* Boston, 1962.
Bond, Brian, ed. *Chief of Staff: The Diaries of Lieutenant-General Sir Henry Pownall*, vol. 1. London, 1972.
Chatfield, Lord. *It Might Happen Again*, vol. 2: *The Navy and Defence.* London, 1947.
Churchill, Winston S. *The Gathering Storm*, Bantam ed. New York, 1961.
Cooper, Alfred Duff. *Old Men Forget.* London, 1953.
Dalton, Hugh. *The Fateful Years: Memoirs 1931–1945.* London, 1957.
Dilks, David, ed. *The Diaries of Sir Alexander Cadogan, 1938–1945.* New York, 1972.
Harris, Marshal of the Royal Air Force Sir Arthur. *Bomber Offensive.* London, 1947.
Harvey, John, ed. *The Diplomatic Diaries of Oliver Harvey, 1937–1940.* London, 1970.
Henderson, Sir Nevile. *Failure of a Mission: Berlin, 1937–1939.* New York, 1940.
Ismay, Lord. *The Memoirs of Lord Ismay.* London, 1960.
Jones, Thomas. *A Diary with Letters, 1931–1950.* London, 1954.
Kelly, Sir David. *The Ruling Few.* London, 1952.
Lawford, Valentine. *Bound for Diplomacy.* London, 1963.
Leasor, James, and General Sir Leslie Hollis. *The Clock with Four Hands* (English title, *War at the Top*). New York, 1959.
Liddell Hart, B. H. *The Memoirs of Captain Liddell Hart*, 2 vols. London, 1965.
Macmillan, Harold. *Winds of Change, 1914–1939.* New York, 1966.

Macready, Lieutenant General Sir Gordon. *In the Wake of the Great*. London, 1965.

Nicolson, Sir Harold. *Diaries and Letters, 1930–1939*. New York, 1966.

Peterson, Sir Maurice. *Both Sides of the Curtain*. London, 1950.

Rhodes James, Robert, ed. *Memoirs of a Conservative: J. C. C Davidson's Memoirs and Papers, 1910–1937*. London, 1969.

Selby, Sir Walford. *Diplomatic Twilight, 1930–1940*. London, 1953.

Simon, Viscount. *Retrospect*. London, 1952.

Slessor, Sir John. *The Central Blue: The Autobiography of Sir John Slessor, Marshal of the RAF*. New York, 1957.

Strang, Lord. *Home and Abroad*. London, 1956.

Strong, Major General Sir Kenneth. *Intelligence at the Top*. New York, 1969.

Swinton, Lord (Philip Cunliffe-Lister). *Sixty Years of Power*. London, 1966.

Templewood, Viscount (Samuel Hoare). *Nine Troubled Years*. London, 1954.

Vansittart, Lord. *The Mist Procession*. London, 1958.

Wellesley, Sir Victor. *Diplomacy in Fetters*. London, 1944.

BIOGRAPHIES

Carlton, David. *Anthony Eden: A Biography*. London, 1981.

Cecil, Robert. *A Divided Life: A Biography of Donald Maclean*. London, 1988.

Charmley, John. *Duff Cooper: The Authorised Biography*. London, 1986.

Cross, J. A. *Lord Swinton*. Oxford, 1982.

Dilks, David. *Neville Chamberlain*, vol. 1: *Pioneering and Reform, 1869–1929*. Cambridge, 1984.

Feiling, Sir Keith. *The Life of Neville Chamberlain*. London, 1946.

Gilbert, Martin. *Winston S. Churchill*, vol. 5: *The Prophet of Truth, 1922–1939*. Boston, 1977.

Macleod, Iain. *Neville Chamberlain*. London, 1961.

Middlemas, Keith, and John Barnes. *Baldwin: A Biography*. London, 1969.

O'Halpin, Ennan. *Head of the Civil Service: A Study of Sir Warren Fisher*. London, 1989.

Reader, William J. *Architect of Air Power: The Life of the First Viscount Weir of Eastwood, 1877–1959*. London, 1968.

Rhodes James, Robert. *Anthony Eden*. London, 1986.

Rose, Norman. *Vansittart: Study of a Diplomat*. London, 1978.

Roskill, Stephen. *Hankey: Man of Secrets*, vols. 2 and 3. London, 1972 and 1974.

BOOKS AND DISSERTATIONS

Adamthwaite, Anthony. *France and the Coming of the Second World War, 1936–1939*. London, 1977.

Allison, Graham T. *Essence of Decision: Explaining the Cuban Missile Crisis*. Boston, 1971.

Andrew, Christopher. *Her Majesty's Secret Service: The Making of the British Intelligence Community*. New York, 1985.

Andrew, Christopher, and David Dilks, eds. *The Missing Dimension: Governments and Intelligence Communities in the Twentieth Century*. Urbana, Ill., 1984.

Ashton-Gwatkin, Frank T. *The British Foreign Service*. Syracuse, 1950.

Baer, George W. *The Coming of the Italian-Ethiopian War.* Cambridge, Mass., 1967.
——. *Test Case: Italy, Ethiopia, and the League of Nations.* Stanford, Calif., 1976.
Barnett, Correlli. *The Collapse of British Power.* New York, 1972.
Beaufre, André. *Deterrence and Strategy.* London, 1965.
Beer, Samuel H. *Treasury Control: The Co-ordination of Financial and Economic Policy in Great Britain,* 2d ed. London, 1957.
Bialer, Uri. *The Shadow of the Bomber: The Fear of Air Attack and British Politics, 1932–1939.* London, 1980.
Birch, A. H. *Representative and Responsible Government.* Toronto, 1964.
Bishop, Donald G. *The Administration of British Foreign Relations.* Syracuse, 1961.
Bond, Brian. *British Military Policy between the Two World Wars.* Oxford, 1980.
Braybrooke, David, and Charles E. Lindblom. *A Strategy of Decision: Policy Evaluation as a Social Process.* New York, 1963.
Bridges, Lord. *The Treasury.* London, 1964.
Brodie, Bernard. *Strategy in the Missile Age.* Princeton, 1959.
Burton, J. W. *Systems, States, Diplomacy and Rules.* Cambridge, 1968.
Cameron, Fraser M. "Some Aspects of British Strategy and Diplomacy, 1933–39." Ph.D. diss., Cambridge University, 1972.
Ceadel, Martin. *Pacifism in Britain, 1914–1945: The Defining of a Faith.* Oxford, 1980.
Charmley, John. *Chamberlain and the Lost Peace.* Chicago, 1989.
Chester, D. N. and F. M. G. Willson. *The Organization of British Central Government, 1914–1956.* London, 1957.
Claude, Inis L., Jr. *Power and International Relations.* New York, 1962.
Cockett, Richard. *Twilight of Truth: Chamberlain, Appeasement, and the Manipulation of the Press.* New York, 1989.
Coffey, Joseph I. *Arms Control and European Security: A Guide to East–West Negotiations.* New York, 1977.
Cohen, Emmeline W. *The Growth of the British Civil Service, 1780–1939.* London, 1941.
Connell, John [John Robertson]. *The "Office."* New York, 1958.
Coverdale, John F. *Italian Intervention in the Spanish Civil War.* Princeton, 1975.
Cowling, Maurice. *The Impact of Hitler: British Politics and British Policy, 1933–1940.* Cambridge, 1975.
Craig, Gordon A., and Felix Gilbert. *The Diplomats.* Princeton, 1953.
Crossman, Richard H. S. *The Myths of Cabinet Government.* Cambridge, Mass., 1972.
Crozier, Andrew J. *Appeasement and Germany's Last Bid for Colonies.* London, 1988.
Del Boca, Angelo. *The Ethiopian War, 1935–1941,* trans. P. D. Cummins. Chicago, 1969.
Dennis, Peter. *Decision by Default: Peacetime Conscription and British Defence, 1919–1939.* London, 1972.
Edwards, Jill. *The British Government and the Spanish Civil War, 1936–1939.* London, 1979.
Ehrman, John. *Cabinet Government and War, 1890–1940.* Cambridge, 1958.
Emmerson, James T. *The Rhineland Crisis 7 March 1936: A Study in Multilateral Diplomacy.* London, 1977.
Etzioni, Amitai. *The Active Society: A Theory of Societal and Political Processes.* New York, 1968.
Fry, Geoffrey K. *Statesmen in Disguise.* London, 1969.

Fuchser, Larry W. *Neville Chamberlain and Appeasement: A Study in the Politics of History.* New York, 1982.

Funke, Manfred. *Sanktionen und Kanonen: Hitler, Mussolini und der internationale Abessinienkonflikt, 1934–1936.* Düsseldorf, 1970.

Gannon, Franklin Reid. *The British Press and Germany, 1936–1939.* Oxford, 1971.

George, Alexander L., and Richard Smoke. *Deterrence in American Foreign Policy: Theory and Practice.* New York, 1974.

George, Alexander L., David K. Hall, and William E. Simons. *The Limits of Coercive Diplomacy: Laos, Cuba, Vietnam.* Boston, 1971.

Gibbs, N. H. *The Origins of Imperial Defence.* Oxford, 1955.

Gilbert, Martin. *The Roots of Appeasement.* London, 1966.

Gordon, G. A. H. *British Seapower and Procurement between the Wars: A Reappraisal of Rearmament.* London, 1988.

Gordon, Hampden. *The War Office.* London, 1935.

Halperin, Morton H. *Bureaucratic Politics and Foreign Policy.* Washington, D.C., 1974.

Hankey, Lord. *Diplomacy by Conference.* New York, 1946.

——. *Government Control in War.* Cambridge, 1945.

Haraszti, Éva. *The Invaders: Hitler Occupies the Rhineland.* Budapest, 1983.

Hardie, Frank. *The Abyssinian Crisis.* London, 1974.

Higham, Robin. *Armed Forces in Peacetime.* Hamden, Conn., 1962.

——. *The Military Intellectuals in Britain, 1918–1939.* New Brunswick, N.J., 1966.

Hill, Christopher. *Cabinet Decisions on Foreign Policy: The British Experience, October 1938–June 1941.* Cambridge, 1991.

The History of the Times, vol. 4: *The 150th Anniversary and Beyond, 1912–1948.* New York, 1952.

Howard, Michael. *The Continental Commitment.* London, 1972.

Howson, Susan, and Donald Winch. *The Economic Advisory Council, 1930–1939.* Cambridge, 1977.

Huntington, Samuel P. *The Soldier and the State: The Theory and Politics of Civil-Military Relations.* Cambridge, Mass., 1957.

——, ed. *The Strategic Imperative: New Policies for American Security.* Cambridge, Mass., 1982.

Huth, Paul K. *Extended Deterrence and the Prevention of War.* New Haven, Conn., 1988.

Jacobson, Jon. *Locarno Diplomacy: Germany and the West, 1925–1929.* Princeton, 1972.

Jennings, Sir Ivor. *Cabinet Government,* 2d ed. Cambridge, 1951.

Jervis, Robert. *The Meaning of the Nuclear Revolution: Statecraft and the Prospect of Armageddon.* Ithaca, N.Y., 1989.

——. *Perception and Misperception in International Politics.* Princeton, 1976.

Jervis, Robert, Richard Ned Lebow, and Janice Gross Stein. *Psychology and Deterrence.* Baltimore, 1985.

Johnson, Franklyn Arthur. *Defence by Committee: The British Committee of Imperial Defence, 1885–1959.* London, 1960.

Joll, James, ed. *The Decline of the Third Republic.* London, 1959.

Kaiser, David E. *Economic Diplomacy and the Origins of the Second World War: Germany, Britain, France, and Eastern Europe, 1930–1939.* Princeton, 1980.

Kelsall, R. K. *Higher Civil Servants in Britain.* London, 1955.

Kennedy, Paul M. *The Realities Behind Diplomacy: Background Influences on British External Policy, 1865–1980.* London, 1981.

——. *Strategy and Diplomacy, 1870–1945.* London, 1983.

Kieft, David O. *Belgium's Return to Neutrality.* Oxford, 1972.

Knox, MacGregor. *Mussolini Unleashed, 1939–1941: Politics and Strategy in Fascist Italy's Last War.* Cambridge, 1982.

Liddell Hart, B. H. *The Defence of Britain.* New York, 1939.

Lindblom, Charles E. *The Intelligence of Democracy: Decision Making through Mutual Adjustment.* New York, 1965.

Lippincott, John M. "The Strategy of Appeasement: The Formulation of British Defence Policy, 1934–1939." Ph.D. diss., Oxford University, 1976.

Louis, William Roger. *British Strategy in the Far East, 1919–1939.* Oxford, 1971.

MacDonald, C. A. *The United States, Britain and Appeasement, 1936–1939.* New York, 1981.

McKercher, B. J. C., and D. J. Moss, eds. *Shadows and Substance in British Foreign Policy, 1895–1939.* Edmonton, Canada, 1984.

Mackintosh, John P. *The British Cabinet,* 2d ed. London, 1968.

May, Ernest R., ed. *Knowing One's Enemies: Intelligence Assessment before the Two World Wars.* Princeton, 1984.

Mearsheimer, John J. *Conventional Deterrence.* Ithaca, N.Y., 1983.

——. *Liddell Hart and the Weight of History.* Ithaca, N.Y., 1988.

Medlicott, W. N. *Britain and Germany: The Search for Agreement, 1930–1937.* London, 1969.

Meyers, Reinhard. *Britische Sicherheitspolitik, 1934–1938: Studien zum aussen- und sicherheitspolitischen Entscheidungsprozess.* Düsseldorf, 1976.

Middlemas, Keith. *Diplomacy of Illusion: The British Government and Germany, 1937–1939.* London, 1972.

Millett, Allan R., and Williamson Murray, eds. *Military Effectiveness,* 3 vols. Boston, 1988.

Mommsen, Wolfgang J., and Lothar Kettenacker, eds. *The Fascist Challenge and the Policy of Appeasement.* London, 1983.

Morgan, Patrick M. *Deterrence: A Conceptual Analysis,* 2d ed. Beverly Hills, Calif., 1983.

Mosley, Richard K. *The Story of the Cabinet Office.* London, 1969.

Murray, Williamson. *The Change in the European Balance of Power, 1938–1939: The Path to Ruin.* Princeton, 1984.

Naylor, John F. *Labour's International Policy: The Labour Party in the 1930s.* Boston, 1969.

——. *A Man and an Institution: Sir Maurice Hankey, the Cabinet Secretariat, and the Custody of Cabinet Secrecy.* Cambridge, 1984.

Peden, G. C. *British Rearmament and the Treasury, 1932–1939.* Edinburgh, 1979.

Peele, Gillian, and Chris Cook, eds. *The Politics of Reappraisal 1918–1939.* London, 1975.

Petersen, Jens. *Hitler-Mussolini: Die Entstehung der Achse Berlin-Rom, 1933–1936.* Tübingen, 1973.

Posen, Barry. *The Sources of Military Doctrine: France, Britain, and Germany between the World Wars.* Ithaca, N.Y., 1984.

Post, Gaines, Jr. *The Civil-Military Fabric of Weimar Foreign Policy.* Princeton, 1973.

Pratt, Lawrence R. *East of Malta, West of Suez: Britain's Mediterranean Crisis, 1936–1939.* Cambridge, 1975.

Preston, Adrian, ed., *General Staffs and Diplomacy before the Second World War.* London, 1978.

Quester, George H. *Deterrence before Hiroshima: The Airpower Background of Modern Strategy.* New York, 1966.

Ridley, F. F. *The Study of Government: Political Science and Public Administration.* London, 1975.

Robertson, Esmonde M. *Mussolini as Empire-Builder: Europe and Africa, 1932–1936.* New York, 1977.

Rock, William R. *Chamberlain and Roosevelt: British Foreign Policy and the United States, 1937–1940.* Columbus, Ohio, 1988.

Roseveare, Henry. *The Treasury.* New York, 1969.

Roskill, Stephen. *Naval Policy between the Wars,* vol. 2: *The Period of Reluctant Rearmament.* London, 1976.

Schelling, Thomas C. *Arms and Influence.* New Haven, Conn., 1966.

Schmidt, Gustav. *England in der Krise: Grundzüge und Grundlagen der britischen Appeasement-Politik, 1930–1937.* Opladen, 1981.

Shay, Robert P., Jr. *British Rearmament in the Thirties: Politics and Profits.* Princeton, 1977.

Simon, Herbert A. *Models of Man.* New York, 1957.

Smith, Malcolm. *British Air Strategy between the Wars.* Oxford, 1984.

Snyder, Glenn H. *Deterrence and Defense: Toward a Theory of National Security.* Princeton, 1961.

Snyder, Richard C., H. W. Bruck, and Burton Sapin. *Foreign Policy Decision-Making: An Approach to the Study of International Politics.* New York, 1962.

Steinbruner, John D. *The Cybernetic Theory of Decision.* Princeton, 1974.

Stern, Paul C. et al., eds. *Perspectives on Deterrence.* New York, 1989.

Thompson, Neville. *The Anti-Appeasers: Conservative Opposition to Appeasement in the 1930s.* Oxford, 1971.

Till, Geoffrey. *Air Power and the Royal Navy, 1914–1945.* London, 1979.

Tilley, Sir John, and Stephen Gaselee. *The Foreign Office.* London, 1933.

Toscano, Mario. *Designs in Diplomacy,* trans. and ed. George Carbone. Baltimore, 1970.

Trotter, Ann. *Britain and East Asia, 1933–1937.* London, 1975.

Waley, Daniel. *British Public Opinion and the Abyssinian War, 1935–6.* London, 1975.

Wark, Wesley K. *The Ultimate Enemy: British Intelligence and Nazi Germany, 1933–1939.* Ithaca, N.Y., 1985.

Warner, Geoffrey. *Pierre Laval and the Eclipse of France.* London, 1968.

Watt, Donald Cameron. *How War Came: The Immediate Origins of the Second World War, 1938–1939.* New York, 1989.

——. *Personalities and Policies: Studies in the Formulation of British Foreign Policy in the Twentieth Century.* Notre Dame, Ind., 1965.

——. *Too Serious a Business: European Armed Forces and the Approach to the Second World War.* London, 1975.

Weinberg, Gerhard L. *The Foreign Policy of Hitler's Germany: Diplomatic Revolution in Europe, 1933–1936.* Chicago, 1970.

Welch, Howard G. "The Origins and Development of the Chiefs of Staff Subcommittee of the Committee of Imperial Defence: 1923–1939." Ph.D. diss., London University, 1973.

Wendt, Bernd Jürgen. *Economic Appeasement: Handel und Finanz in der britischen Deutschland-Politik, 1933–1939.* Düsseldorf, 1971.

Wilensky, Harold L. *Organizational Intelligence.* New York, 1967.

Wiseman, H. V. *Parliament and the Executive.* London, 1966.

Wolfers, Arnold. *Britain and France between Two Wars.* New York, 1940.

Yarmolinsky, Adam. *The Military Establishment.* New York, 1971.

Young, Oran R. *The Politics of Force: Bargaining during International Crises.* Princeton, 1968.

Young, Robert J. *In Command of France: French Foreign Policy and Military Planning, 1933–1940.* Cambridge, Mass., 1978.

ARTICLES AND BOOK CHAPTERS

Alexandroff, Alex, and Richard Rosecrance. "Deterrence in 1939." *World Politics* 29 (1977).

Ashton-Gwatkin, Frank. "Thoughts on the Foreign Office: 1918–1939." *Contemporary Review* 188 (1955).

Beck, Robert J. "Munich's Lessons Reconsidered." *International Security* 14 (1989).

Beloff, Max. "The Whitehall Factor: The Role of the Higher Civil Service, 1919–39." In *The Politics of Reappraisal,* ed. Peele and Cook.

Betts, Richard K. "Conventional Deterrence: Predictive Uncertainty and Policy Confidence." *World Politics* 37 (1984–85).

Boadle, Donald G. "The Formation of the Foreign Office Economic Relations Section, 1930–1937." *Historical Journal* 20 (1977).

Bond, Brian, and Williamson Murray. "The British Armed Forces, 1918–39." In *Military Effectiveness,* ed. Millett and Murray, vol. 2.

Bosworth, R. J. B. "The British Press, the Conservatives, and Mussolini, 1920–34," *Journal of Contemporary History* 5 (1970).

Cohen, Michael J. "Direction of Policy in Palestine, 1936–45." *Middle Eastern Studies* 11 (1975).

Craig, Gordon A. "The British Foreign Office from Grey to Austen Chamberlain." In *The Diplomats, 1919–1939,* ed. Craig and Gilbert.

Crozier, Andrew J. "Prelude to Munich: British Foreign Policy and Germany, 1935–8." *European Studies Review* 6 (1976).

Darwin, John. "Imperialism in Decline? Tendencies in British Imperial Policy between the Wars." *Historical Journal* 23 (1980).

Dilks, David. "The British Foreign Office between the Wars." In *Shadow and Substance in British Foreign Policy, 1895–1939,* ed. McKercher and Moss.

——. "Flashes of Intelligence: The Foreign Office, the SIS and Security before the Second World War." In *The Missing Dimension,* ed. Andrew and Dilks.

——. "'The Unnecessary War'? Military Advice and Foreign Policy in Great Britain, 1931–1939." In *General Staffs and Diplomacy before the Second World War,* ed. Preston.

——. "'We Must Hope for the Best and Prepare for the Worst': The Prime Minister, the Cabinet, and Hitler's Germany, 1937–1939." *Proceedings of the British Academy* 73 (1987).

Dunbabin, John. "The British Military Establishment and the Policy of Appeasement." In *The Fascist Challenge and the Policy of Appeasement,* ed. Mommsen and Kettenacker.

——. "British Rearmament in the 1930s: A Chronology and Review." *Historical Journal* 18 (1975).

Elliot, Walter. "Co-ordination of Imperial Defence." *Journal of the Royal United Services Institute* 75 (1930).

Frank, Willard C., Jr. "The Spanish Civil War and the Coming of the Second World War." *International History Review* 9 (1987).

Fry, Michael G. "Historians and Deterrence." In *Perspectives on Deterrence*, ed. Stern et al.

Goldman, Aaron. "Sir Robert Vansittart's Search for Italian Cooperation against Hitler, 1933–1936." *Journal of Contemporary History* 9 (1974).

Gruner, Wolf D. "The British Political, Social and Economic System and the Decision for Peace and War: Reflections on Anglo-German Relations, 1800–1939." *British Journal of International Studies* 6 (1980).

Hall, Hines H. "The Foreign Policy-Making Process in Britain, 1934–1935, and the Origins of the Anglo-German Naval Agreement." *Historical Journal* 19 (1976).

Hamilton, Sir H. P. "Sir Warren Fisher and the Public Service." *Public Administration* 29 (1951).

Harrison, Richard A. "A Presidential *Démarche*: Franklin D. Roosevelt's Personal Diplomacy and Great Britain, 1936–37." *Diplomatic History* 5 (1981).

——. "Testing the Water: A Secret Probe towards Anglo-American Military Cooperation in 1936." *International History Review* 7 (1985).

Holton, Gerald. "Introduction." *Daedalus* 106, no. 4 (1977).

Ismay, Major General H. L. "The Machinery of the Committee of Imperial Defence." *Journal of the Royal United Services Institute* 84 (1939).

Kennedy, Paul M. "The Tradition of Appeasement in British Foreign Policy, 1865–1939." *British Journal of International Studies* 2 (1976).

Knapp, W. F. "The Rhineland Crisis of March 1936." In *The Decline of the Third Republic*, ed. Joll.

Knox, MacGregor. "Fascist Italy Assesses Its Enemies, 1935–1940." In *Knowing One's Enemies*, ed. May.

Lebow, Richard Ned, and Janice Gross Stein. "Beyond Deterrence." *Journal of Social Issues* 43 (1987).

Levy, Jack S. "Quantitative Studies of Deterrence Success and Failure." In *Perspectives on Deterrence*, ed. Stern et al.

Luard, Evan. "Conciliation and Deterrence: A Comparison of Political Strategies in the Interwar and Postwar Periods." *World Politics* 19 (1966–67).

McKercher, B. J. C. "'Our Most Dangerous Enemy': Great Britain Pre-eminent in the 1930s." *International History Review* 13 (1991).

Marder, Arthur. "The Royal Navy and the Ethiopian Crisis of 1935–36." *American Historical Review* 75 (1970).

Meyers, Reinhard. "British Imperial Interests and the Policy of Appeasement." In *The Fascist Challenge and the Policy of Appeasement*, ed. Mommsen and Kettenacker.

Millett, Allan R., Williamson Murry, and Kenneth H. Watman. "The Effectiveness of Military Organizations." In *Military Effectiveness*, ed. Millett and Murray, vol. 1.

Naylor, John F. "The Establishment of the Cabinet Secretariat." *Historical Journal* 14 (1971).

Niedhart, Gottfried. "Appeasement: Die britische Antwort auf die krise des Weltreichs und des internationalen Systems vor dem Zweiten Weltkrieg." *Historische Zeitschrift* 126 (1978).

Overy, R. J. "German Air Strength 1933 to 1939: A Note." *Historical Journal* 27 (1984).

Parker, R. A. C., "Economics, Rearmament and Foreign Policy: The United Kingdom before 1939—A Preliminary Study." *Journal of Contemporary History* 10 (1975).

[353]

——. "The Failure of Collective Security in British Appeasement." In *The Fascist Challenge and the Policy of Appeasement*, ed. Mommsen and Kettenacker.

——. "Great Britain, France and the Ethiopian Crisis, 1935–1936." *English Historical Review* 89 (1974).

Peden, G. C. "A Matter of Timing: The Economic Background to British Foreign Policy, 1937–1939." *History* 69 (1984).

Post, Gaines, Jr. "The Machinery of British Policy in the Ethiopian Crisis." *International History Review* 1 (1979).

——. "Mad Dogs and Englishmen: British Rearmament, Deterrence, and Appeasement, 1934–35." *Armed Forces and Society* 14 (1988).

Quartararo, Rosaria. "Imperial Defence in the Mediterranean on the Eve of the Ethiopian Crisis (July–October 1935)." *Historical Journal* 20 (1977).

Robertson, Esmonde M. "Hitler and Sanctions: Mussolini and the Rhineland." *European Studies Review* 7 (1977).

Robertson, James C. "The Hoare-Laval Plan." *Journal of Contemporary History* 10 (1975).

Rothwell, V. H. "The Mission of Sir Frederick Leith-Ross to the Far East, 1935–1936." *Historical Journal* 18 (1975).

Sakwa, George. "The Franco-Polish Alliance and the Remilitarization of the Rhineland." *Historical Journal* 16 (1973).

Schuker, Stephen A. "France and the Remilitarization of the Rhineland, 1936." *French Historical Studies* 14 (1985–86).

Slessor, Squadron Leader J. C. "The Co-ordination of the Fighting Services." *Journal of the Royal United Services Institute* 76 (1931).

Steiner, Zara. "Decision-making in American and British Foreign Policy: An Open and Shut Case." *Review of International Studies* 13 (1987).

Steiner, Zara, and M. L. Dockrill. "The Foreign Office Reforms, 1919–21." *Historical Journal* 17 (1974).

Walker, Stephen G. "Solving the Appeasement Puzzle: Contending Historical Interpretations of British Diplomacy during the 1930s." *British Journal of International Studies* 6 (1980).

Wark, Wesley K. "British Intelligence on the German Air Force and Aircraft Industry, 1933–1939." *Historical Journal* 25 (1982).

Warner, Geoffrey. "France and Non-Intervention in Spain, July–August 1936." *International Affairs* 38 (1962).

Watt, Donald Cameron. "British Intelligence and the Coming of the Second World War in Europe." In *Knowing One's Enemies*, ed. May.

——. "Divided Control of British Foreign Policy—Danger or Necessity." *Political Quarterly* 33 (1962).

Whealey, Robert H. "Mussolini's Ideological Diplomacy: An Unpublished Document." *Journal of Modern History* 39 (1967).

Wrench, David J. "The Influence of Neville Chamberlain on Foreign and Defence Policy." *Royal United Services Institute Journal for Defence Studies* 125 (1980).

Young, Robert J. "French Military Intelligence and the Franco-Italian Alliance, 1933–1939." *Historical Journal* 28 (1985).

——. "Spokesmen for Economic Warfare: The Industrial Intelligence Centre in the 1930s." *European Studies Review* 6 (1976).

Index

Library of Congress Cataloging-in-Publication Data

Post, Gaines, Jr., b. 1937
    Dilemmas of appeasement : British deterrence and defense, 1934–1937 / Gaines
Post, Jr.
       p.   cm. — (Cornell studies in security affairs)
    Includes bibliographical references and index.
    ISBN 0-8014-2748-7
    1. Great Britain—Politics and government—1936–1945.   2. Great Britain—Politics
and government—1910–1936.   3. Great Britain—History, Military—20th century.
4. Great Britain—Foreign relations—1936–1945.   5. Great Britain—Foreign relations—
1910–1936.   6. Great Britain—Foreign relations—Germany.   7. World War, 1939–
1945—Causes.   I. Title.   II. Series.
DA578.P65   1993
327.41'009'043—dc20   92-27606